THE WORLDS AND I

Ella Wheeler Wilcox

www.GeneralBooksClub.com

Publication Data:

Title: The Worlds and I;
Author: Wilcox, Ella Wheeler, 1850-1919
Reprinted: 2010, General Books, Memphis, Tennessee, USA
Original Publisher: New York, George H. Doran company;
Publication date: 1918;
Subjects: Poets, American; Journalists; Spiritualism; Biography Autobiography / Literary; Biography Autobiography /
Editors, Journalists, Publishers;
BISAC subject codes: BIO007000, BIO025000,

How We Made This Book for You
We made this book exclusively for you using patented Print on Demand technology.
First we scanned the original rare book using a robot which automatically flipped and photographed each page.
We automated the typing, proof reading and design of this book using Optical Character Recognition (OCR) software on the scanned copy. That let us keep your cost as low as possible.
If a book is very old, worn and the type is faded, this can result in numerous typos or missing text. This is also why our books don't have illustrations; the OCR software can't distinguish between an illustration and a smudge.
We understand how annoying typos, missing text or illustrations, foot notes in the text or an index that doesn't work, can be. That's why we provide a free digital copy of most books exactly as they were originally published. You can also use this PDF edition to read the book on the go. Simply go to our website (www.GeneralBooksClub.com) to check availability. And we provide a free trial membership in our book club so you can get free copies of other editions or related books.
OCR is not a perfect solution but we feel it's more important to make books available for a low price than not at all. So we warn readers on our website and in the descriptions we provide to book sellers that our books don't have illustrations and may have numerous typos or missing text. We also provide excerpts from books to book sellers and on our website so you can preview the quality of the book before buying it.
If you would prefer that we manually type, proof read and design your book so that it's perfect, simply contact us for the cost. Since many of our books only sell one or two copies, we have to split the production costs between those one or two buyers.

Frequently Asked Questions

Why are there so many typos in my paperback?
We created your book using OCR software that includes an automated spell check. Our OCR software is 99 percent accurate if the book is in good condition. Therefore, we try to get several copies of a book to get the best possible accuracy (which is very difficult for rare books more than a hundred years old). However, with up to 3,500 characters per page, even one percent is an annoying number of typos. We would really like to manually proof read and correct the typos. But since many of our books only sell a couple of copies that could add hundreds of dollars to the cover price. And nobody wants to pay that. If you need to see the original text, please check our website for a downloadable copy.

Why is the index and table of contents missing (or not working) from my paperback?
After we re-typeset and designed your book, the page numbers change so the old index and table of contents no longer work. Therefore, we usually remove them. We dislike publishing books without indexes and contents as much as you dislike buying them. But many of our books only sell a couple of copies. So manually creating a new index and table of contents could add more than a hundred dollars to the cover price. And nobody wants to pay that. If you need to see the original index, please check our website for a downloadable copy.

Why are illustrations missing from my paperback?
We created your book using OCR software. Our OCR software can't distinguish between an illustration and a smudge or library stamp so it ignores everything except type. We would really like to manually scan and add the illustrations. But many of our books only sell a couple of copies so that could add more than a hundred dollars to the cover price. And nobody wants to pay that. If you need to see the original illustrations, please check our website for a downloadable copy.

Why is text missing from my paperback?
We created your book using a robot who turned and photographed each page. Our robot is 99 percent accurate. But sometimes two pages stick together. And sometimes a page may even be missing from our copy of the book. We would really like to manually scan each page. But many of our books only sell a couple of copies so that could add more than a hundred dollars to the cover price. And nobody wants to pay that. If you would like to check the original book for the missing text, please check our website for a downloadable copy.

Limit of Liability/Disclaimer of Warranty:
The publisher and author make no representations or warranties with respect to the accuracy or completeness of the book. The advice and strategies in the book may not be suitable for your situation. You should consult with a professional where appropriate. The publisher is not liable for any damages resulting from the book.
Please keep in mind that the book was written long ago; the information is not current. Furthermore, there may be typos, missing text or illustration and explained above.

1

THE WORLDS AND I

ELLA WHEELER WILCOX

THE WORLDS AND I

ELLA WHEELER WILCOX

AUTHOR OF "POEMS OF PASSION," "SONNETS OF SOBBOW AND TBI-UMPH," ETC.

ILLUSTRATED

NEW XBJr YORK GEORGE H. DORAN COMPANY

FOREWORD TO CRITICS AND CLERGYMEN

BEFORE you express your opinion too loudly regarding the last chapters of this book, the author respectfully suggests that you read the following editorial which appeared in the "Harbinger of Light."

"Communication is possible, but one must obey the laws, first finding out the conditions. I do not say it is easy, but it is possible; and I have conversed with my friends over yonder, just as I can converse with any one in this audience now."

Sir Oliver Lodge.

"Only a few weeks ago a Captain Chaplain drew a pathetic picture of the deaths of some of 'the boys' at the front and comforted his hearers with the inspiring assurance that 'they had passed painlessly into the night from which no mortal has ever returned! He is evidently another of the clergy who 'do not know. As a matter of fact, the gallant souls referred to did not pass into night at all–either painlessly or painfully! They passed into the spiritual dawn, and as they gradually recovered consciousness the light around them increased, and, to their inexpressible joy, they eventually found themselves in an environment of translucent brightness. Night, indeed, for such self-sacrificing heroes! Then, again, what authority, apart from Shakespeare, has this 'spiritual guide for the assertion that these departed warriors cannot return? His Bible certainly contradicts him. A battalion of old Israelitish fighters returned when Elisha was hard pressed by his foes, and if they could return in those times, why cannot our brave lads return to-day?

"Samuel also returned and spoke to Saul; one of the old prophets returned and conversed with John; and at the time of the Crucifixion the streets of Jerusalem were thronged with the so-called 'dead. If these things could happen in the past, why cannot they happen in the present? Does God work by fits and starts, or are His ways the same yesterday, to-day, and for ever?

"But independent of all Scriptural testimony, we know, on the authority of modern-day scientists and millions of other witnesses, that the return of the departed is an indisputable fact, and that, as Sir Oliver Lodge points out, if the conditions' are provided, they can converse with us, as spiritual intelligences conversed with mortals in olden days. Thousands of 'the boys' who lost their physical bodies on the battlefield of this world-wide war have returned to their homes and talked with their parents and friends. And the reunion has been so real that 'the blinds have been pulled up, and a flood of soul-uplifting sunshine has dissipated the clouds of gloom. These facts are now becoming common knowledge, and are being shared by all sorts and conditions of men– the majority of the clergy excepted!

"To put the question to a clergyman who has no knowledge of the PROOFS of survival supplied by the evidence of psychical research, is tantamount to going to a butcher and asking him to solve a problem in electrical science! What does a butcher know about electrical voltage or the principle upon which the voltameter is constructed? And what does a clergyman know of the change called death, and what happens afterwards, if he has neither investigated personally, nor studied the amazing evidence which demonstrates beyond cavil that the dead do return and do communicate? In every other department of human inquiry, if we desire a solution of some abstruse problem, we instinctively consult an expert in the particular science or study involved. And why should not the same principle be followed in seeking knowledge of human survival and the interblending of the spiritual and material worlds? We should go to those who know–not to those who do not know.

"We would, therefore, advise all those who resort to their minister for information on the transcendent subject under discussion to ascertain the extent of his knowledge, and con- sequently his authority for the attitude he assumes. Let them ask him these questions:–

"i– Are you familiar with the experiences and declarations of Sir Oliver Lodge, Sir William Crookes, Sir William Barrett, Dr. Alfred Russel Wallace, Sir Arthur Conan Doyle, Professor Zollner, Professor Lombroso, Professor Richet, Professor Hyslop, Bishop Welldon, Archdeacon Wilberforce, Rev. Dr. Dearmer, Rev. Dr. F. Holmes-Duddon, Rev. Dr. Norman Maclean, Archdeacon Colley, Rev. P. Fielding-Ouid, M. A., Rev. Arthur Chambers, Rev. Chas. L. Tweedale, F. R. G. S., and a multitude of other authoritative investigatorsf

"2– Have you ever sat with a well developed medium, or in any other way personally investigated what are known as psychic or Spirituaiistic phenomena? If the replies to these questions are in the negative–and they certainly will be in nine cases out of ten–it may very safely be assumed that the clergyman does not possess the necessary qualifications for expressing any opinion whatever on the subject. He may, however, express it all the same, but it should not be allowed to carry the slightest weight.

"Surely no exception can be taken to these terms! They are based upon reason and commoa sense, and should be accepted without demur."

CONTENTS

CHAPTEK PAGE I The Little Days 17 II First School Days and Early Pets 33 III The Beginnings or Success Si IV "Maurine" AND "Poems OS Passion" 72

V Two Amusing Near Romances 85
VI The Compelling Lover 92
VII Steps Up Spiritual Stairways 102
VIII Life IN Meriden 114 IX New York 125
X The Bungalow 138
XI Little Efforts AT Brotherhood 155
XII Interesting People Met in New York 170
XIII Lunatics I Have Known 180
XIV A Royal Funeral., 193
XV Happy Memories of Well-known People. 209
XVI The Battlefield of Love. 232
XVII High Lights on Places and Personalities Seen in Travel 252
XVIII On Historic Ground 266
XIX Hawaiian Queens and the Sultan of Java. 283
XX Marriage Customs and Polygamy 300
XXI People, Abroad and at Home 316

XXII The Beginning of the End 337
XXIII The Search of a Soul in Sorrow 346
XXIV The Keeping of the Promise 361
XXV From France 389
Epilogue 413
A Pictorial Summary of the Life of Ella Wheeler
Wilcox 421

THE WORLDS AND I
THE WORLDS AND I

CHAPTER I

The Little Days IITY literary career was in a large measure begun before " my birth through prenatal influences.

The mother who wishes her unborn child to possess certain tastes, talents or qualities, cannot bring about the desired result by merely thinking of- it. Thought is only constructive when it is charged with intense feeling and emotion. Powder scattered lightly over a large surface does not project a bullet to the mark, but compressed into a small space and given the right impetus, the lead is sent to the bull's-eye. So, desultory thought is wasted, while focused thought creates that which it desires. The expectant mother whose thought is focused intensely in any special direction attracts to herself out of space the Ego awaiting reincarnation best calculated by its former lives to use her thought; and she impresses upon its embryo mind, in the important months which ensue, the nature of her wishes.

My mother, always a devotee at the shrine of literature (and having in her own mind the seed of poetic fancy) found herself for the first time in her life with a large library at her command during the months preceding my advent. She committed to memory whole cantos of Byron, Moore, and Scott, and mentally devoured the plays of Shakespeare, as well as various works of fiction. Curiously enough, she believed that the child she was carrying under her heart was to be a novelist. Always she spoke of me before my birth (so aunts and a grandmother as well as she have told me) as a daughter who was coming into her ripened life (I was the youngest of four children) to carry out her own unrealized ambitions. "My child will be a girl," she said, "and she will be a writer; she will follow literature as a profession; she will begin young, and she will travel extensively and do all the things I have wanted to do and missed doing."

When, at the age of seven and some months, she found me printing on scraps of paper a story about the love of Mr. Larkspur for Miss Hollyhock, and the jealousy occasioned by a roving bee, she did not join in the surprise of other members of the family, but said, "I expected her to do these things." So my crude, early efforts met with encouragement from the start, and my ambitions were fired by my mother's often expressed belief in my abilities.

I think I did not differ from other small children in any particular, save, perhaps, in my lack of interest in dolls. AH my dolls were carefully laid in a drawer until some doll-loving little visitor came, when they were produced. I wanted kittens or puppies for playthings, particularly kittens. Dolls were so cold and inanimate, kittens so warm and responsive. I have all my life found wonderful companionship in cats. Dogs, too, have been dear friends and comrades. The only doll which left any memory in my child life, was a crooked-necked yellow summer squash whidh I dressed up in a bit of lace and tied a string about its waist and called "Mary." I insisted that she strongly resembled a little blonde neighbor, Mary Hart by name. A few years afterward, my sister was amused because I saw a resemblance to this same Mary Hart in a shock of yellow wheat tied in the middle. Mary was very slim of waist and very golden in coloring.

I believe I was rather an amiable child, yet I had very naughty spells when quite young. Visiting my grandmother and aunts at the age of three, I was (unwisely) allowed to sit at the table with my elders and partake of all the goodies under which the table groaned. When pie time came, I grew obstreperous, because hot mince pie, not cold, was served. I kept shrieking, "I want a piece of cold mince pie!" My mother wished to take me away from the table, but

Aunt Abigail said, "The poor little dear must have what she wants." So she hurried to the kitchen and cooled a piece of pie by holding it in a pan of cold water. When she returned, I was kicking my heels on the floor, screaming lustily, and, refusing the cold mince pie, I declared I wanted my pie hot! My mother applied a hot hand instead. In all my mother's life afterward, whenever I expressed an intense desire in her hearing, she would say: "Oh, yes, I know, you want a piece of cold mince pie."

Another droll little story was told me about myself between the ages of two and three. A small boy, named Eddie, came to call with his mother, who said she thought Eddie and Ella would make good playmates. I looked at the boy intently for a moment, ran into the kitchen, and reappeared with a tin wash-dish and a rag in my hand. My mother in amazement asked me what I was doing. I replied, "I am going to wash Eddie's face before I play with him." When, in later life, I showed an impulse to try and improve people physically, mentally, or morally, without any requests on their part, I was reminded of this early incident. In the country neighborhood, I was recognized, from the age of eight to fourteen, as a child prodigy, and my teachers gave me praise, far in excess of my merits, as I recall those early efforts in prose and verse. I loved to give my imagination full sway, and "Composition Day," the dread of most children, was to me a delight. Two of my teachers instituted a monthly school-magazine (made of sheets of note-paper fastened by a ribbon) to which the scholars contributed. My effusions were prominent under my own name and several pen-names. Various narratives, essays, verses, and a special line of conundrums and httle jokes about my schoolmates, appeared in each number of the magazine. Before this, however, I had finished, at the age of nine, a novel whose title page read as follows:

Minnie Tighthand and Mrs. Dunley A True Story By Ella Wheeler

The novel contained ten chapters; and was "bound" in paper torn off the kitchen wall. The first four chapters were headed by lines of original verse. This, my maiden effort in verse, described the heroine–

A head covered with pretty curls;

A face white as the snow. Her teeth are like handsome pearls;

She's tall and stately too.

Mrs. Grant, the "woman villain" of the story, was described as "Neither handsome nor pretty, but always fretty."

Under the sub-title of "A Death," in one chapter the following couplet appears:
Death came down so stilly So softly, so chilly.

After the fourth chapter wis finished, the family discovered my occupation and the reason for my continual requests for scraps of paper. An older brother, then man-grown, hearing my story and verses, volunteered the information that novelists never wrote the verses which headed their chapters, but selected them from the works of a poet. I distinctly recall my mental depreciation of novelists, and an accompanying augmentation of respect for poets, after my brother's statement. I permitted the remaining chapters to go into my book without couplets.

The next verses which I recall were composed for the school-magazine and were of a: somewhat personal character. A little girl living just across the road from my home was named Ophelia Cramer. Down the road, on the way to the school, lived Homer Benson, who chanced, that summer, to be the chosen cavalier of Ophelia, always waiting for her before he went to school and walking on her side of the road as we returned home. Naturally, they were subjected to much teasing from other children. In my own home, an aged and toothless dog was fed on a corn-meal diet, which my mother prepared for his sustenance. To the school-magazine I contributed the following classic stanza:

"An old dog's bread is made of meal," Said Homer Benson to his Ophel.

"I know it, love," she said, with a sigh, "And if they did not eat it, they'd surely die."

From that early stage onward, through my teens, my literary proclivities and mental powers were influenced by reading tiie New York Mercury, New York Ledger, Waverly, Peterson, Godey, and Demarest's Magazine, and novels of Ouida, Mary J. Holmes, and Mrs. Southworth. This emotional literature naturally had its influence upon my imagination, and caused me to live in a world quite apart from that of my commonplace farm environment, where the post-office was five miles distant, mail came only two or three times a week, and the call of a neighbor was an event. Instead of this life, I was mentally living in enchanted realms, surrounded with luxury and beauty, and enjoying the romantic adventures of the heroines of fascinating fiction. I think I was nine years old when I saw my first editor.

He came from Madison with a railroad official to ask for subscriptions for some proposed new line of railroad. He came in a "covered carriage"–my idea of elegance and wealth, as I rarely saw anything better than lumber-wagons or runabouts. I came from school, a long mile walk, on a hot summer afternoon, tired and curious to know who was within. As I entered the room, some member of the family presented me, and the editor took me on his knee.

"You look as delicate as a city girl," he said. "You ought to be more robust, living in this fine country air." Editors have said many kind things of me since then, but nothing which ever gave me such a sense of being a superior being as that. To look like a city girl–what joy! Yet I had never seen a city girl then, I am sure.

During my fourteenth year, the New York Mercury, which had been sent us by Aunt Abigail, living near Jamesville, Wisconsin, ceased to come. Aunt Abigail no longer subscribed for it. I missed its weekly visits with an intensity scarcely to be understood by one who has not known the same lonely surroundings and possessed the same temperament. There was not money enough floating around in those times to permit a subscription to the Mercury, and if I were to possess it, I knew I must either obtain a long list of subscribers, which would be a difficult and laborious undertaking, or earn it by my pen. I resolved to try the latter, but, feariiig failure, I did not want the family to know of my attempt. Finally, I decided on a stratagem. I was corresponding with a young girl, several years my senior, who was in the freshman class at Madison University. j I confided in her and enclosed the Mercury letter. Jean posted my letter and watched the news-stand for results. Two months later, long after I had relinquished all hope, she wrote me that my essays had appeared. Whereupon, I wrote a stern reproof to the editor for not sending the paper, "at least, as pay for my work," if he could afford no other remuneration! Shortly afterward a large package of back numbers of the New York Mercury came addressed to me through the country post-office. Now, even at that early age, I had an admirer, naturally disapproved of by the family. When the enormous roll of newspapers, direct from the editor's office, came to me, a stern member of the household at once concluded that the would-be "beau" had subscribed to win new favor in my eyes. This accusation was made before I was questioned on the subject. Perhaps the most triumphant and dramatic hour of my life was when I stepped forth, in short skirts and long ringlets, and announced to the family that not my admirer, but my "literary work," had procured the coveted Mercury for our united enjoyment.

In later years, I frequently heard of statements made by various unknown individuals who claimed to have "discovered" me and to have given my first efforts the light of day, but the advent of my muse into prose was also through the medium of the Mercury and wholly through my own efforts. The prose essays were published under the name of "Eloine," and immediately after their appearance I sent, under the same name, an ambitious poetical effort describing a highly emotional experience, to the editor of the "Ladies'

Promenade" column. The verses appeared anonymously with a half-column of sarcastic ridicule by the editor, which he closed by saying that the author of the lines so crucified was able to write very acceptably in prose, and he trusted she would "never again attempt poetical expression." Humiliated and crushed, but only temporarily, I rose to new attempts, and my first published verses appeared under my own name, in the Woverly Magasine, shortly afterward. Three short poems sent to Frank Leslie's publishing house brought me a check for ten dollars. This aroused in me such ambitions, that I proceeded to the nearest book store, twelve miles distant (riding to town on a high spring seat beside my brother in a lumber-wagon filled with bags of wheat for market), and there I wrote down the addresses of a dozen magazines and weeklies and began to bombard them with my effusions. Having had my first manuscripts published (even though one had been riddled by ridicule), I believed that the path to literary attainment was a flowery one; but at the end of the next three months I had become so accustomed to the "respectfully declined" note from various editors that a check for forty dollars, which was finally sent me by Frank Leslie's house, proved almost a nervous shock.

To possess such a sum of money all at once was a wonderful and inspiring experience, and it set my brain afire with new fancies. Many of the poems appeared in the Leslie and Harper publications without my name attached, as was the custom in those days, and I at once proceeded to send them, properly autographed, to country newspapers in Wisconsin. This led some of the editors no doubt to the belief that they had "discovered" and launched me, while in truth my verses had previously been published and paid for by New York and Boston editors.

Until I began to earn money, the neighbors had criticised my mother for keeping me out of the kitchen and allowing me to "scribble" so much. But when they found me able, with one day's work at my desk, to hire an assistant in the house for a month they began to respect my talent.

I wish the score " grown men and women who write to me for "aid and influence" in getting into print could know just how I found my way into the favor of editors. It was by sheer persistence. It never occurred to me to ask advice or assistance of others. I am glad it did not, for the moment we lean upon any one but the Divine Power and the divinity within us, we lessen our chances of success. I often receive letters now from writers in the West, asking me to use my influence with editors in their behalf and saying, "You must realize from your own early struggles how impossible it is to get a start in an Eastern periodical without a friend at court." No more absurd idea ever existed. Eastern editors are on the lookout for new talent constantly, and if a writer possesses it, together with persistence, he will succeed whether he lives in the Western desert or in the metropolis, and without any friend at court. All such literary aspirants are requested to read these pages and learn how I found my "friend at court"–the will in my own soul, and the patient and persistent effort of mind and heart and hand. Miles from a post-office, more miles from a railroad, and far from any literary center, without one acquaintance who knew anything about literary methods or the way to approach an editor, I pounded away at the doors of their citadels with my childish fist until they opened to me.

I recently came across a curious set of little home-made books where I kept my accounts long ago–a page for the poems sent to Frank Leslie's, another to Harper's Bazar and Weekly, another to Demaresfs, and so on through the list; and then the various journeyings of a poem, eight, nine, ten times to New York or Boston and back again before it folded its wings and rested in some editor's nest of "accepted manuscripts." I am sure I made many blunders and wrote much trash, and when advice was volunteered I did not value it as highly as I should. I felt I alone must make my climb toward the heights I sought, and no one could "boost" me up.

I soon filled the house with all the periodicals we had time to read, and in addition the editors sent me books and pictures and bric-a-brac and tableware–articles from their prize-lists, which were more precious than gems would have been to me.

They served to relieve the bare and commonplace aspect of the home, and the happiness I felt in earning these things with my pen is beyond words to describe.

About the time I appeared in print, I left the country school. My record there had been wretched in mathematics, while excellent in grammar, spelling, and reading. I lost interest in study, and my mind would not focus itself upon books. I lived in a world of imagination, and pictured for myself a wonderful future. In this I was encouraged at home by the ambitions of my mother, who despised her life and felt herself and her family superior to all her associates, and was forever assuring me (and them as well!) that my future would be wholly apart from my early companions.

Fortunately for me and for all concerned, I was a healthy and normal young animal, fond of my comrades, and enjoying their sports, into which I entered with zest, despite my mental aspirations and literary tendencies. But feeling I must receive a better education, the family made great sacrifices to send me to Madison University.

I was not happy there; first, because I knew the strain it put upon the home purse; second, because I felt the gulf between myself and the town girls, whose gowns and privileges revealed to me, for the first time, the different classes in American social life; and third, because I wanted to write and did not want to study. I had lost all taste for schoolbooks.

On composition-day, I undertook to distinguish myself by writing a "narrative," as the class was requested, but my ardent love-story only called forth a kind rebuke from gentle Miss Ware, and I was told to avoid reading the New York Ledger.

After one term, I begged my mother to allow me to remain at home and write, and she wisely consented. I took to my profession with a new ardor and enthusiasm after that.

My world grew larger with each sunrise, it seemed to me. People from Madison, Milwaukee, and Chicago began to write to me and seek me out. I was invited to visit city homes, and while this was a delight bordering on ecstasy and a relief from the depressing atmosphere of home anxieties, it yet brought with it the consciousness of the world's demands, which, added to those of duty and necessity, made a larger incoijie imperative.

There was continual worry at home; No one was resigned or philosophical. My mother hated her hard-working lot, for which she was totally unfitted, and constantly rebelled against it like a caged animal beating against iron bars, while she did her distasteful tasks with a Spartanlike adherence to duty, doubting the dominance of an all-wise Ruler who could condemn her to such a lot. Like thousands of others in the world, she had not learned that through love and faith only do conditions change for the better. The home was pervaded by an atmosphere of discontent and fatigue and irritability.

From reincarnated sources and through prenatal causes, I was born with unquenchable hope and unfaltering faith in God and guardian spirits. I often wept myself to sleep after a day of disappointments and worries, but woke in the morning singing aloud with the joy of life. I always expected wonderful things to happen to me. In some of the hardest days, when everything went wrong with everybody at home and all my manuscripts came back for six weeks at a time without one acceptance, I recall looking out of my little north window upon the lonely road bordered with lonelier Lombardy poplars, and thinking, "Before night something beautiful will happen to change everything." There was so much I wanted! I wanted to bestow comfort, ease and pleasure on everybody at home. I wanted lovely gowns–ah, how I wanted them! and travel and accomplishments. I wanted summers by the sea–the sea which I had read of but had never seen–and on moonlight nights these longings grew so aggressive I often pinned the curtain down and shut out the rays that seemed to intensify my loneliness, and I would creep into my little couch under the sloping eaves, musing,

"Another beautiful night of youth wasted and lost." And I would awakenhappy in spite of myself and put all my previous melancholy into verses–and dollars.

Once I read a sentence which became a life motto to me: "If you haven't what you like, try to like what you have."

I bless the author of that phrase–it was such a help to me just as I was nearing the borders of the family pessimism and chronic discontent. I-tried from that hour to find something I liked and enjoyed in each day–something I could be thankful for; and I found much, though troubles increased and conditions did not improve about me.

Slowly, so slowly, it seemed to me, my work and my income increased. I longed for sudden success, for sudden wealth. It was so hard to wait–there was so much to be done. There was a gentle hill south of the house; often on summer evenings, after writing all day, I climbed this ascent at sunset and looked eastward, wondering what lay for me beyond the horizon. I always had the idea that my future would be associated with the far West, yet it was to the East I invariably looked. My knowledge of the East was bounded by Milwaukee–the goal of happy visits two or three times a year.

Sometimes I walked through the pasture and young woods a half-mile, to call on Emma, the one friend who knew and sympathized with all the family troubles. And Emma would walk back with me, and we would wonder how many years longer these walks and talks would continue for us. I would tell her of my successes in my work, and she and her gentle mother rejoiced in them as if they were their own personal triumphs. Such restful walks and talks they always were!

Looking backward, I recall few mornings when I did not greet the day with a certain degree of exhilarating expectancy. Even in times of trouble and sorrow, this peculiar quality of mind helped me over obstacles to happiness which, retrospectively viewed, seemed insurmountable. A peculiar spiritual egotism possibly it might be called, for it led me to look for special dispensations of Providence in my behalf, and a setting-aside of nature's seeming laws and regulations, as well as the violating of reason's codes, that I might be obliged.

Facing the deadly monotony of the commonplace, I always looked for the unusual and romantic to occur. Environed by the need of petty economies, I always expected sudden opulence. Far from the world's center of life and action, I felt that hosts of rare souls were approaching, and, while hungry in heart and brain, I believed tfiat splendid banquets were in preparation for me. What would otherwise have been lonely, troubled, and difficult years were made enjoyable by this exalted state of the imagination.

Such concentration of expectancy, of course, brought some degree of result. Unusual things did happen, and that same virile, vivid imagination magnified them and made them seem colossal confirmation of my hopes. The commonplace meadows blossomed with flowers of beauty, and buttercups and daisies looked to me like rare orchids and hothouse roses. Between what really happened, and what I continually expected to happen, the world widened, existence grew in interest, and earth palpitated with new experience as the years passed. Always I expected more and more of life, and always it came in some guise.

Everything was material to me in those days;–the wind, the bees, the birds, and every word dropped by my elders in conversation which had a possible romantic trend, and all that I read in my favorite sensational novels proved fuel for my fire of ambition. Like most young poets, I sang more in the minor key than the major. The first poem which I considered of sufficient merit to copy in a manuscript book and which brought me four of the ten dollars of my first check was entitled "Two Lives":

An infant lies in her cradle bed;
The hands of sleep on her eyelids fall. The moments pass with a noiseless tread.
And the clock on the mantel counts them all. The infant wakes with a wailing cry.
And she does not heed how her life drifts by.
A child is sporting in careless play;
She rivals the birds with her mellow song. The clock unheeded ticks away.
And counts the moments that drift along. And she does not heed how her life drifts by. But the child is chasing the butterfly.
A maiden stands at her lover's side In the tender light of the setting sun. Onward and onward the mom-ents glide.
And the old clock counts them one by one. But the maiden's bridal is drawing nigh, And she does not heed how her life drifts by.
A song of her youth the matron sings, And dreameth a dream; and her eye is wet.
And backward and forward the pendulum swings In the clock that never has rested yet.
And the matron smothers a half-drawn sigh
As she thinks how her life is drifting by.
An old crone sits in her easy chair;
Her head is dropped on her aged breast. The clock on the mantel ticketh there,
The clock that is longing now for rest. And the old crone smiles as the moments fly And thinks how her life is drifting by.
A shrouded form in a coffin-bed,
A waiting grave in the fallow ground;
The moments pass with their noiseless tread. But the clock on the mantel makes no sound.
The lives of the two have gone for aye
And they do not heed how the time drifts by.

A clock always possessed a subtle charm for me and almost human qualities of companionship; and I can recall the sense of loneliness that came over me when, on rare occasions, our clock ran down–or was temporarily out of order.

Ofttimes I wrote four or five bits of verse (I called them "poems" then) in a day. Once I wrote eight. Unless I wrote two in twenty-four hours, I felt the day was lost. I received from three to five dollars for each poem accepted, and those that failed to bring me money served to supply me with weekly or monthly periodicals, and also with more material things. At my suggestion, articles from the prize-list of objects given by editors to those who secured subscribers were sent in payment for my verses (those which had failed to bring me money from other editors). A curious incident occurred in connection with this. I had accepted a half-dqz a silver forks from one editor, and many years afterward–in fact, several years subsequent to my marriage–I discovered that the forks were manufactured by the firm with which my husband was associated the greater part of his business life.

The subjects which I covered in this outpouring of early fancies were quite varied as will be seen by the following selections of verses written in one week, while still in my teens.

GODS MAJESTY I look upon the budding tree; I watch its leaves expand; And through it all, O God, I see.

The marvel of Thy hand. And all my soul in worship sings, 0 praise tiie Lord, the King of Kings!

1 look upon this mortal frame So wonderfully made; I note each perfect vein and nerve

And I am sore afraid; I tremble, God, at thought of Thee So awful in Thy Majesty. I look upon the mighty sun.

Upon the humble flower; In both, O great and heavenly One, I read Thy wondrous power; And in an ecstasy I raise A song of thankfulness and praise.

I look upon the lightnings flash; I see the rain drops fall; I listen to the thunders crash.

And find Thee in it all; In earth and sky, and sea and air. Thou, O my God, art everywhere.

DEPARTED

Love reigned King in my heart one day,

Reigned with his courtiers three– Belief unspoken. Trust unbroken.

And Faith as deep as the sea.

And I cried in sweet pain, "Oh long may they reign, And my heart be their kingdom alway."

But the Courtier's Belief slipped down from his throne

And died at the feet of King Love. I saw him falling, all vainly calling

To the King and the Courtiers above. And he struggled with death and he labored for breath, Till he died with a heart-broken moan.

"But the King and his two noble courtiers still reign.

And shall reign forever," I said; But lo, on the morrow, I wept in keen sorrow.

For Trust in his beauty lay dead. And I buried him low, and I said, "Now I know How to value the two who remain."

But Faith drooped and died; and Love sat alone. And he pined for the ones who were dead;

A king without reason he reigned for a season But his strength and his glory had fled.

And no pain stirred my breast and I said, "It is best,"

When he tottered and fell from his throne.

HEARTS EASE

Give me work for my hands to do.

Whenever I have a grief; There's no other balm so good I ween

For a wounded Heart's relief.

And give me something to think about.

Something beside my pain; And let me labor throughout the day

With a busy hand and brain.
From the flush of mom till the gloom of night
With never a time to weep; And then in the gloaming let me turn
Like a weary child to sleep.

As I read over the scores, yes, hundreds of these verses, written those first years of my literary career, and note the memorandum above them, stating the prices received and in many of them the periodicals wherein they appeared, I realize how much more exacting to-day are the requirements of all editors. Small as were the prices paid me (varying from three to fifteen dollars), I am sure no young writer to-day could sell so many verses of this type for any price. Literary standards are higher, and literary tastes of readers more cultivated. But at that time I was fortunate in finding editors who liked just what I was able to supply, and when urged by older people of larger culture to try historical themes my first effort in that line met with ignominious rejection; and the last of the editors to reject them said, "Give us heart-wails;–that is what our readers like; they can read history in books."

CHAPTER II First School Days and arly Pets

MY first day at school was when I was less than seven, I think. I know it was only a temporary schoolhouse, half a mile away. I cried to go, and was allowed to accompany the older children of the neighborhood and my brother. I recall the fact that it was the summer season, because the noon school dinner-pail contained strawberry shortcake. I asked at recess for my part of the shortcake: instead of waiting till noon, I ate it and then ran home.

Later, there was the other schoolhouse a mile distant from my home: a short mile, I think; yet we called it that. In the winter it often seemed a long mile. But when the drifts were higher than the fences, and hard and firm, there used to be an exhilaration in racing over them to school. Sometimes when the big storms came and the roads were badly drifted, there was excitement in seeing the neighbors and our own men and horses turn out plowing the road to school; and then, too, many times in very inclement weather, neighbors took turns in carrying the children. The Howies, the Harts, the Hol-dens, the Mcginnises, all lived west of us, and when they came along, I could ride with them. But the roads needed to be very bad when we felt we could not walk. Those walks no doubt helped to develop the very robust health and great vitality I have always enjoyed.

Two early summers of schoolgoing were shadowed by a curious fear of earthquakes which assailed me. I think there must have been somewhere an earthquake, which had been talked of by the family–very likely at the extreme ends of the earth. But it impressed my imaginative mind, and when the summer sun baked the black soil in Wisconsin and cracked it open in places, I suffered untold agonies as I walked home from school, feeling great pity for the laughing children beside me, who were going, all unsuspectingly, to their doom. I would think of this as I went to my little bed under the eaves, never expecting to see the dawn. The second summer this fear seized me, I told my mother about it, and was assured by her that we lived in a place where no such calamities occurred. So positive was she that the fear left me forever. When I did participate in a real earthquake, long afterward, in the island of St. Kitts, it came upon me without warning and was over just as I realized what it was. Although I had half a night of justified expectation of other quakes to follow, I did not experience in that half-night a hundredth part of the terror of those hours of my childhood.

When I was very small, I used to "play horse" a great deal. After I was married and went back West on a visit wearing my best clothes and feeling myself a very dignified matron, an old farmer, Mr. Coolidge, came to call. He said to me, "EUy" (the old farmers always called me that), "do you know what you were doing the first time I ever saw you?"

"No; tell me," I answered.

"Well," replied Mr. Coohdge, "you were four years old; and your brother Ed was driving you about the yard with a pair of lines over your neck, and he was using a whip on you and yelling at the top of his voice, Gol darn it, why don't you whinny louder?"

One of the things which linger in my memory like an old fragrance in the air, is "Mrs. Elliott's Spring." An English lady lived half a mile through a pasture, where the creek ran; and at the foot of a hill there was this ever-flowing clear cold spring of water, about which peppermint grew in a thick border. It used to be the delight of the school children when two of them were chosen by the teacher to take the school pail, and go to "The Spring" and fill it. We always picked bunches of peppermint to bring away with us. Mrs. Elliott had a mildly insane son, who lent a touch of the dramatic to these trips. He walked all day in a circle, talking to himself

FIRST SCHOOL DAYS AND EARLY PETS 35 and smiling, and paying very little heed to any one. His circle was a beaten path, such as horses make on a threshing machine. His mother said he had overstudied; and others said he had been crossed in love. The house was quite apart from the spring; and we did not see "Crazy John" unless we made an effort. When we wanted a real thrill to change the monotony of life, we ran up, and took a look at the sad yet smiling lunatic.

A touch of the dramatic was added one summer by another John: "Big John", who came to live in a house near the school. It was built by a Norwegian, and the lower part was dug into a hill; and above this basement rose a whitewashed cabin. I had read stories even then of robbers' caves, and this house from the first gave me creepy feelings. When Big John occupied it, I am sure we school children were the first aggressors. I am certain we made faces at him or teased him in ways known only to children. I know my parents were neglectful as are nine-tenths of American parents, in giving their children that education of the heart which makes them courteous and thoughtful toward all lesser creatures. My family had that New England prejudice toward "foreigners" which springs from a curious provincial American conceit: and we, like all American children, grew up thinking we were made of finer clay than the children who sprang from Irish, Scandinavian, or, in fact, any blood save "American." So looking back, I am quite sure Big John was more sinned against than sinning, when he chased the school children as we passed his "dug-out," and hooted at us until our parents had him arrested as a nuisance, and a menace to the peace.

I had as a child very white hands, and very red cheeks; and after one of the times when Big John pursued us, Homer Benson said to me, "My! but you were scared, EUy! Your cheeks got as white as your hands."

The arrest of Big John made a decided commotion in the neighborhood. I was called as one of the witnesses; and the trial took place in the school house in the district where the Justice of the Peace, Bill Wilson, lived. A Justice of the Peace was my idea of a great man. Bill Wilson was a large man, with a heavy voice, and helped along my impression of an awe-inspiring official. Now I had read some story, I think by Mrs. E. D. E. N. Southworth, where a girl is called to the witness stand and saves the life of someone condemned to death, by her dramatic testimony and her striking personality.

With this in my mind, I lay awake the night before I was to be a witness at the trial of Big John, and tried to rehearse my part. Albeit I knew the size of the room in the school house, I visualized a large auditorium, with stately steps leading up to a rostrum. I saw myself ascending-fliis stairway, and I felt the large audience was holding its breath as I moved along. I knew I would wear a little shawl which was my "Sunday best"; and I wondered whether I had better drape it over my shoulders at first, and then let it carelessly trail down, as I stood before the Justice, or whether it would be more effective if I let it trail first, and then drew it up with a "queenly gesture" as I began my impassioned testimony. I do not remember how I decided. I only remember feeling how small and inferior the school room looked, as I entered that next evening and how dreadfully near me, only over the aisle, was the Justice. When he called my name, I started to cross the aisle and stumbled: forgetting all about my shawl and my queenly gestures. When I stood before the Justice, very red and frightened, he bellowed, "Well, Elly Wheeler, what do you know of this man's actions?" Tremblingly I began: "I think–I think," and again the Justice bellowed–"I don't want to hear what you think; I want to hear what you know." The remainder of the case is forgotten now. I only recall my broken dream of a great hour, and a sense of depression, as I rode home. I am sure the case was decided against Big John, for he never troubled us again, to my recollection.

I believe my teachers, as a rule, were fond of me. But I know I was very mischievous and disagreeable one winter. I played all sorts of pranks on a good old man who came to take charge of the school and who had no idea of system or order. I feel tears in my heart to this day when I remember

FIRST SCHOOL DAYS AND EARLY PETS 37 it. My shame and remorse awoke when the good old man came to our house to "board a week" and talked continually to my mother of the wonderful gift he thought I possessed in composition, while never a word of complaint was made about my bad conduct. The coals of fire burned deeply into my head and heart. And they burn to this day. I can still see the. uncouth old man sitting tilted against the kitchen wall with his feet on the rung of the chair, and his knees high in the air (he was very long of limb), talking to my handsome mother while she prepared the dinner, and telling her what a wonderful child I was in his estimation; for, in my heart, I knew he should have said, "Madam, that little brat of yours has made me more trouble at school than all the other children."

To be overpraised has always been more painful to me than to be undervalued, and, that day, I experienced my first mortification of this kind. I ran out into the yard, I remember, to escape hearing his eulogies.

My father never took the reins of government over us. He left that to mother. Once only have I any recollection of being chastised by my father.

I was less than six–not over five, I am sure. I had been disjippointed in something, and I began to cry. My mother paid no attention. I went into the front room where my father was talking with a neighbor, and I lay down on the floor and kicked my heels against the wall just beside the stairway that led to the upper rooms. I believe I could point to the exact spot to-day, so memorable was made that moment by what fouovifed.

My father rose from his chair, and still continuing his conversation with the neighbor, came over and delivered four rousing slaps on that part of my anatomy which was uppermost at that moment. Then, without addressing a word to me, he resumed his seat and his conversation. I was so astonished that I rose to a proper position and state of mind at once.

This, I think, was the end of my very naughty habit of lying down on the floor and kicking when displeased. My older brother used to sing a school-song when I did this. He would look at me and begin to sing the refrain, which in olden days they employed to memorize the state capitals. He sang always for me as I kicked my legs in the air.

Upper California, Upper California, the capital is Monterey.

And yet my elders tell me I was really a very amiable child!

I loved cats with a tender passion. My mother was kind to animals, but she thought their placewas outdoors or in the barn. My older brother also loved cats, but my sister was peculiarly afifected by the sight of one. She became violently nauseated if a cat approached her.

My brother Marcus, as well as my father and brother Ed, had just one bad habit. They used needlessly strong language when moved by great emotions. When they took the name of the Creator in vain, it always hurt me like a blow in the face. They were such good men and such brainy men, and this seemed a blight on their otherwise noble characters. It was a mere habit but a bad habit.

Once, my brother Marcus wanted some cats he loved to come indoors in stormy weather. My mother objected, and I remember what my brother said. He said, "When I have a home of my own, I will have a hell full of cats." Well, he married an angel, an American-French girl,–sweet Lois; and she let him have all the cats about he wanted. But it was a heaven full, not a hell. For she made home heaven.

I somehow induced mother to let me have my pet cat in the house daytimes, but it was always put out at night. Mother had a habit of picking the cat up any sort of way and tossing it out in the yard, when bedtime came. She told me of a plea I made to her when quite small which impressed her greatly. I ran after her as she went to the door with the cat and I caught her skirts and cried, "Mother, put him out a-walking; put him out a-walking." All through later life mother quoted this to me when I suggested gentler methods of doing anything.

I was fond of little calves and colts and chickens which came on the farm. One event stands out clearly. One

FIRST SCHOOL DAYS AND EARLY PETS 39 morning my brother Marcus came to my bed and woke me gently, and, bundling me up, carried me out to see a new colt before breakfast and before Ed saw it. There was a little lady calf which allowed me to sit beside her and pretend to milk her, while my brother filled my little wooden school-pail with milk from his large tin pail; and, later, the family was quite astonished to find I really knew how to milk a cow. But my mother never allowed me to do this, save on a few rare occasions when the men were driven with work. She hated outdoor work for women. And she said my hands would be spoiled–my hands which were her pride and delight– assuring me that some day I was to dwell among people who would appreciate beautiful, well-kept hands. Never did mother lose sight of her ideals for me. There was a wonderful chicken which became my pet when I was of chicken-pox age. I had taken care of the mother hen while she sat on twelve eggs, feeding her and watering her with care. When I heard the first peep of chickens, I was thrilled with the maternal instinct. The old hen allowed me to help pick off the bits of shell from her brood. Every one of the twelve eggs had produced a chicken, but one was afflicted with a strange malady.

When the mother hen clucked her eleven flufify balls of life to follow her and showed them how to pick up crumbs and seeds, the twelfth chicken walked backward with his head high in the air. Vainly the mother hen called and fluttered about him; he could not walk straight. So I called him "Tipsy" and took him into the house, and put him under the stove in a tin pan with warm cloths about him. I fed and coddled him and for days tried to put him back with the brood, but he could not live among them. Although he could pick up food, and drink water, he invariably walked backward when trying to move about. So Tipsy became my house pet, and deep was my affection for him. When he was six weeks old Tipsy crowed! I was startled and filled with apprehension. Never was a six-weeks-old little rooster known to crow before, I knew. I felt that Tipsy had not long to live. I ran upstairs where my mother was making beds and told

THE WORLDS AND I her. Mother was hurried and tired, and she paid no attention to me, save to say I was in her way. Shortly after that I fell ill of chicken-pox. It was a light attack, as I was a most robust child, but I had to keep in bed for a week. At the end of the week, when I was told I could dress and sit up, I asked to see Tipsy. My mother very gently told me the sad news. Tipsy had walked backward just as a door blew shut in a gale of wind, and he was killed. They had buried him in the yard. Mother's tender sympathy was very comforting then. Afterward I exhumed the body, and buried him by a stone in the pasture where reposed several of my pet cats, and I planted flowers over his grave.

An old blue hen became my favorite later. She followed me about, and let me carry her in my arms. I must have been eleven years old. It was a summer day and I was helping my mother, churning the butter while she baked. She was making a cake and asked me to go out and bring in some eggs. I ran out full of the joy of life. As I looked in all the accustomed places for the eggs, I passed by the corn crib, and saw on the south side, huddled against the crib, my blue hen. Her eyes were partly closed, and when I touched her she seemed to be unconscious. My heart fairly froze in my breast with fear and sorrow. I knew my blue hen was dying. Yet I could not stay and try to save her, as my mother had told me to hurry back with the eggs and to finish the churning before the men came in for dinner. I went back to the house and finished the churning. I turned my back so my mother could not see that I was weeping. Tears always annoyed mother. They affected the men folk, but they displeased her. I knew she would think me very silly for crying over the blue hen, but I could not help it. The day seemed to have lost all luster for me as I thought of my pet dying alone by the corn crib. She was dead indeed when I went out after the butter had come, and the table had been set. I hollowed out a grave for her, and picked some flowers to scatter over her corpse.

It was after I had grown up that I told my mother of the sorrow of that hour.

FIRST SCHOOL DAYS AND EARLY PETS 41

There are still living in the village of Windsor, Wisconsin, a man and wife bearing rather unusual "given names," who had each a somewhat peculiarly beneficial influence on my early life. I refer to Brazier Ellis and his wife, Olyette. "Bra" Ellis, as his chums used to call him, frequently came to visit with my brother, and to hear my sister sing, and to argue on all sorts of subjects with my mother. When, before my fifteenth birthday, there was much comment in the neighborhood about my having had "pieces published in the papers," Brazier Ellis, during a call on the family, looked at me critically and said, "Well, by the time she is sixteen Ella will be a regular bluestocking, round-shouldered, and wearing spectacles." The words were spoken in jest, but they filled me with a cold horror. It was the first intimation I had received that the shining shield of literary talent and achieve–ments could have a dark side.

I remember asking my mother what "Bra" meant; and she told me that people who devoted their whole time to study and writing often grew round-shouldered and also overtaxed their eyes; but she did not believe that this was necessary. I then and there resolved that it should not prove a necessary accompaniment to my profession (for from the beginning I knew literature was to be for me not an amusement or a fad but a life-work).

I began, the day after Brazier's words were uttered, to walk about the house and the yard, for at least half an hour, with a yardstick or a rod of some kind across my shoulders, and my arms linked over it. This made a very erect attitude, a high chest, and deep breathing compulsory. I often sat in this way while reading some book, and a more healthful or beneficial exercise was never taught in physical culture schools than this, which I evolved out of my own vanity; for it was really a desire to "look pretty," rather than any more sensible motive, which caused me to devote a little time each day to this practice. All the heroines in my favorite novels were described as erect and willowy, with beautifully poised heads, and I did not intend to acquire any habit which they would scorn to possess I was troubled because nature had not given me a

"long, swan-like neck," but, at least, the neck I had should not be sunk between round shoulders.

The spectacles, too, I was determined should be avoided. My eyes were naturally very strong, and rather far-sighted. I could read signs at the roadside at a much greater distance than any of my school companions; yet the corresponding difficulty to read at a normal distance, which frequently accompanies far sight, was not mine. With such excellent eyes, there was often a temptation to overtax them; but the ogre of the "spectacled bluestocking" kept me from many an indulgence in night reading and writing through many lonely evenings when the only alternative was to go early to bed.

One mile east of my home lived the Sabin family; and Ellen, the oldest of an ever increasing family, was my great friend. She was the most brilliant scholar in three districts, and at fifteen had surpassed all her school mates in education. At sixteen she was teaching pupils older than herself. I used to look forward to walking over to see the new baby which came every year to the Sabin home; but Ellen did not greet each new arrival as enthusiastically as I did. She felt that her mother was overtaxed, and when twins arrived one year Ellen looked at me with blazing blue eyes, and said, "Come next year and we will have theee to show you." Yet she proved the good fairy to all the brood and her unlimited generosity, affection and unselfishness gave them all larger opportunities for education. Ellen Sabin became a powerful educational factor in the middle West and the far West, and is to-day President of Downer-and-Milwaukee College. I remember a brilliant June day when Ellen and I saddled our horses and took a wonderful ride to Token Creek seven miles away, where she went on errands for home. The locust trees were in full bloom and Ellen recited for me a poem I had never heard until that day: "O what is so rare as a day in June? Then, if ever, come perfect days." Ellen's dear mother always hailed with delight my little literary triumphs: and when in my teens, I ran to the Sabin house to show my first book, "Drops of Water," there was as much rejoicing as if I had been one of their own brood.

Two miles west lived another family of eight children (the Howies). When they moved into our town, they seemed to bring a breeze from a larger world to us. They were Scotch people of fine blood and brain, and our families became very intimate. Jean and Mary, though both older than I, were very devoted to me. Jean posted my first efforts at literary achievements and kept my secret until they appeared in print. Mary chose me for her bridesmaid when she was married; and my first check paid for my gown. Mary and I have not met in many years, but we still write and love each other as of old. I used to ride my horse up to the Howie house; and these rides always savored of adventure to me. When I set forth, it ever seemed to me that romantic experiences would occur before my return. I fancied I might perhaps be thrown from my horse at the feet of some Knight who would be touring through the country at that exact moment; or it might be that the steeds of his coach would be frightened by the equestrienne, and that he would be thrown at my feet to be succored and cared for.

Olyette Ellis was at that time a Miss Smith, and my very dear school-teacher for a term or two in the little Westport schoolhouse. She impressed upon her pupils the benefit to be derived from daily cold baths, which, of course, meant a cold rub in a cold room, as we had no running water or porcelain tubs or steam heat in our environment; and she laid much stress on the care of the teeth and other hygienic habits which were of lasting value to me. Besides which, she possessed artistic and poetical talent, and by her praise greatly encouraged me in my early ambitions.

My opportunities for acquiring education and accomplishments in my childhood were limited. There were no kindergartens then, and the nearest schoolhouse was a mile distant. My father taught me my letters from the outside of an almanac, and I believe I learned to read quickly at an early age. I was fortunate in having parents who used excellent English; and the older children had been taught to regard ungrammatical expressions and poor spelling as something bordering on disgrace. So I absorbed the foundation of grammar and orthography without being conscious of it. My sister taught school and music and when she came home, at vacations or week-ends, brought well-educated friends into the home; and I heard many dissertations between my sister and oldest brother (a great reader and fine grammarian) and school-teacher friends which were helpful to me on the pronunciation of words.

My mother was gifted with a wonderful power of expression, and had, by constant reading and a marvelous memory, acquired a rich vocabulary. My father, too, used good English, often somewhat stilted it seemed, when he was talking with strangers. I remember he was fond of using long words and I have seen a very puzzled look on the faces of some of his very simple-minded listeners (like the Norwegian hired men and women who helped us out at harvest-time). He once asked a green maid to do some bit of mending for him, and instead of saying, "when you have time," he said, "when you have opportunity." Of course, that is a common word; but it was Greek to the Scandinavian girl, and she came to my mother and asked: "What is opportunity? Mr. Wheeler said I must have it."

My father had been, during his youth in Vermont, somewhat delicate in health; and he had never performed any real manual labor until he came to Wisconsin to seek his fortune (and to lose all he had). His family, on the maternal side, was related to Ethan Allen, and his grandmother was the first white child born in Kew Hampshire. I believe some four generations back he traced Welsh ancestry. My mother's family, which was also American for four generations (her grandfather fought in the American Revolution), went back to French, Spanish and Irish forebears, and there was a rumor, which was her great pride, that the blood of Pocahontas filtered down through some branch of her family. I never knew how authentic this rumor was, but certainly my mother's sister. Aunt Abigail, looked strikingly like a squaw. She was as brown as' an Indian, with straight, black hair, and she had a horror of being indoors. She loved the open, and lived into her eighties on the old Pratt farm, near Johns-
FIRST SCHOOL DAYS AND EARLY PETS 45 town, Wisconsin, taking care of stock and avoiding shoes and stockings when the weather would permits Surely this does speak of Indian blood. Aunt Abigail boasted of the fact that she never had a proposal in her life, and never saw the man who possessed the least attraction for her as a lover.

The mixture of blood in my mother's ancestry was strikingly illustrated in her sisters. The younger. Aunt Mary Ann, was distinctly Spanish in her type and nature, handsome, coquettish and fond of dress; and her Latin temperament led her into two marriages. Aunt Amine was typically New England through and through, classically handsome, excessively neat and frugal, and austere in her ideas. I always stood in awe of this aunt. She was the wife of a prominent lawyer and judge in Wisconsin, and the mother of one of the eminent educators in the West, Professor W. D. Parker, long president of a college, now retired and living in California. He inherited his mother's austere moralities.

My mother was a strange commingling of French and Irish temperaments,–wit and brilliancy. The Irish blood, no doubt, owing to the narrow ideas prevailing in New

England for so long a time, was never acknowledged by the family (despite the fact that my grandmother's name was OConnor) until I grew old enough to insist upon it. Once I took this stand, my mother accepted the fact with open pride.

My father had, in Vermont, been the inheritor of a very roomy old ancestral house; and he had made an income by teaching the violin and dancing and deportment. In the Vermont house at Thetford, there was a large ballroom, where the "elite" used to come to learn these polite accomplishments from my father. Not until after he was eighty did he lose the upright figure and the easy, graceful deportment that always distinguished him from other farmers in our Wisconsin environment.

My motiier was taken as a bride to this Thetford house from Bradford, Vermont, her birthplace, and my brothers and sisters were born there. I did not appear on the scene until the family had lived some time in Wisconsin.

As my father's financial ventures were not successful in the new life of the West, and as the family purse needed replenishing, he resumed his old occupation again in a measure; and when I was eight years old, he had formed a class in dancing at Token Creek, a little burg some seven miles from our home. There was an inn there known as "Fields' Tavern," where the dancing class was held. I was permitted to attend, and there learned my first steps in an art that always fascinated me. It seems to me now that beautiful dancing contains all the other arts; it is poetry, music, sculpture, and painting all in one.

My love for it was so intense and my aptitude so great that I am sure had my home been near any metropolis I should have been made a member of some ballet company before I grew out of childhood. Apropos of this, after my marriage, I was one of four young women who studied dancing under an old French ballet master. Two of the class took up the study to reduce their weight, and two of us for the benefit to our health and for the pleasure it afiforded. (One of these was Marie Millard, the sweet and gifted daughter of Harrison Millard, the composer. She sang in opera for a season, and then married Louis Gottschalk, composer and musical director, now of California.) This old French master of the ballet was, of course, devoted to his profession, and he could not imagine that there was any position or vocation in life which recompensed a woman for missing the career of a successful ballet dancer. Several times during the two terms of lessons I had with him, he wrung his hands and cried out that it was "such a misfortune Madame had not fallen into his hands in her early childhood; he could have made such a wonderful artist of her." My sister was a most beautiful dancer, and she was very much of a belle among the beaux at Fields' Tavern; I found food for some of my early verses and stories, by hearing the family and friends discuss the jealousy of her rival admirers.

Mr. Fields was the father of four very handsome daughters, and two of them possessed remarkable singing voices, as did my sister. Both my sister and Ann Fields, I remember, were the wonder of my father; when, after playing a whole com-
FIRST SCHOOL DAYS AND EARLY PETS 47 position of dance music on his violin, like "The Lancers" for instance, they would sing it through perfectly–their voices like flutes. Had either of these girls been given the opportunity to study, they would have made operatic stars. I have heard my mother relate how, at the age of

three years, my sister used to astonish my father's pupils in Vermont by singing fully twenty songs distinctly and correctly.

Ann Fields was a handsome Amazon and prided herself upon her physical prowess. Such girls were not as frequently met with in those days as now, and Ann seemed to my childish mind like some radiant creature who had dropped from another planet. I am quite sure that the remarkable qualities I ascribed to Minnie Tighthand, the heroine of my first "novel," were suggested by Ann Fields.

A wonderful day came when my sister had a piano and soon after (at the age of fourteen) I began lessons. I received only a few terms of instruction as my sister was teaching elsewhere, and, shortly after, she married and moved to another state. But I was a faithful student, and gained the foundation knowledge of music which has enabled me all my life to obtain pleasure and recreation through some sort of an instrument. For this privilege I feel profoundly grateful to my family.

After my sister's piano was sent to her, my father, who had been speculating a bit in cattle and had made a little profit, bought me an Estey organ, which was my heart's delight for many a day. I even obtained such prestige as a performer on the organ that I consented to teach the rudiments of instrumental music to a neighbor's girl. I look back upon this experience of my life with amazement at my own self-confidence and the confidence of my neighbor in my ability. After my marriage and removal to the East, where I came in contact with world-famed musicians, I dropped my crude piano-playing in fright, realizing how little I knew. Then there came a time when again I felt I must have musical expression, and I took up the mandolin, which musical toy resulted in giving me great distraction for five years. I formed an orchestra (we called it "The Bungalow Band") among the cot- tagers at our lovely seashore home, and with two mandolins, a guitar, flute, cello, and piano, we studied good music and were able to give and receive much pleasure. We gave home concerts for charity. My mandolin, too, accompanied me on a tour of the world, and in every country I obtained national airs and practiced them many hours in our quarters on the ship or in quiet corners of the big decks during long voyages. Once in a compartment which my husband and I had all to ourselves in a long railway journey in northern Africa, I whiled away otherwise tedious hours by practicing some Arabian melodies which I had been fortunate enough to find after much search in a shop in Tunis.

The Arabs, like all Orientals, do not write their music; it is sung by one generation to another: but in Tunis I found a book of the Arabian airs which had been written down by an enterprising Frenchman who went and lived in the Arab tents, for months, for the purpose of studying and transcribing their national airs. (Antonin Laffarge was the musician's name, and his book, "La Musique Arab: Ses Instruments et Ses Chants," is a treasure which I highly prize. I doubt if any one else in America or perhaps in England possesses a copy of it.)

My husband and I spent the week of the full moon, in April, 1913, at Hamman Mousquitine, where there are the wonderful natural boiling spring baths of northern Africa; and each evening he liked to have me take my mandolin out under the big terebinthe tree and play the Arabian airs while he smoked his cigar. (Oh, week of wonderful memories!) Again, in India, I found a book of old Indian songs without words, which helped me to enter into the spirit of India after I left its historic shores.

In 1914, I abandoned the mandolin for the harp, and now find all my former dalliance with music a helpful preparation for a more serious study. Music is an important factor in mature life, and looking back across the years I realize that some wise, kind "Invisible Helper," urged me on always in every attempt I made to express myself in music, so that, in my later years, I might have this consolation and means of mental and spiritual development. I wish FIRST SCHOOL DAYS AND EARLY PETS 49 all young people could realize the value of music in later life, and apply themselves accordingly. Musical vibrations are important factors in helping our spirit friends to come near.

Very early in life, I felt an intense longing to be a linguist. Especially did I desire to learn French. One summer, my brother told me there was a French boy on a farm a few miles away. He was working for an old gentleman who had emigrated from France a half-century before; that old gentleman said that the boy, George, spoke an excellent French. (We learned afterward that he had been sent to a French reform school for some early misdemeanor, had proven himself an apt pupil, and had come out after four years, speaking the "language of courts" quite correctly.) I at once negotiated with George to come to my home each Sunday and give me a French lesson. I obtained books and learned to read quite easily, but was impatient of the study part, and so did not make the progress I might otherwise have done. Yet, when marriage took me to the East and my husband urged me to begin the study of French seriously, I found that my Sunday afternoons on the farm in Wisconsin with the reform-school boy had been of real value to me.

In New York city I beceune the first pupil of a dear French lady, Madame Sorieul, just from France and scarcely able to speak or understand a word of English. A friendship of a quarter of a century has resulted. Madame Sorieul, now a resident of Bridgeport, Connecticut, still teaches French.

Swimming was an accomplishment which, as a little girl, I longed to acquire, but my mother thought a girl who swam, skated, or whistled was a tomboy. (Broad as she was in so many ways and so in advance of her associates and time, she nevertheless had her limitations.) We were not near any body of water larger than "Cramer's Pond," which relied upon frequent rains to keep it from being merely a marshy hollow; but over at Token Creek there was a stream of considerable depths, especially after a spell of rainy weather. One fatal day I was allowed to go and spend the afternoon with one of my friends, Helen Fields, and there found several other little girls. Helen told us that the creek, where it ran so THE WORLDS AND I through the woods, was very deep and very clear, and that we could go swimming there and no one see us. It was a hot summer day, and the idea seemed fascinating. So off we went, and off went our clothes, and into the creek we splashed. Terrible thoughts of what would happen if my mother chanced along came to blight the brilliant moment for me; but we came out, dried ourselves off (in the sunlight and with leaves, no doubt, as I am sure Helen took no towels along), dressed, and returned home without being discovered. Just how the story leaked out I do not recall; but I do recall the terrible scolding I received, for my mother's brilliant flow of language was never more noticeable than when she was angry. She never used a vulgar or coarse word, but she could be sarcastic to an unbelievable degree, using very choice expressions. She believed I had disgraced myself and the family and all womankind by immodest conduct, and I was in disfavor for many a day.

It was not until after my marriage that I had the privilege! f acquiring the very healthful and useful accomplishment of swimming. My mother spent the last seven of her ninety ears at my seashore home and lived to see me swimming every summer day, and learned to accept the fact that I swam well with considerable pride. Yet she would almost invariably add, after any complimentary remark that was made on he subject: "It was not considered nice for girls to swim in iy day."

CHAPTER III The Beginnings of Success IN my early teens, before the railroad came to Windsor, our post-office was at Westport, five miles distant. Mail came, I believe, only twice a week. My early effusions were posted in that office, and when the men were busy with farm-work I used to go into the pasture, put a bridle and blanket and surcingle on single-pacing Kitty, take a cross-lot ride to the home of Alice Ellis, whose father had brought her a pony from California, and off we would speed to the Westport post-office. There was great joy of life in thosg rides, but they were restridted before long, because a "Mr. Butt-In" from somewhere along the route told a male member of my family that "Elly and Ally rode like the very devil and would break their necks if allowed to go on in that way." Soon after this, a post-office was established at Leicester, four miles west of us, and still later at Windsor, three miles east of us, where the railroad had formed the nucleus of a little town. Leicester about the same time became merged into Waunakee, two or three miles to the south, but the same distance from my old home. I believe Waunakee is now quite a thriving town; but even in the early years of my marriage it was so modest in size that it led to a droll sarcasm from the pen of my humorous husband. I was making my second visit to Wisconsin after my marriage. My husband went with me, but left after a few days for the East, on a train passing through Waunakee to Chicago. I wrote him the next week that a citizen of Waunakee said Mr. Wilcox was the handsomest man he ever saw. To this my Robert replied:

"Which of the residents of Waunakee was it, my dear? The one who lives in the red house north of the railroad track, or the other one living in the white house south of the track? With such a continual rush of crowds passing before his vision continually, I should think the Waunakee citizen a most competent judge of manly beauty."

To return to those earlier days when Leicester was our post-office carries me back to several prosperous years on the farm when the family owned a "top buggy" which seemed to me like a queen's chariot as I rode with my brothers to the Good Templars' lodge-meetings, where we met a circle of our "best society." There was much talk, papers were read and songs sung, after which was a general good time.

There were two winters also about that time made joyous by a singing school. Mr. Padley, who possessed a fine tenor voice, was our teacher, and his skill was so great that he developed a voice in me, and I became his first soprano.

Then there was a sort of semi-annual or quarterly ball at Miller's Hall, which was always a brilliant function. The hall was engaged by a dozen young men who issued invitations by word of mouth to those deemed worthy by merit of good behavior and good dancing to be in "our crowd." Each man invited his "lady" and paid his share of the expense for music and supper. I was sixteen years old when Miller's Hall was at its height of popularity, and I still think of it as a sort of illuminated Temple, brilliant with lights and dazzling with youth, beauty and elegance. I know that it was in reality a crude building, lighted with kerosene-oil lamps and peopled with farmers, and their wives, daughters, and sons, in home-made clothes. There were too, of course, storekeepers' families and clerks, bookkeepers and schoolteachers, all of whom were regarded as a little higher in the social scale. We used to dance from early evening to the break of day and then regret that dawn had come so soon.

My romantic temperament and the sensational reading I fed upon caused me to imagine m)rself the heroine of sentimental experiences at an early age. Quite unknown to any one, I believed I was a victim of unrequited love at the age of thirteen. Ignoring boys of my own age, I fixed my attention upon a young man of twenty-five who often came to the house to see my brothers, and who was engaged to be married to a girl in her twenties.

My hero was a clerk of some sort, which enabled him to dress more nattily than the farm-boys; and he seemed to me like one of the "younger sons" of the aristocratic families described by Mrs. Southworth and Mary J. Holmes. Regarding me as the little girl I was in reality, and quite unaware of my romantic attitude toward him, he made something of a pet of me, thus fanning the flame in my imaginative heart, to what I quite enjoyed believing was a hopeless passion which would send me to an early grave.

Emily, the sweetheart of my hero, was brown as a Gypsy, with coal-black hair and eyes, and a protruding under lip– what the surgical dentists call, I believe, "the bulldog jaw." In my eyes she was altogether beautiful, because she was the chosen one of my hero; and for a period of several weeks I went about the house with my tongue thrust against my under lip, hoping to resemble Emily, if I could not he she.

My sister one day asked my mother what in the world was the matter with Ella's mouth: "It looked so strange lately." They made solicitous inquiries as to whether I had any pain or swelling of the mouth, and so much attention was bestowed upon that feature that I was obliged to let it resume its natural shape.

The day Emily became the bride of my hero I confided to a sympathetic chum the fact that I never expected to smile again. In return, she told me that she had been thwarted in love by cruel parents (she was fifteen), and that earth for her,. too, was henceforth a barren waste.

A few months afterward, my first effusions appeared in print, and life assumed a new aspect and my hopeless passion was forgotten. I was fifteen when the next hero appeared on my horizon. He was twenty-six, and he came from a lumber-camp in the northern part of the state, and told tales of adventure that made him seem like a second Othello. He possessed a very good tenor voice and sported a black moustache, which his jealous rivals said was originally a sickly yellow in color. Dark tales were afloat that he had been seen to drink a glass of beer; and also that he was in arrears at the country store for rather flashy neckties and waistcoats which he had purchased. His evident interest in me at the lodge-meetings and the singing school and at Miller's Hall caused my family uneasiness, as I evinced decided pleasure in his attentions. He was given to understand that he was not welcome as a caller at my home. The next night at the lodjge-meeting he announced his immediate return to the logging-camp.

Being on the entertainment committee for a song, he gave with great passion "The Pirate's Love-Song," gazing at me as he sang,

"This night or never my bride thou must be."

I drove back across the prairies feeling that I had blighted one man's life and that Ouida could find in me a wonderful heroine for a new novel. A few days afterward, the man sent me his first, last, and only love-letter, so terribly misspelled and so ungrammatical that my second romance died a sudden and ignominious death. His "blighted life" continued, however, to send forth new shoots, and he buried four wives and was living with the fifth the last I heard of him.

After my early advent into the magazines and weeklies, the current of my life very rapidly changed. New acquaintances and new interests came, and I drifted from the lodge meeting, the singing school and Miller's Hall into other circles.

A correspondence with several contributors to The Mercury and other periodicals popular at that time ensued, and lent a new interest to my life. Helen Manville wrote charming verses, and I was greatly flattered when I one day received a letter from her commending some verses of mine and asking me to write to her. The little poem she liked was the following:

STARS

Astronomers may gaze the heavens o'er.

Discovering wonders, great perhaps and true–

That stars are worlds and peopled like our own; But I shall never think as these men do.

I shall believe them little shining things, Fashioned from heavenly ore and filled with light;

And to the skies above so smoothly blue An angel comes and nails them every night.

And I have seen him. You, no doubt, would think A white cloud sailed across the heaven's blue;

But as I watched the feathery thing, it was An angel nailing up the stars I knew.

And all night long they shine for us below. Shine in pale splendor till the mighty sun Wakes up again. And then the angel comes And gathers in his treasures one by one.

How sweet the task; and when this life is done And I have joined the angel band on high.

Of all that throng. Oh, may it be my task To nail the stars upon the evening sky.

Mrs. Manville lived at La Crosse, Wisconsin, and she came to visit me afterward– my first visit from a literary celebrity, for she was a celebrity in the West at that time. My return visit to Mrs. Manville was an epoch in my life, and I felt more widely traveled on my return than I felt in later life after a tour of the earth.

Besides her poetic talent, Helen Manville possessed exquisite beauty, which she transmitted together with her talents to her lovely daughter, now Mrs. Pope, whose works have been pubhshed over her name, Marion Manville Pope.

Eben E. Rexford, author of "Silver Threads Among the Gold," was another Wisconsin poet with whom I corresponded for a considerable time; but we never met. Mr. Rexford was a shy bachelor, hiding away among his books and flowers all his life. He passed on to higher worlds of poetry and flowers only two or three years ago, still a resident of Wisconsin.

Although my correspondence with a more famous poet occurred several years later, this seems the appropriate place in my life story to relate it. I refer to my acquaintance with James "Whitcomb Riley. He wrote, praising some things of mine, particularly the following verses, to which he gave unstinted words of approval:

THE STORY
They met each other in the glade–
She lifted up her eyes; Alack the day, alack the maid!
She blushed in swift surprise.
Alas, alas, the woe that comes from lifting up the eyes!
The pail was full, the path was steep;
He reached to her his hand; She felt her warm young pulses thrill
But did not understand.
Alas, alas, the woe that comes from clasping hand with hand!
She sat beside him in the wood;
He wooed with words and sighs. Ah, love in spring seems sweet and good
And maidens are not wise.
Alas, alas, the woe that comes from listing lover's sighs!
The summer sun shone fairly down;
The wind came from the South. As blue eyes gazed in eyes of brown.
His kiss fell on her mouth.
Alas, alas, the woe that comes from kisses on the mouth!
And now the autumn time is near;
The lover roves away. With breaking heart and falling tear
She sits the livelong day.
Alas, alas, for breaking hearts when lovers rove away!

This letter of appreciation from Mr. Riley, who was just coming into public notice, led to a most interesting correspondence which must, I think, have covered more than a twelvemonth. It is a veritable loss to literature that this spirited and sparkling series of letters which were exchanged no longer exists. We often interspersed our letters with verse; and I recall a parody which Mr. Riley wrote on the above poem which was a gem of wit. He wrote of an imag- inary visit which he hoped to make me in my home in Wisconsin, and I remember that one stanza ran something hke this:

He sat beside her in her home;
He let her call him "Jim." She let him hold her hand in his.
Which was great fun for him.
Alas, alas, the woe that comes from calling fellows "Jim!"

The wit and sparkle and beauty and pathos of his letters and my replies would, I know, have been delightful reading for the world to-day–had Mr. Riley and I remained correspondents only and never met. The meeting was precisely like the encounter of a canine and a feline. Mr. Riley certainly barked in a way which caused my feline back to rise, and instead of calling him "Jim," I hissed in his face.

It all came about very suddenly at the first of our three meetings. I was visiting in Milwaukee; Mr. Riley was on a hunting trip of a few days with Reverend Myron Reed.

He called on me; in fact, stayed over a day for that purpose. I attired myself for his call in a new gown—one of the first really modish gowns I had ever owned. I remember it was black with little pipings of pale blue, simple, but quite in the fashion. My hair also was arranged in the fashion of the hour. The front was cut in a full flufify "bang" which everybody feminine wore just then. I had at that time a radiant bloom; and I went to meet my caller, thinking my black and cerulean gown was very becoming. Not so Mr. Riley. He began at once to criticize me, announcing himself as bitterly disappointed in my "frivolous appearance." My "fashionable" dress and banged hair he thought most inappropriate for a "genius," and hearing that I had attended a lawn-party that afternoon where there had been dancing, he expressed himself still more violently. Only idiots with their brains in their feet, he said, cared about dancing. I should be above such things.

My own shock when I first saw Mr. Riley had been very great. He was very blond and very ugly. I was never at- tracted by blond men, even when handsome, and his whole personahty was most disappointing to me. I did not, of course, tell him so, but I did tell him that I considered him most impertinent in his comments.

He went away and wrote a letter still worse than his spoken words, and I replied accordingly. Then he came back from the hunting-trip, and, on his way to the train, he called at the door just a moment, and asked to see me. I had an engagement, and he was hurrying to the train, so in five minutes he tried to be a bit conciliatory— paid me a compliment—and said he hoped we would be friends after all. But his next letter was so disagreeable that I wrote and asked him to return, at once, every letter I had ever written, as I did not want posterity to know I had wasted so much time on an impossible person. I sent his letters all back by the same post, and received mine shortly after. A few months later he wrote, begging me to resume the correspondence as it was before we met; but after two letters that proved impossible.

In one of his letters, Mr. Riley asked me how I thought that "God-woman," Mrs. Browning, would have looked in a fashionable gown and with a "bang," and I replied that I thought she would have looked very much better than she did with the corkscrew curls prominent in the pictures I had seen of her. This reply still further disgusted Mr. Riley.

The only other time I ever met James Whitcomb Riley was something like eighteen years after, when he was famous and opulent and making a visit to his publishers in New York.

I was living at the Westminster Hotel, a very happy matron, and I was giving a luncheon that day to Theodosia Garrison, who was just coming into the early glow of her present brilliant fame. I saw Mr. Riley sitting in the reception-room and at once knew him, he had changed so little. After greeting him, I told him of my luncheon-party and that ten lovely young girls and women were coming down in the next elevator, and asked him to give them the great pleasure of meeting him for one minute. Mr. Riley shrugged his shoulders and said:

"I never do that sort of thing; it bores me."

"But," I urged, "these young girls will be so pleased, and it will be a memory for them to cherish always. Please meet them. I promise no more than five minutes of your time shall be taken."

But Mr. Riley firmly declined.

"You do not deserve your great success," I said, and that was our parting. Some time after that, Mr. Riley wrote me a letter saying that he had recently, on a lecture tour, talked with a man about me, who had, to his consternation, proved to be a newspaper reporter, and that the reporter had distorted and exaggerated some criticisms he had made on me. He begged me to pardon him for having been led to talk with one who misrepresented him. The article, which I afterward saw, was indeed very disagreeable, and I simply wrote to Mr. Riley that I thought it an excellent habit to talk to strangers regarding other writers and all women in a way that one is not afraid to have appear in print. And that was our final word.

This being in full my entire acquaintance with James Whit-comb Riley, one can imagine my state of mind when, last year in California, a lecturer on the work and life of the Hoosier Poet stated at the close of every lecture that Mr. Riley and Ella Wheeler Wilcox had been at one time engaged to be married, but that Fate intervened. I looked up the bureau which had sent out the lecturer, only to learn that the man had recently died; so death had stilled the voice which had repeated this untrue tale, and I could only await the proper moment to deny it myself, which is now. Mr. Riley was greatly beloved by all who knew him; he was full of wit and charm and kindliness, I am told. But–he and I were not suited to be chums.

Returning to the period of Ufe when my early verses gave me local fame, I recall the first time a poem of mine was read in public. It was a poem for the decoration of soldiers' graves in Madison, Wisconsin, and the request came in a very official-looking envelope right from the state-house and signed by the governor, the one-armed hero of Gettysburg, Lucius

Fairchild. Great was the excitement in the little brown house in Westport when that letter came, and great was the joy of all when my verses were pronounced even more than good for the occasion. I declined to read them myself, as I felt that I had not the talent or the self-confidence needed for that role, so Major Myers, an accomplished elocutionist, was chosen for the reader, and gave them with great effect. The verses began:

Gather them out of the valley,
Bring them from moorland and hill. And cast them in wreaths and in garlands
On the city so silent and still;
So voiceless and silent and still. Where neighbor speaks never to neighbor.
Where the song of the bird and the brown bee is heard But never the harsh sounds of labor.

The audience on that very beautiful May day gave the little country girl poet a veritable ovation; but not so remarkable was the demonstration as that which occurred the same year a few months later, when the Grand Army of the Tennessee met for their reunion in Madison, and I was again made the poet of the day and evening, and Major Myers again read my poem, this time before an audience of some five thousand people, in the largest auditorium of the city. I had been told that, from among the many generals to be there, Sheridan would be absent, much to the disappointment of the committee. As my poem was written in the present tense, therefore, I made no mention of him. Of Grant, I wrote:

Let Grant come up from the White House
And grasp each brother's hand; First chieftain of the Army,
Last chieftain of the Land.
Come, heroes of Lookout Mountain,
Of Corinth and Donelson, Of Kenesaw and Atlanta,
And tell how the day was won.

After I had entered the hall and was sitting in the audience near the stage, where the speakers were to give their addresses and my poem was to be read, Major Myers came to me in great perturbation and said:

"After all, General Sheridan is here; he came at the last moment. It is a great pity you did not mention him in your poem."

"Give me a pencil and pad," I said, "and I will write a verse now."

"What! Right here, in all this excitement?" the major asked, and he gave me the implements, demurring and doubting.

To my signal, a few moments later, he came back and received with great delight the following stanza:

As Sheridan went to the battle
When a score of miles away. He has come to the feast and banquet
By the iron horse to-day. Its pace is not much swifter
Than the pace of that famous steed That bore him down to the contest,
And saved the day by his speed.

When the poem was read and Major Myers produced the new verse and explained it had been written since I came to the hall, there was such a demonstration as never had been known in that auditorium before, so people said, and there was still another after the poem was finished. It was my first call before an audience to receive its cheers; and to respond only with bows and tears, for never have I been able to make a speech in public.

General Sherman said to a man near him on that occasion:

"If this goes to that girl's heart, it will do her good; if jt goes to her head, it will spoil her."

The next morning, the charming man and beloved governor of the state. General Lucius Fairchild, came to call on me and bring his congratulations; and, as he took my hand, he said:

"I wish I had two arms to put around you, little girl. I am so proud of you."

It was not very long after this that an editor came from Milwaukee to offer me a position on his trade magazine, at what seemed to me a princely salary. I was to edit the magazine literary page and furnish original prose and verse each month. The family demurred: the men objected, but my mother, ever anxious to have me widen my horizon, consented.

It was my first breaking-away from the country home and my second trip on a railroad when I went to Milwaukee. I knew one family there and through it secured board with friends–an eminent judge and his wife. For three months I held the one and only position which during my lifetime took me from my home into an office. Then the trade magazine failed, and I went back to the country. But I had left a new circle of friends which was to be a center of social pleasure and benefit to me for many years to come.

The judge at whose home I boarded those three months was, through a late marriage, the father of two little girls. I became deeply attached to these children and they and their mother to me. I put little Eva to sleep every night by telling her fairy-stories. One evening, however, an editor came to call before Eva had her hour with me. She was in the back parlor with her parents, and I received the editor in the front parlor with only heavy plush portieres between. Eva could not understand why I did not come to her. Her mother explained that I had a caller; suddenly the editor and I were startled at seeing the heavy dark portieres part and a cherub in a "nightie" standing between them, while a baby voice, with a peculiarly fascinating alto chord in it, ejaculated, "I'd like to shot him." Then the curtains closed and the cherub vanished. On Eva's third birthday, I wrote the following lines, which welded the heart of her parents to me forever:

SOMEBODY SWEET

A robin up in the linden tree.
Merrily sings this lay: "Somebody Sweet is three years old,
Three years old to-day." Somebody's bright blue eyes look up.
Through tangled curls of gold. And two red lips unclose to say,
"To-day I am free years old."
Clouds were over the sky this morn,
But now they are sailing away; Clouds could never obscure the sun
On Somebody Sweet's birthday. Bluest of skies and greenest of trees.
Sunlight and birds and flowers. These are Nature's birthday gifts
To this sweet pet of ours.
The pantry is brimming with cakes and creams
For Somebody's birthday ball. Papa and mamma bring their gifts
But their love is better than all. Ribbons and sashes and dainty robes.
Gifts of silver and gold Will fade and rust as the days go by,
But their hearts will not grow cold.
Then laugh in the sunlight. Somebody Sweet,
Little flower of June; You have nothing to do with car-e.
For life is in perfect tune. Loving hearts and sheltering arms
Shall keep old care away For many a year from Somebody Sweet,
Who is three years old to-day.

Only a few years before the war I was in Paris and spent a happy evening with "Somebody Sweet," where she lived with her fine husband and interesting family of five boys, which included sturdy twins.

I belonged in Milwaukee for a season to the O. B. J. Club. It was a select company of young people who organized with the one object, "Oh, Be Joyful." Dancing was its chief method of expression. Hattie, my especial chum at, that time, lived in what seemed to me a palatial home. She was a graduate of two colleges, a fine musician as well, and brilliant in recitation, often giving public recitals. Her particular admirer that season had a friend, John, who was in Milwaukee for a few weeks on business. John lived in the South and was engaged to be married to a very lovely young widow, so Hattie told me, but John was a fine dancer and he had been invited as a guest of the O. B. J. Club. Hattie and "Vin" wanted me to accept him as an escort to the ball, which took place on the night of my arrival at Hattie's house from my country home. So John was presented, and proved a very handsome young man and a wonderful dancer.

Dancing and music always stirred my muse to action; so the morning after that ball I wrote some verses called "A Dirge," beginning:

"Death and a Dirge at midnight, Yet never a soul in the house Heard anything more than the throb and beat Of a beautiful waltz of Strauss."

The verses proceeded to relate that a girl's heart broke and died, as she floated about in her partner's arms to the waltz music, because she knew he loved another. When John called the following evening I read him the verses and said: "I had to utilize you and the music to pay for the slippers I danced through last evening." John replied: "Then you are just a broker, Miss Ella, and we fellows are the stock you manipulate." The verses brought me 3.00 and bought new slippers–and led a number of people to think I had passed through a great sorrow of the affections.

"The Waltz-Quadrille," one of my most popular early verses, was similarly conceived. I had promised the quadrille at a commencement ball at Madison University to a man on the eve of a journey, who was unable to find me when the number was called. Although I did not have the pleasure of a dance with him, I wrote the poem and sent him a copy of it, saying: "This is the way I should have felt had I been in love with you and had I danced the waltz-quadrille with you just before your departure from Madison."

THE WALTZ-QUADRILLE

The band was playing a waltz-quadrille. I felt as light as a wind-blown feather, As we floated away, at the caller's will. Through the intricate, mazy dance together. Like mimic armies our lines were meeting. Slowly advancing and then retreating, All decked in their bright array; And back and forth to the music's rhyme We moved together, and all the time I knew you were going away.

The fold of your strong arm sent a thrill
From heart to brain as we gently glided
Like leaves on the waves of that waltz-quadrille;
Parted, met, and again divided–
You drifting one way, and I another.
Then suddenly turning and facing each other.
Then off in the blithe chassez.
Then airily back to our places swaying.
While every beat of the music seemed saying
That you were going away.
I said to my heart, "Let us take our fill
Of mirth, and music, and love, and laughter;
For it all must end with this waltz-quadrille,
And life will be never the same life after."
Oh, that the caller might go on calling.
Oh, that the music might go on falling
Like a shower of silver spray.

While we whirled on to the vast Forever,
Where no hearts break, and no ties sever,
And no one goes away!
A clamor, a crash, and the band was still,
Twas the end of the dream, and the end of the measure;
The last low notes of that waltz-quadrille
Seemed like a dirge o'er the death of Pleasure.
You said "Good-night" and the spell was over– Too warm for a friend, and too cold for a lover– There was nothing else to say. But the lights looked dim, and the dancers weary, And the music was sad and the hall was dreary After you went away.

During one of my visits in Milwaukee, the next year, I had my first experience with the occult world. I had been reared in a home where a question mark always was used after any statement made by people or books regarding the future life. Yet from the hour I could think, I always thought with reverence and love of God, the Great Creator of this wonderful universe. Faith was born in my soul and as a little child my belief in prayer and in my guardian angels haloed my world.

I think I could not have been more than nine years old when, sitting one day, on the stairs leading from the "front room" to the sleeping apartments, I heard the grown-ups talking in an agnostic manner about things spiritual. I recollect just how crude and limited their minds seemed to me and in my heart was such a soft wonderful feeling of faith and KNOWLEDGE of worlds beyond this world.

I realize now, that the family was not atheistical as that word is understood to-day. It was merely too advanced intellectually to accept the old eternal brimstone idea of hell and the eternal psalm singing idea of heaven; it refused to accept the story of the recent formation of the earth, knowing science had proof of its vast antiquity. Unfortunately, the larger and far more reverent religion of the present day, which is in perfect accord with science and reveals heaven to us as a most beautiful place if we so build it while here, was not then talked or understood generally; so the Wheeler family was regarded as heretical by the church people. My father and two brothers were strictly moral men and possessed a fine sense of honor in money matters. My oldest brother sacrificed his personal ambitions and aims to devote his early youth to aiding the family through very hard times. His whole youth was one; of service and sacrifice for others. I remember one Christmas when money was very close indeed.

This brother rode seven miles on horseback on a bitter day to get two little books for the Christmas of my brother and myself, so our day would not be wholly blank. With such characteristics it was difficult for my parents or brothers to believe that some of the orthodox church-going men and women of their acquaintance who evaded debts, ignored duty and fell from morality easily, were nevertheless to be "saved" through their periodical "repentance" and return to faith of the church, while these men who were living the Sermon on the Mount were to be lost. Very much vital force and many words were wasted by them all in discussing these subjects with minds not awakened enough, or brains developed enough to comprehend any idea not cut and dried for them by some supposed authority.

I used to dread these arguments and always when anything really bordering on. irreverence was uttered it hurt me like a blow. In after years I understood why this was. Being an old soul myself, reincarnated many more times than any other member of my family, I knew the truth of spiritual things not revealed to them. I could not formulate what I knew, but I felt myself the spiritual parent of my elders; and I longed to help them to clearer sight.

In later life my mother grew to accept my belief in guardian angels and in prayer, seeing the wonderful way my own prayers were answered, and how I was protected and helped by the invisible forces about me. Of course an)d: hing which related to Spiritualism or communication with those who were gone from earth met with the loudest ridicule from the whole family. Nevertheless my mother used to relate strange dreams and forewarnings which came to her. But with the same independence which marked all my thoughts I held my own ideas on these matters and always hoped for an opportunity to investigate. It came during the visit to Milwaukee mentioned above. I had become involved in one of the transitory romances which lent illusion to my otherwise commonplace life–only this romance seemed to threaten a more serious phase, as the man was bent on marriage. While I liked his very earnest love-making and felt flattered by his attention, as he was a "city beau," I did not want to end my girlhood by marriage. Older friends assured me he was desirable and that I had received a "good offer," and ought not to refuse it. Still I demurred. Life was to me a book I had just begun to read, and it seemed to me the hand of marriage would close it. Yet I was loth to give up the attentions of my "city beau." In this state of mind I one day donned the garments of a friend who was in deep mourning, rented a bright red wig from a costumer, and proceeded to a psychic lady who was creating excitement in Milwaukee by her slate writing. Men were consulting her regarding the wheat market and she was very prominently before the public eye. Of course I was a country girl, not universally known in Milwaukee, but I felt I wanted to be absolutely incognito and so disguised myself in the weeds of my friend.

The first message which came upon the slate was: "Ella, why don't you come to us honestly; we all know and love you. Alice Gary." The next was, "Ella, you must not marry this man; he is not the one for you; great sorrow will result if you do. Harvey."

Now the only Harvey I knew had died suddenly of heart disease some six months previously. He was a connection by marriage (his uncle married my cousin), and he had always been much concerned about my kaleidoscopic panorama of romances.

Well, it was not the message but the natural course of events which prevented me from marrying the man; but time proved that he was, indeed, not the man for me.

After that experience I naturally made other explorations into the world of occultism–with all kinds of results, of course. I learned that one psychic in twenty (or medium, as they were called in those days) who made a business of occultism, possessed real powers in that line and the other nineteen mistook the ability to read the thoughts of people for second sight. Telepathy is a word much in use nowadays; but that in itself is a very wonderful thing. It does not, however, give its possessor the right to claim that what she feels, sees or hears, regarding the people who come to her, is a message from the realms beyond. Often the psychic believes she sees a spirit when she sees only a thought form; yet my experience has proven to me beyond question that certain sensitives do see the astral forms that frequently appear in our midst. Until my very recent investigations in this realm of the invisible, which will be dealt with later, there was only one other period of my life when I gave the subject serious attention. That was after the death of my baby boy. I think I must have visited one hundred clairvoyants, mediums and psychics of various types, in many cities and states. Always during the years following my loss, I went into the presence of these sensitives with one dominating thought and desire; the desire to be convinced that other children were coming to bless my life. And here was where I eventually learned my lesson of the power of thought forms. Every psychic I visited, with one exception, foretold the birth of children for me. Often the very dates of birth were given and the sex of the various children. So powerful was my desire, it made a picture which the mediums mistook for the spirit child to come. One of the women, a trance medium, was an absolute seer. She said no other child would come to me in this incarnation; that my only child was in the spirit world; and then she proceeded to outline my future. Now, after more than a quarter of a century, I am able to say that every event she foresaw has transpired, events which seemed impossible of becoming realities at the time she foretold them.

These experiences made me realize the folly and danger which lie in this investigation of invisible realms for the people who are merely curious and who have no basic foundation of knowledge of occult matters. The hysterical and jealous woman who goes to a medium to learn whether her lover or husband is true to her will, of course, know that her worst fears are well founded, for her intense jealous thoughts will make a form visible to the eyes of the psychic. The psychic is not a fraud, but a self-deceived mind-reader.

Once afterward the real psychic came across my path. This was not a professional but a woman of wealth and social position who, since early childhood, had been pursued by psychical phenomena and who was able to produce messages on slates which were held in full sight of the sitter and never opened by her. Owing to the objections of her husband to this phenomenon, the lady had not used her powers for twelve years until in my apartment at a New York hotel she consented to try to obtain a message for me. I procured two slates from children in the hotel but there were no slate pencils available. "Let us try sheets of paper," I said, "with an atom of lead pencil between them." "I never tried that," she said, "but we can experiment." She insisted that I make all the preparations; so I placed a sheet of hotel paper from my desk between two slates and with it the tiny end broken from a lead pencil–an atom impossible to hold between thumb and finger. I strapped the slates with an elastic band, and the lady held one end while I held the other. They were spasmodically jerked about in our hands, but I clung to them. The room was brilliantly lighted. After some three or four minutes three taps came on the slates. My caller, who had just asked me what work I was doing that winter, remarked that the taps indicated a message.

"You open the slates," she said. "I do not want to touch them." So I opened them and there in a delicate spider-like scrawl were these words legibly written:

"God gives a part of Himself to you with each new work: and my own dear boy makes you my daughter,

Maria Wilcox, mother."

My husband lost his mother when he was but seven years old; and she died, as she had lived, in a little Connecticut town. Her name was Maria Wilcox. I never saw her, of course; and she was but a vague memory to my husband. That this absolute stranger from another state, who had never met my husband, should be able to produce this message filled with tender motherly pride, impressed me with a sense of awe and reverence for God's marvelous universe. I believed then, and I believe now, that in some manner impossible for the finite mind to explain, the curtain of infinity had swung aside for a moment, and that the lovely spirit that had been the mother of a rare son sent a word of greeting to me. I felt so satisfied and at peace that I did not for many years make any further attempts to communicate with worlds beyond. I had my message, without money, and without price, and with no possibility of collusion or fraud. I was satisfied to rest on that conviction.

Several other messages were written for me on the slate that same evening; nd one was signed "Shama Baba." Asked who he was, the answer came, "Shama Baba is your near guide. He is one of a band which dominates you. Do you not feel how much we have for you to do?"

My husband, who was an earnest student of njatters spiritual, felt great interest in this message. Ever afterward he spoke of Shama Baba as a real personality in my life. If I was disappointed in any aim or desire, Robert would say: "Ella, Shama Baba is back of this; it must be for the best." Not two weeks before the sudden illness which ended his earth life he made this remark to me.

CHAPTER IV "Maueine" and "Poems of Passion"

IN the late seventies and early eighties there was much talk in the Western and in some of the Eastern newspapers, of the "Milwaukee School of Poetry." My name was used as its leader; though never at any time in my life have I ever wished to be regarded as a leader in anything. To work out my own life problems, and find my own way through earth's interesting, while puzzling, mazes, has seemed to me quite enough responsibility, without attempting to lead others. In this "School of Poetry" the editors named Carlotta Perry, Hattie Tyng Griswold, Sarah D. Hobart, Estella Aiken, Fanny Driscou, Charles Noble Gregory and Grace Wells, besides other lesser stars. All of these writers were well known throughout the West, and several of them had attained recognition in the East. There was a brilliant clergyman in Milwaukee at that time, a man in his late sixties, who had surprised his congregation by marrying a handsome young school teacher in her middle twenties.

The lady was very ambitious to make a shining place for herself socially; not among the purely fashionable people, but among the intellectuals. She desired to establish a Salon and to become the Madame de Stael of Milwaukee. Her husband was recognized as one of the leaders of thought– progressive religious thought of the day; and he seemed, to many people, a composite Henry Ward Beecher and Ralph Waldo Emerson of the West. He possessed a handsome home and the best minds of Milwaukee gave him homage. His young wife felt her newly acquired high position to be one of pleasurable responsibility; and she aimed to supplement her husband's intellectual supremacy by her own mental graces. Unfortunately she lacked that subtle quality of tact; and while seek-

"MAURINE" AND "POEMS OF PASSION" 73 ing to make herself a personage in her husband's congregation, she was apt to antagonize instead.

I had read of her gatherings of shining lights in the intellectual world of Milwaukee and I had regarded her from afar as a planet of the first magnitude. It can be understood, therefore, with what a mingled sense of awe and pride I went to my friend, Hattie, one day, and told her and her family a wonderful bit of news, namely: that Mrs. Salon (so we will call her) had spoken to me on the street and introduced herself; that she had said her husband was greatly pleased with a recent poem of mine entitled "The Voluptuary," and that they would both like to have me spend a few days with them before I left the city. Hattie and her people thought it was a decided compliment; and I went forth to Mrs. Salon's home with great expectations in my imaginative heart. I pictured to myself brilliant gatherings of rare people to whom she would introduce me as her new-. found protegee, and from whom I should imbibe inspiration and culture. Instead of this I passed two of the most wretched days of my existence under this lady's roof. I found the very first evening that she had invited me there to pick me to pieces, intending, I am sure, to rearrange the particles in a new order; and with an unquestionably worthy desire to benefit me. Very possibly she meant to exploit me after my re-creation was complete.

She began her work by endeavoring to destroy every feeling of pleasure or satisfaction I had had regarding the kind words and praises of Western editors. She said these men only belittled me by their approval, as they knew nothing of real poetry or of what constituted good literature. One word from an Eastern editor or writer was worth more than columns of Western adulation, she said. Having finished the editors, my hostess proceeded to attack all my Milwaukee friends, declaring they were not the proper people to advance my interests. The attentions I had received from several young men she thought most compromising; and she thrust a fierce sword of criticism into my poems containing sentiment; the "little love-wails" the editors had liked. She said I was going on in a way calculated to spoil all chance of a desirable mar- riage; and she finished her oration by declaring that sentiment, romance and passion were all illusions, and that real marriage was based wholly on mental comradeship and respect. I listened to all the lady had to say and, being her guest, withheld the retort which sprang to my lips. Only when she attacked my good friends did I make my protest.

But after I left her house and went to my country home I wrote her a letter. I thanked her for her hospitality, but I assured her that, while I appreciated her motive, her attempt to make me over must be abandoned. "I prefer," I said, "to be a poor original of my own individual self than a good imitation of you. I must follow my own life, choose my own friends, and learn my own lessons as I go through life. If I make mistakes I must profit by them; and profit will be more lasting than if I followed some course of conduct laid down by another which does not appeal to me."

Mrs. Salon spoke of me afterward as an impossible young person who could not be helped by any one, and she seemed to see a disastrous end to my career. Her own career, however, was not one which made me regret the position I had taken. Much trouble befell her in many ways and she became a victim to nervous disorders. The Salon was never established.

This experience, like all other experiences, led me to write some verses. They were entitled:

ADVICE I must do as you do? Your way I own Is a very good way. And still, There are sometimes two straight roads to a town,

One over, one under the hill.

You are treading the safe and the well-worn way.

That the prudent choose each time; And you think me reckless and rash to-day

Because I prefer to climb.

Your path is the right one, and so is mine. We are not like peas in a pod,

"MAURINE" AND "POEMS OF PASSION" 75

Compelled to lie in a certain line, Or else be scattered abroad.

Twere a dull old world, methinks, my friend, If we all went just one way; Yet our paths will meet, no doubt, at the end.

Though they lead apart to-day.

You like the shade, and I like the sun;

You like an even pace, I like to mix with the crowd and run.

And then rest after the race.

I like danger, and storm and strife,

You like a peaceful time, I like the passion and surge of life.

You like its gentle rhyme.

You like buttercups, dewy sweet.

And crocuses, framed in snow; I like roses, born of the heat.

And the red carnation's glow.

I must live my life, not yours, my friend.

For so it was written down; We must follow our given paths to the end,

But I trust we shall meet–in town.

The poem which had pleased Mr. and Mrs. Salon was:

THE VOLUPTUARY

Oh, I am sick of love reciprocated,

Of hopes fulfilled, ambitions gratified. Life holds no thing to be anticipated.

And I am sad f rom being satisfied.

The eager joy felt climbing up the mountain Has left me, now the highest point is gained.

The crystal spray that fell from Fame's fair fountain Was sweeter than the waters were when drained.

The gilded apple which the world calls pleasure. And which I purchased with my youth and strength,

Pleased me a moment. But the empty treasure Lost all its luster, and grew dim at length.

And love, all glowing with a golden glory.

Delighted me a season with its tale. It pleased the longest, but at last the story

So oft repeated, to my heart grew stale.

I lived for self, and all I asked was given, I have had all, and now am sick of bliss, No other punishment designed by Heaven

Could strike me half so forcibly as this.

I feel no sense of aught but enervation In all the joys my selfish aims have brought,
And know no wish but for annihilation. Since that would give me freedom from all thought
Oh, blest is he who has some aim defeated;
Some mighty loss to balance all his gain. For him there is a hope not yet completed;
For him hath life yet draughts of joy and pain.
But cursed is he who has no balked ambition.
No hopeless hope, no loss beyond repair. But sick and sated with complete fruition.
Keeps not the pleasure even of despair.

I had in my first score of years published two little books of verse. Then I grew ambitious to write a story in verse– something that I felt must be as notable as "Lucille." There was, it may be seen, no limit to my faith in myself, or rather in the powers I believed were working through me. This belief I once expressed in a poem which has through all the years proved a mental and spiritual tonic to me in times of doubt or depression:

ACHIEVEMENT

Trust in thine own untried capacity As thou would trust in God Himself.

Thy soul Is but an emanation from the whole. Thou dost not dream what forces lie in thee.

"MAURINE" AND "POEMS OF PASSION" 77

Vast and unfathomed as the grandest sea; Thy silent mind o'er diamond caves may roll. Go seek them–but let pilot will control Those passions which thy favoring winds can be.

"No man shall place a limit to thy Strength;
Such triumphs as no mortal ever gained
May yet be thine if thou wilt but believe In thy Creator and thyself. At length
Some feet will tread all heights now unattained–

Why not thine own? Press on; achieve! Achieve I I therefore set about thinking up my plot. I was at the old farmhouse in Westport and I used to drive over to Windsor for the mail in a little "buggy" behind a mature horse named "Burney," that my father had bought for such purposes; and I often used to stop at Emma's house and take her along with me. It was on a May day when, as I drove alone to Windsor, I thought of the plot of "Maurine"– the sacrifice of a maiden who discovered that her fragile girl friend loved the man who had won her own affections, but who had not yet declared himself. It was wholly imaginary, and, of course, had I ever experienced a real love, I could not have written such a story, because my tale made my heroine much stronger in her friendship than her love. As soon as I reached home and had unharnessed Burney, and put him in his stall, I began "Maurine." The name was suggested by a short poem I had read recently by Nora Perry, called "Norine."

I resolved to write ten lines each day on my story and if I missed one day from any cause, to write twenty the next. In this way I completed the book in October, besides doing much other literary work. In those days I used to write prose stories to help eke out my income. I sold these very crude and uninspired tales for ten or fifteen dollars, to the lesser magazines and weeklies. I remember feeling so elated when Peterson's Magazine published a story of mine in the same number with Frances

Hodgson Burnett. She had not then come into her great fame, but I had recognized her genius, and felt honored to have my name appear near hers. My stories were all ground out with hard labor, and I dreaded the work of writing a story as much as I loved the writing of a poem. One tale was refused by ten editors and then sold to an eleventh, who paid me 75.00 for it. Such an hour of joyful surprise as that was! Particularly so because the tenth editor had sent the worn manuscript back from his office with a marginal note: "This is a dead dog–better bury it." Instead, after a few tears of mingled grief and anger, I gave my "dead dog" a new cover and sent it forth to crown me with triumph.

That was a summer full of pleasure and hope–and happy dreams–the summer I devoted to writing "Maurine." My mother, always deeply interested in my work, felt I was to make a great success; and I planned a summer somewhere by the sea for her and me (the longed-for sea I had never yet beheld) through the proceeds of the book.

My friend Hattie came from Milwaukee to visit me and was most enthusiastic over the poem; and Hattie was possessed of fine and cultivated taste, so I valued her criticisms.

Ella Giles, an accomplished and intellectual young woman, author of several books, came from Madison, and added her words of praise. Ella Giles afterward became Mrs. Ruddy, of Los Angeles, California, and died there recently, leaving a lustrous name as a brilliant club woman and active suffragist, and writer of both prose and verse. I spent many hours with her the last year of her life.

When my book was completed I made a visit to Chicago and called upon Jansen and Mcclurg, expecting that staid firm eagerly to seize my proffered manuscript, which I thought was to bring me world-wide fame and fortune. Instead, it was declined with thanks ind I was informed that they had never heard of me. After repeated efforts and failures, I induced a Wisconsin firm to get the book out. It barely paid expenses. But a little later I was made happy by having Jansen and Mcclurg write and request the privilege of republishing the volume with additional short poems. It never, however, became a "best seller," but has seemed slowly to grow in favor with time.

A perpetual dividend of pleasure resulted from "Maurine,"
"MAURINE" AND "POEMS OF PASSION" 79 in the periodical discovery of girls named for my heroine. I had created the name, and therefore each child bearing it seemed to be, in a measure, my own. Once in San Francisco a photographer asked me to come and pose for him. He sent an exquisitely beautiful young daughter to bring me to his studio. She smilingly told me that her name might interest me. "It is Maurine Ramussen," she said. "My mother read your book before my birth."

A few years later, Harrison Fisher "discovered" Maurine Ramussen, and exploited her on canvas and in Sunday supplements as a type of perfect beauty. I saw many portraits of her for a time; and I have often wondered what became of her. She is, I trust, somebody's happy wife. The photograph she gave me at that time but faintly shows her rare loveliness at sixteen. The youngest of my Maurines spends her summers at Granite Bay and is five years old and the possessor of glorious Titian hair–Maurine Manwaring, by name. In Chicago, too, there exists a "Maurine Club." It was the summer I wrote "Maurine" that I made a little song about the old Wisconsin home, beginning:

This is the place that I love the best; The little brown house like a ground bird's nesl. Hid among grasses and vines and trees, Summer retreat of the birds and bees.

The little house was brown from being weather-beaten and lacking paint. I longed to be able to buy paint enough to make it white with green blinds; but painters informed me that, being old wood, it would drink up paint as a toper drinks alcohol. I never attained the financial status which permitted me to buy the paint. But I trained vines to climb over the house, and each summer it was almost hidden by its wealth of wild vines brought each spring from the woods. One beautiful and rapid-growing vine with a fragrant blossom called the wild cucumber was my delight until I made a dreadful discovery. Small snakes began to be seen about our yard every midsummer; and a wise old settler explained the horrible invasion as due to the wild cucumber vine. He declared serpents were attracted by its odor and would come miles to enjoy it. Respecting the artistic temperament of the reptiles, I yet had to abandon the vine and substitute morning glories; and after the wild cucumber was gone the serpents disappeared.

Much of my earlier work was tinctured with melancholy both real and imaginary. Young poets almost invariably write of sorrow- When publishing "Maurine" I had purposely omitted more than twoscore poems of a very romantic and tragic nature in order to save the volume from too much sentiment. Letters began to come to me requesting copies of these verses–ardent love songs which had appeared in various periodicals. This suggested to me the idea of issuing a book of love poems to be called "Poems of Passion." To think was to do–for I possessed more activity than caution in those days.

As just related, every poem in the book had been published in various periodicals and had brought forth no criticism. My amazement can hardly be imagined, therefore, when Jansen and Mcclurg returned the manuscript of my volume, intimating that it was immoral. I told the contents of their letter to friends in Milwaukee, and it reached the ears of a sensational morning newspaper. The next day a column article appeared with large headlines:

"TOO LOUD FOR CHICAGO.
THE SCARLET CITY BY THE LAKE SHOCKED
BY A BADGER GIRL, WHOSE VERSES
OUT-SWINBURNE SWINBURNE AND
OUT-WHITMAN WHITMAN."

Every newspaper in the land caught up the story and I found myself an object of unpleasant notoriety in a brief space of time. I had always been a local celebrity, but this was quite another experience. Some friends who had admired and praised now criticized–though they did not know why. I was advised to bum my offensive manuscript and assured that in time I might live down the shame I had brought on myself. Yet those same friends had seen these verses in periodicals and praised them.

"MAURINE" AND "POEMS OF PASSION" 81

All this but stimulated me to the only vindication I desired–the publication of my book. A Chicago publisher saw his opportunity and offered to bring out the book, and it was an immediate success. It was afterward issued in London also, where it met with wide favor. The book contained scarcely fifty poems, and the criticism turned upon five or six of these. One was "The Farewell of Clarimond" and was written after reading Theophile Gautier's story, "Clarimond," a weird, strange tale, told with the power of great genius; yet although I gave his story credit for my verses,. certain critics insisted on referring to my poem as a recital of my own immoral experiences!

My knowledge of life was bounded by visits to Madison and Milwaukee, Chicago, and some lesser villages; and by books I had read and letters I had received from more or less intellectual people. The works of Gautier, Daudet, Quida, with a bit of Shakespeare, Swinburne and Byron (I had never possessed an entire volume of any of these poets), no doubt lent to my vivid imagination and temperamental nature the flame which produced the censured verses. Were I to live my life over, with the wisdom of years and knowledge of the world to start with, I surely would not publish "Poems of Passion." Yet looking back across the years and realizing all that has ensued since that day, I feel that it was one of the stairs by which I was ordained to climb out of obscurity and poverty, through painfully glaring and garish light, into a clearer and higher atmosphere, and a larger world of usefulness.

The first proceeds of the sale of the book enabled me to rebuild and improve the old home, which was fast going to ruin.

Life, which had been a slowly widening stream for me at this period, seemed to unite with the ocean of success and happiness.

My engagement, not yet announced, occurred the week my book was issued. But there was, as ever in life, bitter in my cup of sweets. The majority of critics, while they increased the sales of "Poems of Passion" by their denunciations of it, also wounded me deeply by their unnecessarily vituperative attacks. Many friends,-who I had believed would be my defenders, took an attitude of patronizing pity toward me which was harder to bear than outright disapproval, and others openly expressed their regret that I had not waited until I was "married or dead" before allowing the poems to appear. To which I replied: "So long as I believe them fit for publication at all, I do not feel I need a husband or tombstone to protect me from assaults of the public."

Mr. Charles A. Dana, in the New York Sun, gave two columns of ridicule and condemnation to the book; but he made the mistake (if he really wished to prevent the book's success) of quoting a full half column of lines wherein the highly disapproved word "kiss" was used. This brought me scores of letters, asking where the book could be purchased; and I wrote a note of thanks to Mr. Dana for his very unique method of advertising my book. Mr. Dana was exceedingly wroth at my note.

In the Chicago Herald appeared this gracious item: "It is to be hoped that Miss Ella Wheeler will relapse into Poems of Decency now that the New York Sun has voiced the opinion of respectability that her Poems of Passion are like the songs of half tipsy wantons." Yet, in spite of all this five hundred citizens of Milwaukee united to give me a wonderful testimonial of their approval. On a May night, at St. Andrew's Hall, eloquent speeches were made, my poems were recited, and a purse of five hundred dollars was presented to me.

Mr. E. E. Chapin, Chairman, spoke of me as "standing forth to-day, a representative of the genius of poetry and song, of democracy and progress, of the young America motto on our State coat of arms."

My friend Hattie came from her new home in Chicago to read, with most effective skill, several of my poems, and Colonel M. A. Aldrich, the brilliant newspaper man (who had first conceived the idea of this testimonial reception), read for me lines I had written as a response in place of the speech which I knew I could not make. My lines were:

"MAURINE" AND "POEMS OF PASSION" 83

Speak for me, friend, whose lips are ever ready With chosen words, to voice another's thought;

My shaken heart would make my tones unsteady; Speak thou the words I ought.

Say that the love I give in lavish fashion,

To all God's living creatures everywhere. Pervades me with a deep and holy passion,

A wordless, grateful prayer.

Say that the gifts I may have used too lightly, As children toss rare gems in careless mirth.

From this glad hour, henceforth shall shine more brightly And prove their honest worth.

Say that my life shall be one grand endeavor To reach a nobler womanhood's fair height;

Say how my earnest aim is to forever Be worthy of this night.

In speaking of the evening afterward one editor compared me to "Corinne at the Capitol." I did not know who Corinne was; and so I looked her up, pleased to find myself compared to the Greek woman poet who in a trial of poetry had conquered the great poet Pindar.

It was a very wonderful night, and many wonderful things resulted from it as well as newspaper publicity, good and bad, pleasant and unpleasant. My brother wrote me that while the family was reading aloud the report of my ovation, the next day, a heavy rain was falling and he was placing pails and pans to catch the water leaking through the roof. My five hundred dollars was used to put a new roof on the old house, also an addition, much needed because of the advent of many nieces and nephews.

The consciousness that I was able to do this for my family, as well as to send a niece away to school, made the ugly comments of many editors and critics endurable. One of these comments was headed, "A Protest against Ella Wheeler," and another compared me to a dispenser of "poisoned candy."

Perhaps best of all the articles which appeared in the pa- pers at that time, I like the following taken from my old scrapbook:

"The people of Milwaukee who interested themselves in giving Ella Wheeler a substantial reception did a graceful thing. The reception, the speeches, and the 500.00 purse will be to the talented, hard-working, cheery little song bird what reinforcements are to troops who have fought well. Thousands beside those who participated in the reception have watched the brave little soldier, valiantly fighting her way from obscurity to her present proud eminence, and have gone out to meet her with congratulations and good wishes.

"The practical Milwaukee detachment was not content to move into line with cheers and platoons of praise only—so it pressed the paymaster into service and golden dollars wreathed the golden words. The reinforcements Ella Wheeler received last week, the columns of praise, the words of encouragement and the handful of gold will improve her generalship–will add new forces to her heart and brain, and the public will see the benefit. She is now no longer an unknown girl, a soldier on the frontier, but a literary general, whose words receive attention. Wisconsin is proud of Ella Wheeler, proud of her history, her courage, her talent and her promising future, and by words of commendation and more substantial aid the Commonwealth has encouraged and will encourage her daughter."

A certain critic, who believed himself to be a prophet, thought the attention bestowed upon the book was most absurd, as its life, he said, at best would not extend beyond a twelvemonth. Yet now, after thirty-four years, the book still lives.

CHAPTER V Two Amusing Near Romances

TWO years before meeting the man who became my husband, I was invited to receive calls on New Year's day, with a lady in Chicago. Among the callers were two men, friends of the hostess; one a bachelor, very distinguished in appearance; one a lawyer close to sixty, very unattractive in person, but intellectual and a devotee of the Muses. My hostess told me he lived apart from a practical wife with whom he was not in sympathy, but there was no divorce– simply an understanding that they were happier apart. Both of these men were appreciative of my poetical gifts; and the bachelor invited my hostess and me to hear Bernhardt two evenings later. My hostess excused herself, on the plea of other engagements, and I, went alone with the very agreeable and entertaining bachelor. After the theater we had a very cosy little supper at a fashionable restaurant; and what was my surprise, in the midst of the clatter of dishes and the surge of the orchestra, and the chatter of voices at neighboring tables, to have the bachelor in a very matter-of-fact manner ask me to become his wife. I gasped in astonishment, unable to take his words seriously. Here was a man I had seen only twice, and of whom I knew less than little, save as my hostess had told me he was respectable and much liked by people who knew him, and a successful financier, asking me on our second meeting the most important question which can be presented to a woman.

"I do not want you to answer me now," the bachelor said. "I merely want you to give me the opportunity to win you. I have been watching your career for two years; and I made up my mind some time ago that you were intended for my wife. I am sure of it now we have met. But all I ask is that you permit me to write to you for a month, and that you give me respectful and serious consideration as a suitor, and at the end of a month I will visit you and talk the matter over again." This was not at all my ideal of an ardent wooer; and although the man was decidedly attractive mentally and physically, so far as personal appearance goes, he did not cause my pulses to quicken or my heart to accelerate its beats. I realized that he was in earnest, however, and consented to his very reasonable request for a month of trial wooing by letter.

I was to pass the next month in Milwaukee, visiting among friends there; and it so happened that a great deal of entertainment was provided for me. Not finding more serious subjects to discuss with my new correspondent, I wrote of the things which were occurring and of my enjoyments. When the month had expired, my bachelor appeared upon the scene, on one of my busiest days, and found me with several engagements and various callers, and a general condition of things not conducive to sentimentality.

It was some hours before he and I were left quite alone. I had been dreading the moment, as I knew I must tell him the utter impossibility of ever regarding him as a life companion. But the wind was suddenly taken from my sails by the bachelor, who said:

"You are dreading what you have to tell me; now let me relieve your mind by saying I no longer desire you to receive me as a suitor. I am convinced by your letters, and your attitude since I came, that you are the type of woman who must have excitement continually, and who could never be satisfied with one loyal lover. I am sure it is necessary to your genius to have a retinue of admirers; but I could never play the role of the complacent husband; and since you are not at all in love with me, I will not attempt to make you so. We will be the best of friends and let it end at that."

This was quite sensible, and the dilemma was solved. Yet it was a new experience to have a wooer take the words out of my mouth and decide such a matter for me! So this near-romance ended as suddenly as it began. The bachelor mar-

TWO AMUSING NEAR ROMANCES 87 ried a very young girl not long there-after; and he lived to amass a large fortune, and carve out a very brilliant career for himself. He lived also to see me most happy and contented with the love of one man, having found the right one. And we were good friends to the time of his death, though seldom meeting.

The grass-widower lawyer, meanwhile, often wrote me letters concerning my literary work. His letters were brilliant and interesting and often helpful. They contained no hint of sentiment. After I had met my lover, I intimated the fact to the lawyer, who warned me, in a fatherly manner, to be careful and not make a mistake which could not be easily rectified. When "Poems of Passion" was about to be published the lawyer asked to see the contract, and suggested some few changes. Once while visiting Chicago he invited my hostess and me to lunch with him in a downtown restaurant after we had been shopping.

It was something like two months after my marriage that I received a bill for "Professional Services" from this lawyer. In surprise I wrote and asked what the professional services had been. The amazing reply was, "The hill is for advice on your contract with your publishers and for a lunch where you ordered such expensive luxuries as frogs' legs!"

I paid the bill and never heard from my intellectual and thrifty-minded friend again. Relating the experience to my hostess at whose house I had met the man, she seemed surprised that I had not realized the romantic nature of the man's interest in me; but no such thought had ever entered my mind. Sixty years old and with a living wife, how could I imagine such a possibility?

In the forenoon of a February day in 1883 I boarded the train at Windsor, Wisconsin, for the ten-mile ride to Madison. Judge and Mrs. A. B. Braley had asked me to go with them to the Inaugural Ball of the Governor that evening. In my suit case I carried a pretty white gown, trimmed wilh narrow bands of swansdown, made for the occasion. The day was bright and clear and my heart was very light. Life seemed a joyous thing. Suddenly as I took my seat in the coach I saw a young woman clothed in deepest black, her face partially hidden by her black-bordered handkerchief, her form, shaking with the sobs she was trying to suppress. It was the bride of a year, the widow of a week, a lovely girl I had last seen radiant with happiness.

I sat beside her for a little while, just as we were approaching Madison, and her great sorrow seemed to envelop me. All the way up to Judge Braley's home I thought of her and felt I could not enjoy my visit because of her grief.

But I found my friends delighted to welcome me, and the young wife of the brilliant Judge had so many interesting plans for my entertjiinment that the incident of the day passed entirely from my mind. That evening, as I stood before the mirror, putting the last touches to my white toilet, a swift vision of the young widow in her weeds came before me. With a stricken conscience I realized how quickly I had forgotten her; and I pictured to myself the dark shadows she must have carried into the home she was visiting, and contrasted it with the brightness of my own environment. It was at that moment the poem "Solitude" was conceived– the first four lines coming at once in their present form.

Laugh and the world laughs with you,

Weep and you weep alone. For the sad old earth must borrow its mirth.

It has trouble enough of its own.

I knew they were the nucleus of a longer poem, and simply tucked them away in the pigeon-hole of my brain until I should have leisure to complete the verses. The majority of my poetical creations have come in this way, a line or a stanza first at unexpected times and in places where I could not, at once, complete them. From the very beginning I learned to carry such an idea with me, and work it out at leisure.

The following morning at the breakfast table I recited the quatrain to the Judge and his wife, acquainting them with the cause of the inspiration. Both were enthusiastic and the Judge, who was a great Shakespearean scholar, said, "Ella, if you keep the remainder of the poem up to that epigram- matic standard, you will have a literary gem." It was not until the second night thereafter that I found time to complete the poem. We came home from a theater-party and I told my friends I was going to sit up and finish the poem.

There are certain small incidents in all our lives which make an enduring impression on memory. Such an incident was that of taking my verses into the library where Judge Braley sat smoking his morning cigar and reading them to him and his wife, after warning them that I felt I had not kept up to the standard first set by my muse. I can still see the look on the very handsome face of the Judge as he listened with increasing interest, and I can still hear his deep voice lifted in quick spontaneous praise, in which his fair young wife joined. The cigar the Judge was smoking had gone out and he stood up to relight it. He was six feet in height and he had a peculiar little trick of bending one knee back and forth when he stood talking. This knee was very active as he puffed at the freshly lighted cigar and said: "Ella, that is one of the biggest things you ever did; and you are mistaken in thinking it is uneven in merit; it is all good and up to the mark."

I sent the poem to the New York Sun, received five dollars therefor, and it appeared in its columns February 21st, 1883, over my maiden name, Ella Wheeler. The verses became remarkably popular and were recited and copied so widely that they became hackneyed. In May, 1883, the poem was included in my book, "Poems of Passion." I have the original manuscript copy in one of the many manuscript books where all the poems I considered worth preserving were copied, with date and place of writing.

In 1885, a year after I had added Wilcox to my name and gone East to reside, a man of whom the literary world had never heard, Mr. John Joyce, of Washington, heard the poem recited and heard some one ask who wrote it. Mr. Joyce immediately declared himself as the author. I have no idea that he was wholly responsible for his words at that time, as I had been told that he was very much addicted to drink– a habit which he afterwards, it is said, overcame, greatly to his go THE WORLDS AND I credit. I, of course, indignantly denied his claim, putting forth my own true story, as given above. Mr. Joyce, however, having uttered his lie, deliberately repeated it on every possible occasion from that day to the day of his death, some three or four years ago. He declared that he wrote the poem in 1861 on the head of a whiskey barrel in the wine room of the Gait House in Louisville, Kentucky. He had published a book entitled "A Checkered Life" in 1883, together with a number of very trashy verses. In that volume Mr. Joyce had given the story of his life from youth to maturity. He even admitted the fact that he had, in his early life, been the inmate of an insane asylum for a period of a few months. To quote his own statement I give the following memorandum in "A Checkered Life."

"Eastern Kentucky Lunatic Asylum, Lexington, Kentucky.

"The records of this asylum show No. 2423, John A. Joyce, 18 years of age; occupation, farmer; habit, temperate; original disposition and intellect good; cause, heredity; form of mania, perpetual motion. Admitted June 20th, i860: discharged September, i860.

W. A. Bullock, M. D. Medical Superintendent."

Mr. Joyce's book was written while he was serving a term in prison for whiskey frauds. The book contained twenty-three so-called poems, supposedly all he had ever written. Naturally it did not contain "Solitude" because I had not then composed it. I have a copy of the first edition of this book in my possession. Yet two years later after my poem became famous, the man claimed that he had written "Solitude" in 1861. Why should he have omitted it from this book? In 1885, Mr. Joyce issued a new edition of the book, inserting the poem under the title, "Laugh, d the World Laughs With You," but retaining the copyright date of 1883.

My husband wished to start a suit for damages, but was urged by acquaintances to drop it, as they said the general impression of Mr. Joyce was that he was "a harmless old TWO AMUSING NEAR ROMANCES 91 lunatic whose words no one took seriously." But Mr. Joyce proved himself seriously annoying up to the day of his death. He never allowed more than two years to pass without finding some obscure paper in which he could again set forth his claims to my poem. I repeatedly made an offer of 5,000.00 to be given to charity, when any one could produce a copy of "Solitude" published prior to February, 1883. I finally offered to present to any charitable institution he might select, in his name, that amount of money, when Mr. Joyce produced his proof. Of course it was never forthcoming; and yet he claimed the poem had been in circulation for twenty years before I wrote it.

I believe my experience one which nearly every author has known at some time in his or her career. Though misery may like company, the fact does not prevent one's own suffering, when made the victim of a man of this type, who belongs to the poison insect order of humanity. He is only an insect, and yet his persistent buzz and sting can produce great discomfort.

CHAPTER VI

The Compelling Lover

T N my dreams of the compelling lover who would one day come into my life, I always imagined a sudden and romantic meeting. Never did it occur to me that I could drift leisurely into love's sea on the river of friendship. At sixteen I was one day at a party where a certain young man named Charlie was the beau ideal of every girl in the room, as well as the favorite of the whole country town. He was tall, handsome, a good dancer, better educated than almost any other of our young men, and was then teaching school in a near neighborhood. I had known him from the time I could remember. At this social gathering, he and I sat side by side during the repast; and Charlie grew a bit sentimental and said to me: "Ella, why is it you never seem to care for me as the other girls do?" "I do care for you," I replied: "I like you immensely and am always glad to see you." "But you do not care for me as other girls do," Charlie replied, with a very tender glance of his beautiful black eyes. "If you mean sentimentally, that is true," I answered. "I know most of the girls are very much infatuated with you in that way. And now you mention the matter, it is rather curious that I do not feel any sentiment for you. You are just my type; your looks please me; and you are in every way the sort to arouse my romantic nature. The only explanation I can give of your failure to do so, is that I have played I spy around the hay stack with you since I could walk; and there is no novelty about you. Perhaps if you went away for five years and came home new I might become interested." Charlie laughed and said he thought he would try the experiment.

Curiously enough he did go away to college soon after, and it was just five years before we met again; but he had broken two girls' hearts in the meantime, and was then studying for the ministry; and Ufe for me had utterly changed, as well.

When the real lover who was to dominate my life through time, and to retain my love through eternity, came upon the scene, all the romantic elements of which I had dreamed entered into the experience. I was visiting at the home of Colonel and Mrs. Benjamin on Prospect Avenue, Milwaukee. An evening entertainment was to take place, and I was making a few purchases for the occasion, in the way of gloves and ribbons. Fearing the hour was growing late, I stepped inside the largest jewelry establishment of the city and asked the proprietor (who was an intimate friend of my host) for the time. I was there but two or three moments, at longest; but those moments were the turning point of my destiny; the great crisis of my earth existence; the psychological moment which had no doubt been arranged by the Lords of Karma for my future happiness and development.

I was so occupied with my plans for the evening, and so anxious lest I keep my friends waiting their dinner, that I paid no attention to the occupants of the shop outside of the proprietor, who gave me the time. I departed alt iinaware of the wonderful event which was already registered in my life.

This has always struck me as a peculiarly pronounced expression of the way destiny slaps our self-conceit when we imagine we can foresee the events in our own lives.

Since early girlhood I had been expecting the coming of the Prince Royal to take possession of the kingdom of my heart. No matter what else life held for me or did not hold for me, that was the central event on which my idea of happiness turned.

I was in no haste for his coming, yet Ufe was filled with an agreeable expectancy at the thought of his possible approach, and I was ever on the watch for his arrival. Many false pretenders to the throne had come and gone; yet I knew somewhere waited the rightful Prince, and some day he would come and claim his own.

Of this mysterious being in the realm of the future, I had written years before:

Across the miles that stretch between, Through days of gloom or glad sunlight;
There shines a face I have not seen Which yet doth make my whole world bright.
He may be near, he may be far–
Or near or far I cannot see; But faithful as the morning star
He yet shall rise and come to me.
What though fate leads us separate ways?
The world is round and time is fleet. A journey of a few brief days
And face to face we two shall meet.
Shall meet beneath God's arching skies While sun shall blaze or stars shall gleam,
And looking in each other's eyes Shall hold the past but as a dream.
But round and perfect and complete
Life like a star shall climb the height As we two press with willing feet
Together toward the Infinite.
And still behind the space between. As back of dawns the sunbeams play,
There shines the face I have not seen Whose smile shall wake my world to-day.

And yet at that long-expected moment, when I was really in the same room with my Prince, no least intimation came to me; no sensation of any unusual kind; no impression to prepare me for what was to follow. Completely absorbed in the trivial affairs of the hour, I went my way unconscious that I had reached life's greatest crisis.

It was some three or four days thereafter that in my always large mail there came a very distinguished-looking letter in a blue envelope. I was accustomed to receiving letters from strangers, who from the time I began to write felt called upon to offer me either their criticisms or their praises; their approval or their disapproval. (It has always seemed to me that my path leads through two rows of individuals: one flinging rocks and mud, one casting bouquets at my feet.) Therefore, a strange penmanship did not surprise me. What interested me was the very unusual chirography and the effective stationery. The letter was written from the State of Georgia on a rainy Sunday afternoon; and it stated that the writer, one Robert Wilcox by name, in attending to business for his firm (what is now the International Silver Company, of New York), had been in the jeweler's establishment when I entered that day, and he had inquired of the proprietor who the young lady was; and had learned my name. He asked if it might not be his good fortune on his next visit to Milwaukee, some three months distant, to be introduced by our mutual friend. Unlike the other strangers who wrote me, he made no mention of my poems; he merely asked to be presented. I knew, of course, that any conventionally reared young woman would consider this a most irregular manner of making the acquaintance of a stranger. I knew it was, according to established ideas, bordering on impropriety; yet I so greatly admired the penmanship and the stationery of my would-be acquaintance that I was curious to know more of him.

Having received many letters from men in my life, I did not become a prude at that moment. I replied to Mr. Wilcox that he could not call as I should not be in Milwaukee on the date he mentioned; but I asked him what had prompted him to write me. This, of course, gave him the opportunity to write again. Then ensued the most interesting correspondence it has ever been my fortune to enjoy. They were not love letters; they were beautiful, unusual, educating, broadening, witty, and sometimes a bit daring; but never sentimental. I have them still– more precious than their weight in diamonds.

Mr. Wilcox told me about himself; about his being an orphan at the age of seven; and of the dear "Aunt Hattie" who had reared him along with her five daughters after the death of his lovely grandmother. He told me of his travels through Russia, Norway, and Sweden, as well as all other European countries, and he sent me books to read. The very first book he sent was Thpnias a Kempis's "Imitation of Christ"; the next was the "Cross of Burney"; then some of Gautier's works; "The Magic Skin"; and many others, always good literature. He told me he was a bachelor and would never marry: he had too many duties and obligations to relatives. I told him this made him more interesting as a correspondent, because I was very tired of men who became easily sentimental; that I was a very busy young woman also with many growing obligations to fulfil before I thought of marriage. He came West twice during our correspondence of five months, and I refused each time to see him; I was at my country home, and the house was crowded with little nephews and nieces, and everything was commonplace and every one was worried; and I felt I wanted to enjoy his letters without any jarring note entering into this purely intellectual correspondence. The letters always came in blue envelopes of a very beautiful shade and even the sight of one in my mail lent the day dignity; the crest on the paper seemed to lead me away from everything banal and common. One day a curious little parcel came in the never-to-be-mis-taken penmanship. It was narrow and long and I opened it wondering what it could be. It was an odd paper-cutter of sandalwood and copper, carved with oriental figures, something unlike anything I had ever seen.

Now I do not know how to account for the efffect of this trifle upon me. The home was particularly depressing at that time. There was a great shortage of money, and no one seemed able to provide the needed commodity. Some years before my oldest brother with his lovely wife and two little sons had gone to Dakota to battle with the elements and the beetles and grasshoppers for success as a ranchman. His life was a valiant fight against Nature's obstacles.

My sister, wife of a good man and a good physician, lived in Illinois. Doctors were overworked and underpaid in that locality and time. The climate was malarial. The loss of her first children and her subsequent broken health for a period of years had caused me much solicitude, and had awakened in me a great desire to be of comfort to her and her living children, who had inherited her musical talents. Another brother lived at home with an ever-increasing family. I do not remember that any of them ever asked a favor of me; but my heart was always torn with sympathy for them and for my aging parents: and there was ever an urge from within to relieve needs and improve conditions. My mother was overworked and very irritable. It can be readily understood that there existed that state of internal discord which more frequently than otherwise pervades an atmosphere where in-laws live under one roof.

My nature craved peace. I was born with great longing for harmonious surroundings. My mother, who would willingly have died for me, was yet not willing to control her temper, or restrain the sharp word which brought on family quarrels, as no one of them had learned self-control. I felt sorry for all of them and I was able clearly to see the wrongs existing on both sides. I urged my mother that, as hers was the stronger intellect, it was her duty to show the larger self-control and forbearance toward another woman worn into irritability with excessive child-bearing. I tried also to make her understand that the absence of the pleasures and luxuries of the world which she grieved over in my life were not as painful to me as discord and inharmony at home. Every penny I gave her for family expenses and every bill I paid wrung her heart with anguish, because she wanted me to be able to save my income for myself.

What hurt me most keenly was to have her remind others of my sacrifices–a thing which destroys all the benefit of a gift.

It was into this unhappy atmosphere that the little paper-knife came. At the sight of it something seemed to grip me about the heart with a band that awakened every deep emotion in my nature. A panorama spread before me of beauty, peace, comfort, luxury love. All the mean and unlovely phases of life dropped away, and I was lifted into a world of which I had dreamed sometimes when reading a rare poem, or hearing lovely music, or in the perusal of some of Ouida's exotic descriptions. I was shaken by storms of tears, and yet I did not know what I was crying about. Certainly no thought of the sender of the little gift, as a possible lover, entered my head at that moment. It was only that the gift seemed to be an expression of a world so at variance with my own that the contrast overwhelmed me. I was then preparing to bring out "Poems of Passion." The publishers sent me a telegram one February day to come to Chicago. In the Windsor post-office, on my way to the train, I found a letter in a blue envelope, saying the writer of it would be in Chicago that day and he hoped for a line from me while there. My first impulse was to go to Chicago and return without sending him any word until afterward. I was newly unhappy; matters had come to a critical state at home, and unless certain bills were paid within a few weeks I knew there would be public comment, hard to bear. Money was due me from various editors, but I could not demand it in advance. I was in this state of mind, feeling life was a mere tragedy of the utterly commonplace, when I suddenly decided I would send Mr. Wilcox a note, at the Grand Pacific Hotel, saying I was at the Palmer House and that he might call. I was with a lovely friend who lived there, dear Mrs. Tallman, who with her devoted husband was my faithful friend to the hour of her death. Mr. Wilcox called and I saw him in the hotel reception room. I was so numb and sick with my home worries that I had only a sense of his great aloofness. He was exceptionally fine looking, strong, manly, in the prime of life, very correctly dressed, very cultured in manner, and his voice was remarkable for its deep beauty. He seemed to my poor and troubled mind like a man from Mars. He served to make my own home show more miserably than ever in my eyes by the contrast of what he suggested with his great composure, his quiet dignity, and his air of cosmopolitan breeding. I went back to my country home feeling a vast loneliness. I thought I could no longer enjoy his letters; I believed he must have felt the wide difference between us, just as I felt it.

I was owing him a letter, but I did not write it. After three weeks there came a plaintive note from him saying, "Of course, I know how horribly disappointed you were after seeing my ugly phiz; I saw your disgust in your eyes; but you might, at least, drop a fellow gently and not with a sickening thud; you might, at least, write and tell me if you received the book I sent just before we met."

(This letter was not a pose; as I afterward realized, this most attractive and magnetic man was without one atom of vanity and actually thought himself ugly. I have seen him go out of his way to cross a room trying to avoid looking in a mirror.)

The correspondence was resumed on its purely literary basis. I borrowed money from the bank, and paid the worrisome debts. Money came to me from editors sooner than I expected. My friend, Hattie, in Milwaukee, asked me to be her bridesmaid; and her mother asked me to come to the house and have my gown for the occasion made there. With the suddenness of an April day after a long March of storm my spirits rose to joyfulness again. It was on April 20th, just two months after my first meeting with Mr. Wilcox, that the Lords of Karma again took my destiny in hand.

My correspondent had written me that he would not be in the West again before June; yet there at the post-ofsce, as I took my train to Milwaukee, was another letter from him saying that he had been called West again and would be in Milwaukee on April 20th, at the Plankinton House, and would I send him a line there or to Chicago the following day? Instead, a message was sent to him at the hotel giving him my city address. An hour later came a magnificent basket of flowers (I have the basket yet) and in it a note asking if he could call. My hostess was so charmed with the great floral gift that she urged me to see him; and I sent him a note saying he might call for half an hour only, as we were all so busy with the wedding preparations we had to economize time. My trunk had not yet come up from the station, so I wore a simple little house gown of the bride-to-be when I went in to meet my caller. He remained three hours, and loo THE WORLDS AND I missed his train to Chicago. That night he wrote his first love letter; and after he left me, I went up to my friend's room and, greatly to her astonishment, began to weep wildly. The same strange state of mingled ecstasy and misery which the little paper-knife had caused, took possession of me. I knew I was at last and forever desperately in love. But not until I received his letter the next afternoon did I know that the feeling was mutual.

The heavenly luster which shone over my world for the next few weeks cannot be described. I walked on air; and every breath was a stimulant. Never did bridesmaid glow with such unutterable joy as I when I stood by Hattie's side in the church, during the marriage ceremony, and dared harbor the hope that my own wedding might be in the near future; and that I might hear the sacred words pronounced which would make me the wife of my Prince of Lovers.

We were married a year and two days later. During that year I never met any one who knew Robert Wilcox outside of business acquaintances.

The few friends to whom I confided my engagement were greatly concerned lest I should find disaster and disillusionment at the end of my rainbow of promise. But the disillusionment never came. Instead, during thirty-two years of marriage, life grew in radiance and beauty, and I lived to realize my early poem written years before: I

DREAM

Oh, I have dreams. I sometimes dream of Life In the full meaning of that splendid word.

Its subtle music which few men have heard. Though all may hear it, sounding through earth's strife.

Its mountain heights by mystic breezes kissed,

Lifting their lovely peaks above the dust; Its treasures which no touch of time can rust. Its emerald seas, its dawns of amethyst.

Its certain purpose, its serene repose, Its usefulness, that finds no hour for woes. This is my dream of Life.

THE COMPELLING LOVER loi

Yes, I have dreams. I ofttimes dream of Love

As radiant and brilliant as a star.

As changeless, too, as that fixed light afar Which glorifies vast worlds of space above. Strong as the tempest when it holds its breath,

Before it bursts in fury; and as deep

As the unfathomed seas, where lost worlds sleep, And sad as birth, and beautiful as death.

As fervent as the fondest soiil could crave.

Yet holy as the moonlight on a grave. This is my dream of Love.

Yes, yes, I dream. One oft-recurring dream Is beautiful and comforting and blest.

Complete with certain promises of rest, Divine content, and ecstasy supreme; When that strange essence, author of all faith,

That subtle something which cries for the light,

Like a lost child who wanders in the night. Shall solve the mighty mystery of Death;

Shall find eternal progress, or sublime

And satisfying slumber for all time. This is my dream of Death.

CHAPTER VII

Steps Up Spiritual Stairways

MANY women remember the months preceding their marriage as the happiest, the most romantic time of their lives. Not so I. My somewhat painful prominence as the author of "Poems of Passion" made me desirous of keeping my coming marriage a strict secret from the pubhc. I knew once it was even suspected, there would be a fusillade of newspaper thrusts, which would destroy the sacredness and beauty of the happiness which promised to be mine. I remained very closely in my country home, only going a few times that year to Milwaukee to visit friends, and on those occasions my lover saw me there.

These friends, at whose home I was later married, while meaning to be kind and solicitous for my welfare, made me very uncomfortable. They had urged me the year previous to encourage the attentions of a man of means, living in the East, who was uncongenial to me. They thought me very foolish to expect a great romance to come into my life: they said those things existed more in books than in reality. When they saw me swept away by a great romance, they were suspicious of the lover in the case. They warned me that he was such a man of the world and so attractive to women that I need take much he said with an interrogation mark after it. They also urged against allowing him to visit me in my country home, assuring me that he would never continue his interest in me after a visit there. They were, too, opposed to my spending my money on repairing the old home. Nevertheless I repaired it; and the very first day it was finished my lover came and made his first visit and met my family for the first time.

My experiences in building the new addition on the house STEPS UP SPIRITUAL STAIRWAYS 103 were not all agreeable. My father was aging noticeably, both physically and mentally; and from the time I began to earn a considerable income he had ceased to feel much responsibility about money matters. He used to say: "Let Elly attend to this," when my mother spoke of family needs. My father had shown decided appreciation of my talents from the beginning, even though he used to worry about the amount of postage I used in sending out my various manuscripts. A phrenologist once said that my father's head was strikingly like that of Daniel Webster, save that an enormous bump of caution prevented him from putting into use many of his splendid abilities. It was this caution which made him anxious about the postage I used; but after the checks began to come in and my poems began to win approval, he was very appreciative. I remember one time when he made a business trip out to Iowa for a few days, a very unusual event in his life, his coming up to my room in the early morning of his return and waking me to tell of an experience he had had in Iowa. He had met a man at the hotel who was most enthusiastic about some poem of mine, and he and this man had sat up the whole night talking about me. I think no compliment I ever received from the public pleased or touched me more than this.

In his early life in Vermont, my father had learned to be handy with hammer and saw; and after he came to Wisconsin he put this knowledge to practical use. When I planned the addition to the house I, of course, employed a professional carpenter; but my father was very insistent that he knew how to plan and put up the addition better than the carpenters. There was some small repairing of another part of the house which my father was doing at his own expense; and he seemed to feel that the entire work was of his own doing. Twice he became so critical and fault-finding that the carpenters threw down their tools and told me they were leaving. The last occasion of this nature was only a week before I expected the visit of my lover. I went into a paroxysm of tears and when my father saw this, he relented and so did the carpenters, who resumed work.

I was, as a rule, a very cheerful person, and not given to tears in public: it took some big crisis to produce such a result. But when the house was done, I was almost a nervous wreck. One thing remains to this day, or did the last time I was ever in the old house, to remind me of my father's unreasonable interference. When the wardrobe off the new bedroom was all ready for the masons, I went in and found the beams which were to hold the hooks raised so high that it necessitated a foot-stool to reach them.

I had told the carpenters myself a few days before where I wanted them placed (to accommodate my five feet, three inches and a half in height), but my father informed me that he had raised them, as it was (I am sure he began his sentence with a word beginning with D) "poor carpentry work to have them so low down." The masons were all ready with their plaster when I made the discovery, so the room had to be finished that way. Only an Amazon in height would find it convenient.

It was really the beginning of my father's broken state of mind, which caused him to be a mere child during his later years. From being almost a dandy in his early life and the neatest of men, he had, at this time, grown very careless in his attire. This troubled me, naturally; and I tried to rouse him out of such a state. I was the only one who had any influence over him. Before the coming of my lover I had bought my father a new suit of clothes and a new hat; and I asked him on the morning of the expected visit to don these clothes. He stubbornly refused. I explained the importance of the occasion and he replied that if any city man was coming there and did not like his appearance, he could go right away again; he did not propose to change his habits or his clothes in his own home to suit the whim of callers. I think, perhaps, that was the moment of my life when I touched bottom in despair. My mother started into the fray, but I begged her to desist, as she only served to rouse still further my father's stubbornness. But again my state of abject misery brought on a torrent of tears, and again my father relented and attired himself in the new clothes. (I remember that I took his old hat away and burned it up and that, after the departure of

STEPS UP SPIRITUAL STAIRWAYS 105 my visitor, I had to confess this fact to him, and he was so displeased that for a period of some ten days he went about bareheaded to show me his disapproval of the act.)

Yet in spite of all this, and in spite of the predictions of my Milwaukee friends, my lover was not repelled by my home conditions. I do not remember much happiness during that visit, however. There was a brood of small children and their mother and father and grandparents were all nervously worn with the conditions which had been created by years of wrong thought and lack of self-control. Save the love and pity I sent out to them all, there was little love in the atmosphere: and I was on tenter-hooks every moment of the time my lover was there, lest some painful upheaval occur. Yet I know that every one of them, deep in their hearts, felt love and gratitude toward me and desired my best happiness: and all of them felt an admiring reverence for the splendid man who had come into my life.

They had seen many admirers about me; and through a long girlhood had seen me interested at various times, but never before swept away completely by an overwhelming emotion. So they were really on their best behavior; for which I fervently thanked them when the visit was over, besides thanking God, on my knees that night, as I always did for every least favor.

Before my lover came, I had been anxious in my mind regarding what he might think of my having dabbled, to the extent already mentioned, in matters psychic. I knew he was reared by orthodox relatives in New England, and I knew he was, at the same time, a cosmopolitan who had grown broad in his ideas, through extensive reading and through extensive travel. In his letters he expressed great reverence for the Creator and a strong belief in prayer and in the presence of guardian angels. But I had an idea that he might think me weak or unwise or uncanny, if he knew I had any interest in psychic phenomena. So, when suddenly, in one of our talks, he said to me, "Have you ever looked into this matter of communication with the spirits of our dead friends?" I trembled to the marrow of my bones; but I replied honestly

"Yes, I have, and I believe it sometimes occurs." Then I waited for my sentence of disapproval. Instead, with a very beautiful smile, my lover said: "I am so glad you believe this. I do. The subject interests me greatly." So another hurdle was safely leaped in my adventurous ride toward happiness.

At this moment, as I write of this occurrence, I am filled with a sense of profound awe at the consciousness of the important part this sympathy between us on all subjects pertaining to spiritual matters has played in my life. It has been, indeed, the very rock-bed foundation of my wonderful love life of thirty-two years with this rare soul.

The friends of my husband who knew him only in his business life would, no doubt, be astounded at such a statement of mine. He was not quickly understood by those who met him. A practical business man, with agreeable manners and the most winning voice, and a well read man, was what most people would say of him. Only to a few, possessed of understanding, did he reveal his peculiarly spiritual qualities. Not until the first year of my life with him was I aware of his open vision and his ability to see and hear on planes not visible to the physical eye and ear. When I did become aware of this, he warned me not to speak of it freely, as he, himself, did not understand the laws connected with it and was afraid to have it known. He had, however, he confessed to me, since a child, at times been conscious of the presence of beings not visible to others. While we were in our Meriden house he saw, on three separate occasions, a woman in a gray Shaker bonnet and gray gown pass through our upper hall. The first time he saw her he was confident some one in the house was playing a trick; but when convinced that all the inmates of the house could account for their doings at that moment, he knew he had had one of his "visions."

Nothing of unusual moment happened after these three visitations and he was never able to trace any occurrences in the history of the house to explain the matter.

After the death of our baby he saw the vision of the child

STEPS UP SPIRITUAL STAIRWAYS 107 on several occasions, at two of our New York homes and once in a hotel.

Besides his business qualities, my husband was a popular club man; he played an excellent game of whist, bridge and auction, and was popular with his companions through his wit and his courtesy at the card table.

In my early married life, he was much in demand for the game of poker; and I remember the first time he went to the club after we were in our Meriden house. He told me he was invited to a special game of poker at his club there, and it would be his first meeting with old friends since his marriage. (I know I felt a great glow of pride as he went down the walk, thinking how in all the congratulations his friends would naturally offer him on his marriage I had been the one woman in the whole world selected to wear his crown of "wife.")

That afternoon he had read to me in a New York paper an account of a book, written by Eliot Coues, on theosophy, containing many remarkable statements regarding the worlds beyond the earth.

It was the first time I had ever heard the word "Theosophy." He told me he was going to send for the book, and he said: "Ella, I wish you would write the author and try to meet him some time in New York. I think we ought to know more of this matter." Of course, whenever he expressed a wish of any kindj I never rested until I had done whatever I could to carry it out. I devoted the evening to letter writing and then retired, to enjoy the sound sleep which has always accompanied my nights. I woke to greet him on his return and to hear him express his appreciation that I had been so sensible about his going to the club, and to listen to all the different remarks his friends had made about his marriage. He said he had had a very enjoyable evening, but he said: "All the time I kept wondering if you would remember to write to Eliott Coues." Great was his satisfaction when he learned the letter was written.

That was one of the side lights which helped me to see what a composite nature was possessed by lie man I bad married. At the card table with his old bachelor chums, all unknown to them, he was hoping I had sent out this life line to spiritual worlds. And this was characteristic of him through all his life. His letters to me, extending over a period of thirty-four years, while naturally speaking of domestic and business matters, are yet full of his longings for and convictions of spiritual truths. While he never went deeply into the profound philosophy of Theosophy, he yet bought me every book on that subject which hfe felt would be a help to me and he was greatly impressed with the idea of reincarnation. It explained to both of us the mystery of our quick recognition of each other as mates for time and eternity; and it explained the complexities of this earth life which otherwise would make the Creator seem very unjust.

It used to be a wonder to him, as well as to me, that such ignorance existed in the Christian churches regarding reincarnation. When in the nth chapter of Matthew, Christ says, speaking of John the Baptist: "AND IF YE WILL RECEIVE IT, THIS IS ELIAS WHO WAS FOR TO COME. HE THAT HAS EARS TO HEAR, LET HIM HEAR."

Again in Chapter XVII: "BUT I SAY UNTO YOU THAT ELIAS HAS COME ALREADY AND THEY KNEW HIM NOT; AND THEY HAVE DONE UNTO HIM WHATSOEVER THEY LISTED. LIKEWISE SHALL THE SON OF MAN SUFFER OF THEM. AND THE DISCIPLES UNDERSTOOD THAT HE SPOKE UNTO THEM OF JOHN THE BAPTIST." That John the Baptist himself did not know he was Elias, reincarnated, is not strange. Few of us know who we were in former lives; but the Masters know; and Christ, the latest and greatest of all Masters, knew of what He spoke. Nevertheless His bigoted followers dare to hold up their hands and qry "Paganism" when reincarnation is mentioned.

Our studies in theosophy taught my husband and myself how dangerous were the investigations into spiritual phenomena unless one went about it with the light of knowledge in the brain and reverence in the heart. It taught us we were STEPS UP SPIRITUAL STAIRWAYS 109 not to seek information of coming events through the spirits of the dead, nor ask for advice on merely earthly matters; and that such advice, when obtained, was either given through mind reading or by earth-bound spirits whose progress we impede by continually calling them back to decide matters we should decide ourselves. Theosophy taught us that we should not lean on any power save the God-power in our own souls; and that we are not saved by any power save the power of the Divine Self we develop, as our brother Christ developed it through all His incarnations until He became truly "One-with-God." Theosophy also taught us that we must live the sermon on the mount, not merely believe in it, if we expect to find any satisfaction in the realms after death. And it taught us that all the realms, planes and spheres beyond earth are thought-builded; and that just according to our thoughts, actions and words will our "mansions not made by hands" be heavens or hells.

The continual effort made by my husband to put these beliefs into practice in his daily life were known to me, alone, perhaps. The effort made his business life ofttimes difficult; and had he put these ideals aside, keeping his religion for Sundays only, he would, no doubt, have attained great wealth, with his combined business acumen and his industry. Even in his love of cards and in his monotonous life of travel for the first seven years after our marriage, where card games were his only recreation, he introduced his idea of altruism. This, too, was a matter known only to me. He played games of chance only with men he knew; whatever money he made was kept in a separate purse, and when he came home he asked me to help him distribute it anonymously among deserving people. I remember one year when we both found great delight in sending a poor aging artist, in the Middle West, mysterious packages of money by express. We had met this artist while traveling and had bought a few of his pictures which we had given to friends. But his hand was losing its cunning, and he was too far along in years to take up any other occupation, so we felt a great happiness in bestowing upon him these blind favors. The sick, the lame, the blind.

no THE WORLDS AND I were aided out of this card fund: never any one we knew well: never any of our own dependants: always some one outside, whose needs we knew, but were not supposed to know.

My husband was reared by strictly old-fashioned orthodox relatives. His father believed card playing was wicked, and so did many of his boyhood companions. Some of these I afterward met, and knew they considered Robert had strayed from the fold of salvation by his worldly habits, such as playing cards for money. Yet I never knew one of these friends or relatives of his who lived so near the Christ standard in all his dealings with his fellow men, or who had so devout a heart toward God, year in and out, as Robert Wilcox. Sympathy, generosity, helpfulness, appreciation, all that was worth while; slow to anger and quick to forgive; with keen powers of discrimination, yet never carpingly critical, he surely lived his life along the ideals of brotherhood: never a Church member or a Church goer, yet liberal in his aid to churches and respectful toward all creeds.

The year following the Chicago Exposition and Congress of Religions, the East Indian Monk, Swami Vivekananda, came to New York and gave a course of lectures. My husband was then passing through a business crisis which required all of his courage and self-control. We first heard of these lectures in a somewhat curious way. One evening, just after, dinner, the postman brought a letter; it was from a stranger, addressed to me, and had been three times forwarded. It told of a lecture to be given by Vivekananda, giving the, time and the place, and closed, saying: "I feel sure, from what I read of your writings, that you will be interested." The hall where the lecture was to be given was just two blocks, from our apartment, and the date was just one hour from the time I received the letter. We had no other engagement for that evening, and my husband proposed going.

We reached the hall just as Vivekananda was going on the stage in his robe and turban. We sat in the very last seat of the hall, clasping each other's hands as the impressive orator gave a never-to-be-forgotten talk on things spiritual.

STEPS UP SPIRITUAL STAIRWAYS in

When we went out my husband said: "I feel that man knows more of God than we do. We must both hear him again."

My husband attended with me not only a number of evening lectures, but on several occasions came from his business office during the day to listen to the Swami. I remember his saying, as we went out on the street one day: "This man makes me rise above every business worry; he makes me feel how trivial is the whole material view of life and how limitless is the life beyond. I can go back to my troubles at the office now with new strength." Yet no one among his business associates knew where he had been.

Although I had naturally possessed the concentration which enabled me to sit in a crowded room where people were talking, singing or dancing, and to lose myself in reading or writing, I had yet to learn that concentration was a science.

It was Vivekananda, the East Indian teacher, who gave me my first lessons in concentration. He told us all, that this great law, once understood and acquired, could not only lead us to the summit of self-control, but it would give us the power of achievement and a knowledge of realms interpenetrating our visible and coarser world. After each lesson (and indeed a portion of each day since that time) I made a practice of sitting quite alone for a quarter or a half hour, seeking to bring my too active mind under the check rein of my will. I endeavored to drive out every thought save that of God– the one supreme, omnipotent creator of all the worlds which exist or ever have existed; He of whom Christ said: "Why call ye me good; there is none good but the Father." I sought to fill myself with the sense of His power and to bathe myself in love for Him.

Always, from these moments of concentration, I arose with new strength and poise to meet life.

One night, after coming from a lecture, my husband left me at the door of our apartment, and said he was going up to the Lotos Club for an hour to smoke his cigar and indulge in a game of cards. I prepared for retiring, and then sat down to my moments of concentration. Suddenly I felt that I must go to my desk. I had no idea what I was to do; I had finished my day's work before I went to the lecture; and I had no least thought of writing anything more that day. Yet so strong was the urge that I arose, went to my desk, and took up my pen and began to write. I was perfectly conscious, yet ray mortal brain certainly had nothing to do with what my pen wrote down. It was as if some one thought for me. I watched my hand form the words with interest, as I would have watched a friend write. This is the poem which came under those peculiar conditions: ILLUSION

God and I in space alone

And nobody else in view. "And where are the people, O Lord," I said, "The earth below, and the sky o'er head

And the dead whom once I knew?"

"That was a dream," God smiled and said,

"A dream that seemed to be true. There were no people, living or dead. There was no earth, and no sky o'er head

There was only myself–in you."

"Why do I feel no fear," I asked,

"Meeting you here this way, For I have sinned I know full well. And is there heaven, and is there hell,

And is this the judgment day?"

"Nay, those were but dreams," the Great God said,

"Dreams, that have ceased to be. There are no such things as fear or sin. There is no you– you never have been–

There is nothing at all but ME."

It is the only experience of the kind which ever befell me. And oddly enough, it is the only one of my thousands of verses which I was ever able completely to memorize and never forget. Whoever wrote it through me helps me to recall it.

The verses went begging; no magazine would use them, fearing they were unorthodox. The Century editor (Mr.

STEPS UP SPIRITUAL STAIRWAYS 113

Gilder) liked them very much, he said, but felt they might not be understood by his readers. Finally the Chap Book of Chicago used them, after which they were copied all over the earth, usually without my name. The London Athenceum published them some three years afterwards, and asked its readers to supply the author's name, if possible. I supplied it with the name and date of the magazine first using it.

On several different occasions in New York, or while traveling at different periods of our lives, my husband and I went to spiritual seances and investigated the phenomena. We encountered a few cases of pure fraud, not many; more cases of the presence of earth-bound spirits and again of elementals, mindless creatures that often frequent seance rooms. In no one of these circles did we find any knowledge that benefited us. Once, in a private home in California, through a psychic who only came to her friends, we were conscious of being in touch with higher forces; conscious, indeed, that our little son had grown in the spirit world, and was able to send us a message. The proofs, under perfect test conditions, were convincing to us.

That was fully fifteen years before my husband passed into higher worlds himself, and we never, during that time, made any further investigations. We simply rested satisfied that such truths existed. But always, in talking of th se matters, as we so frequently did, my husband would say: "If I go first, I will come to you and make myself known to you in such ways as I can, if God will permit it. If you go first, you must come to me."

In many of his letters I find these promises and only two weeks before his going out of the body, when he w. s in perfect health, he spoke very earnestly on the subject to me again, saying: "However hard it might be for you to stay here in our dear seashore home, were I to go on ahead of you, it is yet here that I feel I could reach you in spirit and make myself manifest. Both our summer and our winter homes here are so charged with our love-life that I am sure I could make myself known to you." How this promise of his has been kept will be told in later pages.

CHAPTER VIII Life in Meriden

THE first summer of my married life was spent at Thimble Islands, in that most inappropriately named resort, Stony Creek. (The utter lack of imagination which characterizes a large majority of Americans is displayed in the names given their towns. How any seashore resort with the wonder of waves and tides in the perspective, and islands and trees and rocks to lend variety, could be dubbed "Stony Creek" will ever remain a mystery to me.)

My husband had bought a little cottage there before he met me, planning to give some of the relatives who were blessed by his bounty a summer at the shore. (It was a curious coincidence which he and I had discovered early in our acquaintance, that both of us were doing what we could to help ten relatives, with our purses and our thoughts.) It was my first acquaintance with the sea; and although it was the Sound, for me it had all the beauty and majesty and novelty which had been ascribed to the ocean by my imagination. Coming as I did from the inlands of the Middle West, dwelling right on the banks of the Sound with the Prince of my early dreams, materialized into the most adorable of lover comrades, made life almost too full of happiness.

It was my husband who first found the location of our cottage disappointing. He called to my attention the fact that it was only pleasing to look out on the water at high tide. Until he mentioned it, the mud flats at low tide had not registered in my mind. But after a time I realized with him that we would not be satisfied to make that place our permanent summer home. So the little house was sold, for a trifle more than it cost, and at the end of the season we went into a house which had been rented for a term of two or three years, at Meriden, Connecticut, as my husband's business affairs centered about the manufacturing town for a period of time.

It was a pretty home, and when we were together life was full of everything sweet and beautiful. But my husband was obliged to be absent on business of the company in which he was a stockholder, fully half the time. On several of these trips I accompanied him; but that was not always practicable, and when he left me in Meriden I was acutely lonely for lack of congenial companionship. Fortunately I had my work; for while marriage relieved me of the urgent necessity of writing, there was ever the urge from within; and there was a brood of nieces and nephews in the West, needing assistance in gaining an education; a work I had already begun before marriage and which I was glad to continue.

Then I took up the study of French, and I resumed my old long-abandoned exercise of riding. My husband arranged with a stableman in Meriden to provide me with good saddle horses, and I kept up this enjoyment until that wonderful day came when expectant motherhood glorified life with new splendor.

While I made many sweet and lasting friendships in Meriden, I never grew to feel the town was my real home. It was so unlike the West, so much more self-centered and bound up in material ideas, it seemed to me, than was Madison or Milwaukee, or Chicago, as I knew them at that period. I could not, somehow, enter into any

at-one-ment with the purely New England element about me. My family had all been
bom in New England, yet the Wisconsin environment in which I had been reared
was wholly different from that of Meriden. There I had been known from childhood,
and my literary talents had been admired, and I was a sort of daughter of the State,
wherever I went. In Meriden the knowledge of my literary tendencies made people in
general stand a bit aloof, as if they thought I was not quite like other folks. They were
not readers of poetry to any extent, and knew little about my work. I think the word
"poetess" to the average American, until recent years, suggested a sen- timental person
with ringlets and an absence of practical good sense. I greatly desired the respect and
friendship of Robert's friends, and both were given gradually. In the meantime I
experienced much heart-loneliness when my beloved was away from home. Looking
back, I realize that I was supersensitive, and that the Meriden people cared very much
more for me than I understood at that time. But the New England temperament is so
repressed that it does not quickly show its affections. I missed the spontaneous spirit
I had been accustomed to meet in the West.

The social life in Meriden, too, seemed very formal to me. I liked best my informal
calls on a few near neighbors in the evening, and they, too, seemed to enjoy having
me run in bare-headed in my little Josephine house gowns, which I always wore in
those days.

There was a beautiful girl bride, sixteen years old, who had run away from home
to marry a traveling boy entertainer, and who was living at home while the young
husband went on his tour. This girl Sallie was so radiant it was a joy just to look
at her. When she came into my little study in the Colony Street house and talked
about her lover and let me talk about mine, the while our men were away, life lost
much of its loneliness. Dear, blooming Sallie! her life since then has been full of
tragedy. Two divorces, a suicide; the suffering of neglect and infidelity; separation
from children; humiliation and despair; a little season of opulence and happiness, then
again tragedy. But all of these things have not destroyed her radiant spirit, or blighted
her brilliant beauty. Sallie is a living example of what the modern woman can bear
and triumphantly overcome. When I stir the pot-pourri of memory, the perfume of
rose leaves in a closed jar rises at the thought of Sallie as she was then.

The first understanding interest which Meriden felt in me, as a poet, came through
the St. Elmo Commandery, K. T., the Masonic organization of which my husband
was a member. Meriden's very important man, Mr. H. Wales Lines, asked me to write
a poem for an occasion in the near future when the Commandery was to be honored
by the presence of some distinguished guests. Robert brought the request to me and
seemed desirous for me to write the poem. He provided me with such books and
literature as would give me the history of the Masonic Order, an order of which I knew
little, save that it held secrets which no woman could share.

I felt much concern about my ability to do honor to the occasion (or rather, to do
honor to my husband, which was my leading thought, I am sure).

I toiled in my little study for two or three days without being able to write one
satisfying line, and each night, when my husband came in, I was obliged to shadow
the hope in his eyes by a disappointing report. Then he told me that one of his very
best business friends from New York, newly married, was coming with his bride to

spend the week-end with us. He hoped I might finish my poem and be ready to enjoy their visit, but meantime assured me I need not feel anxious about their entertainment, as he would see to that, if I needed the time for my work. However, not a line of the poem came until after tht friends had arrived. We had dined and were in the drawing room; Robert told them of my work and asked them to excuse me if I went up to my study, but in a few minutes I came down with my writing materials and asked them to let me sit in their midst and write. I felt that such a congenial atmosphere would bring an inspiration. And sure enough it did. So, there in that social circle I began and completed the poem which delighted not only my husband but the whole Commandery, and not only the Commandery, for the poem has been used periodically by Masonic orders all over the world at many distinguished gatherings. Just at the beginning of the war my publishers in London wrote me enthusiastically regarding this poem. But, best of all, it brought me, at the time it was written, in closer touch with my husband's friends and made Meriden seem a little more like home to me.

The first suggestion for a poem made to me by the man whose name I was honored by wearing later occurred in Chicago a few months previous to our marriage. We were looking into the window of an art shop where were displayed three charming engravings of the stork.

In the first the stork was standing with his mate beside a pool where babies grew like water lilies among ferns and mosses. In the second the chosen infant was snugged on the back of his consort, while Mr. Stork was ringing a door bell with his foot. The third picture represented the reception of the child at the open door by a smiling woman. The pictures were signed "Rosenthal, 1862."

Curiously enough, I had never heard the legend of the stork until the explanation of the pictures was given me by my lover, who added, "I think you could make a very pretty poem on this topic. With your permission, I will send these pictures out to your home for you." So the pictures were sent, neatly framed, to the Wisconsin farm, where I returned that day: and very shortly afterward the poem was written and became, on its publication, immensely popular with mothers, with musicians and with elocutionists. Through all the long years since its appearance it has been sung and recited in many homes and salons.

BABYLAND

Have you heard of the Valley of Babyland The realm where the dear little darlings stay, Till the kind storks go as all men know And oh, so tenderly bring them away? The paths are winding and past all finding By all save the storks who understand The gates and the highways and the intricate byways That lead to Babyland.

All over the Valley of Babyland Sweet flowers bloom in the soft green moss And under the ferns fair, and under the plants there Lie little heads like spools of floss. With a soothing number the river of Slumber Flows over a bedway of silver sand. And Angels are keeping watch o'er the sleeping Babes of Babyland.

The path to the Valley of Babyland Only the kingly kind storks know. If they fly over mountains or wade through fountains No man sees them come or go. But an angel maybe, who guards some baby, Or a fairy perhaps with her magic wand, Brings them straightway to the wonderful gateway That leads to Babyland.

And there in the Valley of Babyland Under the mosses and leaves and ferns Like an unfledged starling they find the darling For whom the heart of a mother yearns. And they lift him lightly and snug him tightly In feathers soft as a lady's hand: And oif with a rockaway step they walk away Out of Babyland.

As they go from the Valley of Babyland Forth into the world of great unrest. Sometimes in weeping he wakes from sleeping Before he reaches the mother's breast. Ah how she blesses him, how she caresses him Bonniest bird in the bright home band. That o'er land and water the kind stork brought her, From far off Babyland.

My one joy and delight, pure and unalloyed during those two and a half years in Meriden, outside of my hours with my husband, was in my visits to Aunt Hattie and Uncle Lester, and their five daughters (Robert's cousins, with whom he had been reared like a brother) in New Britain, Connecticut. Aunt Hattie's sister was Robert's mother. It proved to me of what rare, broad, sweet and beautifully Christian lineage he sprang (on his mother's side there was kinship to Ralph Waldo Emerson) when this aunt and her five daughters, who had been accustomed to receive both his love and his means without any wife to come between them with claims for either, accepted me with open hearts and arms, and from the hour of our first meeting to this day never has one moment of discord or misunderstanding come to shadow life. Reared in a strictly orthodox atmosphere. Aunt

Hattie Booth and all her daughters were yet as broad as the universe in their outlook on religion and in their understanding of God's requirements of His children. All my ideas which many at that time called Unitarian, and which a year later I knew were theosophical, Aunt Hattie would discuss with me, evincing the deepest interest," and profound was her insight into things psychical. That is no wonder; for if ever a human being was in close touch with the world of Angels it was she. To this day, fully twenty years since she passed out of earth sight, I can not think of this rare and lovely woman without a rush of tender love sweeping through me, and of eager hope at the thought of again meeting her in realms not so far distant from me, I trust.

The commonplace, ordinary type of woman could easily have felt jealousy because of the new and expensive interest of the relative who had been her benefactor; and one encounters in such situations sometimes a nature so narrow and petty that gratitude for past favors is sunk in resentment that any one else should now share the thoughts of the benevolent bestower of material benefits. Such a nature can make purgatory out of heaven and discord out of harmony for all within her environment. Therefore it was then, and ever will be, a source of perpetually flowing springs of love and gratitude mixed with reverence–the gracious attitude of my husband's Aunt Hattie and of her five daughters, all living to-day, and still bestowing upon me their never-changing affection. I have always felt this close bond which united my husband's blood kin to me a far greater satisfaction than the honors I have received from any social or literary source during my whole career. Aunt Hattie was a Bulkeley–a name known and honored in New England–and my husband felt very proud of his blood. Many eminent clergymen and other men of note sprang from the Bulkeleys and they were, too, famed for their keen sense of humor and quick wit.

In my heart's jewel collection of rare souls Aunt Hattie always seemed to me like a perfect amethyst; she was so exquisite, so translucent, so gleaming. She would have adorned courts or shone in the salon of a de Stael, had her destiny called her there.

In my Wisconsin home we had never made much of a festival of Thanksgiving Day, save to prepare a little extra food and perhaps attend some social gathering in the evening. But we had few relatives, and the fifty miles which lay between my grandparents' home and my own were seldom bridged by more than one visitor at a time. Therefore it was a new and delightful experience when, the first Thanksgiving Day after my marriage, I sat at Aunt Hattie's table with twenty-one new made relatives. I was the twenty-second. Aunt Hattie employed no domestics, four of her five daughters being of an age to be helpful, and the sweetest possible atmosphere of loving service characterized the home. I presume they may, being human, at times have had their spats and misunderstandings, but in all the years during which I was a frequent guest at the home for long periods of time, I never heard any discordant words under that hospitable roof: and there was much fun, much mirth, much happiness, despite the fact that two of the daughters suffered from serious physical disorders resulting from the effects of scarlet fever in their childhood, and despite the fact that many anxieties and worries came to the family, as is the fate of most mortals. It was my ideal of a loving home–the atmosphere I had always longed for.

Uncle Lester was given to moods of much depression and fear about the future, but always that rare soul of Aunt Hattie's soared above the clouds and brought sunshine; and always she turned Uncle Lester's sighs to smiles and his fears to hope. I remember how like a big tree brjuich full of birds their table seemed to me on that Thanksgiving Day. At one moment there would be twenty-two people sitting at it; the next moment I would see but a dozen; the others had flown to bring back more food to the table, just as birds fly back and forth to feed their young, and I, the new-comer, was so feted and loved and appreciated that my heart was bursting with love and gratitude for the blessings that God had bestowed upon me.

Dear Aunt Hattie! It is said that the foundation of happiness in Heaven is fonned, not by our creeds and psalm singing and church-going, but by remembrance of the good and kind words and deeds we bestow upon God's children, our fellow beings on earth. It is said, too, that Hell is formed by remembrance of our unkindness to our earth companions. Surely Aunt Hattie rose quickly to a beautiful realm where she trod golden floors made of her own golden deeds on earth. Of such is the Kingdom of Heaven. God and all His great angels bless her forever and ever!

It was a shining hour of my life when I imparted to Aunt Hattie the wonderful news of my expectant motherhood. Again the white soul and big heart and broad-loving spirit were revealed in her spontaneous delight; and all through those radiant months, fully half of them spent without my husband's presence, Aunt Hattie and her daughters and the good Uncle Lester were my strength and comfort and defense against the many anxieties and fears which would, at times, intrude on my great happiness. It can easily be imagined how painful and bitter would have been the situation of a newcomer and expectant mother in a strange land if the husband's relatives had been opposed to the advent of a child, as sometimes occurs in families.

Never was a child more longed for, or more anticipated, than that babe of mine; and never did waiting mother feel herself to be more of a chosen and anointed being than I during those months. Naturally, I felt a deep gratitude towards others who also welcomed the coming child. My first sea voyage was taken during that period of my life. Being in excellent health, the physician thought it no risk, and so the wonderful trip to Havana and back was enjoyed without any disastrous results and with lasting memories of great pleasure.

Some verses written on that voyage, suggested by a remark made by my husband, became extremely popular and have been set to music by more than one composer since. Seeing a scarf of mine fluttering in the sea wind at the open port hole of our cabin, he said: "See how that old flirt of a sea wind is trying to coax that scarf to come out and see the world with him; if she went, he would kiss her a few times and then fling her into the waves to drown." So before the day ended I wrote "The Seabreeze and the Scarf."

Much as my husband desired a son, all the "people-who-are-supposed-to-know" predicted a daughter. So we relinquished the idea of Robert, Jr., and prepared to welcome Winifred Wilcox. All through the Cuban trip we talked of Winifred. She became a real personality to us; and we thought of her as if she had lived many years under our roof.

My happiness was so great that I shared my expectations with all my friends from the very beginning of my hope, and Anna Robertson Noxon, a gifted woman from the South, who was very well known at that time as a writer of bright verse, sent a poem to "Winifred," beginning:

Winifred, when bees are humming We shall listen for your coming.

I have the lines among my treasures laid away.

Once, while my husband was in the West, I wrote him what a happy visit I was having with friends of his in New York, and before me lies a letter he wrote me in reply. He says therein:

"I am glad too you have Winifred with you, in all your happiness in New York. Though she is very young to go into society, I feel she is very safe snugged up so closely to your warm heart; and the little confidences that she receives from its whispered pulsings must be very delightful to her. I should think you would be talking to her all the time. A kiss to her."

But suddenly, one May day, when the expectant father was in Tennessee on business, not Winifred, but Robert M. Wilcox, Jr., came to earth life; and not liking the world into which he had been so unceremoniously ushered, he remained only twelve hours.

Informed by wire of the arrival of his son, my husband wrote me a letter which was replete with beauty and wit.

"Who," he said, "is this Robert M. Wilcox weigliing ten pounds? What was his hurry? Where is Winifred? It is the first instance on record when a Wilcox stepped in so impolitely before a lady. Yet he and his mother have made me the proudest man that walks the earth to-night."

A few hours latet a second telegram called my husband home to find only the beautiful body of his son left for him to see. Through a man's tears, mourning that longed-for son, and trembling for the life of his wife which hung in the balance, he was the saddest man on earth. So brief was the life of this son, and so unprepared were we to think of him as a son, that, as time passed, he became like the memory of a dream to us; while the thought of Winifred has always lingered, as of one we had known and loved and dwelt with.

During the twenty-nine years my husband remained with me after the loss of our child we used Winifred as a sort of mentor when either wished gently to rebuke the other. My husband, who always desired me to be philosophical when any trouble or annoyance came (even if he failed to be so), found me rather rebellious and indignant one day over an unjust and ungrateful action of an inferior, who had received benefits from our hands. "You must control yourself, my dear," he said; "how do you think you would appear to Winifred in such a mood? Would you be an example for her?" Once when he was smoking more cigars than I felt were good for him, and a few reminders of the fact from me, as well as from his physician, did not cause him to desist, I asked him what he thought Winifred would say if she found her father injuring his health by such a habit. So ever this daughter of our imagination walked with us; and we often saw young girls whom we described as of "Winifred" t3 e.

CHAPTER IX New York

AFTER the death of our baby we left our Meriden house, and went to Shelter Island for the summer, where I slowly pulled back to health of mind and body, and that autumn we settled in New York, which became my husband's headquarters for an independent branch of the sterling silver business in which he was engaged. The little apartment we took was my first real home, entirely arranged and planned by myself during my husband's absence, and it was my first experience in being my own housekeeper and doing my own marketing, while a cunning little sixteen-year-old maid, Louisa, came in the morning to assist me and went home at night, as our apartment was not large enough to house her.

I had even selected the apartment alone; and when my liege lord returned he was amused and a bit startled to find how tiny it was. When I explained my dominating desire to be economical, he was greatly touched. I had not yet become accustomed to the thought of spending any one's money but my own, earned by my pen; and there was a certain embarrassment in the idea of using even my husband's purse.

We remained in the little apartment only during the winter; but they were very happy months, and about that small home will ever linger a halo of memory. Our belongings were artistic, and, small as the domicile was, my friends always exclaimed at the charm of the spot when they entered it

During the first two years of my marriage, while living in Meriden, I had made the acquaintance of a number of literary people in New York. My very first introduction to any social life in the metropolis had been at a reception given by Jenny June Croly, who was at the height of her popularity. She was President of Sorosis, and her writings, speeches, and active works for the advancement of women made her a conspicuous figure in the intellectual world of that time, and surrounded her with brilliant people. I felt highly flattered when she asked me to be her guest of honor at one of her Sunday evenings. At her home I met many celebrities, and was invited to various other entertainments from time to time, so when I became a resident of the metropolis I was not a stranger.

I began to ask a few of the people I had met to come to my apartment on an occasional Sunday afternoon, and in my little band-box of a drawing room were frequently gathered a bevy of poets, artists, actors, musicians, and always a circle of charming girls. It has been my good fortune all my life to have as close friends young women of unusual beauty and brain and moral worth.

Young people of both sexes made much of me those first years in New York; for "Poems of Passion" was still in the pubuc eye, and was much read and talked about, and in the East seldom criticized. All the lovers and brides and bridegrooms and dreamers of dreams wanted to meet the writer of the ardent love verses; and many of the literary drawing rooms made a feature of having some actor or elocutionist recite selections from my book. I followed this volume the first year I lived in New York with "Poems of Pleasure," and many of the verses from this volume became extremely popular for recitation, particularly "The Birth of the Opal." This poem came into form through the following chain of circumstances.

The year preceding my marriage I had been made the poet of the day at a large banquet, "A Woman's Congress," given for Julia Ward Howe and other Eastern women of note, at the Palmer House, Chicago. There I met Mrs. Sophia Hoffman of New York, a beautiful and motherly woman, of much intellectual charm, who at once became my devoted friend. I remember feeling the wind go out of my sails that afternoon by something she told me Julia Ward Howe had said: that Miss Wheeler evinced con- siderable ability and she thought it might be developed into real talent with study and hard work. As I had worked with unflagging zeal and persistence ever since I could hold a pen, and had already received many words of commendation from high sources, I felt very much set back by Mrs. Howe's words; but these set-backs have ever come to me periodically in order, no doubt, to save me from that most offensive and blighting sin–conceit and self-satisfaction.

After I came East, I met Mrs. Hoffman at many functions, and one day (to be exact, it was December 13th, 1886), while I was on a shopping trip in New York, Mrs. Hoffman asked me to lunch with her, and then took me to the jewelry establishment of Marcus and Sons, at that time on Union Square. She introduced me to Mr. Marcus, Senior, and asked him to show me the wonderful opal he had in a large piece of rock from somewhere in Honduras. I had never before seen an opal, and was much impressed by it. Mr. Marcus said to me: "I wish you would write a poem about it; it has always seemed to me that the opal was the child of the sunbeam and the moonbeam. I have told several of our New York poets of my idea; but not one of them has grasped it in all its beauty. I think you could." "Yes," I replied, "I am sure I can." "If you do," Mr. Marcus said, "let me see the poem as soon as it is done. I am getting out a little book on gems which it would suit." I went back to Meriden and in my little study, on December 14th, I wrote, in perhaps a half hour's time:

THE BIRTH OF THE OPAU

The Sunbeam loved the Moonbeam,
And followed her low and high. But the Moonbeam fled and hid her head.
She was so shy–so shy.
The Sunbeam wooed with passion;
Ah, he was a lover bold! And his heart was afire with mad desire,

For the Moonbeam pale and cold.
She fled like a dream before him. Her hair was a shining sheen,
And oh, that Fate would annihilate The space that lay between!
Just as the day lay panting In the arms of the twilight dim,
The Sunbeam caught the one he sought And drew her close to him.
But out of his warm arms, startled And stirred by Love's first shock.
She sprang afraid, like a trembling maid. And hid in the niche of a rock.
And the Sunbeam followed and found her And led her to Love's own feast;
And they were wed on that rocky bed. And tiie dying day was their priest.
And lo! the beautiful Opal– That rare and wondrous gem–
Where the moon and sun blend into one, Is the child that was born to them.

I sent the verses to Mr. Marcus, saying I wished to publish them in The Century Magazine first, after which he could use them in his booklet on gems.

Mr. Marcus returned a check of twenty-five dollars and said he desired to be the first publisher of the poem. Fortunately, I obtained his permission to allow the verses to be recited in two or three drawing rooms during the time he was preparing his booklet, for when the booklet appeared my verses were without my name. Mr. Marcus explained that it was owing to an error in the printing room. But, naturally, it was a bitter disappointment to me. It caused me much annoyance, as when a few months later I included them in my new volume, "Poems of Pleasure," several letters came to me from people who said they had seen these lines before, and asking for my proof of their authorship. This proof was forthcoming in the word of the many people who had heard the name given at receptions and seen it on programmes of recitals.

Aubrey Boucicault was then a beautiful lad, a sort of child prodigy in the artistic circles of New York; he was like a young Apollo, and at many entertainments that winter the piece-de-resistance was "The Birth of the Opal," given by Aubrey Boucicault. A young English actor, Courtenay Thorpe, made them a specialty also. But despite the almost universal popularity of these verses, I found my little poetical bark was not yet out of the choppy waves of criticism. Although I had been made a welcome guest in many literary salons, there was one woman, the wife of a successful author, whom I met frequently at receptions and who gave charming evenings at her own home and distinctly ignored me. She even went so far as to invite a protegee staying in my own home, without including me. I was afterward told that the good lady objected to my poem, "The Birth of the Opal." She said I had laid bare all the secrets of married life in that poem.

It was some time after this that a Spanish poet was expressing his enthusiastic admiration for my verses, and I could not refrain from telling him the incident above related; to which the witty Spaniard replied: "My God, madam, did the lady think she, alone, knew those secrets?"

The one and only time I was ever induced to recite in public was that winter, and that poem. Before I relate the incident I must go back to the beginning of my career. It has already been told how Frank Leslie's publishing house sent me my first check for ten dollars, the price of three poems. A benign old gentleman, Benjamin Smith, was the Leslie secretary; he had been many years in the employ of the house, and he was a gallant devotee at the shrine of Mrs. Frank Leslie, who, after the death of her husband, took the business into her own hands, and was able to leave at her death, a few years ago, a fortune of nearly two million dollars.

Mr. Smith wrote me, after I had been a contributor to the Leslie periodicals for a year or two, that my first poems were regarded by him and Mrs. Leslie with considerable sus- picion, as my penmanship was so crude and childish, and the merit of the verses suggested an older hand. He often used to write me very chatty letters, and always was there some compliment for Mrs. Leslie, or some clipping telling of her beauty and brilliancy, which naturally appealed to my imagination. Therefore it was with a tense interest that I made my first call at the Leslie publishing house, where Mrs. Leslie had written me she spent all her daylight hours.

I confess to a feeling of disappointment at the first sight of this lady. The newspaper descriptions of her, and those of Benjamin Smith, seemed overdrawn. She looked older and less radiant than I had imagined, and her pronounced Roman nose, while it indicated her Napoleonic business prowess, militated against her beauty. But her skin, of exquisite texture, was like the finest marble and with that peculiar luster which seemed to shine from within. Her eyes were large and blue, and her mouth almost too small for beauty, too thin-lipped. Her form was molded after the Spanish lines, a little too slender in the waist and too full in the bust for modern ideas of symmetry, perhaps, but at that time small waists were regarded as a necessary accompaniment to beauty. Her feet, too, were out of drawing, so tiny were they. I once saw her crossing a street attired in a heavy fur coat which made her full bust more prominent, and gave her large head and large Roman nose a Juno-like appearance, while from beneath her skirt peeped out those infantile feet. It was an inartistic effect. Mrs. Leslie, however, felt very proud of her feet and very sensitive about her hands, which were small but unlovely in shape. She made a feature of long sleeves and lace falling over her hands in her dressing. Mr. Abraham Wakeman, a one-time Postmaster of New York, told me that he saw Mrs. Leslie when she was Mrs. Squires and in the full bloom of early womanhood, and he said, without any exception, she was the most magnificent specimen of female beauty he had ever beheld. Her brilliant beauty led Frank Leslie to obtain his own divorce and hers, to make her his wife. Mr. Squires was her second husband, although she spoke of him as her first. There had been a brief early marriage (with some elements of tragedy connected with it) which she never mentioned, and only a few people knew of it. She often referred to herself as "a mere child" when she married Mr. Leslie. When I met her, she was probably in her middle or late forties, and she seemed a very tired woman. But she was alive with sentiment and romance–the dominating qualities in her nature, second only perhaps to ambition for power and prestige.

The man known as the Marquis de Leuville was in the foreground of her life; and she was genuinely and unquestionably in love with him. He was a striking-looking individual, very tall, with long hair and a peculiar walk due to very high heels: he was a fluent talker and a great flatterer of women. He was younger than Mrs. Leslie, and it was evident to all who saw him that he had her bank-book account in mind, in his pursuit of her. Their engagement was announced, but the marriage never took place.

With Mrs. Leslie's unquestionable business acumen, her fine intellectual qualities, and her large experience in the world, it seemed almost incredible that she should be so misled by her belief in her powers as an enchantress. Yet, if we study the lives of other women who have been prominent in the eyes of the world through their combined beauty and intellect, we shall not find Mrs. Leslie a solitary instance of such foolishness. The woman who during the time of feminine prowess rules men by her physical charms and her magnetism and her ability to keep them entertained, is quite prone to ignore the fact that she has lost her attractions, long after the sad truth is apparent to every one else. Accustomed for years to have men pursue her because she is physically attractive, she cheats herself with the belief that her attractions, not her bank account, cause them to continue the chase after she is past her prime. When a woman finds her chief interest in life is her power over men, it affects her very much like a drug habit, and is as diffictilt to overcome. And it leads to as many illusions.

Mrs. Leslie used to talk of the many men who frequented her salon as her helpless slaves. Yet, while given to great caution in handing out money for charitable purposes usually, she almost invariably proved an easy mark for her impecunious admirers.

Mrs. Leslie believed herself to be one of the greatest inspirations to the poetical genius of Joaquin Miller. I think possibly she may have been. I was in New Orleans, with my husband, at the Exposition, the second winter after my marriage. Mrs. Leslie, who was at another hotel, called and told me Jdaquin Miller had asked her to bring me to breakfast with him at the Cable House, where he was spending that winter. My husband thought it worth my while to meet the poet of high boots and long hair, whose genius was unmistakable. So I went to the breakfast, and Mr. Miller met me at the door, and looking down upon me from his great height, said, "Why, Elly, I didn't think you were so petite and pinky; I imagined you a big-wristed girl out West milking cows." I remember the poet as very gallant and complimentary toward Mrs. Leslie, though I did not see any evidences of consuming passion in his attitude.

Mrs. Leshe, from the hour I met her, evinced a deep interest in me; and desired my presence at all her functions, which, during the first few years of my life in the East, were really brilliant affairs. And oiie met there, in her crowded drawing rooms, some very worth-while people. I had come from the West, into the presence of people whose names alone in my early youth gave me a thrill, and I felt that I was dwelling in an enchanted land. I lacked the discrimination which comes from experience with humanity, and I was so dazzled with the love light in which I walked that everybody and everything was seen through a veil of illusion. While my husband had often told me that (at that time) my utter lack of any tendency to criticize my fellow beings was peculiarly pleasing to him, he nevertheless became somewhat troubled about my too ready acceptance of everybody I met in New York as an angel in disguise. He wanted me to learn, not to criticize, but to discriminate. Looking back over our wonderful years together, I do not recall one instance where my husband failed in judgment of the people he be- lieved worth taking as friends and those he thought it wise to keep as acquaintances only. He was most anxious for me to meet and enjoy whomsoever was worth knowing. He realized that my life belonged—in a measure—to the public, and he was ever watchful of himself to see that his claims upon me did not restrict the growth of my talents or circumscribe my life. But he was solicitous lest the designing and the unworthy should crowd out others more deserving.

There came a time when he was very much troubled about Mrs. Leslie's constant claims upon me as an assistant at her functions, her desire to have my name appear in print beside hers, no matter whether I had been with her or not, and her unwillingness that I should have friends made outside of her circle. She and the Marquis de Leuville were very much before the public eye in the press, both in America and England, and there was a great lack of dignity about the whole matter which distressed my husband. It led finally to my urging Mrs. Leslie, as a friend, to adopt a different course of conduct toward the de Leuville man, telling her of the wrong impressions she was creating; and this caused Mrs. Leslie to feel hurt, and to regard me as having turned against her. She thought I had been unjust toward de Leuville also; but I am sure she lived to realize her mistake in that matter. There were admirable qualities in Mrs. Leslie's nature. She was quick to appreciate talent of any kind and to aid it where such aid did not call for too much sacrifice on her part. She was free from petty jealousies, and ready to see and praise beauty in another woman. This is a trait not often found in a woman whose stock in trade is her own beauty. And she was amiable and to certain kinds of suffering sympathetic. Then again, one came up against such adamantine streaks in her nature that it was a veritable shock; I have seen her almost angelic in tenderness, and I have seen her as cruel as the iceberg. Surely a strange woman.

While I met Mrs. Leslie frequently afterward at various functions I never continued the old intimacy; and only called upon her once afterward, a few years before her death. The "Marquis," it was learned, at the time of his death, was a son of a barber; and had set forth determined to make a career for himself by hook or crook. His course of procedure was to seek out wealthy women of mature years and flatter them into compliance with any of his wishes. It was an amazing fact that the man had lived in luxury and forced his way into many social circles through such means.

To return to the "Birth of the Opal," and my recitation of that poem, takes me back to the first year of my acquaintance with Mrs. Leslie. It was the last function I attended before my baby came. I know I wore a white satin Empress Josephine gown, belted high under my arm pits and very full in drapery, Mrs. Leslie had planned to have my recitation an effective one; and she had sent to the bank and brought forth a splendid set of opals, in which she decked me. I had never heard then of any evil omen attached to this jewel and I was thrilled with their wonderful beauty. I was given a chair on a sort of impromptu raised dais of some kind, and in my Josephine gown and the splendor of the opals I recited, or rather said, ray verses in a monotone, with no-effort at elocution.

I think there must have been something rather droll about my manner of saying the verses, as "An Imitation of Ella Wheeler Wilcox" was afterward given as an encore on programs by Settle Bloom, a charming reader of that day, who was popular in drawing rooms. I once sat in the audience where this lady gave a reading for charity, and heard myself imitated, and was convulsed with laughter. It made me more determined than ever to let my one appearance in the role of a reciter be my last.

Mrs. Leslie had given me my first shock by her dismay at my coming motherhood. From the first hour she knew of it she had declared it a terrible misfortune; and I recoiled from her when she said, "I would as soon touch a worm as a newborn baby. You will destroy your figure, your complexion, and no doubt lose your husband's love by this sacrifice." After a few such speeches I requested Mrs. Leslie to desist talking on the subject; and almost her only reference to it afterward was on this occasion where three months before my baby came I recited the "Birth of the Opal," and she said to me, "If your baby is a girl you must call her Opal." Mrs, Leslie was four times married; and she was about to be married to a fifth husband, a Spanish Marquis of an old family, when he died suddenly. Yet I am sure in her whole adventurous career she never knew such happiness as was mine in that brief period of expectant motherhood.

Those early years in New York's literary circle would have held dangers for me had I not been so absorbingly and reverently in love with my husband. The literary salons, like all New York circles, teemed with men who were ready for flirtatious experiences, and the author of "Poems of Passion" was, by some of these men, supposed to be a free lance in love matters. But it did not require long to convince them of their mistake. One bachelor said, in speaking of me, "She really bores me; you can not talk ten minutes with her before she bumps you up against a two-hundred-pound husband with whom she seems to be ridiculously enamored."

One of mywomen acquaintances assured me it was very bad form to let other men know I was in love with my husband; that it savored of the country; and that, besides, I was cheating my genius. She thought one of my talents needed to be fed with romantic experiences in order to keep the fountain of expression flowing with fresh waters. Mrs. Leslie warned me that it was very unwise and very unsafe to permit my husband to know I was so deeply in love with him. She said the only way to hold a man was to keep him in doubt and to show him that other men were interested. But I knew these theories were false philosophy; and I knew life had nothing to offer me that could in any way compensate for one moment's loss of my own self-respect or the respect and confidence of the man who made me his wife. To "make good" as a daughter and a sister had always seemed to me a greater achievement than to attain fame or financial success; and to fill the often difficult role of wife, to the very best of my ability, (aided by constant prayers for larger wisdom and more understanding) became my one controlling aim. Therefore the life in New York was only entertaining and amusing, and again sometimes disillusioning, but never dangerous for me.

The materialization into personalities of some of the famous names I had known proved not always satisfying. Talent and genius had ever seemed to me like two white sentinels guarding the door of the human mind from the intrusion of ignoble jealousy, petty envy, and unworthy selfishness. The gifted man and woman I had thought must be the great man and woman. It was not invariably so: and many of the halos I had bestowed upon imagined personalities had to be "cut over" or removed entirely when the actual individual was encountered. Yet about all those early years in New York there was a brightness and beauty that still shines in memory as I look back upon them. It was a constant surprise to me, to think I was really living in the midst of the people of whom I had dreamed during those lonely years on the Westei-n farm; and when I would send a poem to the New York magazines or weeklies, and receive an answer back swiftly, there was always a sensation of novelty in the experience; a happy realization that I was not five miles from the post office and fifteen hundred miles from the editors, but a living part of the great metropous myself, and in touch with the whole world in consequence.

I organized a little French study class and social club at my home, which resulted in much pleasure and entertainment. We talked only French for two hours.; a fine was paid for breaking into English even by one sentence. Then afterward we spoke our native tongue while enjoying a simple repast. The now famous and successful author, then just beginning to be known, Will N. Harben, was one of the circle and a great favorite with every one. He was handsome and witty, and full of southerni gallantry and pretty flattery toward all women. In connection with him I recall such a droll little incident. I am wondering if he will remember it if he reads these pages. One evening during our French hour the door of my apartment was opened into the hall, and quite a draught of air was coming through. A French teacher, who was always engaged for the evening, was giving a recitation. I sat near Mr. Harben, and he was within reach of the door. Feeling the chill of the air, and not wanting to disturb the reading by rising, I whispered to Mr. Harben very softly: "Shut the door; shut the door." This he did after a third repetition. Then when the time came to speak English Mr. Harben assumed a most dolorous air, and said to me, "You can not imagine what a moment of ecstasy followed by dull despair you gave me when you spoke. I thought you were speaking French; and that you said, Je fadore. But with what a thud I fell after your third repetition!"

One day I took a party of some ten young people, Mr. Harben among them, to visit a clairvoyant of whom I had heard interesting things. She proved to be a tall handsome woman, who seemed to feel a great respect for her calling. She charged a nominal price, and proceeded to take handkerchiefs and other objects from the people in my party; and when one young man began to say witty things, she hushed him, remarking that she wished every one to be serious and respectful while in the room. She told us she had possessed this clear seeing power since she was a small child; and that she knew it came from a divine source. Then she went on to tell all those in our party some very interesting and some very remarkable facts concerning themselves, their affairs and their friends. We all came away impressed that the clairvoyant was really possessed of occult powers.

The name of this lady was Katherine Tingley; and she has since become known the world over through her prominence in a certain branch of theosophical work at Point Loma, California. This was the only occasion when I met the lady.

CHAPTER X The Bungalow

DURING my residence in New York (a period of nineteen years) I was enabled to carry out to some extent many of my early longings to be helpful to others.

I brought my sister's daughter, who was also my namesake (Ella W heeler Bond), a born musician, on for a year of musical study in the metropolis. She proved a faithful student and a most grateful and sweet girl. She returned to the West (the family had moved to Nebraska) and has made a most successful career for herself since in musical fields. Daughters of my brother were sent to school (the oldest to college) from the proceeds of my pen; and girls who were not relatives, save through the kinship of talent, came into my life at times in the capacity of protegees. A little story written by one girl in Chicago attracted my attention. I wrote to the author of it, and afterward invited her to visit me.

It resulted in her remaining in New York, either under my roof, or near my home, for a period of seven years, and then going to France as a correspondent for an important periodical, for another period of seven years. She did not develop the talent for story writing which I imagined she possessed; but she developed great industry, and made a most commendable place for herself in the literary, musical and educational world. And, best of all, she grew steadily in nobility of character, which is, after all is said and done, the only kind of growth that counts in life. She is one of my dearest friends to-day, growing more beautiful with years.

In my desire to be helpful to girls of talent, I sometimes made mistakes of judgment. I know now that we should never go out of our way to seek opportunities of service. We should do that which comes directly to our attention. When we hunt for people on whom to bestow our favor, we are implying that the Lords of Wisdom do not know their own business.

One day, in some periodical my husband had brought home, I read a few lines of verse which stirred me deeply with their great beauty. I had never before seen the name which was attached to the verses. I wrote a note to the author in care of the magazine, saying I wanted to know something about her.

She replied from another American city, and it led to a correspondence. I spoke to many people of her, and no one had ever heard of her. She sent me a number of her verses, and they all seemed to breathe forth the spirit of unusual genius.

I became obsessed with the idea of making the girl known to all the literary people and the critics of New York. She had told me that she was engaged in a rather uncongenial occupation to earn her living, and I imagined her just as eager for a larger life, and for the association of kindred minds, as I had been out on the Wisconsin farm. I felt as if I might act the part of Fairy Godmother to her– the Fairy Godmother I used to dream would come into my life as I lay under the sloping eaves of the old farm house, but who never came. I thrilled with the thought of the happiness and benefit I might bring into this gifted girl's life.

I asked her to come and visit me and let me give a reception in her honor. My husband saw how eager I was to do this, and gave me carte blanche to go ahead. I was living in a small apartment, so put the guest up at a nearby hotel. The reception was arranged to take place at one of the then prominent New York hotels, a hotel where my husband had often lived as a bachelor, and therefore attractive to me. My delight and enjoyment in this affair cannot be described. I had the verse which had first attracted my attention printed on a ribbon as a souvenir for each guest. I invited everybody I had ever met at any of the literary salons–at Mrs. Croly's, Mrs. Leslie's, Robert Ingersoll's, Nym Crinkle's (then famous as a critic and writer, and whose daughters gave charming literary evenings), and at Harriet Webb's (a leading light among readers and teachers of elocution), and there was a sprinkling of theatrical people, and all the newspaper critics were asked, whether I knew them or not. Fully one hundred guests responded to my invitation, and the carriages extended many blocks down the side street of the hotel where the reception took place.

One then eminent literary man of the city, who had been very gracious to me after I came East, called on the day of the reception, saying he could not be present in the evening, but he wanted to pay his respects to the young lady, whose decided talents he, alone of all New York, had noticed before I brought her to his attention. I remember how this man, while praising my impulse to do the girl honor, expressed a doubt regarding its wisdom. He said it was a matter one must go about with great care–this making of acquaintances in a metropolis. At that time I still saw all my Eastern friends through haloes, and I wondered at his remark. It was evident, however, that his words impressed my guest.

The reception was a very joyous and well-ordered affair. Several of the young woman's poems were recited; there was some good music and a tasteful repast. There were notices in all the papers, and the young lady went home the next day expressing herself as very grateful for my courtesy.

She wrote me one brief letter, reiterating her thanks, after she reached home. Then, although I wrote her again, a chatty letter, she dropped out of my horizon. At Christmas time I sent her a little token. A most formal note of acknowledgment was received by me. Then to my amazement I learned that she had been in the city, the guest of the eminent literary man to whom I had introduced her, and she had never called, or written me of the fact. I wrote and asked her how I had offended her, and begged for the opportunity to apologize if I had in any way hurt her. She replied with a cold note, saying she preferred not to say anything about her reason for not calling or writing.

To this day (that is thirty years ago) I have never known the explanation of her conduct. I think, however, the literary gentleman was very critical of some of my guests who came to do her honor. I know he was severely critical of Mrs. Leslie, and the poor girl, despite her great talent, was too meager in soul development to realize that she would not be contaminated by a casual meeting with some one she might not wish to keep as a constant companion, and too stunted in heart to grasp the fact that my impulse had been absolutely without any motive other than to give her pleasure while I repaid many social debts, through a unique and worth-while reception in her honor.

There was at that time a New York daily paper which prided itself upon its personalities of a sarcastic and disagreeable kind. Its editor had already made me the subject of some unkind items. He indulged in a half column of caustic comment on the reception I gave the unknown poet, declaring it was done with the desire to hoist myself into public notice. No more unjust words were ever written, but my guest must have felt they were true; thereby she displayed still more painfully her lack of perception and lack of the delicate qualities which make real womanhood. To this day, when I see the occasional gems of beauty which still fall from this poet's pen, I feel the old wound ache in my heart. My impulse was so absolutely spontaneous and kind, and the hurt I received was so needless.

Worse than the personal hurt was the blow to my ideal of the poet. A mortal on whom God had bestowed the divine power of creation, in any art, seemed to me one who must be incapable of any belittling fault, and of the petty sins like envy, jealousy or ingratitude. I could understand those gifted beings falling through mighty passions and colossal temptations, bom of their intensity of emotions. But the mean and ignominious sins I had not associated with genius until that experience. Such people are, T am sure, mere vehicles through which at times disembodied inteligences work. They are no more the real creators than is the telephone wire or receiver the person speaking.

Life, however, always applies a balm after it has wounded us. The spring following this experience my husband selected a larger apartment, where we moved, to remain five very happy years, and where it was my privilege to enjoy a circle of delightful friends. Later we spent several beautiful years at the old Everett House, and both of these places were joy filled for me. Our summers we had for six years spent at various resorts; three of them at Narragansett Pier. But one fortunate day, on our return from the latter place, we stopped off at New Haven, and my husband engaged a horse and light carriage, and we drove out seven miles to Short-Beach-on-the-Sound, to call on dear Aunt Hattie, who with her married daughter (wife of Gardner Reckard, the artist) was spending a few weeks there. We had never seen this place, which is only a few miles from Thimble Islands. Its wonderful and rare beauty, of pink granite rocks, majestic trees, and wide expanse of water, seized us both in a grasp which never relaxed; the next summer saw our darling house built on the rocks overhanging the Sound; and in this house (which was the first cottage east of the Rockies to be called "The Bungalow") and the living house built afterward, which was named "The Barracks" by my husband, we spent every summer of our united lives afterward.

Shorter and shorter grew my months in New York, longer and longer the season at the shore home. And finally when my husband was wise enough to go out of business (without waiting to acquire millions as most American men do), we spent all the time not given to travel in this Earthly Eden.

We made the resolution that no one should ever be invited to partake of our hospitality in the Bungalow save those for whom we felt a genuine affection or regard. No mere business acquaintants, and no one to whom we merely owed social obligations; those should be entertained elsewhere; but the Bungalow at Short-Beach-on-the-Sound (Granite Bay) should be kept for the near and dear ones bound to us by ties of affection. This house was the first home which ever satisfied my husband's heart. While we made home quickly of any place we occupied, the true home feeling and every home craving found expression and satisfaction in our adorable nest on the pink rocks.

As my years went on in New York, fate brought into my life a circle of gifted and beautiful girls who were destined to play a large part in my happy social and domestic life, at Granite Bay.

Two very charming girls, sisters, who were in the habit of calling on me frequently, one day urged me to accept an invitation to a large suburban house party. I had never met the host and hostess, but they urged the sisters to bring me, after sending me a very sweet letter of invitation. I went– and among the twenty-two guests, the most strikingly beautiful and interesting person there was Julie Opp, now Mrs. William Faversham. She was just out of the Convent, where she had been educated, and her statuesque beauty and charm of manner at once appealed to me. Finding her home was in New York, I asked her to come and be my guest the next Sunday afternoon, and ever since that hour we have been fast friends. Julie had not the slightest idea of becoming an actress at that time. She did plan a little later to write, and after translating a fashion article from a French magazine she sold it to a New York editor, and the money therefor she used in buying me a gift–a silver glove mender! I still have it in my sewing bag.

Mrs. Henry Plant was a gracious friend of Miss Opp's, and many other ladies who entertained much found her attractive presence, her agreeable manners and her gift at conversation drawing features for the entertainment of their guests. Julie was immensely popular with her own sex, which is not supposed to be usual with a pronounced beauty. At somebody's "Afternoon" a few months later Julie introduced to my husband and me (it chanced to be one of the occasional affairs of that nature which my man attended), two beautiful sisters, Kate and Martha Jordan. Kate was in the public eye because of stories she had written at a very early age. She had just received a prize from Scribner's Magazine for the best story in a competition. She was striking in appearance, a voluptuous brunette, with a very pale skin, scarlet mouth and quantities of blue-black hair which curled naturally. Martha, her sister, was petite, of the Cupid build, very blonde, and her eyes were pure sapphire. Both girls were possessed of the real Irish wit and power of repartee; and both were musically inclined. My husband admired them greatly find we made them at once a part of the circle we planned to have visit us in our Bungalow.

The three girls came together a few months later. We met them with our launch at Branford Harbor and took them over a tossing sea to our eyrie on the rock; and such happy, beautiful days followed–that summer and many summers thereafter. So enamored were they of the place that they rented a little cottage adjacent to our own, which my husband had just purchased, and bringing another girl friend, "Adele" and a chaperone, they came back after a week or two in the city, for the summer.

Because of the purely feminine nature of the household they named the cottage "Amazonia"; and that name clung to it until two years ago, when we changed it to "Arcadia." Kate was writing a new novel that summer, and Julie was writing also, and Martha was supplying a syndicate with some tales of emotional adventure which she did under a pen name. All were good swimmers, and after their work was done there were boating and swimming and dancing at the old Branford House, and there were wonderful hours of gathering in the cabin of our Bungalow and indulging in long intimate talks and reading the newest books. Intellectual and interesting men, of course, followed this attractive trio of girls to our retreat. The girls declared they would never feel satisfied with a honeymoon which did not include a week at the Bungalow. We promised the three we would help them to carry out this desire if they supplied the bridegrooms, and Martha and Kate spent the first week of their subsequent marriages, some years later, in our Bungalow. Until the summer of 1909, when her lovely soul took flight from earth, Martha Jordan was always our guest some time during our yearly sojourn at the seashore home. And Kate still comes to the spot hallowed with wonderful memories, and Julie Opp Faversham and her gifted husband and her beautiful sons have often been our guests.

Next in the order of succession, there dropped into our midst an adorable girl in her teens, with the joy of life in her blue eyes and the soul of a poet in her radiant breast. This was "Theodosia Garrison," then Theodosia Pickering, of Newark, New Jersey, and now Mrs. Frederic Faulks, of Elizabeth, New Jersey–and of the whole world, for her rare poetical talents have made her universally known.

It was through my husband's acquaintance with her father, Silas Pickering, that this lovely friend came into my life, to make such an important feature of it.

Mr. Pickering told my husband he would like to have his young daughter meet me, so Robert arranged to bring her down for a week end one September day. I had no idea before she came what she was like; and during the first half hour of her visit thought of her as a typical summer girl, golden of hair, turquoise of eye, slender of form, and very young indeed. The next half hour I learned that she was a sea nymph, excelling in swimming and diving; and an hour later at dinner, where we had guests, discovered she was dazzling with wit, astonishingly brilliant in conversation, and acquainted with the works of every author living and dead. The next morning I learned that she had written a poem while in her room, a real poem worthy of the name. She told me she had always, since a child, written verse; but had published only two or three bits. Before she had reached her middle twenties, however, Theodosia Garrison was a name universally known.

First as a girl, then as the wife of a man who became a helpless invalid, then as a fascinating widow, and now as the happiest wife on earth, she, who is known to the public as Theodosia Garrison, has been my guest and friend during all the wonderful years since first we met. Her poetical gifts were so natural and spontaneous that she did not at first realize their importance—as a child might pluck and play with rare orchids, unconscious of their value; but gradually the meaning of the gift God had bestowed upon her grew into her understanding, and with each year her talents ripened. I know of no other poet in America possessed of a more lyrical power of expression. Had she possessed ambition for achievement.

there are no heights Theodosia Garrison might not have attained; but curiously enough she has not the least desire to shine or to be thought great. She sings as the larks sing, with the joy of life.

My memory treasures golden summer hours when "Dosia" Sat at one desk and I at another writing poems which we afterward read to each other, each glad of the honest criticism of the listener

Then there were swimming bouts to "Green Island" and back to our Pier; and long talks in the sun on the seawall where we dried our hair. Then the beloved Master of the House would steal our guest away for a whist, bridge or auction game, wherein she excelled, like the female "Admirable Crichton" she is.

Lovely of personality, absolutely free from belittling jealousy or small gossip; as unselfish as she is brilliant, it is no wonder we felt privileged to be the friend and entertainer of Theodosia Garrison. She is the wittiest woman living and an incomparable mimic. Kate, Martha and Theodosia, meeting first on our Bungalow veranda, formed an enduring friendship; and star weeks in our memory are those when we entertained them all together.

Theodosia Garrison and I were sjtnpathetic on still another point; we both loathed mathematics, and both had distinguished ourselves in early youth by our failures in figures.

One day she was writing a lyric at the Bungalow, and I was filling an editor's request to write an article on giving daughters an independent income. Undertaking to calculate how many dollars would result from a penny a day for eighteen years,

I became confused and appealed to my poet friend. "Dosia," I called, "how much money would a girl have at eighteen if her parents had saved a penny a day from the time she was born?" "Wait a minute," Dosia replied, "and I will tell you." After a few moments she called forth, "I make it about seven thousand dollars." "Well," I said, "I made it six and over so I am safe to say it would be over five thousand." I sent in my little article and the kind and trusting editor used it without blue-penciling. It appeared in an evening paper while my husband was on a trip West. He read it and wrote me, "Great Heavens, Ella, some mathematician! You are safe on verse, my dear, but do go carefully when you approach mathematics." A stranger wrote me a few days later: "Madam, I have considered you a good poet and very much of a philosopher but God knows you are no mathematician. Are you aware that your blushing bride in order to have that amount of money for a dot would be ninety-five years old?" Since then I have never consulted Theodosia on figures.

Another rare gem in my collection of lovely girl friends was Helen Pitkin, of New Orleans, daughter of the then minister to the Argentine Republic and Ex-Postmaster of New Orleans, now Mrs. Christian Schertz of that town. Beauty, culture and numberless accomplishments made Miss Helen a belle at sixteen and good fortune lent her to me every summer before and after her marriage until the beginning of the present war. Helen of Orleans is a skillful harpist, a linguist, and a combination of Mesdames Recamier and de Stael in that she is as beautiful as she is brilliant. She is, too, the author of two books of prose and of many lyrics in verse.

Before the electric lights came to Short Beach we used to set apart one night in the summer, which we called "Illumination Night." Every cottage and all the piers and the boats were illuminated with colored lanterns, each family vying in friendly spirit to produce the finest effect. This occasion always ended up with a ball in the cabin of "The Bungalow." One year I conceived the idea of lighting up a big barge and having it towed about the Sound near the shore by our launch, with the Goddess of Liberty and the thirteen original states represented by fourteen beautiful girls in classic draperies. This I carried out, with the cooperation of my friends, most successfully, Julie Opp being my Goddess of Liberty. Her slender statuesque beauty was just in its early dawn and I am sure in all her later stage appearances she was never more wonderful than on that perfect August evening.

I am sure, too, there was never a part more fitted for this beautiful and progressive woman than that of Liberty.

From the hour I first knew Julie Opp to the present day, she has always suggested to me freedom from small thoughts, aims and prejudices. She has always been big in her ideals of life. Very early she endeared herself to me at one of my Bungalow Balls, where she was the belle of the evening. Coming to me quietly, she said, "I do not want to fill my dancing card right away. I want you to tell me if you have any awkward boys or old bachelors who are not popular with the girls. I may as well help them to have a good time by dancing with them; and then let me introduce to the wall flowers some of these Yale men who are flocking about. I know how hard it is for a hostess to manage things like that sometimes. Between us we can give everybody a good time."

Even to talk with Julie Opp Favershara over the telephone gives me a sense of larger horizons. She has from her early youth drawn the best and most worth-while people in every line of art and endeavor to her.

Her power of overcoming difficulties of all kinds is almost abnormal. When her first longed-for son was lying still-born in the house, and she was almost at death's door, she fairitly whispered, "Two years from this time I shall give my hus band a living son; and two years after that another."

This was told me by one who heard it, and who was angry with her for not feeling that her one sacrifice had been enough. "She will never be a well woman after this," the friend said, but Julie grew well and more beautiful than ever and bore her husband the two sons.

Some years later she was told by specialists that she was the victim of a fatal mjdady; but again she overcame, and all signs of this malady have vanished before her courage and will.

The next year following the Goddess of Liberty tableau I planned "Cleopatra going up the Nile in her Barge," and all my historic characters were prepared and anticipating the event, which was destined not to occur, because of a wild northeast storm which swept over the coast on that particular night. Later in the season, however, I did carry out a very effective water scene wherein Miss Pitkin appeared as "Tennyson's Elaine" upon "The Barge of the Dead Steered by the Dumb." Miss Pitkin's luxuriant hair was just the color of moonlight and she appeared like a moonbeam phantom rather than a real personality in her role. She has been known to her friends in Bungalow Court since then as "Elaine."

During our early summers at the Bungalow, my husband and I became greatly interested in a most unusual child, named Elna Harwood. Her parents were New Yorkers; her mother a cultured young English woman. Elna was very blond and very fair to look upon, and even as a child she swam and dived like a mermaid and rode a horse like a cowboy and won all the medals in the sprinting races for the children. Added to this she was the leader in her studies at school, and my attention was first called to her by reading some verses she had written. One day in a big thunder storm she rushed into the Bungalow, all out of breath, saying a poem had come to her and she wanted to sit at my desk and write it: and it really possessed lines of true poetic worth. I watched her development each summer with interest; and was not surprised when she carried off the literary prizes in two schools, the last being the Normal College. She had, in the meantime, been a year in England and France, and when she finally took up the work of a teacher, I felt considerable regret, feeling her pen should be her prop, rather than the teacher's rule. Then one bright day Elna married the finest of her many suitors; and the three vigorous children which came into her life seemed to fill it so full that we felt she would have neither time nor inclination for developing her latent literary gifts. I, for one, was not troubled over this. The woman who is married to the man of her heart and is the mother of his children seems to me to have found the highest possible mission which life can offer.

Destiny, however, had other plans for Elna. One day her husband fell ill–a very serious illness which necessitated his spending months in a hospital. That was only a few years ago, but now the name of Elna Harwood Wharton is al- ready recognized by the readers of various magazines where her stories and other contribution's have made her a feature. During her husband's illness, to distract her mind, and with an ultimate hope of supplying something of the missing income from her husband's inability to pursue his profession, Elna Harwood took up her pen. Her talent, supplemented by thorough education, and ripened by the deep experiences of wifehood and motherhood, sprang almost full grown into power. The very first story she ever submitted to an editor brought her five hundred dollars. She is destined to become one of American's brighest literary lights as time goes on. Elna Harwood Wharton (Mrs. George Wharton) lives in Washington, D. C, where Mr. Wharton holds a desirable position in the employ of the Government. She likes to call herself "one of the Bungalow girls," and it was in the early years of her beautiful teens that I wrote the following verses wherein she figures prominently. Our launch, which my husband named "The Robella" by combining our two names, gave us and our friends great pleasure for twelve years. My special delight was to take it out in a rolling sea, filled with girls and boys who were all fine swimmers, and to bound over the big waves and take the spray and "the tenth wave" in our faces: then, as we neared shore, on the return, to see our most adventurous swimmers leap into the water and swim to the pier. Elna was always one of these.

MY LAUNCH AND I

What glorious times we have together, My launch and I, in the summer weather! My trim little launch with its sturdy sides And its strong heart beating away as it glides Out of the harbor and out of the bay, Wherever our fancy may lead away, Rollicking over the salt track Hurrying seaward and hurrying back.

My boat has never a braggart sail,

To boast in the breeze, in the calm to quail;

No tyrant boom deals a sudden blow.

Saying, "You are my lackey, bend low, bend low!

No mast struts over a windless sea To show how powerless pride may be. But sure and steady and true and staunch It bounds o'er the billows,–my little launch.

Ready and willing and quick to feel The slightest touch of my hand on the wheel It laughs in the teeth of a driving gale, Or skims by the cat-boat's drooping sail. Its head held high when the Sound is still. Then dipping its prow like a water bird's bill Down under the waves of a rolling sea– Oh, my gay little launch is the boat for me!

Ofttimes when the great Sound seethes and swirls I carry a cargo of laughing girls.

Bare-armed, bare-limbed, and with hanging hair

They are bold as mermaids and twice as fair.

They swarm from the cabin,–they perch on the prow,

When the tenth wave batters them, breast and brow,

They bloom the brighter, as sea flowers do

While their shrill, sweet merriment bursts anew.

And oft when the sunset dyes the bay Oer a mirror-like surface, we glide away, My launch and I, to follow the breeze That has jilted the shore for the deeper seas. When the full moon flirts with the perigee tide On a track of silver, away we ride– Oh, glorious times we have together. My boat and I, in the summer weather.

Larry Chittenden, the "Poet Ranchman" and the globe trotter, was one of our literary and aquatic celebrities in those days and found his chief pleasure in teaching pretty girls new strokes in swimming. Edwin Markham and his cultured and brilliant wife visited us when their tall son, Virgil, was. a child cherub. We have, in our Log Book, a most attractive snap shot of the Jove-headed poet holding his rebellious baby boy in his arms after treating him to an undesired dip in the waves.

In later years we added to our list oi illustrious masculine names that of Charles Hanson Towne, poet, editor and wit.

My husband conceived the idea one day, when we were entertaining Oliver Herford (that combination of poet and artist), of substituting the walls of our dining-room for a guest book. So Oliver Herford wrote a witty quatrain, with illuminated colors, on our wall: and since that time a small army of gifted guests have added thereto either poems, original sketches, bars of music, or, in the case of actors, quotations from plays made famous by their talents. One which always attracts a great deal of attention is a droll sketch made by Jack Barrymore, called "The First Night," which was drawn on the wall the day after he opened in New Haven with his "Fortune Hunter."

For fifteen years in succession we gave a costume ball at the season's height. After the scattering, through marriage, death and time, of many of those who made these balls distinctive, we discontinued them and substituted Sunday afternoon musicales during July and August for the entertainment of our little colony, to whom we introduced ofttimes many rare artists. On two occasions Ruth St. Denis (who is lovelier and greater in character even than as an artist) gave us some of her most artistic delineations of the religious dances of history. On another occasion, straight from study in the Orient, Eva Gautier, niece of Sir Wilfred Laurier, ex-Premier of Canada, gave us the wonderful Javanese songs which later proved a great success professionally. Ofttimes, as I looked about my rooms on such occasions, and saw the beauty of my environment, the culture and worth of my friends, and, best of all, realized the holiness and sweetness of the love that enveloped me in my home, I recalled the hour when the little Oriental paper-knife came to me on the Western farm and all that it represented to me at that moment, in a strange half vision–a vision which has been so more than realized in my actual life.

Although space has been given in these Memoirs only to those of my acquaintance who have figured since to some extent in the public eye, the story of my life would seem incomplete to me without more detailed mention of Martha Jordan, afterward Martha Jordan Fishel. From our first meeting Martha and I became very close friends; and her position in our home was very nearly that of a daughter. Of good Irish lineage, Martha possessed the keen sense of humor, the quick wit, the artistic temperament, the gift of song and the love of poetry which that land bestows upon its children. Her beauty, too, told of a line of high-born Irish forebears. Outside of the stage world, no one we ever knew could tell a story or sing a song or give an impersonation like Martha Jordan. Her discrimination in music, literature and art was that of a connoisseur; and her taste in home furnishing would have given her an occupation had she desired it. Had she chosen the operatic stage as a means of expression, her voice, her beauty and her magnetism would have placed her in the front ranks. Martha was a center about which bright and gifted people loved to revolve. Caring absolutely nothing for general society, Martha distinguished herself as a giver of brilliant little dinners where good viands and good taste and good minds united to make the occasions distinctive.

Martha occupied for several years prior to her passing onward, a slim and proud-looking little brick house on Irving Place, just around tlae corner of Seventeenth Street. Its outward appearance was individual, but its interior was impressive with artistic taste, and even the walls seemed to breathe forth the personality of its unusual mistress. A record of Martha's dinners should have been kept, for I doubt if in all New York more memorable ones have occurred. Everybody who sat at Martha's table was worth knowing; and she had a habit of keeping her guests at the table instead of scattering and separating the men and women after dessert. Those post-coffee hours were so genial and brilliant that they sometimes trespassed upon the season supposed to belong to slumber.

Martha went out of earth life in the full bloom of womanhood: went before life had too cruelly disillusionized her, although she had known sickness and suffering: went, leaving us all with the memory of her radiant personality and her vivid interest in the things of earth.

With her going, a certain youthful epoch in the social life of our Bungalow seemed to end. After the first deep shadows lifted we still saw life through sunshine, and still found pleasure in our friends. But we all felt older; more subdued; and something was lacking from our gatherings which has never since been supplied.

But that Martha still lives and still feels interest in us, and that she is very happy in her celestial world, some of us have had proof, now after eight years; and she does not seem so lost to us.

Of this, later.

CHAPTER XI Little Efforts At Brotherhood

THE leading desire of my husband's heart, from the time we became convinced that our one spirit child was to be our only offspring, in this incarnation, was to found some beautiful charity for children.

After we built our nest on the rocks at Granite Bay (Short-Beach-on-the-Sound) we added to our possessions four little cottages which were so near our bungalow that their proximity was embarrassing. My husband purchased them, moved them back a short distance, remodeled them, and each summer found ready tenants for three of them. The fourth we had entirely removed from the premises, in order to erect our living house, "The Barracks," in its place–a most desirable location, within a stone's throw of the beach and affording a beautiful outlook.

Something like a half mile from our little cluster of houses there was an old farmhouse for sale, on the corner of th road leading to Double Beach and surrounded by tall trees. My husband for years cherished a dream of purchasing this house, with several acres of ground, and making it a summer home for orphan children. He even named it "The Ella Wheeler Home." Many were the plans he made regarding it, and bitter was his disappointment when he came to realize that the fortune necessary for the carrying out of his ideal would not come during his lifetime.

But one summer the tenants in our smallest cottage (which we named "The Midge") left in mid-August; and I proposed to my husband that while we were waiting to carry out the large ideal of helpfulness we might proceed on a smaller scale. My suggestion was that we give "The Midge" rent free and provide transportation and sustenance to some worthy person or persons for the remaining weeks of the summer. At that time Rose Hawthorne (the daughter of Nathaniel and the sister of Juhan) had embraced the Roman Cathouc religion and was active in works of charity in the lower part of New York City. I wrote to Sister Rose and explained my idea; I wanted three tired women, or a woman with two children. who needed a change of air and the benefit of the seashore life, for a month. I preferred people who would be cleanly in their habits and not liable to bring any contagious diseases, and people believed to be honest. Otherwise, I had no strings tied to my little benefit.

Sister Rose sent me a pallid young girl of twenty who was weak from the result of a slow fever and unable to go back to her work–it was, I believe, some small clerical position, I have forgotten just what; and I have forgotten her name. But I remember her sweet face and manner; and her wonderful joy at her first sight of a boat; a row-boat, in which she went out each day all by herself, after she learned how to row. And I remember how like a plant brought out of a cellar into the sunlight she blossomed forth in that month.

Besides this girl there was a gaunt pale woman of perhaps fifty who had for many years, the better part of her life, been employed in a tailor's shop, where she wielded a heavy pressing iron. She had become too weak to keep up this work; and for the space of a year she had been taking care of a wee boy named Jimmie, whose mother had died at his birth, and whose father, a day laborer, gave this woman two dollars a week to take care of Jimmie. There were older children at home, but no one old enough to care for the little mite.

I think Jimmie was three that summer; but he looked no larger than many children of a year. His mind, however, was very bright; and we all grew to love little Jimmie and to watch for his small form and short legs to come toddling across the lawn to make a daily call. He had been taught to salute his elders like. a soldier; and it was the delight of my husband to receive and answer this salute. I had told the pale protector of Jimmie, who was the housekeeper for the three, to obtain whatever she desired for the table at the little country store, and charge it in my name. When, at the end of the first week, I received my bill, it was so insignificant a sum I felt there must be some error. The storekeeper assured me it was correct. Then I approached the pale tenant on the subject, saying I was confident she was not providing sufficient food for the three of them. She looked at me in amazement. "Why, dear Lady," she said, "we are living on the fat of the land. I think you have never known what real economy means; and never learned, through being obliged to count your pennies, how to buy with care. I assure you we have all we need or could eat, and you can see how we are all improving."

The young girl and Jimmie were, indeed, showing decided improvement; but the pale protector of little Jimmie remained pale and attenuated; and I learned afterward that she was the victim of an incurable malady. I often wish I knew what became of the pretty girl and little Jimmie. It was fully sixteen years ago when we had the pleasure of giving them that month of recreation, and with the exception of a letter received the first few months afterward, I never heard from them or of them again.

Some time later, we gave that same cottage rent free for two summer months to some very intellectual acquaintances who were passing through a season of hard luck; and to save them from being penned in a hot city flat during the summer we suggested their occupying our cottage. They occupied it; but the experience did not prove as pleasant or as gratifying to us as had the presence of the little city clerk and Jimmie and his pale protector. It is heart and not head which renders the association with our fellow creatures satisfying, the ability to feel gratitude and appreciation rather than the ability to criticize.

Our intellectual acquaintances prided themselves on their ability to dissect their fellows and to pin the dissected portions on the wall and analyze them. They dissected their host and hostess and all their friends, declaring that we were quite too democratic in our ideas and were lacking in dig- crimination. They proceeded to point out all the faults and failings of our guests until we cried a halt and requested them to vacate the cottage.

Finding we could not always carry out our desire to bestow some of our blessings on the really deserving in the ways described, we made a resolution to let no one who came to our doors go away without feeling that life was a bit sweeter than before they approached us. We taught our helpers and employees to treat mendicants with sympathy and peddlers with respect; when it was impossible to bestow money on the mendicants, at least to offer food; and when it was impossible to patronize peddlers, to make-it understood courteously, not brusquely. In fact, to live our religion of brotherhood, which is the basis of theosophy.

When we first made our home at Granite Bay, and for several years thereafter, the resort was only reached by a four-horse stage from East Haven, or by boats. Those were picturesque days and we loved our isolation from the modem methods of travel. I used to feel I was living in medieval times as the four-horse stage swung around the sharp curves of "Snake Hill," and I clung with both hands to the seat of the vehicle to prevent being tossed out. As the town grew in population the discomforts of this mode of travel became manifest, yet when the railroad first talked of putting the trolley service through Short Beach most of us fought it tooth and nail. We feared an invasion of undesirables, and dreaded seeing our romantic resort turned into a Coney Island. It was sympathy for over-taxed stage horses that led us finally to desire the trolley. After that mode of travel was established the little matter of entertaining peddlers became more difficult. They had heard of our hospitable habits and they came upon us in shoals. We could not buy even trifles of six peddlers in a day; but we could at least keep in mind the fact that these men and women were trying to earn a livelihood, trying to keep themselves from becoming beggars, and we did what we could to help them retain their self-respect while we did not patronize all of them.

Neither my husband nor myself contributed to foreign missions, and after we had abandoned the hope of establishing a large charity, we tried to make both the Bungalow and the Barracks, in a small way, represent my husband's original idea of an "Ella Wheeler Home." Many beggars, many cripples, many "down and outs" and a few ex-convicts came to our doors during the twenty-five years we lived together. Doubtless there were many cheats and frauds among them, but I do not believe we ever sent any one away without some little feeling of uplift. I remember one man who came and told me a tragic story of his life, saying he was just released from prison, and asking for money to go to Boston, where he had an old mother. I helped him and felt glad to think I could do so. Shortly afterward my husband learned that the man had indeed been a prison inmate, but that he lived near us and that he used the money I had given him to treat all his boon companions to drinks within an hour after he left me. The man came again a month later, and I allowed him to tell his new story of being detained by illness, and to ask me for more money. Then I told him what I had learned about him. The unkindness of his deception toward me turned the anger I felt at first into grief, and I began to cry. The man looked at me a moment in silence; then he rose up and came and stood before me. "This is the first time," he said, "that I ever saw a woman cry for me. I want to tell you I will never trouble you again; I was born crooked and I guess I will always stay crooked; but I will never bother you again. Will you shake hands with me?"

I took his proffered hand and tried to make him promise to turn over a new page in life's diary. But he shook his head. "I'm crooked, I tell you. I can't help lying and stealing. But youll never have any trouble from me again." And I never did.

The frankness of some of our back door callers was as amusing as amazing. I gave a soiled and husky-looking man food one morning. He said he had slept under a tree and wanted breakfast before tramping on to Boston where he had an old mother. I asked him where he came from. "Oh, from serv- ing time in Joliet," he smilingly answered. "What was your crime?" I asked. "Oh, taking things that didn't belong to me," he said. "You see, I drink. It just comes on me by spells; and then I go all wrong. I get good positions and then I lose them that way." And again he smiled and went away smiling.

Another came to the door smelling of drink. He confessed he had used his last dime for a drink. "What is the use trying to be decent?" he said. "No decent people will have anything to do with a man after he has made a bad record. Ive tried; it's no use. So I may as well just get what little cheer there is in a drink now and then."

During all those twenty-five years at our Bungalow, where we spent five months every summer, we never locked a door at night and we were never molested nor did thieves break in and steal.

While my husband was ever liberal in his helpfulness to the Chapel at Short-Beach-on-the-Sound, we did not attend the services there. This grieved a few of the very orthodox residents, who saw no road to God save through the path they trod. Yet in all that town I never knew another soul so reverent as that which dwelt in the strong body of my Robert.

So great are the natural beauties of Short-Beach-on-the-Sound that it has always seemed to me that one who had the privilege of dwelling there must become reverent and religious.

I have circled the world almost twice and I have seen so much beauty that the memory of it is like a panorama of glory upon glory. I have seen the wonders of the drive from Sorento to Amalfi; the majesty of the drive over Mt. Diablo in Jamaica at dawn; the tropical splendors of the drive from Colombo to Kandy in Ceylon; and I have stood on the edge of glaciers in Switzerland awed at the picture spread before me. I have seen Stromboli sending a flame of fire hundreds of feet in the air at night while its river of fire ran down the volcano to the sea below; and I have sat in the old Greek theater in Taormina, Sicily, 8,000 feet above the earth, and gazed on Mt. Etna in the distance lifting itself 11,000 feet over the Ionian Sea; I have watched the sun turn sapphire sea and azure clouds to vermilion, as it went down on this glorious scene. These and many more wonders of God's earth have I beheld, yet nowhere have I found any other spot which seemed to me to combine so much beauty, comfort, convenience, and charm for the enjoyment of simple and wholesome life as Short-Beach-on-the-Sound at Granite Bay. Its sunrises and sunsets are as exquisite as those of the Orient; its rocks change from pink to amethyst and then to gray with the change of climatic conditions; its waters show a thousand moods and a hundred shades and provide a far greater variety of effects than do the waters of the greater ocean. They shine and murmur in the dawn, they ripple and glow like vibrating molten diamonds in the morning; they leap and threaten at noon; they roar and rage and grow in power with the incoming tide, and they lie at the feet of the rocks in the evening, singing a lullaby.

GRANITE BAY

At Granite Bay, such beauty lies. In rocks, in waters and in skies. As poets dream of Paradise.

The rocks that clasp fair Granite Bay First saw her charms at break of day And flushed to pink from somber gray.

To guard this bay from rude alarms And shelter her from all that harms Great trees reach out protecting arms.

Down to the very water's edge, Between the granite rocks they wedge, And watch in silence from each ledge.

Defending points and islands stand And reefs of rocks run out from land. To keep rude billows well in hand.

The river and the bay are friends; One slender arm the river bends And all her anchored boats defends.

So much one island loves her grace, He fronts all dangers in his place, To shield the beauty of her face.

Loved by the forest and the shore, While sun and moon, and skies adore. The strong rocks hold her evermore.

At Granite Bay the wild winds rest; The sunlight is her welcome guest; The moon goes mad upon her breast.

Not here is heard the sea gulls' scream. They come, but only come to dream: Far out at sea their sorrows seem.

At Granite Bay, far out at sea My cares and troubles seem to me; Love, joy and hope remain, these three.

Though forth my wandering footsteps stray. To realms and regions far away, My heart dwells here, in Granite Bay.

When in 1891 we first built our Bungalow on the pink granite rocks at Short-Beach-on-the Sound, the leading business emporium was Knowles' Store. It was combination store, post-office, express and business office in one. Everybody went to Knowles' store for everything. Mr. E. B. Knowles, the owner and manager, was an important factor just then in local politics. He was a tall man, fully six feet in height, square of shoulder, full of chest, ruddy of skin and very good-looking. His voice was deep-toned, and possessed unusual musical cadences. Mr. Knowles had all the attributes which with early educational advantages would have made him a man of parts and power in a larger world. As a small lad he had attracted the attention of an old hermit of some means. The old hermit, it was said, had been crossed in love and so hid away in these then remote regions, and drowned his sorrow in drink. But his heart was tender and his perceptions keen. He offered to send the Knowles lad to a military school; but his parents were poor and felt they could not spare him. I think it was always a bitter memory in Mr. Knowles' heart–this lost opportunity. He felt he was capable of so much more in the way of achievement than he had been able to do without education. He loved to read, and was always well informed.

There was an aggressive quality about him which, with his political interests, made him enemies. Our very first weeks in Short Beach, some one of his enemies had spoken disparagingly of him. As soon as I met him, however, I felt a great liking for the man. I had been down at the post-office for the mail; and when I came home I said to my husband, "I have met Mr. Knowles; and I like him immensely. Next to your own, he has the most beautiful voice of any man I ever met. It sends little shivers down my spine the way some music does." On the next occasion when I went to the post-office store, my husband asked me on my return, "Well, did you see Shivers' this time?"

From that day until Mr. Knowles passed over the border, Robert spoke of him to me as "Shivers." He and Mr. Knowles were very good friends; and he was sincerely grieved when, just two months before God's sudden call came to him, Mr. Knowles' obsequies took place with all Masonic rites in Short Beach.

Mrs. Davies-Jones and I sent our two harps to the little Short Beach Chapel, and played simple old sacred hymns while the funeral cortege passed in and out.

One summer evening I walked down the street and saw Mr. Knowles sitting quite apart from others, looking up at the starry skies. Stopping to chat a moment, he said, "I have been wondering about those stars. I am sure some of them are just as important worlds as this earth. And I have been wondering if we will ever know about it all in any life. I wish I might have studied astronomy." No doubt this desire of his for greater knowledge is being gratified now.

Mr. Knowles had a brother, called Captain Knowles because he owned a boat which used to convey people about the Sound. That was in the days before trolley cars or automobiles were with us, and visitors to the shore resorts relied upon boats for their pleasures and their sight-seeing.

Captain Knowles was a different type of man from his brother; and had never given much time to reading, and I think he never meditated about the stars. While "Shivers" was very fond of poetry and always followed my writings with interest, the Captain simply knew that I was a literary woman, and let it go at that.

It was not until after his death that a droll little story was told me by some New York people who had gone down to pass a week-end at Short Beach in the early days. They engaged the Captain to take them out in his boat; and he showed them all the places of interest. He called their attention to new cottages which had been erected, and he pointed out the picturesque home of Bishop Goodsell, perched very high on the rocks. Then, with a wave of the hand toward the Bungalow, he said, "And there lives one of the most notorious women in America. She has come here to make her home."

The delicate shade of difference between the words "famous" and "notorious" the Captain ignored. But I am quite sure he would have given any one who purposely applied an unpleasant epithet to me a blow of his big fist.

In our early summers at Short-Beach-on-the-Sound swimming was almost an obsession with many of us. We used to go in the water twice a day, sometimes three times; and we were all prouder of our achievements in the brine than out of it, I fear. I know at that time a new stroke in swimming, or a new high dive, gave me more of a thrill than a new style of verse, great as my love and devotion to the Muses was and ever has been.

One day, as I was swimming across "Little Bay," whose waters caressed the rocks on which our dear Bungalow was built, I met a lovely sea nymph. Her wonderful stroke was only second to her physical beauty. She was a mere child, scarcely thirteen years old, but a little pocket Venus in form, and with a face of delicate loveliness. I learned her name as we paddled leisurely along to a rock, where we sat and rested and chatted. She was Rhoda Burnham, she said; from Kenwood, N. Y. I knew this meant that she was one of the descendants of the Oneida Community, that interesting organization which for a period of thirty years persisted in an attempt to demonstrate the value of eugenics, or thorough breeding, in the human family. When the Government of the United States lifted a protesting hand, and commanded this organization to disintegrate, many of its members came to Short-Beach-on-the-Sound and located there. (This place, and Wallingford, Conn., had been, in fact, popular with the Oneidans, as resorts, previous to the disbanding of the Community.) My husband and I had made the acquaintance of several of these families, and we had found them particularly interesting because of their simple, kindly, trustful and unselfish traits; and we had observed with keen interest how above the average, in physical and mental qualities, were the young people who had been born in the Community.

The Oneida Community was based on the idea of unselfishness, and carried its ideals to the utmost extreme. The little handful of people who first founded the cult believed their leader, Mr. Noyes, had received a revelation; and that they were justified in cutting loose from all established laws and rules regarding marriage and the relation of the sexes and the accumulation of property.

No woman was to bear a child unless she desired motherhood; and she was then to select the father for her child. But before she was allowed to become a mother a committee of twelve wise men investigated the mental, moral and physical conditions of the two contracting parties, and of their ancestors. If any cause was found which seemed to menace the desired offspring, the parties were expected to abandon their idea for the good of the world. Personal feelings and affections were to be sacrificed on the altar of Universal Love. Had the Oneida Community stopped there they might have carried on their purpose to a higher goal of realization; but unfortunately they demanded of their adherents a still greater proof of unselfishness. If the man and woman wanting offspring were found to be unsuitable parents by the Com- mittee, each was expected to accept a mate chosen by that Committee, as better suited to produce wholesome children. Evidence of romantic attractions between two people was cause for criticism and reproof; and they were at once separated and sent to outside resorts, to overcome what was deemed selfishness. One of the sweetest and most admirable women I ever knew talked with me regarding this law of the Community and told me she had been one of its victims. She had entered the Community when only three years old, her parents being among Mr. Noyes' first converts. She had been happy and her life, while one of continual work, was bright and sunny, until at sixteen she found herself romantically stirred by the presence of one of the young men of the Community. The Committee found him unsuitable for her as a mate, so they were separated. She was sent to Wallingford and he remained at Oneida. They believed her, however, to be a desirable mother, and selected for her the man they deemed best for the father of her child. To refuse the mandates of the Committee would have been insurrection; so with love in her heart for another man she bore the child of the one chosen by the "Wise Men." Of course, women are doing these things in fashionable society every day– smothering their afifections and giving themselves to men they do not love, and for the ignoble motives of money or position; so we cannot declare too loudly against the extreme altruism of the Oneidans in this matter, for they at least believed they had a high ideal, while the fashionable father and mother who force their daughter into an unholy alliance know they have only followed the most material impulses. The expectant mother in the Oneida Community was treated like a holy being, and surrounded with every care and protection; and as soon as her child was born it was given into the care of those who were particularly endowed by nature to rear it on the most scientific lines. Children, like property, belonged to the Community, not to individuals.

The children born during the thirty years of the existence of the Community were just coming into adolescence when the United States Government commanded the dissolution of the organization. Where it was possible, the fathers married the mothers of their children; but naturally this was not always expedient. Mr. Noyes, for instance, had been regarded by many of the women of the Community as a divine being, and to mother his children seemed to them a sacred privilege. Mr. Noyes could not espouse all the mothers of his children; and there were other popular men equally embarrassed.

One of my most valued friends became the wife of the father of her son; and she afterward bore him a daughter, born in wedlock. The son was at the time of which I write a youth of exceptional intellect and talent; and he is to-day (twenty-two years later) one of America's most gifted men in the world of artistic expression. The boys and girls born in the Oneida Community were distinctly above the average of those bom in conventional circles where laws of State and Church prevail but where high ideals of the sacredness of the sexual relation and of motherhood do not prevail as a rule.

Therefore, it will be understood how I felt a peculiar interest in the pretty sea njmiph who told me her name was Rhoda Burnham, and that she was bom in Kenwood, N, Y.

Rhoda grew into lovely young womanhood, spending every summer in Short Beach and her winters in Kenwood. One day Rhoda married well and happily. Then she bore a daughter. I was in Europe when this child came; and in Europe I received a letter from Rhoda's aunt, telling me Rhoda was writing poems, and asking me if I would read them if sent. I knew Rhoda was fond of poetry and literature of all kinds; but I had never thought of her as creative. When I opened her MSS. I anticipated the usual girlish amateurish work so often laid before me. The very first lines attracted my attention, so distinctly were they creations of a genuine poet– a genius.

A letter accompanied the verses saying two of the poems had been accepted by the Atlantic Monthly. Later work of Rhoda Burnham Dunn (Rhoda Hero Dunn was her pen name) appeared in the Century, Harper's and Scribner's.

It is the only instance where I ever knew a young poet to begin at the top. There was an almost Shakespearean quality to her verse. It seemed to have suddenly developed after her experience of motherhood; but, unfortunately, a serious heart malady also developed, and for years the young wife and mother was an invalid and is only now coming back to health. She is not yet allowed to use her pen, even to write her friends.

One day, after she had published some of her most brilliant verses in the magazines, Rhoda Hero Dunn was calling while Theodosia Garrison visited me; and an enterprising man with a camera captured the three of us and posed us on the Bungalow sea wall. My own portrait was the only one of the group which did the original justice; both of my fair poet friends were libeled by the camera save as the pose was artistic and the setting excellent.

On that same wall one summer day, two other poets of national reputation sat while it was my good fortune to be their hostess and my bad fortune not to have them photographed. They were Zona Gale and Ridgeley Torrence–both in the early glory of first youth, and both fair to behold. I remember telling them as they sat on the wall, outlined against a scene of exquisite beauty, that I was sure ancient Greece never brought into juxtaposition a more wonderful combination of mental, physical and nature attractions than my eyes beheld at that moment.

Zona Gale had first come to my notice on one of my visits to my old Wisconsin home. I was at the house of Judge Braley, in Madison, and Mrs. Braley told me a young girl wished to meet me. A pretty creature in the short skirts of early youth, and with her hair hanging in braids down her back, came in and modestly asked me if I would look at some of her writings and tell her if she had talent.

This was Zona Gale, whose verse and prose has since given her a wide fame, and whose earnest work for Equal Rights has made her beloved by all the sufifrage organizations.

Ridgeley Torrence, too, has become a name dignified by great ideals carved in enduring lines of high poetic expres- sion, both in lyric and dramatic form. And his work is but begun.

Elsa Barker is another American poet who has graced and vitalized the Bungalow with her presence.

At the time of her visit, she had written only one prose work, "The Son of Mary Bethel." It was a striking work, yet her poetry was to me her real inspiration.

"The Frozen Grail," dedicated to Peary and his band, is an epic of august beauty. It has the distinction of being the only poem that went to the Pole.

Another of her poems ranks with the great sonnets of the world. It is entitled "When I Am Dead," and its fourteen lines are just so many splendid poetical solitaires.

Elsa Barker went to live in Paris shortly after she visited us; and later, when we were in London, she came there to make her home. She spoke to me of a strange experience through which she was passing, and vaguely hinted that it was of a psychic nature. Before we left Europe I had gathered from her that she was receiving messages from some disembodied intelligence, and that the result would be given to the world in time. She seemed profoundly impressed by her experience. When her "Letters of a Living Dead Man" were published and made so pronounced a sensation, I was able to understand why she was impressed. That, and its sister volume, "War Letters of a Living Dead Man," have stirred the intellectual world and made the name of Elsa Barker known ever3rwhere. They are among the notable books of the century. Yet still it is the poetry of Elsa Barker which endears her to me– her poetry and her worthwhile character.

To be a gifted poet is a glory; to be a vrorth-while woman is a greater glory.

CHAPTER XII Interesting People Met in New York

AMONG the interesting people who came into my life during the nineteen years we resided in New York, Anne Reeve Aldrich stands forth in my memory as one of the most unique types, and one most difficult to classify. Miss Aldrich sent me a note, enclosing some very striking lines she had written, and asking if she might call. Her dramatic, melancholy, yet delicate poems had already attracted my attention, and I hastened to set an hour for her call.

The tragic muse who dominated the young woman's mind was not expressed in her personality. The girl was, instead, bubbling with mirth and the joy of life in the early twenties. She had a slight lisp in speaking, which was fascinating; and her sense of humor was her most prominent peculiarity. She made sport of her own tendency to write of death and despair, and laughed over the impression her verses gave of a broken heart. She confessed to having had many transient love affairs, and to using them as the shoots on which she grafted all kinds of strange, exotic poetical fancies.

Miss Aldrich was well born and of the best American stock. She was worshiped by her sweet and gentle mother, who was, if memory serves me right, the widow of a clergyman.

After a year or two of acquaintance with this young poet, I was impressed with her lack of real interest in life; she still laughed and bubbled, but she seemed to tire easily of everything which girls of her age find amusing or entertaining. From her spoken words I gained no hint of this; but from her manner and her aura it breathed forth. Her poems grew more and more exquisite, and she attracted the attention of the best literary minds. But this did not seem to give her real pleasure. It was not very long before the rumor reached me, on my return to town after a summer's absence, that Miss Aldrich was ill. Her sickness was as difficult to define as her mentality had been. She had no malady, so the physicians said, but she felt no interest in anything, and seemed in a state bordering on melancholia. I fancied it to be a slow fever, which would- wear itself away in time. But one night the young poet, not yet five and twenty, fair to look upon, and endowed with rare talents, asked for writing materials, and shortly handed back to the suffering mother the MS. of the beautiful poem:

"I shall go out when the dawn comes in: Would it might leave one ray with me; It is so dark between two worlds How is a soul to see?"

It is one of the most exquisite lyrics in the language on the subject of death. Miss Aldrich died at dawn the following day–died peacefully and sweetly, in the dawn of womanhood and the dawn of day, and in the dawn of her splendid poetical powers.

Another young poet and later editor of a successful magazine (and, like Miss Aldrich, sired by a clergyman) became a part of my little social circle a few years later. This was Arthur Grissom, a fair youth with a diamond mind, and a heart of gold. He was popular alike with men and women, and both my husband and I prized his friendship highly. He possessed a dainty lyrical gift, which would have grown into something greater had he not merged his powers in filling with much success the somewhat difficult position of first editor of the Smart Set. One day we heard with surprise and interest the news of the sudden and romantic marriage of Arthur Grissom. The father of his bride had large wealth, and objected to the marriage, but seemed to accept his talented and noble young son-in-law after a time. I hastened to call on the bride and invite the young couple to my seashore Paradise. Afterward we visited them in their suburban home. So complete seemed their happiness, and so en- thusiastic was the wife regarding her husband's ability to provide for her, in spite of her father's predictions to the contrary, that our surprise may be imagined when a few years later (possibly two) we heard that Mr. Grissom was being sued for divorce on the grounds of failure to support his wife.

We heard, too, that Mr. Grissom had entered a counter suit against the father-in-law, asking damages for alienating the affections of his wife. I wrote a letter of sympathy to Mr. Grissom, in which I said: "This is the first time either my husband or I have felt any interest in a man or woman who could ask for financial benefits to soften the wounds inflicted by unfaithful love. But we well know how you gave up your important position in New York to go West to satisfy a whim of your wife. We know how you catered to her many idiosyncrasies; and we heard from her own lips, not once, but many times, how well you provided for her. Therefore, we feel you are justified in demanding damages for your broken business affairs, and you do right to combat a suit which places you in an ignoble and undeserved position in the eyes of the world."

My letter pleased Mr. Grissom, naturally; and one day shortly thereafter I met him on the street and he turned and walked with me saying how he wished his attorney might hear me state what I had expressed to him in the letter. "If you could let him put down your statements as a part of my defense," Mr. Grissom said, "it would have weight when the case comes to trial in the West." I readily agreed to this, and consented to go with Mr. Grissom to his attorney's office, a day or two later. I had supposed there would be present on that occasion the attorney, a stenographer, Mr. Grissom and myself. What was my consternation on arriving at the office, to find the lawyer of the father-in-law, a prosecuting attorney, and a half dozen stenographers, reporters and others, in all something like fifteen or twenty individuals. Instead of sitting down quietly and talking to Mr. Grissom's attorney, I was called to the stand as if it were a regular court room, and put under a fiery fusillade from the enemy. I was amazed, frightened and angry. The first question the prosecuting attorney flung at me was:

"I beheve your name was first heard in public as the author of some very erotic poems called Poems of Passion. Is that true?"

"No," I answered, "it is not true. Intelligent people had heard of my name a number of years before that book was published."

There was a snicker in the court room, and the attorney proceeded to change his method of attack.

"You are, I believe," he said, "a contributor to a Yellow Journal in this city, are you not?"

"I have the privilege of contributing some ideas of more or less value to the world to a large educational daily," was my reply.

"Well," continued my persecutor, "you know you are associating your name with Yellow Journalism, do you not? And you know the meaning of the words Yellow Journalism?"

"Yes, sir; I think I do," I replied.

"Well, what is it?"

"It means, according to my belief," I replied, "a newspaper which glows with the color of sunshine and throws light into dark places; I would advise you to read it persistently."

The snicker in the court room grew to a loud laugh. Order was demanded.

Again mine enemy changed his tactics.

"I believe you knew Mr. Arthur Grissom intimately, and for a long time," he said. I assented.

"You knew him as a husband of the lady now suing for divorce; and you considered him a good husband?"

Again I replied in the affirmative.

"Well, how was he a good husband?" was the next query.

I replied that he was faithful, kind, loving, and, according to his wife's words to me, a good provider.

"Then you consider him the very best husband you ever knew?" sneered the prosecutor.

"No, sir," I rq)lied. "If I did, I would be here in tfie position of a co-respondent instead of a witness,"

The court room became so noisy with laughter that the case was dismissed. I was blazing with anger at Mr. Gris-som and every one else, feeling I had been trapped into an unpleasant situation. However, the result of this experience was so satisfactory to Mr. Grissom that I was pacified. Curiously enough, it seemed that the lawyer employed by the father-in-law, to riddle me with annoying questions, was in his heart deeply in sympathy with Mr. Grissom. He telegraphed the purport of the "session" West, and the case was settled out of court in favor of Mr. Grissom.

Arthur Grissom did not live many years after that. But it is a satisfaction to me to know, what only his best friends knew, that his heart was wholly healed of the wounds inflicted by a fickle woman, and that he died loving another woman with the deep, fervent love of his ripe manhood. Four months previous to his death, when he was in seeming perfect health, he gave a very brilliant dinner at "Old Martin's" in honor of my husband and myself. There were to be fourteen covers; at the last moment one guest wired his inability to arrive on time. So we sat down, thirteen at table. Mr. Grissom was last to be seated; and there was the usual jesting on the subject. We called him a very healthy-looking ghost.

Of course, it was a mere coincidence that he died in so brief a time afterward. It was the only occasion on which I ever sat thirteen at table; and if circumstances made it necessary for me to be again of that number I should insist on seating myself last.

Early in the winter of 1892 I received a book of verse and a request for my criticism from a young lad who later became one of our most loyal friends. Although this youngster had lived much with nature and was in love with the wilds, he had known a good deal of city life without much guidance. He was conscious of the pitfalls for youth, however, and seemed glad that he had "escaped with his self-respect," as he put it.

In one of his early letters, speaking of his ideals, he said: "It has been a dream of my life since I can remember, that at marriage the husband should dower his wife with the same purity of heart—the same virtue—that he expects of her. I think that their love-life should be the holiest of all human relations; that it is better to worship a wife with reason than a Creator through faith alone; and that a true husband can never be chivalrous enough to a true wife."

This was so interesting that I turned to his verses with pleasurable anticipations, surprised to find them most erotic, yet, withal, full of real power and lyric charm.

I wrote to the young poet and asked him to call on one of my Sunday afternoons, which he did. And such a shock of spun gold hair—such red blood in boyish cheeks—such a virile young child of the woods and fields was never seen, I am sure, save in Ralcy Husted Bell at that early period of his life.

From that time on his friendship has endured, growing stronger with time, as have, indeed, all my worth-while friendships through life.

Ralcy Husted Bell is a man of many talents. Perhaps he has scattered his forces too widely; and yet that very scattering may have given him his breadth of vision and his deeper enjo3anent of life.

Mr. Bell graduated as a physician, having a competence. He practiced medicine only briefly, meanwhile establishing a successful magazine; then he traveled extensively, adding to his collection, and finally settled down in Paris to study art.

His first book of value was "The Worth of Words"; but he has published at least two books of excellent verse besides. Then followed "The Changing Values of English Speech," "The Religion of Beauty," "Words of the Wood," "Taor-mina," "Art-Talks with Ranger," "The Philosophy of Painting," etc. He has also done much scientific work of value.

Remaining a bachelor. Dr. Bell did not put his early ideals of marriage to the test.

Lovely Edith Thomas, Madeline Bridges, Mary Ainge De Vere, John Ernest Mccann, Bart Kennedy, all gave me their friendship in those early days. Since then John Ernest Mccann has passed on to other worlds, and those remaining have steadily added to their laurels. Bart Kennedy was just beginning his career as a fiery and untamed socialist, who wrote excellent epigrammatic prose—prose that was really the free verse of to-day. He sent me some specimens through a friend, and I wrote him a note of appreciation. I asked him to call on a Sunday, and he came with contempt and distaste in his face and mien for my little social circle of well-dressed people of talent. He was a handsome youth, clear cut of feature and gaunt of form, and he was burning to demolish society, to dynamite all conventions, and to divide the millions of the idle rich among the world's needy poor. He left my small salon scowling his disapproval of my manner of life. But he sent me other MSS. which were also praiseworthy, and asked if he might call and receive from me some advice about his work.

I had gone to Short-Beach-on-the-Sound and wrote him he could some day run down there. He happened to choose a day when I was preparing to give my annual costume ball. He found me with a bevy of beautiful girls and attendant young men waxing the floor ready for the dancing. I had no moment to give him and his MSS. naturally. I turned him over to my bevy of girls to entertain, after providing him with a bathing suit and enjoying the exhibition he gave of his aquatic prowess. The day wore into evening and the guests began to arrive, and the dancing was in full swing when Mr. Kennedy appeared to me with a face of fury. He reviled me as a frivolous and unworthy woman of genius who was wasting my time and gifts in ignoble social amusements; and after a few moments of conversation in this vein, which I decidedly resented, Mr. Kennedy flew down the pathway and walked seven miles to catch a night train to New Yoi-k.

I never saw him again until the Spring of 1912, in London. We met at a large banquet where Mr. Kennedy was one of the speakers. He had gained honors and avoidupois in the intervening years, and he was far more lenient toward the world and its social conventions. We met smiling friends, who had parted scowling foes; and we enjoyed a brief time of amusing reminiscence. Mr. Kennedy had a large audience in the old world and was a recognized man of talent. Success had made him more tolerant toward life and people, as is frequently the case with the youthful socialists and social dissenters.

Edgar Fawcett was in his man's prime when I met him in the early nineties. I treasure a letter full of wit which he wrote me in reply to my request for a book and picture to sell at a Charity Kermiss; and which ends with some words of praise for my work–words which at that time filled me with gratitude and pleasure. Though I never knew him well, I sincerely grieved over his death, which seemed to silence a poetical voice of power. The one thing I missed in Edgar Fawcett as a poet was a lack of faith in any life after this. That always limits a poet's power, for poets are given their voices to be heralds of greater lives beyond. Perhaps Mr. Fawcett had to be called onward to gain new knowledge before singing further songs. Perhaps he will come back again and finish his singing in a higher strain.

Walter Malone was another of my young poet friends in those early days. He was a Southern boy, who had studied to become a lawyer, but was so filled with poetic fervor and longing that he left a promising outlook as an attorney in his native State, Tennessee, to come to New York and carve his name on Fame's monument. He passed through various vicissitudes, and after two or three years became exceedingly discouraged and despondent, and went back to his Southern home and resumed the practice of law. Before a decade had passed Judge Walter Malone was a name known and respected in the legal world. But he had not forgotten his early love. Poetry still lured him: and all his leisure moments, which other young lawyers devote to pleasure or social distractions, Judge Malone devoted to the Muses.

As a result one of his poems has become a classic. It is entitled, "Opportunity," and is a reply to the very pessimistic and wholly untrue poem (although a literary gem) of In-galls', written on that subject.

Here is Walter Malone's "Opportunity":

"They do me wrong who say I come no more When once I knock and fail to find you in;

For every day I stand outside your door And bid you wake, and rise and fight and win.

"Wail not for precious chances passed away.

Weep not for golden ages on the wane! Each night I burn the records of the day–

At sunrise every soul is born again.

"Laugh like a boy at splendors that have sped, To vanished joys be deaf and blind and dumb;

My judgments seal the dead past with its dead, But never bind a moment yet to come.

"Thougfh deep in mire, wring not your hands and weep; I lend my arm to all who say, I can. No shame-faced outcast ever sank so deep.

But yet might rise and be again a man!"

This poem has been, and will be, an inspiration to thousands of discouraged men and women. It is widely quoted, frequently without the author's name, as is often the fate of universally appreciated verse.

The work to which Judge Malone gave ten years of his life was an ambitious epic, based on the life of Ponce de Leon. While abounding in brilliant lines and gems of lyric beauty, it will never endear him to his readers as has "Opportunity."

Judge Malone died suddenly of heart failure in the prime of life. He never married. His epic, he said, was his life love. Two years before his death, while arranging to publish his epic, he came and spent a few hours with us at Short Beach. The boyish dreamer I had known years before had grown into a typical Judge–somewhat over weight, serious to gravity, and all intent on his forthcoming book.

There was a melancholy about him which seemed in the light of his sudden death, so soon afterward, to have been something like a prevision of his near departure.

His death seemed sad to us who loved him, yet perhaps it was a happier fate for him to go just after he had completed his Hfe work, instead of waiting to feel bitterly that this work was not properly appreciated. Such a spirit as his is now occupied with so many greater tasks that all he did here will seem to him a mere preparation.

Marshall P. Wilder, the little dwarfed humorist, was also one of that old circle. Marshall's good heart, bright wit and scintillating mind all united to dominate his handicap of a deformed and dwarfed body. He was a living sermon to the pessimists. He made his way into homes and hearts, even among royalty; and King Edward was a devoted friend to the little man at the time of his death.

Marshall married a charming girl, and made a great success of his life. Both he and his wife died before middle life, but I believe there are two or three children left to bear his name.

CHAPTER XIII Lunatics I Have Known

DOUBTLESS every man and woman who is in any-capacity prominently before the public has peculiar experiences with people of disordered minds. But my own have been so varied and so continual that the story of my life would not be complete without a brief account of these amusing and often disturbing occurrences.

I remember when I was first launched as a girl poet being told by my brother that he had read an article declaring all poets and all creative artists to be partially insane. The wholly sane brain did not create; only when the brain began to be overripe, and therefore diseased, did genius develop.

This theory would perhaps explain the cause of my being pursued by the demented so frequently–like seeking like.

A young woman of astonishing beauty, looking something as Lilian Russell looked at twenty-two, appeared one day at my seashore home.

When I went in to learn what was the object of her call, she fell at my feet, kissed the hem of my garment and declared she had come to spend the remainder of her life with me. She could "iron beautifully," she said, and do many other useful things. She had journeyed from Nebraska for this purpose. When assured I had no place for her she showed mingled grief and anger. I told her I would find her a room in a summer hotel nearby until she could return home. I sent for a physician, and he declared her mildly insane on this one topic, but not dangerous. She was provided for at the hotel, but spent much time sitting on my lawn writing me long letters, wherein she declared herself disappointed that I had not lived up to my writings. A letter came from a sister of hers in Nebraska, saying she had

LUNATICS I HAVE KNOWN! i8i just learned of Ellen's destination, and she hoped I would find her useful; that she was really an excellent girl with just one mania, that of living with me. I forwarded to the sister some of Ellen's letters, which had assumed a menacing tone, and begged her to send for her and place her under medical care. This she did, and for years I was snowed under with letters from Ellen, written from this Asylum for the Insane in Nebraska. Then she was sent home to her mother in Canada, cured, the mother wrote me, of all her manias save this one. She begged me to make no reply or else to write severely to Ellen if I heard from her again. I did receive several very wild letters, but now for a period of some five years have been relieved of this annoyance.

While living at the Everett House in New York I received word one morning that a man wished to see me. I asked for his name; and a slip of paper was brought up with the name written thereon; and the bell boy said the gentleman wished to see me about "some plants." I was giving a lunchj-eon (for Julie Opp Faversham, who had been recently married), and the idea occurred to me that probably the florist of the hotel was to make a floral decoration for the occasion. I went down into the parlor to meet my caller, and found a young man of perhaps thirty, very good looking and very well dressed. He came close to me and in an agitated voice asked: "Are you married?"

In astonishment, I replied: "Certainly I am married; but what has that to do with the plants I was told you wished to speak about?"

"No, no; the plans, the plans," wailed the youth; "they said you weren't married." Seeing the man was mentally unbalanced, I suggested he would better take leave;

and he speedily departed, never to appear on my horizon again. The following day a letter came to me from my seashore home, saying a strange-appearing young man had called there seeming much distressed at my absence, and had been given my address in New York. That was how he had learned my location.

The next winter I received a series of well-written but decidedly unbalanced letters from St. Louis. The man said he was a physician, and that there had come to him a revelation of his true sphere in life, and of mine. We were meant for each other; and not until we were united would the purposes of Destiny be realized. Not until the tenth letter came and announced the writer's determination to visit me in New York, did I take any notice of his letters farther than to read them to a few amused friends, who had nicknamed me "The Lunatics' Own."

I sent this tenth letter to the Chief of Police in St. Louis and asked that its writer be looked after by medical and police authorities. The reply assured me that this was done; and that the very intelligent and reputable physician was found to be suffering from acute mania. The doctor himself shortly afterward wrote and apologized for his former letters, saying he had attended a religious revival and studied Shakespeare and read some of my poems all at one time, and the combination had unsettled his reason. After the receipt of this sane and apologetic letter, another insane missive reached me, and then silence.

The next season I spent in California; and during ray absence a pitiful half-witted youth presented himself one cold February morning at my door (our seashore house was kept open for my mother) and announced that he had come to "marry Ella." Assured that I was satisfactorily provided for in marriage, the caller wept wildly and said I had told him to come. Some four months after my return, one summer morning he appeared again at my door. The friend who had seen him on his first call recognized him, and my husband went in and informed him that Mrs. Wilcox was not at home to him, and advised him to take his leave. This he did, only to return on. five occasions. Once he came at midnight, and it necessitated a special conveyance to get him to the train. Previous to this I had sent him four doughnuts and a dollar as he was leaving my door; but the conveyance cost ten dollars, with the fee of the sheriff who accompanied him to the train.

A letter to the Chief of Police in Brooklyn caused the poor lunatic to be placed in an Asylum after his third visit. But a year later he was liberated and immediately set forth to Short Beach to "marry Ella." After the fifth visit the police were again called into counsel. This appeal finally settled the matter and I was relieved of his periodical pursuit. His history made one realize the need of eugenics in the land. His father had been insane; the youth was born insane; yet he had been allowed to marry, and already possessed a wife while he made his romantic peregrinations to Granite Bay in pursuit of another consort.

From Montreal, Canada, the next young Lothario hailed. He began his pursuit while we were living at the Everett House, and by the means of mysterious telegrams which woke us from sleep at the dead of night. One read: "Neither of us can attain success alone. We must be together. I am coming." The name signed denoted Canadian French nativity. Finally a message came announcing his arrival the next day. My husband conceived the idea that some one had been posing under my name, and that the man was coming for some definite reason. Robert engaged two private detectives seven feet tall (or thereabouts) to hide behind a curtain in our apartment and told me to let the mysterious caller come up to my room and to engage him in conversation until I learned what plot was back of the matter. The plan was carried out; but five minutes sufficed to show the poor fellow to be a pitiful lunatic who talked in the most incoherent manner. Not realizing the trouble I was making for myself and everybody else, I called to the detectives to come out; which they did, and to my amazement, clapped handcuffs on the poor wretch. He was scarcely five feet in height, and did not weigh over one hundred pounds; and the two giant detectives looked like Royal Danes worrying a small spaniel. Despite my protest they hauled the foolish lad off to the station house, and my husband and myself were compelled to appear the next day at Jefferson Street Court.

The detectives were determined to send him to the Island for six months, declaring him a dangerous case. I saw no good in such a procedure, and I insisted that a promise be obtained from him that he would never trouble us again and that he be sent back to Montreal. This was finally done and out of the matter my husband made a very droll story. He said when called before the Judge the name of the prosecutor was demanded, and that he gave it as Robert Wilcox: then the Judge asked who defended the man, and that I immediately said, "Mrs. Robert Wilcox." The affair cost my husband a matter of fifty dollars.

Another thing which amused my husband greatly was that I asked to see the prisoner a moment alone, and he found me reading his palm. I wanted again to prove how the palm verifies every mental peculiarity and I found this boy's hand indicated congenital insanity.

A few years ago affectionate postal cards and letters came to me frequently signed simply "Albert." They were from a town in the Middle West. Then came a very handsome fountain pen by post addressed by the same hand. No address was given and of course none of these missives received any reply.

Then came in December 1914 the following letter:

Chicago, 111., 12, 17, 1914.

Dearest Love: While here on business of importance for a few days, and Christmas time is so near, my thoughts are of you. I will love you and think you are the best girl for me. It would be a pleasure to know your choice as a present you would like the best.

This city has large places with fine jewelry in the line of wedding rings to choose from, if you can only make up your mind and come right away when you receive this letter. My address is (The address was given). When you arrive telephone to , and I will come and meet you at the depot. Will have on a dark blue suit, a hat of the same color. Be confident, take my photograph with you so you can recognize me. Inclosed you will find a cash check for railroad fare. I am ever your loving

Albert.

I sent the money order back to the Chicago Postmaster, saying it was from a man of disordered mind. He replied that it had been returned to the sender. I supposed that to be the end of this incident. But my lunatics are ever per- sistent. Another letter came from his Illinois town saying he felt he must come on and see me and talk matters over.

I did not know whether this Illinois town possessed a Chief of Police or not but I risked sending a letter, enclosing Albert's last, and saying I must be relieved of his annoying attentions.

The following letter from the Chief of Police tells the remainder of the story:–

"Dear Madam: I beg to acknowledge your letter relative to the doings of Albert. Albert lives in a tent on Street and with his people; and for a number of years has helped make both ends meet by angling for catfish in the mud of the Mississippi River near his home. Albert is a little fellow about four and a half feet tall; and weighs nearly one hundred pounds. His people hav average intelligence and are very much disturbed by his actions and will try to curb him in any further attempt to annoy you. It is hardly necessary to tell you Albert has been feeble-minded for a number of years."

Albert had sent me his picture on a postal card one time; at least he wrote on an accompanying slip of paper "From Your Valentine." The picture looks better than the description of the Chief of Police, however, and seems of questionable authenticity.

Having no recollection of any period of my existence when I had not been before the public eye, it naturally never occurred to me to feel sensitive regarding that public's often exhibited curiosity concerning my private life. As a young girl, it served as an amusement, and the surprise which was shown now and then by people who met me, and saw no evidence of dark trajjedies or brooding sorrow in my very healthful and happy appearance, was always entertaining.

Even when I heard the tales afloat, which represented me as either suffering from blighted affections or as having been a heartless vampire who destroyed men at a glance, I was never greatly disturbed. I argued philosophically that as the benefits and pleasures of my work were greater than those of girls in private life, so must I expect to feel some thorns in my roses. Better the roses and thorns than empty hands.

It was not until the great satisfying happiness cf my life came, from belonging to the man whose name I wore, that the thorns of my professional life began to pierce and wound. Until I was a wife, all that life gave me, which in any way was satisfactory or pleasing to my tastes and ambitions, came through my use of my talents. Only through my work had I been enabled to help others while blazing my way out of obscurity; therefore to complain of any annoyances resulting from my career which marred my happiness seemed as silly as ungrateful.

When every blessing which I prized came through my husband, however, I found the curiosity of the public and its misrepresentations most difficult to bear with equanimity. It was hard to maintain the reputation for amiability which my husband had given me, when tales floated to me which represented my husband as having deserted a wife and children for me; or reporting him as a brute and a drunkard from whom I was about to obtain a divorce. From time to time we would hear such stories; and always I would burn with rage, while my husband would laugh and calm me down with his quiet, beautiful voice.

On the twentieth anniversary of our marriage, we were living at the Everett House in New York; and we had planned an evening at the theater with a little supper afterward. We were sitting at our special table alone, enjoying our dinner quietly, when a man and a woman came in and took the table directly behind me. The hotel was crowded that night, and the tables were in close proximity. The man sat with his back to mine; and the woman facing him. I had noticed them as they entered, but both were perfect strangers. There came a lull in the dining room–one of those occasions when every one seems to cease talking at once. And just as this lull occurred I heard the man whose back almost touched the back of my chair say in a very distinct and positive tone, "Oh, I know what I am talking about, she was divorced at least TWICE before she married Wilcox." Then the woman replied, "But I thought she was Ella Wheeler when she wrote her Poems of Passion; and that she added the Wilcox by-marriage."

The man raised his voice and spoke with impatience:

"I tell you I know she was divorced at least twice before she married Wilcox."

My husband, who sat opposite me, had been giving some order to the waiter and did not hear this conversation. I have to this day regretted that I did not follow my first impulse, which was to rise and go quietly to the gossipers, announce myself as the object of their conversation, and deny the twice-uttered libel.

But instead I leaned over and whispered the story to my husband and then told him I was going to speak to them.

He at once objected. "It would be undignified," he said. "Instead, call the head waiter and have him ask them to change the topic of conversation, or their table, as Mrs. Wilcox is sitting here."

The head waiter was called and the message delivered. There was a deep silence at the table behind me; and I rose and made a little visit to the tables of three parties of friends, telling them the incident and causing so much mirth and calling so much attention to the gossipers that they left the hotel with an unfinished dinner.

But my twentieth anniversary had been clouded by this small yet irritating incident.

It was only a few years ago when a friend (it was Kate Jordan, the author and my friend of many years) heard my name spoken in a manicure parlor. She had just come from my home and she naturally listened. A patron of the establishment was regaling the young woman who polished her nails with a story of the faithless man who had deserted his family to elope with me. My friend walked over to the loquacious one and informed her of her error, and advised her to be careful what she repeated in the way of disagreeable gossip regarding people she did not know. The woman expressed great indignation at being addressed by a stranger whose words she no doubt questioned. People of that type prefer to believe the unpleasant tales of men and women before the public.

These are but two incidents of many similar cases which have occurred during my married life; and they have hurt far more keenly than any other kind of blow which has been inflicted by the brutal hand of publicity.

The rose of fame is only an artificial flower at best; and if my right to wear it is questioned by critics, or if mud is thrown upon it, it does not matter greatly. But the rose of a perfect love is a rare and exquisite thing; and to have the rude hand of the public clutch at it, or attempt to tear it off one's breast, means real suffering. It is, indeed, a difficult thing for a woman to shine in a public career of any kind and not subject herself to innumerable keen pains in her love life.

There is often such a lack of delicacy in one's very good friends when it comes to placing the celebrity before the woman at the expense of the pride of the man she loves.

When my husband built our Bungalow, its artistic charm and unusual type of attractions caused much comment. The majority of our friends who saw it for the first time would express themselves something in this manner:

"Well, it shows the poet's hand; it is what I would expect of a poet." "But," I would hasten to explain, "the poet had nothing whatever to do with it save to walk into it, all completed. It is all the work of my husband; he planned and conceived the idea, and I never saw it until almost complete." Then they would smile and answer, "Oh, you are very generous to give him all the credit, I am sure."

By that time I would be blazing with anger and reply:

"Why am I generous to tell the truth? I feel it far more a matter of pride to be the wife of a man who cares enough about me to plan this lovely home than to plan it myself. Almost any woman can write; but only one woman could or did become the wife of Robert Wilcox."

Yet the next relay of callers would bring a similar babble of banality from those who were so sure they saw "the poet's work in the house."

These were, of course, the friends who had not been privileged to meet and know my husband intimately. Those of our inner circle who really knew him understood his rare qualities of mind, and brain, and heart. They knew him to be the possessor of unusual powers of discrimination in all matters of art; and of the clear keen judgment of a connois seur. He taught me to regard a home as a jewel to be set beautifully and to be kept choicely. Until my marriage I had not given the home much thought outside of keeping it clean and comfortable. The table, too, I had recognized merely as a place where one satisfied the appetite. My husband taught me to think of it as a thing of beauty and refinement where choice appointments, correct service, and the best moods of the family should lend charm and appetite to the delicately prepared food. After we began our travels he was delighted to see me more anxious to make a collection of rare table linen than of things for my own adornment. Yet as a girl (poet though I was) I could have dined on a bare table without thinking of it, because my mind was full of other things: and that idea of putting poetry into the material things of life had to be developed through my love for, and my desire to please, my husband. No praise ever bestowed upon me by the world ever thrilled me like his praise for my becoming a good housekeeper, and presiding over his table in a manner satisfying to his tastes.

The management and care of his home was to me a delight; never a task or a worry; and perhaps because of this attitude of mind we were blest most of our married life with excellent employees and helpers in our home—which we made their home as well as ours.

One guest endeared himself to me by coming in from a. walk one day and saying, "Do you know your husband is twice the poet you are? He has told me more interesting things about insects and plants and sea animals than I ever heard in all my life."

I am quite sure were I a man, I would fly to the uttermost parts of the earth if I found myself becoming too interested in a woman with a "career."

Much as I have appreciated my talents and enjoyed the benefits and pleasures resulting from them, I do not think I would want to be bom again to earth life with talents which necessitate a career of any kind. Such a career is incompatible with the deeper delights of earth's most exquisite happiness, of a perfect love life. It rudely interferes with privacy, and intrudes on the most sacred moments. The world, like a lawless street urchin, presses its face against the window pane of a celebrated woman's boudoir and either grins or makes grimaces—and then goes away and lies about what it has seen.

Were I allowed to choose my next incarnation, I would ask to come back an accomplished, capable and agreeable companion of my beloved, and to be the mother of his sons and daughters as my only distinction in the eyes of the world.

Sometimes my sense of humor overcame my anger when I heard or read absurd stories about my private life. The following, sent me by my irate English publishers, appeared after I had been on a visit to England:

"Ella Wheeler acquired the name of Wilcox by marriage with a doctor of that name, and her married life, which is of the happiest, has many strange features. The couple live on a vast estate, several hours by rail from New York, each having a residence and household of their own. If the poetess feels a real inclination to have the doctor for breakfast, lunch, or dinner, she sends him a formal invitation and he walks or drives over to his wife's house just like any other friend. Occasionally she repays the doctor's visit, and gives him a pleasant surprise, but, as a rule, she accepts dinner invitations from him no oftener than from other friends. When the doctor has been to New York and brought from there some rare game or fish not obtainable at their place of residence, he makes a point of sharing it with his wife; otherwise the two menages are run on separate lines entirely, yet there never was a cross word between the poetess and the doctor, the latter always remaining the respectful admirer, counselor, and friend.

"The Poetess of Passion has successfully adopted several creeds of liberal tendencies, but the creed she has most faith in is herself. She once said to a friend: After my morning bath I don a kimono and enjoy myself before an immense cheval-glass for ten or more minutes, while I keep saying to myself: "This effigy of mine reflects the handsomest, the happiest and the most gifted woman in the world." And, whether it be true or not, I thoroughly believe in the pleasant fiction, and my day is felicitous throughout. If people would only stop making themselves miserable over a nose that is too broad, or hands that are too red; if they would drop envy and hatred, how much happier this world would be!"

Messrs. Gay and Hancock and Dr. (now Major) Frank Howard Humphries sent indignant corrections of these statements to the London editor, and wrote me letters of S3mipathy. But somehow the whole tale was so amusing it lost its sting for me. I tried to recall what I could have said to "a friend" which assumed such grotesque form in print, and decided it was a simple remark, stating my belief in the power of the spoken word to create that which we desire.

In this sad world we owe a debt to whomsoever makes us laugh, so I owe one to the creator of the two fairy stories given above.

On another occasion a friend of ours was sitting on the deck of a ship when she overheard an animated conversation between two ladies regarding the nationality of my husband.

One woman declared that she positively knew Robert Wilcox was a Hebrew, while the other as emphatically asserted that she knew he was American for many generations back. To this discussion my friend finally added her word, saying that she knew the Wilcox family to be Americans for generations. Yet it is to be questioned if the first speaker was convinced. Somewhere in the far distant past my husband had Spanish and Welsh ancestors; but there was in his appearance a strong resemblance to the very handsome Semitic race. Yet why should a woman who saw that resemblance, say with positiveness that she knew him to be a Hebrew?

Are women really as Lombroso has declared, naturally untruthful?

I once received a letter from a man who asked some sort of favor; just what has passed from memory. But this man reminded me of the days, "when," to quote his words, "we sat side by side in Chicago in a newspaper office." He said he well remembered my longing to be recognized and he was glad my dreams had been realized.

I wrote to the man and assured him I had never sat in a newspaper office in Chicago or any other city, that I had never held any office position and that my writing had all been done at home.

The man was quite indignant and wrote me a second letter trying to convince me that I had forgotten. I believe, however, that I eventually proved to my correspondent that he had made a mistake in my identity. Yet, how many times must he have related that tale to people, confident that he was telling the truth!

These experiences taught me to be very slow in believing anything which is told me regarding people who are in the public eye. The Know-It-AUs are a large family, but their testimony can not be taken, even on oath.

One of the youngest members of the family of Know-It-Alls only recently informed a lady with whom she was talking that Ella Wheeler Wilcox was a man who used a woman's pen name. She knew it to be so. The lady had left my presence only a few hours previously, but she found it difficult to convince Madame Know-It-All, nevertheless, of her mistake.

The very youngest at the present writing, a man who has known me for some fifteen years, remarked to an earlier friend that he was told my first husband was a charming individual.

It required considerable emphasis on the part of this older friend to convince the man that I had been married only once. He said he had been informed of my early marriage by some one who knew.

Even after the relation of all these absurd and annoying tales, I am sure there are many individuals who will read these pages and still need this final and positive and easily proven statement of mine, to-wit: I was never the wife of any man but Robert M. Wilcox, and he never possessed any wife before me. Neither of us ever passed through the divorce court. And we lived in growing happiness together until the hour when God called him to a larger life on more wonderful planes.

CHAPTER XIV

A Royal Funeral

"C ACH year, from the time of our marriage, my husband– planned some trip, which he thought would be a benefit and pleasure to me.

We visited most of the States, and Canada, and all the important seashore resorts. We went twice to Cuba and three winters to other West Indian islands. Always I said that I did not want to go to Europe until my husband had time to remain there with me several months. We hoped to go some time in the early summer and remain until late autumn.

But destiny had other plans for us.

From the hour of my marriage my husband had wished me to write only verse. He felt it was a waste of my energies and talents to attempt prose. I had begun a novel before our marriage, and I completed it the first year afterwards: and this convinced me I had no real ability in prose and that I should keep to my gift of poetry, and seek to develop it more fully.

Then, after a decade of years, I came one day to a question of duty. I had made a habit of sending my mother a check each month, besides doing what I could toward the education of nieces. Each year in my visit back to the old home I saw with a catch in my heart how my parents were aging, and how difficult were the financial conditions. There were eleven in the family, and I realized that more money was needed to tide the family ship over the shoals. My father and brothers were never intended for farmers. My older brother (then in Dakota) should have been in editorial work and would have been but for his sacrifice to what he believed to be duty– the duty to stay at home and work at uncongenial labor, when given the diance to start in educational lines.

My other brother had distinct mechanical gifts. As a young lad, he had made with a jack-knife, out of sticks no larger than knitting needles, a little threshing machine, which, attached to a water wheel, also of his own construction, actually threshed out wheat. I remember how I thrilled at the sight of it in action, and what dreams I had of his future greatness. Those dreams might have been realized had he been placed in a school for mechanics.

Meantime, while other neighbors, and Norwegian immigrants, all about us, developed less valuable farms into profitable returns, our farm steadily degenerated. I knew the fault lay at home. But I pitied rather than blamed our men. They were simply out of their orbit.

At the hour of which I write, in the early nineties, there was a financial crisis in the land. I knew my husband was anxious and troubled. Through friends of mine in Milwaukee, who meant more than well, and believed they were making him a millionaire, he had been induced against his inner wish, and will, to invest in Gogebic mines the first year of our marriage. Had the money he used remained where formerly invested, it would have enabled him to retire with a competence in our early married life, as time proved. One of the most wonderful evidences to me of his beautiful nature, and his sense of delicacy, is the fact that never once did he by word or act make me feel that but for my friends he would have had no business worries. The one request he did make of me was, that I should not ask him to meet or entertain these friends who had, by over-persuasion, induced him against his inner feelings to invest in these mines–a request I granted at the cost of being regarded by them ever feeling and ungrateful for their former friendship. Just at this particular juncture, when grave financial disasters were imminent in the country and the needs of my relatives in the West seemed pressing, an offer was made me by a syndicate for a series of prose articles at very excellent rates of remuneration. I accepted the offer, thinking to write the series of fifteen articles and to let that be the extent of my prose work.

My husband was always wishing to do something to help my mother. I have before me a letter he wrote in 1890, while I was visiting my parents in Wisconsin, which says, "I wish you could do more to make your mother's life happier. I would gladly contribute anything toward such a plan. I think we should pay more attention to those who are dear to us and nearing the end of life than to those who have the long road ahead of them. You must think up something I can do for the good mother who brought you into the world where I could find you." Once he had insisted on sending my mother a substantial check, because he said I had often bestowed gifts upon his relatives, paid for out of my own purse. But I did not like to have my husband add my family to his own long list of dear ones who still looked to him for help. Therefore, I accepted the editor's offer to write the prose series; so successful were the articles that another series was requested, and for many years thereafter I seemed never able to extricate myself from an arrangement which permitted me to do so many goodly and gracious acts toward others; while the work I sent out in this way made its place with a large audience not approachable through the medium of poetry.

It was because I had reached this large audience that the editor of the New York American sent a representative to me one cold winter night with a surprising proposal, just as my husband and I had finished dinner and were preparing to go to the theater. At dinner that evening Robert had remarked that he was so driven by business matters that he scarcely knew where to turn. When the editor's card came to me I left him sipping his coffee while I went in to see my caller. Presently I spoke to my husband, saying, "Robert, please come in and inform this insistent man how wild and impossible is his suggestion. He has asked me to sail in three days for London, to write an American poet's impression of a royal funeral. Queen Victoria is dying, it seems; they have their reporters and correspondents there, but they want me to go as their poet. I would as soon think of flying to Mars as of taking such a commission. Imagine me crossing the ocean for the first time, in mid-winter, and alone!"

To my amazement, my husband said: "Go, and I will ac- company you. We need not be gone more than a month, and it is really a great thing for you to see." Neither of us ever understood afterward how he came to make such a sudden resolution; or how he was able to carry it out with all the business affairs he had demanding his attention. So instead of the leisurely voyage over summer seas we had always planned, we crossed in mid-winter on a hurried, hurly-burly trip, lasting six weeks. Yet it was truly a wonderful experience and worth all the discomfort and suffering from climatic causes which followed.

A place had been provided for me to witness the great funeral procession and I was escorted to it by one of the special correspondents. My husband, meanwhile, had taken under his wing a very charming girl we had met on the ship, who had crossed on a matter of business and was quite alone. Robert obtained seats for her and himself in the Park where the procession was to pass. As they set forth, he remarked that it was fortunate for me that such careful plans had been made for my comfort, as I was exceedingly timid in a large crowd; that it was the only situation where he had found me unable to keep my poise. The young woman replied that she did not mind crowds at all, but rather enjoyed them.

As they entered the Park, searching for the number of their seats, the crowds increased rapidly, and they were very much jostled about. Two stretchers passed them with women who had already fainted. Ten minutes later, in what seemed the center of a solid human wall, my husband was touched on the shoulder by a London "bobby," who called out, "Look out there, sir, for your lidy!" Feeling a weight on his arm which he had supposed to be caused by the pushing crowd, my husband saw to his consternation that his companion was toppling over in a dead faint. It seemed ages before a stretcher was obtained, and ages before he was able to get his charge out into the open space, where they remained until the crowds dispersed. And that was all my Robert saw of the royal funeral!

Meanwhile, I was seeing the entire procession from so close a proximity that I could have tossed a flower on the head of every king of earth. They were all there following the small coffin of the little great Queen with real sorrow in their hearts. It was a majestic sight; but the emptiness of earthly glory never impressed me so forcibly as when I saw that tiny casket being carried away to its final resting-place. The Queen was scarcely five feet in height, and it seemed almost like the casket of a child. Now as I sat there, almost within touch of all the crowned heads of Europe, I suddenly recalled a very curious incident which had occurred ajx weeks before the death of the Queen; before her illness, even. I had attended an afternoon musicale and tea in New York. Over our teacups, an acquaintance had told me of a droll little person in the city who looked like a country school-maam and who lived in a funny little apartment not so far from the locahty where I dwelt that winter. This droll person possessed a strange pack of weird-looking cards; and for the sum of twenty-five cents she read your fortune. On my way home, I hied me to the card person, who, after receiving my remittance, laid out her cards and began to tell me the usual things one hears on such occasions. Then suddenly she said, "You are going very soon on a long sea voyage, are you not?" I laughed in derision, and replied in the negative. "But, you are," persisted the droll person, "and you are to be surrounded with royalty. Look at the Kings in your, cards; every one in the pack, and Queens! You are surely going to be among them and much honor will come to you and you will go very soon." I left the droll person who had made her absurd predictions, feeling my time and my twenty-five cents had been wasted. Yet, here I was, in less than eight weeks afterward, recalling this incident, right in the center of the procession which contained all the Kings, Princes and royal personages of Europe. I could not explain it. Can you? It makes one think there must be truth in the idea that whatever is happening now in the visible realms has first been rehearsed in the realm of the invisible. I relate this incident exactly as it occurred. When I came back, I tried to see the droll person to tell her of the truth of her predictions, but she was gone and I never knew what became of her.

I cannot describe the mental agitation I endured on that whole trip. I had never in my life before taken a commission of any kind. I had never gone out anywhere to write descriptions of anything. All my writing had been from within, and done in my own time and way. From the hour I reached London I was depressed by the purple and black drapings of the whole city; and the climate began to affect me unpleasantly. It did not seem to me that I could write one thing of value for the editor who had sent me out expecting great things.

We arrived in London several days before the funeral ceremonies were to take place. It was not until the night before the event for which I came that one single atom of inspiration came to me. I had been driving about the gloomy city with my husband and I returned to Hotel Cecil feeling ill in body, paralyzed in mind, and despairing in heart. I sat in the reading room a few moments after dinner, idly glancing over an old copy of The Gentlewoman, one of the monthly English magazines. My eyes chanced on an item which had been printed some weeks previously in the column devoted to the doings of royalty. It said: "The Queen is taking a drive to-day." The sentence sent a thrill through me. The Queen was surely taking a drive–her last, on the next day. I was so tired and ill that I could not sit up longer, so retired to my room. It was heated by a gas grate, which proved to be out of order, so that only half of it lighted. I crept into bed between cold Irish linen sheets feeling very discouraged despite the thought which had entered my mind for a poem. I woke at three with the first four lines of the poem clearly defined. I felt an immense sense of relief. I knew I could write something the editor would like; something England would like. The representative of the editor was coming at nine o'clock in the morning expecting material from my pen. I went to sleep again, and awoke at seven. I wrapped the down comfortable about me, lighted the impotent little gas grate, and sitting on the floor, while my husband still slept, wrote the poem which opened the heart of all England to me.

I had never been especially interested in the Queen, but as I wrote I began to feel very deeply her worth, and the pathos of her last ride; and I wept copiously. My husband woke suddenly and saw me sitting by the grate on the floor, weeping, and asked with concern what I was crying about. "I'm crying about the Queen's last ride," I said, "and because I am really writing something worth while."

When I read the verses to him, he was most enthusiastic. And when, at nine o'clock, the dreaded American man came to get my copy to cable it to New York, he found me, for the first time since my arrival in London, smiling. The poem was cabled to the New York American, and was cabled back again by them to an evening paper in London (I think it was the Mail) that same day, crossing the ocean twice in twelve hours. Its publication brought me quantities of letters from English people, and, later, words of appreciation from royalty itself.

THE QUEENS LAST RIDE

The Queen is taking a drive to-day; They have hung with purple the carriage-way. They have dressed with purple the royal track Where the Queen goes forth and never comes back.

Let no man labor as she goes by On her last appearance to mortal eye; With heads uncovered let all men wait For the Queen to pass, in her regal state.

Army and Navy shall lead the way

For that wonderful coach of the Queen's to-day;
Kings and Princes and Lords of the land
Shall ride behind her, an humble band;
And over the city and over the world
Shall the Flags of all Nations be half-mast-furled;
For the silent lady of royal birth
Who is riding away from the Courts of earth;
Riding away from the world's unrest
To a mystical goal, on a secret quest
Though in royal splendor she drives through town. Her robes are simple, she wears no crown: And yet she wears one, for widowed no more, She is crowned with the love that has gone before;

And crowned with the love she has left behind In the hidden depths of each mourner's mind.

Bow low your heads–lift your hearts on high– The Queen in silence is driving by!

The poem was set to most effective music by a friend of King Edward, and a year from that day was sung at the memorial services, in the presence of all the royal family. This poem was the only thing I wrote while abroad that was of any value whatever, and this experience decided me that never again, under any circumstances, would I take a "commission" to go anywhere and write on any subject.

From London we went to Holland, and just one week from the day of the Queen's funeral we were witnessing the bridal procession of the Queen of Holland, seeing her and her liege lord at very close range, and afterward I was shown through the Royal Palace. The most interesting part of that experience was the night we passed in a hotel in the forest near Scheveningen, a summer hotel which had been opened up just to accommodate the influx of guests on this festival occasion. The deep snows all about the hotel, the dark forest of trees, the candle-lighted rooms, the thick frost on the window panes of our sleeping apartment, all lent the night a weird charm. It gave us a sensation of being a cave man and woman. Several years afterward we went back there in the summer season and spent ten days at this popular watering place. But that winter scene is the picture which stands forth distinctly in memory's picture gallery.

My husband had been planning the long-dreamed-of saun-terings through Europe when we might at least spend a whole summer in the Old World. The dream seemed about to be realized when the unexpected happened, and again duty stepped in and took the place we had prepared for pleasure at life's board. My father, who had been for some years a child in mind, and a growing care in the old home which was filled with nephews and nieces of all ages, was suddenly released from his body at the age of ninety. My mother two years before, this had suffered from an illness which the family attributed to a fall. I was sent for and even after she arose from her bed of sickness the word "stroke" was never mentioned by the family or the physician. I alone seemed to realize that my mother had experienced a slight stroke of paralysis which had produced that fall.

My mother had been very eager always on my visits home to have me bring the latest novels and the latest books of poetry, and read aloud to her. I had provided myself with reading material on this visit, and after she was able to sit up and walk about the house I began reading the newest novel of the season. It was Hall Caine's "The Christian," I remember. Unforgettable is that hour when I first realized that she did not remember one word that I had read to her at the previous sitting. After that I only read the simplest short tales or anecdotes to her, and even then her mind would wander, and she would begin to talk of her family troubles in the midst of my reading. I knew then that the wonderful mind of my mother was only a cracked vessel.

The last visit I made to the old home before my father's death was one of indescribable anguish. He had no recollection of me, and when I tried to recall myself to his mind, he replied that he was not expected to recognize every stranger who came into the house. It is an intensely painful experience to see one's parents go back to the weakness of childhood without childhood's charms. Father had a mania for building fires, and it was necessary to watch him continually that he did not set himself and the house on fire. He was very irritable toward the children and in return they were irritable and disrespectful toward him. (We must inspire respect before we receive it.) I had kept up my assumption of courage and cheer while at home, for the sake of the broken old mother, the worn and harassed sister-in-law, the unfortunate children reared in such an atmosphere, and the discouraged brother trying blindly to pull through such miserable conditions as best he could. That these conditions might all have been different through a different mental attitude in years past, did not make the situation seem any more hopeful. Most of us realize in the midst of our troubles that we might have done a great deal to avert them; but unless we are sustained by religion and philosophy, this consciousness is more painful than otherwise. My brother had no bad habits, his heart was kind, and mine was very tender toward him. Both of my brothers had served their country in the Civil War and were never robust afterward. One went in as a mere lad.

When I left home to meet my husband in Chicago, I obtained an end chair in the Pullman car from Madison, and, turning my back on the fortunately few occupants, let the long restrained flood of tears flow. Never in my life had there been a wilder downpour; and still weeping, I took my pencil and paper from my traveling bag and wrote the following verses:

UNTO THE END I know not where to-morrow's path may wend. Nor what the future holds; but this I know. Whichever way my feet are forced to go I shall be given courage to the end.

Though God that awful gift of His may send. We call long life, where headstones in a row Hide all of happiness, yet be it so; I shall be given courage to the end.

If dark the deepening shadows be that blend With life's pale sunlight when the sun dips low. Though joy speeds by and sorrow's steps are slow I shall be given courage to the end.

I do not question what the years portend– Or good or ill whatever winds may blow It is enough, enough for me to know I shall be given courage to the end.

It was a very broken and weepy wife that crept into the strong arms of her husband that night in Chicago. I think the spirits who go from Purgatory to Paradise must feel something as I did. After he had sympathized and comforted all he could, I remember that my husband became very stern and he said: "You shall do everything for your people that you can financially, and I will help you if you will let me; but I'm not going to allow you to visit there any more when it puts you into such an hysterical condition. They cannot possibly receive enough benefit by your presence to pay for the vitality you lose."

Destiny arranged that I should not make another visit; only to go and bring my mother back East after my father's death; and that was the duty which intervened and prevented our foreign wanderings for a period of seven years.

It had been the dream of my mother's life, since I began to earn money, to live with me in some beautiful spot by the sea, free from all care and trouble. This dream was late in being realized; and the habit of her mind was such that she failed to find the happiness and peace she had looked for with me; failed because happiness and peace must first be sought for within. I brought my mother into a paradise of beauty and comfort and gave her every tender care, every comfort, every possible distraction. She heard nothing but words of cheer, praise and affection spoken in the house, yet the old habit of thinking of herself as a martyr to unkind fate had become a sort of an obsession with her and gave her a morbid pleasure. When I had visited the old home in the West, a great deal of my time was passed in listening to her relation of the annoyances to which she was subjected by having so many noisy children in the house. Yet, here in my beautiful, restful home, she frequently complained because of her loneliness in being deprived of the association of the children in the West. My mother had never liked cats, and she found much fault with us for allowing out beautiful Angora pets in our living room. This was my first experience since I started in my little artistic apartment in New York City (a period of some seven years) of hearing any complaint or fault-finding in my home. The early cry of my heart for a peace-filled, love-ordered home had been realized, both in New York, and in our beautiful bungalow; but now I was obliged to contend again with that element of discontent which had marred my girlhood life.

The only one whose word or wish could influence my mother was my husband. She adored him, and when he reproved her for her fault-finding and her complaints, telling her how unhappy she made me, she would become as penitent as a little child, and "behave" for days. Of course, I realized that it was not an easy matter to adjust a life at the age of 84 to entirely new conditions, and my husband urged me to be philosophical and not take my mother's complaints too seriously. He met the difficult problem which had come into our free and happy home. life so wonderfully that if I had not loved and respected him to the limit of my powers before, I surely would have placed him on a pedestal then. I tried to be as calm as he was; but my failure to make her contented and appreciative of our paradise was a severe blow to me. It was, however, a great lesson: a lesson on the importance of cultivating a grateful and contented state of mind, no matter what our situation may be: in the darkest conditions to look for some ray of light and to be thankful for it, for the mind like the body grows into the attitudes we give it. If we sit with sunken chests over our tasks we eventually find it impossible to straighten up. So if we train our minds to critical and gloomy thoughts when we come into the sunlight we still see gloom. As my mother talked much of her early life in Vermont, I decided to take her to the scene of her childhood and youthful married life, and let her see the old places once again. Some years previously I had made a trip to Vermont with my husband, and knew there was a very good hotel at Bradford, the town of her birth. So we set forth and during the day's journey I more and more realized how near to childhood my mother had returned despite her still fine vocabulary and sharp wit in repartee. Many people who talked with Mother saw no evidence of her broken state. On this trip she seemed very much confused about our destination and mixed up her remarks regarding Wisconsin and Vermont continually. Arrived at the hotel, I proceeded to look up my mother's old acquaintances and succeeded in finding fully a dozen whose ages varied from 75 to 90. A dinner was given for my mother at which ten of these old people appeared, and they made much of her, recalling incidents which she had quite forgotten. Yet she did not enjoy this event. She was greatly displeased with the signs of age in her old friends; and said she would have preferred to remember them as they were in her early life. So this attempt to make her happy was also a failure.

Even at this age, Mother was a strikingly handsome woman. She had kept her very beautiful form, her well poised head was still erect, and her hands would have served as models for a sculptor, despite the hard work they had done. Her large eyes, of a deep violet shade, were still clear and unusual in their beauty, and her very delicately chiseled features had not lost their outlines. On the train and at the hotel every one turned to look at her; and one stranger came and said to me, "The moment I saw your mother I remarked to myself, There is a true aristocrat; a grande dame who has always moved in high circles."

I remembered my mother getting the dinner for fourteen Norwegian harvest men, and wondered if the lady would call that "high society." But in her appearance she certainly did represent the aristocratic and cultured side of life.

When we returned to our home, she seemed a little more appreciative of its comforts, and now and then she would surprise me by an almost happy mood in which she expressed gratitude and pleasure. But I do not recollect that these moments ever continued through an entire day. Gradually she became less irritable, and with each month her adoration for Robert increased.

After two years of a constant effort to entertain my mother, my husband told me I must find some one to assist me in this care of her, in order that he might enjoy the old-time days and weeks of my companionship, uninterrupted by thoughts of my duty toward her. Guardian angels provided me just at the crucial moment with the right helper for this difficult position. A letter came to me the very day I had told my husband that I would follow his wishes, from a young lady who had recently lost her mother. She wrote me that she was disappointed in her ambitions to follow an artistic career, and that she would like to find a position as a companion to an old lady. It was one of the many instances in my life where difficult problems were solved for me by invisible helpers. The young lady came to remain six months. She remained during my mother's life, a period of five years, and for several years thereafter. She was indeed a member of my household until she was married from my home, leaving its beautiful environment for a home of her own, almost as beautiful. My mother was devoted to her, and very happy in her companionship. Disliking old people, she enjoyed and was delighted with this handsome young lady.

The winter before my mother died she was in her usual good health and my husband took me to the West Indies for two months. We were sailing home in March, on a boat which had left two weeks sooner than we desired to leave, but we had decided to take it because its next passage would bring us back too late. Forty-eight hours before we reached Boston, a heavy snow-fall made us wish we were back in Jamaica. I went down into the dining salon for a cup of tea. The grounds in my cup looked interesting; and I asked the stewardess laughingly if she could "read tea-cups." It would amuse me to have mine read. She replied that the cook was very wonderful in all those ways, and, of course, I sent for him immediately. He was a large and quite black man; and he assumed an air of vast importance as he took my cup to the light and examined it with rolling eyes. Then he came back to me and said solemnly, "Mistress, you'se agoin home now, but not to stay. You'se agoin to be there just a little while; then you'se goin on the longest sea trip you'se ever had. You won't get back again for about a year." I laughed and assured him he was mistaken. "I'm going home to stay a year before I budge out of my house again," I said. "I never go on voyages save in the winter." He insisted that he was right, however, and that I would find it so.

And I did.

When we landed in Boston, a long distance call informed us that my mother had had another stroke; she died in my arms 24 hours later. She died praying, "Oh, mother, come and take me home. I am so tired." In just six weeks, we left our house in the hands of a friend who was convalescing from illness, and we went to Europe to remain almost a year.

I should like to know what quality it was in the mind of the black man that permitted him to see such an unexpected event! It was fortunate for me that my husband could spare the time and take me on this long trip. My mother was within seven months of her ninetieth birthday when she died, and her going was not a great sorrow; yet it was a great emotional ordeal to pass through. It was the fourth time I had been very closely associated with death. In my early girlhood I had been alone with the first wife of Judge Braley, of Madison, when she breathed her last. Both her husband and her mother had felt they could not witness it, but I remained. Again I had been the lonely watcher while the mother of my hostess in Milwaukee, at the home where I was afterward married, breathed her last. I had held my own dead baby in my arms; and now I had held my mother while she drew that last breath which never went forth again. It caused me to dig deep into the profound emotions of life, to live my whole existence from childhood to the present day over and over; to realize all my mistakes and shortcomings; to grieve newly over the thought that I had not succeeded in my effort to make my mother perfectly happy the last years of her life and to regret ever having been irritable to her. Yet there was great satisfaction in the thought that I had given her happiness through having so many of her ambitions for me realized; and in the remembrance of her often repeated assertion that I had never disappointed her, and never been unkind to her. To her continual faith in my abilities as a child and young girl, and her constant anxiety for my attainment of a larger life, and her willingness to sacrifice anything which would help me up and onward, I owed a debt which could never be paid in this incarnation.

The distractions of travel, and the delightful wanderings which I enjoyed with my husband during the next seven months enabled me to rise out of the state of depression in which I departed from America, and to return to my paradise, enriched in mind and soothed in heart, to enjoy the most beautiful years which life had yet offered me.

As a little child and afterward I remembered my mother's often expressed horror of burial and her wish that she might be "either put in the sea or burned" when she died. This idea used to shock all her neighbors; and was therefore more frequently uttered by her. My mother's chief distraction in her monotonous life lay in shocking her neighbors by her unusual ideas. When she came to live with me she showed a distinct disappointment that this wish of hers shocked no one. Cremation had become an every-day event; and she was told that her desire would, of course, be observed. In a talk with her one day on the subject I asked her if she wished to have her ashes sent to Wisconsin to be buried beside my father (with whom she had lived fifty-six years in marriage). She replied emphatically, "No, no, I want them to be scattered in the open air, and not put in the ground." So my mother's ashes were placed in an urn until rose-growing season and then, on a beautiful spring day, they were scattered about a rose bush.

CHAPTER XV Happy Memories of Well Known People

WE made five separate voyages to the West Indies; and always Port Antonio, Jamaica, was our central point of interest. We loved its rare beauty, the wonderful location of its Hotel Tichfield, and the atmosphere which pervaded that delightful hostelry, and we grew to feel much at home within its walls. One year we happened to be in Port Antonio when Jack London arrived there on his wedding trip with his second wife, delightful Charmian–his real mate destined for him since the beginning of time.

My husband and I became good friends of the Londons; and that New Year we four went swimming together in Port Antonio Harbor, where the waters look like a big glass filled with pousse-cafe–so many are the wonderful shades of color reflected therein. Afterward, the Londons visited us at our bungalow, after they had returned from their adventurous and exhausting voyage on the Snark, and both were showing the strain they had undergone. Such dear lovers as they were! In Jamaica I had looked at Jack London's palm; and I had told him that he must conserve his vitality, and not give such complete rein to his love of adventure, or he would not live fifteen years. He lived eleven, I believe, after that.

The proprietor of the Tichfield made a feature of highly artistic menus, and had as his able aide a most gifted artist printer, Mr. Hadley. One day we arrived at the Tichfield at noon; and the proprietor came to me saying that as it was Lincoln's Birthday he desired an extra feature to do honor to the occasion in the way of a beautiful menu card. The artist had done his part, and now he wished I would do mine by writing a verse for the outside of the card. The verses would be needed in an hour in order to have the printers supply the cards by dinner time. It seemed rather a hurried order to give my Muse; but she was obliging and supphed the following verses in time to satisfy the printers and to please mine host:

LINCOLN

When God created this good world A few stupendous peaks were hurled From His strong hand, and they remain, The wonder of the level plain. But these colossal heights are rare, While shifting sands are ever)nvhere.

So with the race. The centuries pass.
And nations fall like leaves of grass.
They die–forgotten and unsung.
While straight from God some souls are flung
To live, immortal and sublime.
So lives great Lincoln for all time.

Having proven myself able to meet such a situation successfully, the proprietor repeated the request on my next visit to his hotel, which occurred January i6, 1909.

We had noticed a striking-looking couple in the dining room at noon, the day of our arrival, and had been told they were Sir Henry and Lady Blake. Sir Henry was for a period of eight years the Governor of Jamaica; then eight years Governor of Newfoundland; then of Hong Kong. This was his first visit to Jamaica since he went away to assume other duties. A dinner was to be given him that night–a stag dinner, and a very beautiful souvenir was planned for the occasion–and would I write some verses for it? I asked for more information regarding Sir Henry's association with Jamaica; and learned that he had caused fine bridges and streets to be made; and had done more to exploit the beauty and the worth of Jamaica than any other Governor had done. He was, in truth, Jamaica's favorite ruler. I endeavored to put these facts into twelve lines, which was all the space accorded me by the printer. The lines were:

JAMAICA

The fairest Island in the seas,
The darling of the Sun; Her friends abide on every side
But in her heart dwells one Who loves her for her own dear sake, Blake, Blake, Blake.
He decked her with colossal gifts
And flung them at her feet; He showed her worth to all the earth In splendid bridge and street; Then let his name the echoes wake. Blake, Blake, Blake.

The verses were read aloud by one of the forty guests with great effect; and after dinner Sir Henry and Lady Blake asked to be presented. Lady Blake and I began to converse, and we found so many topics of mutual interest that we suddenly discovered the lights were about to be turned off in the room where we sat and observed we were the only guests in the hotel who had not retired. My husband had gone to our room after chatting with Sir Henry, leaving me deep in conversation with this very entertaining woman. This was the beginning of a most interesting acquaintance. Lady Blake wrote me after she returned to Ireland, where they made their home. Sir Henry was Irish, Lady Blake, English, and their marriage had been a very romantic one. When we visited England the following year Lady Blake asked us to come to Youghal and spend a few days at their home. Myrtle Grove. This we did, sailing from Queenstown afterward.

The house in which we visited was built thirty years before America's discovery. It had been occupied at one time by Sir Walter Raleigh, and his room was mine during my visit: my husband slept in the room where Spenser wrote one part of his "Faerie Queene." Lady Blake had turned an old stable into a most artistic studio, where she painted a few hours each day. She was an accomplished artist, and her paintings of the ferns and flowers of the various lands where her husband's official duties had caused them to reside occupy a dignified place in England's collection of that nature.

The house was filled with the rarest of Chinese furniture and objects of art. In several rooms we observed old prints of various kinds of Nell Gwynne. We knew that Lady Blake was the sister of the Duchess of St. Albans and later, looking through the book of English peers, we found that the first son of Charles II and Nell Gwynne was legitimatized by the King and made the first Duke of St. Albans. The present Duke of that title is the eleventh.

Lady Blake is one of the most brilliant women of her period–a linguist, an artist, profoundly read, and gifted in conversation. It was indeed a privilege to meet her and her famous husband in their interesting domain.

In the garden of Myrtle Grove Sir Walter Raleigh, after returning from Virginia, planted the first tobacco and potatoes used in Europe, and it was under a yew tree in this garden, while enjoying his first smoke, that his servant dashed a bucket of water over him, thinking his master was on fire.

While I was at Myrtle Grove the New York American cabled, asking me for a sentiment on the death of Mark Twain. I sent the following:

A radiant soul with genius bright Now lends to other realms delight; Let Heaven be glad, let earth rejoice Since unto us was left his voice.

During this visit to Europe, my very enterprising publishers, Messrs. Gay and Hancock, arranged a unique testimonial for me. I was the guest of honor at a luncheon party of sixty men– publishers, editors, bookmen of all kinds, newspaper men, and some invited guests from other circles. It was given at the Holbom Restaurant. Beautiful editions of my works were displayed in the windows of all the London book stores. Mr. William T. Stead was one of the speakers of the day. AH the menus were heart-shaped with my portrait on the cover. That same season I was the guest at the Poetry Recital Society. This society is composed of the descendants of distinguished names in the world of poetry, and the occasion was particularly interesting to me. I saw there the Earl of Lytton, a Rossetti, several Shake-speares, a Wordsworth, a Southey, a Dryden. Then there were representatives through the female line of Burns, Spenser, Watts, Tennyson, Hemans, Proctor, Swinburne, and a score more of well-known names. It was an evening full of thrills for me.

On our next visit to England we had the most delightful day with Marie Corelli in her exquisite home at Stratf ord-on-Avon. She invited our good friends. Dr. and Mrs. Frank Howard Humphries, to bring us to luncheon, and we motored out from London to that historic spot on a glorious June day. This brilliant author proved to be a most entertaining woman and a fascinating hostess. The day is marked in memory's calendar with a red letter.

As we came away I glanced back at the river Avon where I saw a single swan floating, and later the following verses were the result of that glance:

ON AVONS BREAST

One day when England's June was at its best I saw a stately and imperious swan Floating on Avon's fair, untroubled breast. Sudden it seemed as if all strife had gone Out of the world; all discord, all unrest.

The sorrows and the sinnings of the race

Faded away like nightmares in the dawn:
All heaven was one blue background for the grace
Of Avon's beautiful, slow moving swan
And earth held nothing mean or commonplace.

Life seemed no longer to be hurrying on With unbecoming haste, but softly trod As one who reads in emerald leaf, no lawn. Or crimson rose, a message straight from God. On Avon's breast I saw a stately swan.

One of the most unaccountable and exciting experiences of my life took place at the Pan-American Exposition in Buffalo.

My husband was unable to attend this exposition, but he thought I ought to go; and as there were many of our acquaintances in Buffalo at the time, he felt I would be well looked after.

I had been requested by the editor of the Cosmopolitan Magazine to write a poem about the exposition; and I recollect the tons of material in the way of histories he sent me to read up before I wrote the poem. I read thoroughly and wrote carefully; and he was pleased with the poem, but I doubt if any other human being ever cared for it. I know I did not. It was written wholly from my head; my heart was not in it. Having written the poem, however, I thought I ought to visit the exposition. I went about the different departments with interest, accompanied by various friends, and found it instructive and enjoyable; and was about to return on an evening train to New York, when in the early afternoon I met a friend from Little Rock, Arkansas, then residing in New York. This was Mrs. Hollenberg, a typical Southern woman of great charm, universally beloved. Learning that I was leaving that evening, Mrs. Hollenberg urged me to go and see Cummins' Indian Congress. "You like to see dancing," she said, "and these Indians do remarkable war dances. I am sure Mr. Cummins will be glad to meet you; you know he used to be a leader socially in the South and a great man for cotillions, but now he has taken up this work among the Indians and is making a success only second to Buffalo Bill."

We entered the Indian tent and Mrs. Hollenberg brought Mr. Cummins and introduced him. Mr. Cummins told me the Sioux were about to do their war dance; and he pointed out the old Apache Geronimo, then ninety years old, who was a war prisoner with a terrible record of savagery, but who was carried about with the show as one of its attractions. After a moment Mr. Cummins was asked by one of his assistants to come into the tent of the Sioux, from which he emerged shortly to tell me that the Sioux had learned of my presence and wished to adopt me.

"What in the world are you talking about?" I asked, in amazement. "How do the Sioux know anything about me, and why do they want to adopt me?"

Mr. Cummins only smiled. "I simply tell you what they told me," he said. "Come up by the tent and we may find out more."

I accompanied him to the tent, and left Mrs. Hollenberg sitting near old Geronimo. Mr. Cummins disappeared into the tent, and in a very short interval appeared, followed by the whole Sioux tribe. They were in full war paint and feathers, and carried all sorts of death dealing implements. They at once began the most horrible dance about me–shrieking and shaking their knives and pistols in my face. Mrs. Hollenberg saw me growing very white, and came and stood beside me. Mr. Cuinmins had gone over to speak with old Geronimo. Presently the dance ended and each "brave" laid his knife and gun at my feet, rose and said "How" and shook my hand; and the squaws came from the tent and followed suit. Mr. Cummins said I was now a Sioux, and that he had asked old Geronimo to give me a name, and Geronimo had said at once, "Princess White Wings." As I was dressed in a black traveling suit I do not know what suggested the name to him. In truth the whole occurrence has always been most unaccountable to me.

Had Mr. Cummins known that I was to be present that afternoon I should have suspected him of preparing a spectacular bit of advertising, but my visit was wholly impromptu; and, besides, no newspaper account was ever given of the incident so far as I know. How the Indians should have been aware of my presence and why they should have been interested in me, has never been explained.

Two years later I visited the St. Louis Exposition and learned that Cummins' Indian Congress was to give an evening entertainment, and accepted the invitation of friends to occupy a box. Mr. Cummins came to the box and said his Indians had expressed a desire, on being told I was in the house, to speak to me after the entertainment closed. So they filed up, and again shook hands and said "How." The next day to my hotel came a beautiful bead reticule, containing a pair of beaded moccasins and the following letter, which was in Indian dialect, but which Mr. Cummins had translated. I have both the original and the translation:

St. Louis, October 22, 1904. Mrs. Ella Wheeler Wilcox, "Princess White Wings," St. Louis, Mo. Dear Princess: Your coming to visit us in the Indian Congress gladdened our hearts like the Star in the North sky, that guides us when we are far away, back to our wigwam home on the filains.

Our hearts bleed with happiness when you shake our hands at the Indian Congress.

We feel much good and beg the Great Spirit of the Red Man to make the wind blow nice and the great forest bow its leaves and limbs in the presence of the big sun in the skies, whenever you are present.

We shake your hand and send a little present, bead pocket-book, to fill with the Paleface money and hope it always be big full, so our Princess have always plenty in the Paleface land.

We always meet you gladly and protect you when come among our people.

Chief La Kota, he too help to guide you to where all our people live. We shake your hand,

Signed, Chief Red Shirt, Chief Red Star, Chief Spotted Tail, Chief American Horse, for all the Indians at Cummins' Indian Congress.

As interpreted by me, Henry Standing Bear.

That next summer I gave a costume ball, and endeavored to improvise a "Princess White Wings" costume for myself. It was far from being true to the tribe, however.

I wore a plain little white silk gown, over which I hung a wonderful belt of Indian workmanship, and white feathers were stuck in my hair. My wings consisted of white tulle draperies; and I am sure any real Indian Princess would have despised me, but the guests thought the effect pleasing, not being overcritical.

It was the following summer that we gave a series of garden fetes for the benefit of our "Women's Improvement Society" of Granite Bay. This society had become a very enterprising one, building pavements and keeping the streets in condition, lighting dark byways and in every manner improving our beautiful resort.

One of our early experiences had been both amusing and vexing. Finding it impossible to hire men to clean our streets, one of our leading young ladies, daughter of a prominent railroad official, suggested that we do it ourselve. I agreed, saying we would all wear white wash gowns and white hats, and call ourselves the "Short Beach White Wings."

The whole young feminine population went into it enthusiastically, and so much had it been talked about and discussed, that, to our amazement, when we sallied forth, broom and pick in hand, we found a New Haven newspaper man and camera following us about. We were photographed and written up in a way that caused the most discordant results. We had said that we did this work because we could not get the men to do it. We meant because we could not hire men for the work. The editor chose to construe our words to mean that we could not interest our husbands, brothers, sons and fellow citizens in making the town neat. This reflection on our fine men angered us, and pained our men; and dreadful was the muddle in which the poor well-meaning White Wings found themselves. After that we decided to wait and hire men to do our work at any cost.

Our society grew in power and our annual summer benefits provided it with money to enlarge its sphere of activity. The Bungalow lawns were adapted to outdoor fetes, and we gave some effective entertainments for our society and for charity. Having brought costumes from each country in our travels, the pretty girls of Granite Bay found pleasure in being robed as Oriental sirens, and acting as ushers at our musicales; and these fantastically, yet historically, robed beauties, always proved drawing cards, bringing the people from neighboring resorts to pay their entrance fee to our Court, for these occasions.

One of our most recent fetes was a purely social event given in honor of Mrs. Frank Howard Humphries of London, who was visiting me. We gave an outdoor minuet, with golden weather and blue seas and green trees to make the environment perfect.

Wonderful memories! wonderful hours to recall sitting alone in the twilight of life!

Wonderful realizations of the vision which came with the little Oriental paper knife, in the old farmhouse in Wisconsin!

I wrote to a friend in August, 1906, the following lines, from Mayence, Germany:

"We saw the Kaiser to-day, reviewing his troops. Twenty thousand. It was a great sight, but made one feel that Universal Peace, so much talked about, is a million years away. It is. The Kaiser looked older than we had imagined from his pictures. We were very near him, and as we drove back to the hotel, he passed our carriage so closely we could have touched him."

To that same friend I wrote from Cologne:

"The Church of St. Ursula is built on the spot where Attila, the Hun, returning from a pilgrimage to Rome, with his soldiers, slaughtered St. Ursula and eleven thousand virgins. The interior of this Church is decorated with their bones.

"In jeweled cases repose skulls, many of them in lovely lace caps embroidered by devout worshipers. One room of the Church has its walls fairly papered with the bones of these slaughtered nuns."

How little any of us imagined at that time, the nearness of a similar slaughter of the innocents!

The following winter I wrote of my audience with the Pope, Pius X–that beautiful-faced man who never wanted to be a Pope, preferring his quiet priesthood, and whose personality expressed his sense of serious responsibiuty under the burden of his position.

"I have had an audience with the Pope. That expression suggests sitting down in a stately room, alone with this august personage, and engaging in intimate conversation. Instead, it means waiting for a lengthy period of time, in a more or less crowded room, until a tired and overtaxed man, with the weight of an enormous responsibility resting upon him, comes, in the performance of a duty which must grow monotonous to him, and in his brief transit bestows a general blessing on every one in the room. Each one bends the knee, and kisses his hand. I, like all others, carried many rosaries and strings of beads over my arm, and all these came in for their share of the general blessing. Naturally, no individual was privileged to converse with the Pope, but the Audience left one with the satisfaction of having been in the presence, and having seen at close range, one of the world figures. Pope Piux X is a tall man, with a beautiful, sad face. I felt drawn to him."

My blessed chains and rosaries gave great pleasure to many sweet Catholic friends afterward; and only this year (1917) I gave the last one to a dear girl who sent it to a Catholic soldier, telling him it had been blessed by the Pope.

My husband and I were on board the Olympic, sailing to England, when the Titanic went down. At the breakfast table our steward told us that news had been received that the Titanic had struck an iceberg, but was saved with all on board. He said, however, he feared more serious news might come later. Mr. George Marcus, of the firm of Marcus and Company, of New York, was one of the Olympic passengers, and an intimate friend of my husband. Shortly after breakfast we walked on deck, and Mr. Marcus and his artist son walked with us; Mr. Marcus recounted a curious dream he had had the previous afternoon. He said, "I told my son after waking from my afternoon nap, that I had dreamed of the Titanic. I thought I saw it sailing over a smooth sea, and then suddenly run up the sheer straight side of an enormous iceberg and turn a somersault and sink into the sea." The son said both he and his father felt the fate of the Titanic was more serious than had been reported. It was not until the afternoon that the terrible facts were received on board the Olympic. It made the remainder of our voyage very gruesome indeed, as nearly all the crew and half the passengers had friends and relatives on the Titanic. Our room-steward lost his father and two brothers. And it was during this voyage, that we, for the first time, realized fully the wonderful power of poise and self- control possessed by the Englishman. I wrote some verses, entitled "The Englishman," as a result of this experience; and they appeared in an English paper the day we landed. Only on the arrival of the Olympic at the English port was the whole awful truth revealed to us. It was a dramatic hour never to be forgotten.

THE ENGLISHMAN

Bom in the flesh and bred in the bone,
Some of us harbor still A New World pride: and we flaunt or hide

The Spirit of Bunker Hill. We claim our place as a separate race
Or a self-created clan: Till there comes a day, when we like to say
"We are kin of the Englishman."
For under the front that seems so cold
And the voice that is wont to storm, We are certain to find a big broad mind
And a heart that is soft–and warm. He carries his woes in a lordly way.
As only the great souls can: And it makes us glad when in truth we say
"We are kin of the Englishman."
He slams his door in the face of the world.
If he thinks the world too bold: He will even curse: but he opens his purse
To the poor, and the sick and the old. He is slow in giving to woman the vote.
And slow to pick up her fan:
But he GIVES HER ROOM IN THE HOUR OF DOOM
And dies– like an Englishman!

In England I had my attention called to a story by Morgan Robertson, which had been written more than a decade befort the Titanic disaster, and which was being republished because of its peculiar plot. The story was entitled "Futility," and described the building of an enormous ship, the Titan, and of its destruction by an iceberg the second day after being launched. At the time the story was first published no such monster passenger ships were known; but Mr. Robertson's imagination had given a picture of the Olympic and Titanic which was almost photographic in detail, and had called his ship the Titan.

I was curious to know more of the matter; so after my return to America I wrote to Mr. Robertson and received the following reply:

"As to the motif of my story, I merely tried to write a good story with no idea of being a prophet. But, as in other stories of mine, and in the work of other and better writers, coming discoveries and events have been anticipated. I do not doubt that it is because all creative workers get into a hypnoid, telepathic and percipient condition, in which, while apparently awake, they are half asleep, and tap, not only the better informed minds of others but the subliminal realm of unknown facts. Some, as you know, believe that in this realm there is no such thing as Time, and the fact that a long dream can occur in an instant of time gives color to it, and partly explains prophecy."

Interesting as Mr. Robertson's letter may be, it leaves the reader of "Futility," written and first published fourteen years before the Titanic was built and sunk, with a strange and. creepy sensation. In the realm of unknown facts, was it already recorded fourteen years previously that the Titanic should sink?

And how should Mr. Robertson fix on almost the very name which was afterward given to the ill-fated sea monster?

In the year 1917 a similar puzzling and mysterious incident occurred. Miriam French, a beautiful American woman, was on board The City of Athens, sailing from Cape Town, Africa, to America. During her voyage Mrs. French amused herself by writing a story about the ship and imaginary passengers, and ended the tale by having the ship strike a mine and sink into the sea. Two months later The City of Athens met that exact fate. How can the purely material reasoning mind explain such occurrences?

One winter we spent several weeks in Biskra, the "Garden of Allah." Major and Mrs. Thomas, of England, were much in our party, and Mr. Thomas and I grew to be very good friends. Walking about the fascinating desert town one day, we came upon a sand diviner. He claimed, of course, as they all did, to be the sand diviner of Hitchens' famous novel. We had him read our destinies; and I do not now remember what he told me; but he assured Mrs. Thomas she was to receive very sudden news of the sickness of some one at home–an accident, he thought. And he said she would change all her plans of travel and go home. We parted company the next day; but weeks afterward there came a letter from Mrs. Thomas, saying she had received sudden news of an accident which had befallen her son, and they had gone back post-haste to England. How the old Arab with his dish of sand could foresee this is not in my power to explain. All I can do is to state the facts as related above.

My first winter in Jamaica, I had caused myself much suffering, and given annoyance to Robert, and made myself unpopular with the native drivers, by taking note of all the cruelty shown horses and mules in that land. I was constantly reprimanding these drivers, and trying to make them more merciful; and while my husband was full of pity for the animals, he felt I had undertaken a large contract in trying to change their ways during my brief tour. The next winter I decided to go about my humane work more systematically. I told each driver we engaged that I was taking notes on how the drivers treated their animals, and at the end of my stay in Jamaica it was my intention to give a medal and five dollars to the most humane driver. This plan worked very well, and saved many a poor beast needless blows, The medal and prize were bestowed upon Toppins, up at Moneague, on Mt. Diablo, of the Blue Range.

The third winter, we were stopping some weeks at the beautiful Tichfield Hotel, at Port Antonio. My table, where I wrote letters, faced a scene of exquisite beauty; but just beyond the lawns and lovely trees there was a steep road, up which was being hauled by mule teams material for a new bungalow. The drivers were beating these mules one morning unmercifully: and after a half hour I threw down my pen and declared I could endure it no longer.

"Why do you not go out and talk to the drivers?" my husband suggested. "Perhaps if they knew you were the medal and five-dollar-prize lady, they would be more merciful, at least while you stay."

I acted on his suggestion, and sallied forth under my parasol to talk with the darkies. They listened respectfully and then their spokesman answered: "Mistress, yo' don't know the nature of de mule. Yo' can't make a mule go widout beatin him."

"I know better," I replied wrathfuuy. "That is just what the old slave-drivers used to say about your grandfathers."

This remark, I fear, lost its point with my audience. Then I continued: "I have made a very tired and lazy and balky mule start his load by holding an apple in front of his nose. He got the apple and went on briskly. Try it."

The darkey stared at me, and then burst into a loud gufifaw, and said, "Good Lord, Mistress, I hain't had a taste of apple in five years; can't get money enough to buy em for myself, much less for mules." And the drivers went down the hill shouting with laughter at me.

My husband delighted in telling this story all over Jamaica. The apple is, or was at that time, an expensive luxury in Jamaica.

It was an interesting day, the one we spent with Luther Burbank, at his home in Santa Rosa, on our return from the Hawaiian Islands.

Mr. Burbank had arranged his busy life in advance of our coming, so that we could enjoy to the full his hospitality and companionship. It was a few years after the great earthquake, and Santa Rosa, his home town, had suffered greatly during that calamity, which California people all refer to as "The Great Fire," never speaking the word earthquake. I asked Mr. Burbank to tell me his personal experiences, and this was what he related, speaking of it as a curious incident merely; but to me it has ever seemed an evidence of invisible helpers protecting an absolutely unselfish soul.

Mr. Burbank, always an excellent sleeper, never troubled with wakefulness, no matter how great his mental responsibilities, retired at his usual hour the night preceding the earthquake; and found himself unable to close his eyes in slumber. He was not nervous, but simply lay awake until dawn, when he was shaken out of bed by the shock. His house was not badly damaged. His first thought was of his valuable negatives, worth thousands of dollars to science, which were being developed in the photographer's rooms, in the village. He walked down to the village, and saw the large six-story brick building (I think it was that height) in ruins. It required six weeks of daily hauling away of the debris, later, to remove the wreck. Yet when this was done, the photographer came one day to Mr. Burbank in much excitement, to show him a remarkable thing. The entire cases in which the precious nega-i ives of rare plants and bulbs and shoots were placed had remained undisturbed and uninjured. They were wedged in among bricks which served to make a wall about them.

But this was not all. A field which Mr. Burbank had prepared for transplanting his shoots required harrowing. It was a large field and the time and expense would have been considerable. When Mr. Burbank drove out to see its condition, he found it perfectly harrowed and quite ready for his transplanting. The earthquake had at least done one good turn.

These incidents Mr. Burbank regarded as mere accidents. But knowing that when any human being arrives at a state of absolute unselfish consecration of his life to the good of the race, and has no personal ambitions or greedy desires, that he is ever afterward guarded and protected by the Lords of Love, I felt sure the occurrences related were not accidental.

One winter in Cairo I was approached by a very handsome Hindu astrologer, bearing fine credentials, and begging my patronage. He was naturally psychic, he said, besides being a profound student of the old science of astrology, the parent of astronomy. I gave him my patronage and found him quite all that he had claimed to be. So interesting and remarkable was he, that at his request I wrote and signed my approval of him, and recommended him to all who desired an investigation of that phase of occultism. It was five years later that my husband and I reached Port Said in our tour of the world. We had been three weeks on shipboard, and with all the other passengers we hurried down the gangplank and out to the cafe, where we had been told good food could be obtained. We were to be in Port Said only a few hours before starting forth on the Mediterranean Sea for other goals.

No sooner had we set foot on land than a throng of natives (natives of every clime of earth) followed us, importuning us to buy or give or patronize them in some manner. One Arab palmist was particularly persistent. He insisted that he could tell us all that lay in the future, as well as recount all the past held, and he would not be ignored or driven away. He followed us to the cafe, and stood beside us as we ordered, impervious to my husband's frowns.

"You are Americans, I am sure," he said. "I always know Americans. I have read the hand of one of your celebrated Americans–a lady writer, Ella Wheeler Wilcox; she wrote me a letter of recommendation." My husband, for the first time, gave the pest of a man his attention. "Indeed," he said. "Have you met Mrs. Wilcox? Let us see the letter." The man produced a typewritten copy of the letter I had given the Hindu astrologer. The name was changed and palmist was substituted for astrologer.

My husband passed the treasure over to me smilingly. "Have you the original copy?" I asked. "I should like to see her penmanship."

"Oh, I keep that at home," the man replied. "I do not want to wear it out."

"Do you remember how Mrs. Wilcox looked?" I queried. "I have often wanted to know."

"Oh, yes," the man replied glibly. "I met her in Cairo and read her palm there five years ago. She was a very stout old lady with very white hair."

My husband with difficulty restrained his mingled amusement and indignation– his amusement at the expression on my face and his indignation at the man's boldness. He handed back the slip of soiled paper and said, "You are a fraud and a liar; leave here at once; this lady is Ella Wheeler Wilcox, and she is my wife. She never saw you before." I corroborated the statement, asking, "Am I a stout old lady, and have I very white hair?"

"But didn't you have white hair five years ago, and were you"

"I never saw you before in my life," I replied. "And I never want to see you again. Go away and do not dare show that paper to another person."

"Leave instantly," my husband added, "or I will have you arrested." The man vanished, but three different parties of our ship acquaintances told us he had pursued them during the afternoon with the same story and the same soiled slip of paper.

During the next few days I would see my husband chuckling over his cigar, and he would turn to me and ask, "Are you a very stout old lady with very white hair?" And then he would say, "You missed a great deal in not being able to see your own face, Ella, as that man described you."

One time in England my husband and I enjoyed a day of delight by securing seats in the Vanderbilt coach and riding to Brighton and back. Alfred Vanderbilt drove part of the way himself, and others of his friends the remainder of the way.

Naturally, they did not know or care who we were; nor did we want recognition. We were off for our first trip in a coach and four on a beautiful English June day; and a memorably happy time it was. As we rolled along, back of relays of splendid horses, my mind began to fashion a foolish, lilting rhyme which was all ready to be written down when I returned to the Langham Hotel that evening. It ran as follows:

ALL IN A COACH AND FOUR

The quality folk went riding along

All in a Coach and Four–
And pretty Annette, in a calico gown (Bringing her marketing things from town)
Stopped short with her Sunday store. And wondered if ever it would betide That she, in a long-plumed hat, would ride Away in a Coach and Four.

A lord there was–oh a lonely soul,
There in the Coach and Four,
His years were young, but his heart was old
And he hated his coaches and hated his gold, (Those things which we all adore)
And he thought how sweet it would be to trudge
Along with the fair little country drudge
And away from his Coach and Four.

So back he rode the very next day All in his Coach and Four, And he went each day, whether dry or weif. Until he married the sweet Annette (In spite of her lack of lore). But lliey didn't trudge off on foot together For he bought her a hat with a long, long feather And they rode in the Coach and Four.

Now a thing like this could happen we know
All in a Coach and Four,
But the fact of it is, 'twixt me and you.
There isn't a word of this jingle true (Pardon, I do implore); It is only a foolish and fanciful song
That came to me as I rode along
All in a Coach and Four.

While the English people have been most gracious and appreciative in their attitude toward my work, the English highbrow critics (like the American) have had little use for me. The most extraordinary impression has seemed to prevail among them, causing a sort of resentment seemingly, that I am living in the greatest luxury produced by enormous prices paid for poor poems, and endless sales of unworthy books.

A most amusing expression of this idea occurred in a review of one of my books published in England. Referring to my ignoble "wealth" and equally ignoble "popularity," they mentioned my love of flaunting my riches in the eyes of a suffering world, and cited the verses as a proof!

The droll man actually imagined I owned the Coach and Four, never thinking my husband had paid a few shillings for our one and only drive in that kind of vehicle.

Of such brain stuff is fashioned many a critic's mental apparatus!

In my career, I have not often replied to critics. Receiving from the first more appreciation than it seemed to me was my due, I could not complain if criticism, even when not deserved, fell to my lot. Once, when quite young, however, I did reply to a sarcastic critic. A composer of music (a local celebrity) had asked me for some simple "homey verses" to set to music; something pathetic. I wrote a song called "Mother, Bring My Little Kitten."

It was supposed to be a dying child asking for her pet, which she feared she might not meet in heaven. It was mere sentimental stuff, of no value, of course. But the "Funny Man" on the Waukesha Democrat (I think that was the paper) poked much fun at me, and said I ought to follow my song with another, "Daddy, Do Not Drown the Puppies."

I published in one of the Wisconsin papers the following week some verses with the caption suggested, heading them with the Waukesha man's item. The chorus of my verses ran as follows:

Save, oh, save one puppy, daddy,

From a fate so dark and grim– Save the very smallest puppy– Make an editor of him.

They went the rounds of the Western press and caused much amusement. Of all my thousands of verses, I think my brother Ed preferred these. He set them to a tune of his own, and often went about the house singing them. Always when any editor attacked me afterwards, Ed chanted this song.

It was not many years ago when I again replied to a critic. It was a woman critic this time, and she said:

"How may a man be a popular poet and yet save his soul and his art? This is a question which only the select few of any group or period are called upon to answer. Some popular poets, of course, have no souls to save– none at least which emerge above the milk and water current of their verse–the Tuppers and Ella Wheeler Wilcoxes of their generation. Others have no trouble with their souls; they just sing naturally about common sights and sounds, the things all men know or feel or think they know and feel–like Mr. James Whitcomb Riley, Eugene Field, Bret Harte in his brief lyric moods, or, now and then, Joaquin Miller, that high-hearted old democrat who now sleeps in his Sierras."

To which I replied:

"I have just chanced upon your reference to me in your periodical. It gave me a sharp hurt. Skilled criticism is as needed in the world of art as skilled surgery in the world of medicine. But the doctor who thrusts a rusty nail into the flesh of a patient because he chances not to like him is not practicing surgery. You thrust a rusty pen into a poet you chance not to like. That is not criticism. It is spitefulness.

"Poetry to me is a divine thing. I love it with all my heart (yes, even with my soul, which I dare believe is well evolved). There are as many kinds of poetry as there are of intellects in men. I have followed the bent of my own talents since I first thought in verse as a child, and have worked according to my own light. I have never made a bid for popularity. If I chance to be a popular poet it is because I have loved God and life and people, and expressed sentiments and emotions which found echoes in other hearts. If this is a sin against art, let me be unregenerate to the day of my death!

"What have you read of my works? No critic is justified in making such an assertion publicly as yours unless the author has been thoroughly read. Have you read my last collection, Picked Poems, and my recent poems in the Cosmopolitan Magazine and Good Housekeeping f If you have, and call any or all of these milk and water, then there is something the matter with your brain, as well as your heart. If you call my early poems milk and water, then I think you are suffering from arrested emotional development. Something weaker than milk and water must run in your veins in place of blood. That I have written much light verse, which is not poetry (any more than it is doggerel), I know; it is simply popular verse. That I have written many real poems of literary and artistic value, even while of human interest, I also know. There is no more conceit in such knowledge or its avowal than in sajring I know my eyes are brown.

I am as capable of judging the difference between verse and poetry, even when my own, as of knowing the shades of colors, even in my own eyes.

"Hoping you may develop a sense of responsibility which will cause you to study your poets before criticizing them, and that you may grow at least a sage bush of a heart to embellish your desert of intellect, I am.

Sincerely yours."

To which the critic replied:

"Dear Madam: Pardon this delay in answering your letter of September 8th, which was mislaid.

"I can only say that, while I have not read all your poems I have rarely been able to admire those I have read. They seem to be of a kind which lovers of the art must resent; in fact, I have thought of you as so eager for popularity and its rewards as to work solely toward that end.

"We all have our standards, and if your verse is not according to ours, yet it has such a vogue as not to be quite negligible–whence my remark in our May number, which was intended, of course, not for you personally, but for you as an artist. If your feelings were hurt, I am sorry, but the integrity of the art is more important than anybody's feelings. I am. Yours very sincerely."

And to which I again replied:

"The fact that you have read a few of my verses and have not liked them, as you say, is not an excuse for you in the capacity of a critic to speak publicly of my work in your magazine as you did. No critic has a right to make such assertions without having read all a poet's work. Your assumption that lovers of the art resent my kind of work is only true when these lovers chance to be of your special make of mind. There are other kinds! Not knowing me in the least, you have no right to think of me, as you say you have, eager for popularity and its benefits and working solely for those ends. This should not be the reputation of a worthy critic. Something is expected of the critic in the way of noblesse oblige as well as of the poet. Criticism should be big, broad, fearless and kind; just as the surgeon is kind to the patient, although obliged to wound. If you had taken poems of mine (my Sonnets of Abelard and Heloise, for instance, which are regarded as my most ambitious work in a literary way) and then dissected them according to your standards, that would be criticism, even though it might not be universally convincing. What you did was not criticism. Except that I adore cats, I would call it cattish. You lowered your standard as a self-made critic by giving me a nasty stab, without cause or sense. It cannot harm me, because my gifts are too well known, my work too well appreciated, and my own reverence and love for my growing poetical powers too great to be affected by such a stab; but it does harm to you as a critic; and both these letters are written to you with the hope of giving you higher ideals of criticism rather than of in any way changing your point of view toward myself. That does not matter; it is as if I had dropped a wisp of dried grass out of a big glorious bouquet; but it matters much to you to be decent and dignified in your magazine, if you wish to prove your devotion to the integrity of your art.

"America has many poets who are giving the world specimens of real poetry. It has few critics who are giving real

CRITICISM.

"Try to do as earnest a work for your chosen art as I am trying to do for mine, and then we may meet on even ground. But at present you are not even trying to do anything but indulge in personal prejudice. This puts you at a disadvantage, and gives me the position of the true critic with a purpose. For that purpose I am,

Sincerely yours, "Ella Wheeler Wilcox."

CHAPTER XVI The Battlefield of Love

THE world's great battlefields are always shrines for the tourists. Waterloo is yearly visited by thousands of travelers, and pilgrimages are continually made in our own land to Bunker Hill, Yorktown and Gettysburg.

When I went to France it was my desire to visit another great battlefield, a field where waged a strife that has resounded through centuries– that remarkable strife between religion and human passion, in the hearts of Abelard and Heloise.

Guide books point only to the tomb at Pere Lachaise as all that survives of philosopher and pupil, lover and maid, husband and wife, monk and nun; but it was my good fortune to learn more of the lives of this ill-fated pair than the translated volumes of their letters relate; and to see more of the places and objects associated with their names than the tomb at Pere Lachaise.

Guided through the mazes of the cemetery to the tomb of the immortal lovers, by Mr. Charles Moonen, whose card and conversation proclaimed him "homme des lettres," while he acted as professional guide, I learned an interesting fact.

"At Argenteuil," said Mr. Moonen, "you will find the old convent still standing, though no longer a convent, where Heloise received her first communion, and to which she returned afterward to take the vows for life."

So to Argenteuil the next day was the pilgrimage made; at first to meet with many discouragements and baffling contradictions from residents of that ancient and historic environ of Paris, for Heloise lived long ago–and while the poets, and the savants, and the bookworms, and the dreamers of Argen- teuil may all know her domicile, it was not my good fortune to meet any of them that first hour.

Argenteuil, in truth, is more famed for its excellent asparagus than for its lovers of romantic history. But, at last, a gentle-faced nun, telling her beads as she walked before a church door, directed me aright. "It is number 70, Boulevard Heloise, madame, and a private residence," she said. "Here in this church you will find some of the sacred relics taken from the convent when Heloise and her sisters in Christ were forced to leave and go to the Paraclet. You must come and see them another day; we have service now, and they could not be shown."

Driving along the boulevard in the glorious sunshine, the story of Heloise came back to me, in all its force; that old story of mad love, sad suffering, and life-long sorrow.

Heloise had been sent to the convent of Argenteuil for the rudiments of her education by her uncle, the Canon Fulbert. She had returned to his home (now No. 11 Quai aux Fleurs–where an inscription over the door commemorates the fact), a brilliant, beautiful young creature, who was famed for her intellect and learning, while still in the first flush of girlhood. Canon Fulbert was proud of her attainments; and prouder still when she expressed a wish to study the philosophy of the great Abelard, then in the height of his fame, and chief of the school of Paris, the nucleus of what is known

to-day as the great Sorbonne. Abelard was thirty-seven, Heloise a little more than
half that age, perhaps; and one does not need even to recall the fact that the eleventh
century was an era of licentiousness, to understand how Abelard, in his intimate
association with his beautiful pupil, stood in danger of falling from his pinnacle of
religious power. The Canon Fulbert, believing in the prudence and wisdom of his
niece (as men believe only and always in their own), and having faith in the sincerity
of Abelard's ideals, permitted the philosopher to become a member of his household
in order to give Heloise the full benefit of his instruction.

Not only was Abelard given the privilege of teaching the beautiful girl, but he was
authorized to chastise her if she became indifferent or negligent. In his letter to a
friend long afterward Abelard wrote:

"We were under one roof, and we became one heart. Under the pretext of study we
gave ourselves utterly to love. We opened our books, but there were more kisses than
explanations, and our eyes sought each other rather than the texts. Yet, sometimes, to
still further deceive the uncle, I chastised Heloise as a bad pupil, but the blows were
those of love, not of anger. As I grew more and more drunken with passion, I cared
less and less for my school and my studies. It was a violent effort for me to go about
my duties. I lost all inspiration. I could only speak to my students from memory,
repeating old lessons, and when I undertook to write I produced only love verses."

To-day when a priest or a monk becomes obsessed with a woman's charms he
marries her, and is excommunicated from the church, and after a little time ceases to
be remembered by the public. The world has grown too busy and huraanily too broad
to persecute the backslider.

Father Hyacinth was but a passing figure in the court of Church vs. Cupid. But
in 1119 such was the state of public sentiment that the incontinence of a great church
dignitary might easily be condoned, if it was not bruited abroad; but his marriage was
looked upon in the light of an everlasting disgrace, and an unpardonable sin. One
familiar with the history of that period realizes the truth of this statement.

So Heloise regarded it, and so vast and overwhelming was her devotion to Abelard
that she violently opposed any suggestion of a marriage, even after her flight to
Brittany, where at the home of Abelard's sister she gave birth to a son, Astrolabius.
She replied thus to Abelard when he came to inform her that he had promised her
uncle to make her his wife. "It is a dishonor for you to marry; think of the prejudice
you will arouse in the church—what tears you will cost philosophy. How deplorable to
see a man, created for the whole world, serving one woman."

Then this remarkable young woman quoted her lover all the passages prejudicial
to marriage in the Bible and other books, and cited the words of Cicero, who declared
that he could not "at one time attend to a woman and philosophy."

"Think of the discomfort and annoyance of having a nurse and a child in the house
when you are meditating on philosophy; and, when you are inspired to write, the
interruptions of domestic life will destroy your work. Let us remain as we are—
lovers," she said. "The world will forgive our love, but it would never forgive our
marriage. It would understand how I led you to forget your vows of continence, but
would not pardon me for letting you break your vow of celibacy."

Nevertheless, Abelard, held by his promise to Fulbert, made Heloise his wife. She returned to Paris with her uncle after the ceremony, and Fulbert, despite his promise of keeping the marriage secret, announced it to the world. Heloise promptly denied it, knowing that public sentiment would condemn the legal part of his dereliction, while it would condone his amatory sin. So enraged was the uncle by her denials that he subjected the poor girl to the greatest abuses. Abelard, informed of the situation, sent Heloise to the convent of Ar-genteuil, and there she donned the robe of the sisters, with the exception of the veil, and lived ostensibly the religious life of the holy sisters.

But the letters of Abelard–the unexpurgated editions–tell us that the love life of the pair was not interrupted by the convent or the robe. There was a secret passage to the convent, and through this passage Abelard was admitted to his wife. Sixteen years afterward he writes–in answer to her complaint of all they had been forced to suffer: "Do we not deserve our suffering? Did I not secretly visit you at Argenteuil after our marriage? Even in the refectory, sacred to the Holy Virgin, did I not so far forget God as to clasp you unresisting in my arms? That profanation alone merited all we have since endured."

But the love life of Abelard and Heloise at Argenteuil was of brief duration. Secret as they believed their meetings, the story reached the ears of Canon Fulbert, and roused him to fury; robbed of his niece, who in turn was robbed of her good name by Abelard, Canon Fulbert planned a horrible revenge.

Then followed the terrible tragedy, its parallel unknown in all the annals of history. The Canon Fulbert, with his confederates, inflicted incredible mutilations upon Abelard–injuries worse than death; and shortly afterward Abelard entered the monastery of St. Denis, and Heloise, at his wish, took the veil for life in the convent of Argenteuil.

And now here was I approaching that very convent, no longer a. convent but an ordinary Parisian house set back in a court, and bearing the placard, "A Louer." A pretty concierge walked in the garden, and when I explained my errand, her face lighted with sympathy, and taking down a bunch of keys from a nail on the inner wall, she unlocked the door of a room opening upon a small enclosed garden. "This," she said, "was the sleeping-room of Heloise. Her bed stood in that alcove. By the window was once a door which led to the confessional, and outside was her garden where she walked." It was overwhelming– the thought of it all. Here Heloise had first studied, a happy, brilliant, care-free girl. Here she had returned after her marriage to escape the cruelty of her uncle, and here had she taken her vows for life in the bloom of her youth, saying as she accepted the veil which shut her in forever from the world, "Criminal that I was, to bring such misfortune on thee: receive now my expiation, in this chastisement which I must forever bear." Even in that solemn hour it was her devotion to Abelard, not to Heaven, which engaged her thought. It was many years before her heart was given to God.

Later I visited the convent again with a photographer, and was shown, by Mr. Jules Provin, its owner, the subterranean passage through which Abelard used to make his secret entrance, and the old worn stone staircase which his impatient feet trod. This passage, now partly walled up, to form a cellar, used to extend through to the Seine, which is only a ghort disteupce from the Qonv nt. Mr. Provin agsured me tha. t

Abelard made his entrance by boat, and showed me in the roof of the cellar a hook, which had probably served as an anchorage for tying the bark of Cupid.

Mr. Provin did not seem to realize the fortune lying unused in his grasp. He desired to rent his property–for something less than four hundred dollars a year, but could not believe that by making its history knpwn and turning it into a goal for tourists, charging a franc entrance fee, he would soon be independent for life.

Argenteuil is only twenty minutes from Paris, and thousands of tourists would gladly journey thither and pay their franc, did the guide-books direct them to the old convent, where began that long martyrdom of Heloise, that terrible life of solitude and suffering for which she was so unfitted; that crucifixion of the passionate woman on the altar of the (for many years) indifferent recluse.

Sixteen years afterward she wrote to Abelard, "I took the veil to obey you–not to please God."

It was not from this convent that the immortal letters of Heloise were written. Just how long she remained at Argenteuil is not clearly defined.

One historian tells us that the convent brought great scandal upon itself by the mis-conduct of some of its inmates, and that all were driven forth one night by an infuriated abbot. This might be the truth–for there is nothing more contagious than passion–and the example of Abelard and Heloise was more conducive to the propagation of human love than religious fervor, and the age was one of license.

Abelard himself speaks of Abbot Suger, the abbot of St. Denis, as responsible for the violent expulsion of the nuns with Heloise as their superior, and claims that it was wholly a matter relating to the rights of a property-holder, who unduly put in force the law of eviction. At all events, Heloise and her sisters were subjected to great poverty and hardship for some time after the eviction–until Abelard came to the rescue and settled them in the Paraclet, at Nogent-sur-Seine, where Heloise lived as Mother Abbess until her death in 1164.

It wag from the Paraclet the famous letters of Heloise were written. There Abelard's body was brought after his death at the Priory of St. Marcel in 1142, and there Heloise was buried beside him twenty-two years later. No stone remains of the Paraclet; it was destroyed in 1800, and the tomb and its contents conveyed to Pere Lachaise.

It is believed that Abelard and Heloise never met after she took the veil, save during the public ceremonies attending the dedication of the Paraclet to her service.

Any other impression falls to the ground as improbable, after perusing the letters of Heloise written long years after she became a nun–letters which are reproaches for his absence and silence, during all these years–and wild petitions for his favor and affection; letters filled with burning memories of a love that would not die–and with passionate pleas for some word of recognition from the man for whom she had sacrificed honor, name, liberty and the world, in the morning of life.

Abelard traveled and gave discourses at various periods after he took the monastic vows.

Heloise wrote a book of rules for the women of the convents which was blessed by the court of Rome, and entered into the constitution of all the monasteries of the time. She was famed for her erudition and her wisdom during her era. But it is by her letters to Abelard that she is remembered, because those letters reveal the heart of a woman endowed with the rare quality of loving with absolute abandon, unselfishness and loyalty, and of consecrating her life to the memory of that love.

It proves how much greater is a lover than a philosopher, when we realize what a renowned man was Abelard in his day, yet how utterly he is forgotten save as the lover of Heloise. He was the first orator, the first philosopher, the first poet, and one of the first musicians of the twelfth century. He was so broad and so brilliant and so courageous in his ideas that he brought a revolution into the religious world and antagonized the entire tradition-bound clergy. He was persecuted in consequence, but his name grew in glory, and his school of philosophy, the first to teach the liberty of human thought, could not accommodate his vast audience, and he was obliged to address them in the open air.

It is no wonder that this man seemed to Heloise, then seventeen years of age, a veritable god, or that she forgot the world in his love. And so great was that love, that it alone, of all Abelard's glory, is remembered to-day.

Philosophies change: religions alter: creeds die: the minds of men are revolutionized on these subjects, but love lives on, and passion endures–the same yesterday, to-day, and forever in the human heart. Only he who loves is immortal.

While history gives us almost detailed accounts of the lives of Abelard and Heloise, the utmost mystery and silence enshroud the child of this remarkable pair. We know that he was born in Brittany, at the home of Abelard's sister, whither Heloise fled with her lover after her approaching maternity was known to her uncle. From that hour we have no data concerning the child until twenty years afterward, when Heloise writes to the Abbot of Cluny, "For the love of God and me, remember my son Astrolabius; if you can, procure him a living, from the Bishop of Rome, or some other prelate." The Abbot answered: "For Astrolabius, whom I adopt because he is your son, be assured as soon as it is in my power I will do all I can to place him in some great church. For your sake my best endeavors will be exerted." Then a complete veil of oblivion drops over the fate of Astrolabius.

ASTROLABIUS (The child of Abelard and Heloise.)

Wrenched from a passing comet in its flight. By that great force of two mad hearts aflame, A soul incarnate, back to earth you came. To glow like star-dust for a little night. Deep shadows hide you wholly from our sight; The centuries leave nothing but your name. Tinged with the luster of a splendid shiune, That blazed oblivion with rebellious light.

The mighty passion that became your cause, Still burns its lengthening path across the years; We feel its raptures, and we see its tears And ponder on its retributive laws. Time keeps that deathless story ever new; Yet finds no answer, when we ask of you.

At Argenteuil I saw the lonely cell
Where Heloise dreamed through her broken rest.
That baby lips pulled at her undried breast.
It needed but my woman's heart to tell
Of those lonely vigils and the tears that fell
When aching arms reached out in fruitless quest.
As, after flight, wings brood an empty nest.
(So well I know that sorrow, ah, so well.)

Across the centuries there comes no sound Of that vast anguish; not one sigh or word Or echo of the mother loss has stirred The sea of silence, lasting and profound. Yet to each heart, that once has felt this grief, Sad Memory restores Time's missing leaf.

Ill

But what of you? Who took the mother's place When sweet expanding love its object sought? Was there a voice to tell her tragic lot. And did you ever look upon her face? Was yours a cloistered seeking after grace? Or in the flame of adolescent thought Were Abelard's departed passions caught To burn again in you and leave their trace?

Conceived in nature's bold, primordial way (As in their revolutions, suns create). You came to earth, a soul immaculate,. Baptized in fire, with some great part to play. What was that part, and wherefore hid from us. Immortal mystery, Astrolabius?

The Greeks endeavored to defy the sexual impulse. The Christians have tried to crucify it. Ancient civilization gave it full license; modern civilizations have attempted to regulate it by law and to protect it by hygiene, and still the problem of the social evil remains unsolved. Still in every land the scarlet woman walks abroad, whether by the consent or in defiance of the law; and still, despite all painstaking measures of prevention, the dreadful disease approaches closer and closer to the human family.

By their religious rites and their art the Greeks seemed to regard sexual pleasure as the one object of life. In revolt against their excesses the early Christian Fathers strove to surround the procreative act with shame and ignominy. Woman, who had been raised to the pinnacle as a goddess of physical delight by the Greeks and Romans and worshiped for her carnal attributes, was cast into the dust by the fanatical Christian Fathers, and regarded as Satan's emissary of evil. Great as was the woman's degradation in the temples of Aphrodite, where she dedicated herself to sensual rites, still greater was the degradation into which she was flung by morbid Christian minds for centuries. The allegorical tale of Adam's fall was literally accepted; and the odium rested on woman.

Into this reservoir of history time poured its diluting waters; yet from the sediment of that old source filtered down to our Puritan ancestors those mistaken ideas of modesty which caused them to cover the whole subject of sex with a mantle of silence, to stamp the poor coin of ignorance with the insignia of innocence. Even to this day, in most localities in America, it is considered indecent to refer to an approaching birth save in a whisper, and where the young cannot overhear.

The outcome of this system of education, and its attendant rigorous laws, is one which must cause the old gods of Olympus to shake their sides in mirth. And with their laughter must mingle the chuckles of the imps in Hades, as they listen to the statistics of the committee investigating White Slave conditions in America and as they look over the reports of health commissioners, and learn the awful facts of the spread of diseases too long regarded as "unmentionable."

America has endeavored to make the ancient social evil a crime, and to eradicate it by punishment. The Old World has held it to be a necessary evil, discussed it as formally as the tariff, and regulated it by law and hygiene. Yet its problems remain unsolved.

America has seen graft, robbery, black-mail, perjury and murder follow in the wake of its secret sin; and it has come to the consciousness that silence can no longer be maintained regarding an evil which is sapping our national vitality, despoiling our womanhood and subjecting our country to the ridicule of the world.

BUT WHAT ARE WE GOING TO DO ABOUT IT?

France has long had its careful laws providing for the health and convenience of its devotees of Eros, yet can its men proclaim themselves free from acquired or inherited taint, and does the alarming sterility of its wives, as shown in recent birth statistics, speak of normal and robust womanhood?

Two thousand years ago Carthage and Tunis, then among the great cities of the world, governed by pagan ideals, recognized the hetserse as an important part of the population. To-day Carthage is no more; but Tunis, with its two hundred thousand souls, devotes a certain portion of its streets to its licensed courtesans. The old slave market remains intact even to the rings in the walls, where less than seventy-five years ago slaves were exposed for sale and the young and handsome women were offered to the purveyors for harems of opulent citizens.

Now the old slave market is used as an auction place for jewelry, and on special days one may see how little the moral sense of Tunis has changed with the change of laws. Here gather on auction days the modestly shrouded and carefully veiled slaves of the passions of men, their faces hidden save for the eyes, which invite bids for their favors, and wearing on the right hand the symbol of their calling.

Here, too, may be found the Arab of all types and tribes and classes–the rich, the poor; the Bedouin, the Kabyl; each wearing the same impenetrable mask of indifference which hides the Oriental mind so wholly from the most curious eyes, and each with a flower in front of his ear. They show not the least interest in these modestly attired white bundles of sensuality, yet low words are exchanged, prices fixed, dates made, nevertheless. And the white bundles roll away, with the promise of the possession of a new necklace or anklet or brow decoration. The Arab to-day finds a large harem expensive to maintain, but by inheritance, religious training and custom he considers many women necessary to his physical needs. Hence his presence in the old slave market with the flower in front of his ear.

America is horrified with the knowledge of secret organizations of depraved men and women who procure girls and women for immoral houses. It is horrified to know that its trusted guardians of the nation's morals are in collaboration with these procurers. Are the methods followed by all northern Africa, under the protection of France, better in these matters than our own? No two systems could be more diametrically opposed than these two.

In America the fallen woman screens herself from public suspicion by every possible artifice; she goes about her nefarious business with secrecy, and when the law discovers her she is driven from pillar to post like a mad dog in the streets. The emissaries of the law are her natural enemies, and by them she is either punished or blackmailed.

In the office of the Commissioner of Registration in Tunis I was shown wall cabinets filled with neat cards, each bearing a number and a name and a small portrait. When a French girl wishes to pursue the oldest profession known to woman, she calls on the Commissioner, fills out one of these cards, affixes her photograph and promises to pay two francs fifty a week into the city coffer, and to place herself in the care of the physician who has this department in charge.

Thenceforth she is quite free from any molestation from the authorities. For some reason (probably because few of them can write their names) the Arab Phrynes are not asked to make out a card; all are numbered alphabetically, and each one is obliged to pay the same weekly toll and to pass the same weekly medical examination. Also each is expected to follow the custom of centuries among Arab women of her class, and wear a colored handkerchief wrapped about her right hand when she goes upon the street; for that Is the insignia of the Arab courtesan's calling.

Invited by Dr. Gertrude Gordan, the remarkable young Russian woman who has charge of the Asodiki Hospital in Tunis, I went to the clinic with her one morning when she was to give out the certificates of health to her fragile Oriental sisters. "There are nearly three hundred under my care, and there will be ninety this morning waiting for me," Dr. Gordan said; "and you may find it interesting to study them at close range. I have had charge of this work fourteen years, and I can give you much information regarding the subject."

When I entered the long anteroom of the clinic, it seemed to me I must be looking on the participants in a Mardi Gras fete instead of a company of fallen women awaiting a medical verdict.

Ninety women, ranging from the age of sixteen to sixty, and all costumed either picturesquely or fantastically, sat about the long corridor, which suggested the harem of some mighty ruler in the era of the "Arabian Nights" tales rather than a modern hospital. All were unveiled, and every type of Oriental beauty and ugliness was represented. All were powdered and painted, with kohl-tinted eyes and henna-stained finger tips, and nearly all were profusely decorated with tattooed emblems on cheek and brow and chin.

As her number was called, each passed into the consulting-room, and quickly emerged, to proceed smiling and satisfied to the courtyard below, where she would be given her certificate of good health, which permitted her to proceed with her "business" unmolested for another week. On that morning, out of the ninety, only three unfortunates were pronounced tainted, and those three were immediately placed in the care of an officer, and conveyed to the department of the hospital where venereal diseases were treated. For, despite all precautions, these diseases are widespread here as in our own un-protecting land.

Down in the courtyard, after the examinations had been finished, Dr. Gordan led me where the scene defied description. A boarding-school of gay young girls on a fete day never exhibited more joy of life than these Arabian courtesans in the Moorish courtyard of Tunis, happy in the consciousness that they could go forth and sell themselves for a few francs to the first bidder. They sat in clusters on the tiled floor, adjusting their voluminous draperies, arranging their bracelets or anklets, chatting together in the peculiar guttural tones of the native tongue, while they waited their turn to pass into the office and deposit the weekly tax.

Among the ninety, there were four distinctly beautiful faces–such faces as one associates with "A Thousand and One Nights." Perhaps twenty-five were strikingly good looking, and the remainder passed down the line from indifferent to plain and positively ugly.

A number were well past the middle-age mark, and all types were represented: Moors, Algerians, Tunisians, Ouled Nails, Jewesses, and strange-looking barbaric women from the interior with ugly wigs of some coarse fiber drawn low over the forehead, and their necks and breasts covered with innumerable necklaces and odd jewels–every jewel, necklace and anklet testifying to the wearer's success in her career, and worn as proudly as the scarred warrior wears his medals gained in battle. Dr. Gordan named the different tribes and types as they passed along or as they came to speak to her, asking questions or favors. All were evidently fond of the gentle physician, and many of them had been under her care for years.

One girl, of perhaps twenty, showed me her multiplicity of tattoo decorations with great pride– two large chanticleers between the knee and hip, and flowers and mottoes on her breasts and arms, besides various "works of art" on her face.

"Children are not often born to these women," the doctor said, "but when they are it is not difficult to find people who will adopt a child before its birth. Since slavery was done away with, the poor people and these women often sell unborn children to those who rear them for servants or who prepare the girls to be dancers. Among the Arabs, that monotonously licentious dance which is the unchanging diversion of all Arabs, as unalterable and unvaried as the burnous and the gandourah and foutah of their costumes, is taught to little girls of tender years."

Five new faces among her patients caused Dr. Gordan to ask many questions. Before she began this questioning she said to me: "You will find every woman a divorced wife, and when I ask why she chose this immoral career as a profession, each one will answer, It is written, for they are all fatalists." And in fact each of the five responded in those exact words, and each was a wife rejected by her husband.

It seems there is a strict law of the Koran that no Arabic damsel shall live an immoral life. Arabian girls are married so young, and kept in such seclusion previously, that one seldom goes astray; but should such a calamity occur, there is immediate scurrying to find a man who will marry her one day and divorce her the next, whereupon she is allowed to enlist herself among the hetserae. It costs but a few francs to obtain a divorce in Tunis, and most men are willing to pay the price to preserve the sacred commandments of the Koran. Dr. Gordan apologized for the women, even while saying that they are indolent and without moral nature.

"Divorce is so easily obtained here," she said, "and the Arab men are so fickle, and so easily alienated, that if a mother or a sister or other relative quarrels with a wife, or if the wife has no child or only girls, or if the man wants a new wife and cannot afford to keep the old one, he sends her home with all the jewelry he gave her at the wedding. Then what is she to do for a livelihood? She has been reared to believe that there is no work respectable for a woman save to cater to the tastes or passions or pleasures of men. If she cannot do this as a wife, she sees no other way save to go into the world-old profession. She has small ideas of herself spiritually, and so she has no scruples of conscience to combat."

The most beautiful member of the fallen ninety was a newcomer, and had been only one week in her profession. Her husband had divorced her because she bore him a girl child, and she had gone home to her mother, a poor woman. Yes, she had tried to sew, but the prices were so poor and the work so hard she had found it impossible to make a Hving for herself and child. So here she was, quite content with her situation, for "It is written: cest le destin."

Afterward I went into the streets where these women live, and photographed a few of them. The beautiful debutante recognized me, and welcomed me like a friend. She asked us into her suite of two rooms opening off the narrow street, and showed us her wheezy little melodeon, her big unsanitary bed, her two tiny puppy comrades–all with an air of pride. Her patron or manager (a semi-retired professional herself) was most gracious also, and seemed delighted when we posed the "star boarder" for a picture, as did our guide, who, uninvited, placed herself well in the foreground.

Not one of these women by look or manner showed that she regarded herself as unfortunate or her profession as shameful.

When these women go upon the streets they are always veiled to the eyes, because that is the law of the Koran, and because they know all Arab men despise a woman with an unveiled face; but they are easily to be distinguished rom the few respectable old women or servants who walk abroad by their bright foutahs and hose and fanciful shoes showing under the mountain of white haik, and, too, by the colored handkerchief wrapped about the right hand.

As Dr. Gordan and I walked away from the clinic, the streets were lined with Arab men of all ages and classes, the very- young and the old predominating, and many splendid in brilliant mantles and turbans and with a flower in the front of the ear–patrons and lovers, waiting for the big white bundles of licensed sin marked "Sanitary." Surely French law makes all things pleasant and convenient for social sinners.

In Algiers we visited the streets of the women one Sunday morning. It was the finishing touch to an appalling picture of free licensed vice, so awful in its naked boldness and false gayety and lack of shame that it sent us away sick and melancholy. Since converted thought is a mighty dynamic power, what terrible vibrations must go up from those congested centers of sin! Off from narrow untidy streets opened innumerable little rooms, often beautiful with mosaic work and lovely tiling; and from the doors leaned flower-wreathed faces and artistically clad houris, smiling and bargaining with whomsoever might pause at the threshold. Next door and across the street were dance-halls, where fife and drum were making unmusical clamor, and in one a girl as beautiful as an artist's dream was rotating her abdomen in the national dance. A little French girl, seemingly no more than twelve, was making bold overtures to Arabs in burnouses and French soldiers in uniform.

In Algiers there is less orthodoxy than in Tunis, and the laws of the Koran which make it a sin for a Mussulman or woman to affiliate amorously with a Christian are not observed, as in the White City set among the lakes.

All was laughter, brilliant coloring, picturesque costuming, flower-wreathed faces, and unabashed sensuality. At the corner of a street where the revel was at its height sat a noseless woman begging. She was scarcely thirty, and not so long ago had been one of the popular favorites of these quarters. She had paid her penalty by the frightful scars of ravaging disease. Yet the hundreds of licensed courtesans and their innumerable patrons passed her by, giving, seemingly, no heed to the awful warning sight. In her mind was there regret or remorse? Probably not; for doubtless she, too, believes "It was written."

Some of these courtesans, a small minority, having accumulated jewels and money, return to their native towns in the interior and marry. Not often does this happen, but it does happen. Just as among European races are men to be found who are glad to marry tainted money, however malodorous it may be, Arab men are to be found who will take the money and jewels of the Ouled Nail, even though he be to some measure declassed by his tribe afterward.

From the Ouled Nail tribe a large harvest of courtesans is gathered, for the fathers not infrequently bring their daughters to town for this purpose, and regard the profession as quite legitimate. I talked with one of these girls at Biskra and she said her parents were satisfied with her career and she herself was content. She had been two years in the life, and should perhaps stay another two. And when she had money enough she would go home. I asked her if she had no fear of undesired maternity.

"Oh, no," she said piously, lifting her eyes; "the good God protects me."

The week before we left Tunis a theatrical manager took two of those street girls and put them into training for leading roles in a play about to be produced in the Arab theater. Their astonishing aptitude and quickness of perception caused him to predict a great success for them. So might thousands of them find successful careers in decent, self-supporting professions were it possible to shatter the prison walls of tradition about them. But the Arab man has lost his prowess in the great world of affairs, and has found himself unable to cope with modern progress. He has just one domain of power left–his control of the women of his race. It will need a cataclysm and a new incarnation to make him relinquish this domain.

France has established schools all over Algeria and Tunis. Little girls attend until they reach the veiling age; then they remain in the harem and use their manual training knowledge only in the home, and quickly forget their knowledge of any language but Arabic, for the men are opposed to their being able to converse with foreigners. Here and there in large cities where modern life has sounded loud alarm a man may be found who has broken away from old traditions.

At the Excelsior Hotel, Algiers, we saw for the first time in a somewhat extended experience a man and woman in Arabian dress dining together at a table, and even entertaining a European man guest. The Oriental host was a Kabyl member of Parliament, but the Kabyles are as a rule opposed to having the women educated. A school we visited in the Kabyl Mountains contained 300 boys and not one girl. A merchant replied to our queries on the subject that it made women discontented and restless to be educated, and therefore it seemed wiser to keep them at home, ignorant and content. It is the law of the Koran, and not until a new master arises who can appeal more strongly to the Mussulman than Mohammed appealed can we hope for much change to come to the Arab woman's life. She herself is not desirous of a change; but that does not mean that it should not come.

In another Kabyl village we came upon a dancing school where three little girls, the youngest scarcely four, were being taught the Dance du Ventre. Already the little tots were expert in the indecent contortions of that sex dance, created thousands of years ago to stir the sated passions of old mon-archs, and to amuse dull women in crowded harems. Later on these little girls may be dancing in music halls, on tiled floors, in Moorish rooms opening off narrow untidy Streets-of-the-Women in Tunis or Algiers or Biskra; for what is there for them to do with their lives if the men they wed do not keep and protect them?

It is the same old industrial problem. And just what have our modern industrial system and our Christianity to offer in exchange for these fearful scenes of open vice and licensed sin? Between Algiers and Tunis and Biskra, on one side, and London and New York on the other, what is there to choose?

As a Theosophist, believing we are all making a spiral circle of lives toward perfection, I would unhesitatingly choose our own deplorable situation in America. However our civilization has failed in stemming the current of the social evil, it has at least produced a finer ideal of clean womanhood and manhood than was evolved by any older civilization. Ancient Greece established schools for courtesans where seduction was taught as an art, and modern Tunis has only cheapened the same process under French law. The demi mondaine of France dominates most of the theaters and restaurants of Paris and sets the fashions for the world.

If our America is quite as depraved as any and all of these lands, it has at least not lost all shame, and where there is shame for having failed to live up to an ideal there is still hope of ultimate growth. It is only when placid acceptance of evil exists or the bold exploitation of unwholesome conditions prevails that a land or a race is facing destruction.

Such destruction came to Sodom and Gomorrah, to Babylon, Nineveh, Carthage and old Rome, because they had lost all shame. But while there is shame there is an ideal, and where there is an ideal there is hope. Paganism, Mohammedanism, and Christianity have all failed to "bring a clean thing out of an unclean."

But science, under the name of eugenics, has laid the foundation for a new race, which will in time inhabit our earth. Men are being taught the inevitable results of sex excesses, and the plain physical facts, supported by statistics and made as familiar to the young as simple fractions will do more to eradicate the social sin from the world, in generations to come, than all the religions and all the laws have done in the past.

CHAPTER XVII

High Lights on Places and Personalities Seen in Travel

CASTING a retrospective glance over the years of travel in which we encompassed the earth almost twice, there are certain points which stand forth clearly, as mountain peaks shine in the distance when we look back from the deck of an outgoing ship, at a land we have left behind.

In all the beauty and art and fascination of Japan, which held us in thrall for many weeks, the high light falls upon a sad sight–the women of the Yoshiwara district.

There are five hundred and twenty-nine Protestant and many Roman Catholic churches in Japan: and in Tokio alone, the capital city of two million inhabitants, there are over 3,000 Buddhist and Shinto temples of worship. Yet despite all this religious paraphernalia Japan has some difficult problems unsolved regarding the conditions of her women.

There are good women, happy and well-cared-f or women in Tokio. There are culture and progress to be met with everywhere in the daily walks of life, and the women encountered casually and studied superficially seem happier and more content than the women judged in the same casual manner in European or American capital cities.

The streets of Tokio are orderly and quiet at night. Vice does not flaunt itself wantonly in the face of the belated pedestrian along the general thoroughfares, as in London or Paris, or any large American city.

But there are 2,000 women who live in what is known as Yoshiwara district who are moral outcasts. They are under police and medical supervision, and their profession is as old as the world. They are all young; and their ranks are continually supplied by new recruits, when death sickness, marriage or reformation causes a vacancy to occur in the army of two thousand.

The Yoshiwara girls have no disguise or pretense of any secondary occupation like the Geisha girls who are taught to sing and dance and amuse patrons of tea houses and other resorts.

The Yoshiwaras are seldom seen during the day; they never leave their precinct save with police permission and supervision. But as soon as the evening comes, with its artificial lights, they appear in their gilded cages like birds of gay plumage, and await their patrons.

The houses in which these 2,000 "white slaves" live are veritable cages, with gilt bars in front, facing closely on the narrow streets. In the back, and above, are small private rooms. Each cage contains perhaps a score of girls, nearly all pretty, all appearing young and gay and smiling while coquetting with passers by.

At the side of each cage, with his vile face thrust through a window, sits one who calls himself a man–a male creature who in American Coney Island parlance would be called a "barker," and who "employs" the occupants of his special cage, and receives a commission for their services.

Probably nowhere else in the entire world has the segregation of women of immoral lives been systematized in such a manner as this, and while it may, and unquestionably does, protect the city in general from promiscuous vice, yet it is an appalling sight to see 2,000 young girls dedicated to such a life; and scarcely less appalling to think of the despicable class of men created and sustained by this condition of things.

It is stated that the Yoshiwaras' ranks are mainly supplied by parents of extreme poverty who induce their daughters to enter this life rather than face the desperate outlook of the poor in Japan.

It may be urged that there is always honest work to be found by women in any part of the world. But here is what Dr. Kuwada, a philanthropist in Japan, has to say on the subject of working girls in his land.

Dr. Kuwada, a Member of the House of Peers, has given deeply sympathetic attention to the labor question in this country, and has also spent several years in Europe, studying its social problems. Discussing in the Shin Koran, a Tokio monthly, the condition of the female laborers in Japan, he says:

"There are in Japan about ten thousand factories and workshops, employing about a million laborers. Of this total about seven hundred thousand are females. As there is no law limiting the age of factory hands, almost ten per cent of the female laborers are under fourteen years.

"Twenty per cent of the girls employed in the match factories, and one per cent of those in the glass and tobacco factories, are even under ten years of age. We have adopted compulsory education, but how are we to enforce it in the absence of any legislation which forbids the employment of children in workshops and factories? The adoption of a labor law has been talked about more than once during the past several years, but the attempt has been nipped in the bud by the strenuous objection offered by a class of capitalists."

Dr. Kuwada tells us heartrending stories of how the army of 700,000 working girls has been recruited. At first, we are told, the employers hunted the daughters of poor people living in large cities, but as the supply from this source was soon exhausted, they turned to rural districts for a fresh supply. The agents of factory owners go into the country and persuade unsophisticated farmers to send their daughters to the factories, explaining what a fine opportunity the girls will have to acquire refinement and culture in the large cities, and telling what beautiful things and interesting places there are in the city, all of which factory girls are free to see and visit on Sundays.

The good, credulous men of the hamlet and village readily believe the cunning agents and allow their daughters to go, only to see them come home, after four or five years, broken in health and spoiled in character, if, indeed, they do not die before their term expires.

The treatment accorded to these girls is an outrage. Says Dr. Kuwada:

"In some factories it is no secret that the time keepers are instructed to resort to trickery, so that their employees are made to work overtime without receiving any extra pay. In many factories the girls are not even allowed time for meals, but are required to eat while working. Almost all cotton-spinning factories keep their looms in operation day and night. Night work, in which both male and female operatives are engaged together, is found most demoralizing. The methods of punishment are equally inhumane.

"The lash is employed without stint; sometimes girls are imprisoned in dark rooms, or required to work with reduced rations; in many cases their wages are so reduced by fines' that they leave the factory penniless at the end of their contract terms."

Surely Japan has a large problem to solve regarding her women!

THOUGHTS ON LEAVING JAPAN

A changing medley of insistent sounds. Like broken airs played on a samisen. Pursues me, as the waves blot out the shore. The trot of wooden heels; the warning cry, Of patient runners; laughter and strange words Of children, children, children everywhere: The clap of reverent hands before some shrine; And over all the haunting temple bells. Waking, in silent chambers of the soul. Dim memories of long-forgotten lives.

But oh! the sorrow of the undertone; The wail of hopeless weeping in the dawn From lips that smiled through gilded bars at night.

Brave little people of large aims, you bow Too often and too low before the Past; You sit too long in worship of the dead. Yet have you risen, open-eyed, to greet The great material Present. Now salute The greater Future, blazing its bold trail Through old traditions. Leave your dead to sleep In quiet peace with God. Let your concern Be with the living, and the yet unborn;

Bestow on them your thoughts, and waste no time In costly honors to insensate dust. Unlock the doors of usefulness, and lead Your lovely daughters forth to larger fields, Away from jungles of the ancient sin.

For oh! the sorrow of that undertone. The wail of hopeless weeping in the dawn From lips that smiled through gilded bars at night.

Perhaps our most interesting experience in Japan was the visit to Kamakura. In Kamakura, a few miles out from Yokohama, stands one of the world's art wonders, the bronze statue of "Diabutsu"– The Great Buddha. The statue is forty-nine feet in height and represents Buddha sitting in contemplation in a sacred grove. Thousands of copies of this famous statue are to be bought in wood, bronze and photograph form, but not one gives the least impression of its awe-inspiring beauty and indescribable grandeur.

Coming suddenly upon the "Diabutsu" as the visitor must on passing through the outer gates, the effect is overwhelming. No matter what his faith, or lack of faith, or whether he is ignorant or wise in art lore, unless he is of the lowest type of development akin to the jelly fish, he who looks for the first time upon this colossal ideal of an ancient faith must be powerfully stirred.

No artist or sculptor in all the centuries has succeeded in making a perfect representation of Christ–one which embodies love, compassion, wisdom, sympathy and the promise of immortality. Always there is lacking some quality that we feel existed in the Christ, some flaw in the perfect whole.

But all that those oldest extant books of sacred wisdom, the Vedas, describe as the ecstatic state of "realization" which is the ultimate goal of man, and all that Buddha taught three hundred years before Christ regarding that state is expressed in the "Diabutsu." To look upon it is to know the meaning of that much misunderstood word "Nirvana"–not oblivion, not annihilation, but the serenity of attainment and the ecstasy of at-one-ment.

To see this bronze marvel is to grasp the meaning of Christ when he said: "I and my Father are one."

Nothing is known of the artist, but great must have been his faith and large his understanding to have produced work of such enduring magnetism.

Kamakura was the capital of Japan from 1189 until several centuries later. The statue was erected during that period. An earthquake in 1455 and a tidal wave in 1526 destroyed the town, but while calamities wrecked the temples built over the "Diabutsu" the statue itself was unharmed and unshaken. Not so the great religion of which it is a symbol, for he who stands before the glorious figure and feels the full beauty of both turns to modern Japan and seeks in vain for any living expression of that faith, of that philosophy as taught by the Vedas, by Krishna, by Buddha. Conquest of the carnal self, meditation on, and persistent search for, the "God within" until absolute union with the Creative Power was attained– these were the principal supports on which Buddhism in its simple purity rested.

Buddha was an illumined soul and a wise man. He strongly disapproved of the worship of idols and of all beliefs which led mankind away from the one method of salvation through self-conquest. Personal responsibility and character development were bone and sinew of his creed. But Buddhism as it exists in Japan to-day is idol worship, superstition, ignorance and mental indolence combined in a helpless and useless mixture.

At the Buddhistic temple of "Kwannon" in Tokio may be seen any day thousands of the middle and lower class Japanese going through religious ceremonials which must bring sorrow to the soul of Buddha even in Nirvana, so utterly devoid, are they of his spirit and so far away from his teachings.

They are interesting, however, to a foreigner, and there is a certain pathos about the childish performance so seriously entered upon. At one side of the temple may be seen an old woman tossing a coin into a small aperture and then beating violently on a closed door; after which, believing her knock has gained the attention of the spirit god presiding over that department of the temple, she proceeds to utter a brief prayer.

A little farther on three flat bells side by side are rung by means of ropes in order to attract other gods, and three more worshipers toss in their coins, make their petition and pass on. They jostle a man who is clapping his hands before a third shrine to attract the notice of the god he has chosen for some particular appeal.

At the shrine of "Bindzum" there is always a crowd of men, women and children. This deity is supposed to cure all mortal maladies, but first he must be given a coin and then the ailing portion of the body must be touched upon the wooden image. The poor god, who is two hundred and sixty years old, is reduced to a mere misshapen piece of shining soiled wood. His features are worn flat, his fingers are gone, and his digestive apparatus is rubbed away to his spinal cord. And all day long, every day of every year, the throng surrounds this insensate chunk of wood.

In every part of Japan there are such temples and shrines, called Buddhist, where the rank and file go to pray and woo favor from the gods. The priests who dwell in these temples, and live by means of the free-will offering of the people, combine iortune-telling with religion in order to eke out a comfortable income.

All this must grieve the spirit of the immortal Buddha. Yet the serenity of the glorious "Diabutsu" remains undisturbed.

THE DIABUTSU

Long have I searched cathedral, shrine and hall, To find an image from the hand of art That gave the full expression, not a part. Of that ecstatic peace which follows all Life's pain and passion. Strange it should befall

That outer emblem of the inner heart Was waiting far beyond the great world's mart-Immortal answer to the mortal call.

Unknown the artist; vaguely known his creed! But the bronze wonder of his work sufficed To lift me to the heights his faith had trod.

For one rich moment, opulent indeed, I walked with Krishna, Buddha and the Christ,

And felt the full serenity of God.

Hong-Kong is a remarkable city. It is built on an island which was ceded to the English in 1841 and it now ranks third in the seaports of the world. It is a free port, which is a comfort to the traveler. It has a population of 320,000, of which 300,000 are Chinese and the rest Malaysian and English. The fine residential part is called The

Peak, a hill rising 1,600 feet directly back of the business part of the city. This peak has terraced parks, superb residences and a steep cable road going straight to the top.

At the palatial home of Mrs. Ho Tung I met four Chinese women of culture, one in European dress, two in lovely embroidered coats and dark trousers with many valuable jewels in their hair. The father of one of them and the husband of another were present. The young man had been educated in England and held a fine position in a Hong-Kong college. The father in native dress wore a queue and was handsome and courtly. One woman spoke good English, one understood, and one talked not a word. The house was beautiful, and the situation imposing.

Houseboat life in Canton and here on the river is amazing. These same sampan boats are not over forty feet long; some are still smaller. Out of Canton's four millions of Chinese there are one million and a half living in these things. From five to ten people sleep and eat and dwell in each boat, the men working in bigger boats or carrying chairs by day, and the women running the sampans and getting passengers or freight from larger ships. We went to and from our ship in a sampan.

We heard there were only six American families in Hong-Kong, which seems remarkable, for Americans usually are everywhere. In 1911 there were only three motor cars, two for hire and one owned by an American insurance agent. The coolies depend upon the chair business for a living, and would not allow any other means of locomotion to become general.

The chairs are generally delightful when you are not in a hurry, and the way they are borne on the men's shoulders up steep heights is amazing. The fare for long distances is only ten cents. Rickshaws go faster, but can only be used on level roads.

There is something pathetic in the position of the Eurasians, the half-breed Chinese or Japanese. They are like mules, looked down upon by both donkey and horse. They are usually handsome and bright, but can never attain social honors no matter how exemplary and prosperous their lives. Back of this injustice, I suppose, lies a divine law whose breaking when races mix brings punishment on all concerned, except, I fancy, the daddies, who go free from any punishment in this incarnation. In the next they will probably be Eurasians themselves.

There were no horses in Hong-Kong, at least so few that we never saw them, and it was a relief not to have to worry about them. I somehow could not worry about the human animals who carried us about as I would if they were horses. They were so glad to get their ten cents and a tip, and however hard they work they go free after it is over, and are not abused by their employers.

One evening we went to dinner at Government House. The night was glorious with a half moon, and our coolie men carried us up and up for fifteen minutes, each step revealing new beauties. Government House is half way up the peak; and you see the thousand lights above and the many thousand below.

It is the general impression of all European and American residents of China not connected with evangelizing work that our Christian missions are failures so far as making real converts of the people is concerned. But it is also a matter of conviction with these same people that the work of the missionaries is most valuable in its educational efforts, and particularly in its helpfulness to women, in its giving them a new understanding of life, and the self-respect and self-reliance which leads to usef uhiess.

In Canton, a city as large as Manhattan, the destroying of new-born female children is still of frequent occurrence. The bodies of these poor unfortunates are seen floating down the rivers, or found in the streets with other rubbish; but just as, here and there in those crowded, narrow streets, a ray of sunlight sometimes falls, so, here and there, is an awakened mind made conscious of the right of every new-born child to live its life and die a natural death, irrespective of sex.

And through missions, schools, convents, hospitals, there is flowing like a silver thread a clear stream of humane thinking and human responsibility. It is the missionaries who have taught the Chinese women to sew, to take care of their bodies, to bathe, to learn to read and write, and to let girls live. Until the missionaries came only the royal people or a few progressive individuals educated their women. When I went to a convent here which has taken 17,000 abandoned girl babies in sixty years, educated, cared for them and found them positions or husbands, and when I saw the hundreds there now learning useful work and cleanly habits, and remembered the awful city of Shanghai and the mobs in the streets of Canton, the missions seemed like divine institutions.

It does not matter that the Chinese, cleansed though they are by this stream, are not enthusiastic believers of any special Christian creed or dogma; it does not matter if they still cling to some of their old ideas and traditions and superstitions. The fact which is encouraging to the liberal-minded observer is that through the persistent and patient work of our teachers and helpers in the mission schools and hospitals, women are beginning to regard the torturing process of deforming the feet of little girls as barbaric and a relic of a departed era; motherhood is beginning to be understood in its full sacredness; the brain of the girl child is coming to be classed with that of her brother–a divine thing, capable of development–and the woman of this strange, half-awakened old race is coming into her rightful kingdom, slowly, but surely.

Yet, oh, so slowly!

Shanghai, built by the Europeans, is a neat, trim, comfortable modern town; but the walled Chinese city, only twenty minutes away by rickshaws, is a place which beggars description. We were accompanied by a guide who told us that we must leave our rickshaws outside. The streets were so narrow that we could only walk Indian fashion along the tiny pavements, the guide leading, I following and Robert in the rear. Even so well guarded, I felt for the first time in any foreign land a sense of fear. The people on the streets and in the shops which we passed made faces at us, yelled, pointed, and followed us about, passing comments which called forth loud laughter. Robert made apologies for them, saying that Chinamen have been treated as badly in America; but I question if quite to this degree. Even toward their own women who appear on the street they are insulting. I had heard this statement made, but there I saw the fact. We had come from a temple, and a pretty girl in a pale blue coat was emerging with her mother or chaperone. We saw three well-dressed men jostle her and stare and laugh. In Shanghai the old Chinese idea prevails that no respectable woman should be seen upon the streets. We found the shops interesting and made several purchases, though the keepers acted as though they hated us, and would snatch the goods and curios away, if we hesitated about buying.

We visited a remarkable tea house and crossed the bridge familiar to us in our willow pattern chinaware. Then we went to a quaint old Buddhist temple, where the woodwork was blackened with the incense smoke of ages. I said a prayer before Buddha, and the priest burnt joss for both of us, but the crowd of beggars pestered us to such an extent that we were glad to get away to our comfortable modem hotel in the common-place modem town of Shanghai.

It was nine o'clock on a January evening when we found ourselves drifting out of the Hong-Kong harbor and up the river toward Canton. In all our travels nothing so weirdly mysterious is recalled by memory as that river scene– the queer boats mooring about us, the far lights on the aristocratic

"Peak," the low lights of the dim, crowded shores on either side, and the perfect crescent of a new moon flat on its back above us. The sky above the horizon was a deep purple, and the path made by the young moon through it and across the river was unlike anything we had ever seen out of a picture. It seemed to be a path cut through deep water and silver-paved, leading into the Invisible Realms.

After watching it until we were chilly and sleep-hungry, we found our funny little bunks and slept without waking until the boat anchored in Canton harbor, amid the shriek and din of the sampan boatmen and women waiting for cargoes and passengers. In one of these odd houseboats we went ashore, after the guide–named Ah Cum– engaged days in advance, met us on the ship. The sampan was not over forty feet long and only about ten feet of it were under cover; yet in this small craft lived a family of five, sleeping, eating, working, being bom and dying there, as do over one and a half million people. This phase of life in China seemed horrible beyond description to me, yet perhaps it is less horrible than the lives of thousands in the crowded streets of Canton, where two or three million people live so closely packed in together that a nimble-footed sprinter could walk from roof to roof for miles.

Ten coolies and three sedan-chairs were engaged, and the guide and I set forth, each with three men as bearers, while my husband was given four, and then our day began.

Such a day as it was! Such perilous paths we seemed to be carried through; perilous because of the narrowness of the crowded streets and the innumerable corners and stairways and windings which our men encountered in taking us from shop to shop and temple to temple. We found ourselves objects of excited curiosity to the street throng; but there was no such insolence and wild barbaric behavior as characterized the crowds in the streets of the walled city of Shanghai.

We visited many shops and saw very beautiful and very wonderful things. Boys and men were making the cruelly beautiful feather jewelry from the bright plumage of slaughtered birds from Singapore. The infinitesimal particles of plumage were cut by small boys with a tiny knife and glued to the ring, pin or brooch. The boys work four years as apprentices without pay. After a few years of steady application, eyeglasses become a necessity. The work is done in shops on streets where the sun never penetrates.

We saw men sawing apart a block of stone to deliver the pieces of imprisoned jade, and we saw bits of this jade made ready for setting in a ring valued at two hundred dollars.

We visited temples and saw strange and hideous gods, and in one temple I prayed before some of them and burned joss and tossed down two pieces of stone to find out if my prayer would be answered; and the stones cried out "Yes." But a poor woman on a prayer rug at my side asked six times and got five negatives and only one affirmative.

Our guide was most satisfactory and after taking us to see the famous old Water Clock, 1,400 years old, and after having Himself kodak me in a sedan-chair amidst a howling mob, we made again our perilous ascending, descending and winding journey back to the ship. Our ten coolies, for this strenuous and herculean day's task, asked sixty cents each, and our guide told us they had to pay twenty cents out of it for the chair hire.

We took the same ship back, reaching Hong-Kong at noon and feeling that we had seen one of the wonderful sights of the world–a Chinese city of four million people living precisely as they must have lived centuries and centuries ago.

From my husband's diary I quote the following:

"It is ninety miles from Hong-Kong to Canton. It is a night's ride up the Pearl River and the steamers are good. It is well to write ahead for a guide to meet you at the steamer. Your guide is sure to be Ah Cum, as his family have had an iron-bound trust on Canton guiding for three generations; but they do it well and with seeming fairness.

"Canton is twenty centimes old and has never been cleaned. It's ALL there.

"It is the commercial capital of China and has a population of over two million people; they detest foreigners and will let you know it; they will all yell at you before you leave. To explore this human ant-hill of China is the experience of a lifetime. In all Canton there is not a wheeled vehicle, street car or hotel, or a person wearing European clothes.

"The filth-smeared streets are so narrow you can reach out from your chair to the shops on either side and help yourself. The streets are so congested with hordes of human beings that your progress through them is an endless malediction. An oath yelled in tea-chest characters has a frightful sound.

"The Cantonese impress you as great eaters. Braziers with stewing messes are everywhere. Every other store seems a market of some kind. Varnished pigs, ducks, dried fish, dogs and cats (with their heads on) and rat hams, tied with cute little wisps of straw, are all in full evidence and you wonder if you can ever eat again. Peddlers throng the street with large, live flopping fish in bamboo bowls and allow their customers to cut out the slices which they may desire.

"We went to the famous Execution Grounds, a long narrow pottery yard in the center of the city, with fresh clay pots drying in the sun. Here over three hundred criminals are beheaded in a year. They had snicked off two heads the day before, and invited us to stay and see the decapitation of three the next day; but Herself thought our time too limited. The wife of the executioner brought out the terrible two-edged sword and showed us how it was handled. From her voluble explanation we thought she wanted us to kneel down so that she could show us how the trick was done; but we learned when we got away that she wanted to sell us the sword or a pickled head of one of the victims, of which they keep quite an assortment.

"Hundreds of thousands of Cantonese live on junks, sampans, or gayly painted flower-boats, where they are born, reared, married and die. Babies are tied to the deck by long cords and other children are allowed to romp about with a bamboo float fastened to them.

"The flower-boats' are really the boats of dissipation– where women of wobbly morals live and where big gambling is done."

CHAPTER XVIII On Historic Ground

SISTER SUDDHAMMDARA alighted from her bullock cart and walked up to the door of "The Firs," under the stately palms and the blooming "rain trees," which spread their great branches over the path like giant umbrellas of flowered pink and green silk.

Sister Suddhammdara was clothed in a saffron yellow robe thrown gracefully over her shoulder, leaving the right arm free; she carried a large palm leaf fan; she wore straw sandals on her feet, and her head was closely shaven. Despite this most disfiguring custom, she was a comely woman. Had she been aureoled with woman's crowning physical glory, a head of fine hair, one could easily imagine her to be beautiful.

The Singhalese women of Ceylon possess much beauty and, having been allowed freedom and education and association with their men folk for many generations, they are quicker of thought and more at their ease among the people of other races than the average women of the Orient.

Sister Suddhammdara had come to pay her respects to us at our hotel in Kandy, Ceylon, a mutual friend having sent a letter of introduction, and to me she gave her hand in greeting, but to my husband she only bowed, clasping both hanc together, and raising them to her brow. This is the usual Oriental manner of salutation, quite as expressive and less taxing than our eternal handshaking. It was after ten, and we had planned t6 visit the "Temple of the Tooth" with the nun as our guide and interpreter, but she explained that she must first go and partake of her one meal in the day, which she took at II o'clock.

This meal is preceded by a light breakfast of fruit or a cereal at seven in the morning. We persuaded the gentle sis- ter to let us serve her a repast in our apartment and shortly she was provided with rice and curry and delicious papia, and vegetables, and a cup of coffee. She was, of course, a vegetarian, not even using eggs in her diet, "unless," as she said naively, "they are accidentally broken. Then we feel we are not destroying life for the gratification of appetite." After this 11 o'clock repast the nuns eat nothing more until the next morning, but may take lemonade or other cooling beverages. Despite this frugal diet (or perhaps because of it) the sister had the appearance of perfect health and abundant vitality.

We led her to talk of herself and to tell the story of her life. She was born of a Christian mother and grandmother, converted by missionaries of the Church of England. But her mother died when she was quite young, and the father, who had always clung to his faith in Lord Buddha, became blind. His little daughter read to him for five years during a part of every day from the Buddhistic books, and when the blind father passed on the daughter decided to become a nun. Now she was quite happy in her school for poor orphan girls. Besides which she had in coimection with her school a Home for Aged Nuns, an endowment from Lady Blake, the wife of Ceylon's most beloved ex-Governor.

"My bullock and my cart are gifts from this same friend," she said, "and this has enabled me to do much good in getting about among my people."

We asked her what she taught the children. We were curious to know how a Buddhistic school differed from European and American institutions. First of all she told us the children were taught the great precepts of Buddha: right thought, right speech, right conduct; to abstain from taking life, from stealing lying, slander, abuse, or unprofitable conversation. Right mindedness and contemplation in order to attain tranquillity were included in the curriculum. They were given verses for chanting, inculcating these ideas. Then they were taught to pray to Buddha and the four great archangels, who are ever ready, so the Sister believes, to help aspiring mortals seeking for perfection. She told me their names–Datara-see, Verupa, Verupakse and wise Seravana.

Flowers are ofifered daily on the shrine of Buddha, because flowers typify sweet, pure thoughts. Before offering flowers or prayers, the Buddhist must bathe his hands and face and rinse his mouth, and leave his shoes at the door of the temple. Twice each day must the entire body be bathed.

The children are taught to reverence their parents, to appreciate the hardships which parents endure and to offer prayers for them. The noble virtues which produce lovable characters are dwelt upon, and the children are urged to develop these qualities in order to be worthy of loyal friendship and to be able to give such friendship. All the necessary characteristics which go into the making of good wives and mothers are taught the children– patience, amiability, cheerfulness, humility, chastity, industry and love. All this seemed very beautiful to us as we listened, and we wished some of the same methods of instruction might be adopted by the Christian schools of Europe and America.

One of the Buddhistic ideas we found very offensive, just as we have always found the same idea in orthodox Christianity offensive. This is the idea that life on earth, in the body, is to be regarded as a misfortune, and that only in the spiritual state can happiness be found. I urged the good Sister Suddhammdara to introduce a little healthful New Thought and Theosophy into her curriculum, to tell her children that this life was a privilege; that it was one of the rooms in the Father's "House of Many Mansions," and that it was a joy to be one of the workers in this great mansion and to be endowed with power to make the room beautiful and the time passed in it happy.

I told her that many modem and intelligent Christians had abandoned all those old ideas about earth being "a vale of tears" and mortals mere "worms of the sod"; that we knew we were Royal Princes and Princesses of God, and that we had dominion over material things, and could be well, successful, useful and happy if we chose to realize our Divine Inheritance.

But the good nun, like a large majority of our good Chris- tians, could not at once come into an understanding of these ideas.

We went down to the Temple of the Tooth, Sister Sudd-hammdara taking me in her bullock cart, assuring me as we drove along that we were to see many sacred relics in the temple even if the Sacred Tooth was not there. It had been burned, this tooth of Buddha, centuries ago by fanatics of opposing faiths, and a large piece of ivory like an elephant's tooth had been afterward substituted. This is hidden in a jeweled case within a glass shrine in the upper story of the old, old Temple.

We found it surrounded with the heavily sweet frangipani blossoms and by crowds of worshipers. The nun made way for herself and bade me follow, and happy and proud and grateful she seemed when I made obeisance three times, with both hands clasped and lifted to my brow, and when I said a little prayer and flung the frangipani blooms closer about the shrine.

Most pleased was she when I told her I believed Buddha was one of the Great Avatars, one of the Divine Masters sent to help humanity; but, like my Christian friends, she was disappointed because I would not say I believed he was the ONLY Avatar, the God of Creation Himself.

Sister Suddhammdara expressed regret that a good many children in Kandy were attending Christian schools: "because," she said, "they are not taught to respect their parents and their parents' ideas. They are made to regard the faith of their parents with contempt, and to ape European dress and manners. And many times this has produced great unhappi-ness in the homes of the Buddhists."

Perhaps this letter written to a friend in New Orleans, while we were in Ceylon in 1911, gives a more intimate description of all that land meant to us than anything which can be written from memory or from note books:

"We have seen a large chunk of the earth; and we have decided that nowhere have we seen the equal in beauty and charm of Ceylon. And the very heart of this charm lies in Kandy, We stopped at The Firs, a hotel on a cliff over a lake, surrounded by giant palms and other trees as large as our old oak, all covered with a pink flower like a thistle, but soft as a rose. Everybody called it a different name. Heavenly smells were everywhere, and beyond the lake those splendid mountain ranges. The hotel had wide balconies, where we sat and drank in all this beauty, and heard tropic birds make new music. It was like a dream, and hardly seemed real."

The town is 1,700 feet above the sea, and the mornings and evenings were cool, but from 10 to 5 intensely hot. Robert was enchanted with it all, and wanted to begin at once to build a bungalow for winter use. If we were twenty years younger I should urge him to do so, as we could always rent it if we did not feel like taking a 20,000-mile trip to occupy it. I think this is the fifth bungalow Robert has planned for our winter use in the last five years: and certainly he finds a better location each time. Pasadena was the last, and Honolulu before that. We have a fairy, airy castle also in Biskra, and one on the Rhine.

It was at 6 o'clock, on the morning of March 23rd, when we started on our motor trip from Colombo to Kandy. A fine car, an experienced driver, a perfect morning, as beautiful as an opal, and scenery which was created by God's most skilled artists (both marine and landscape) made an environment for us which could not fail to give happiness to any one not suffering from a hopeless sorrow, or a hopeless disposition. Add to this combination of delights the companionship of the dearest one on earth, and you have conditions about as perfect as they are found on earth.

The drive was an unending panorama of interesting pictures. Ceylon is so thickly settled that its cities and villages overlap, and we seemed an endless time in getting out of the city limits, and finding real tropical country, with palm groves, fruit estates, tea and coffee and pepper and cocoa domains, and trees and flowers and vines growing in tropical luxuriance. These things were all revealed to us as we spun along and in between were the villages, the mud houses with the palm leaf roofs, and the people in their graceful native costumes; not as artistic as those of the Indians and Parsee people, yet similar; and all in bright colors, making splendid splashes of red and blue and yellow in the vivid green of the foliage. Finally we came to a rest house, where we stopped for breakfast; and there was a quaint and curious old well in the foreground, and a boy or girl drawing water, and a native ox-cart close by, all food for our camera. The sex of the people is difficult to decide in Ceylon at first glance, because the men wear skirts and long hair, which is done in a Psyche knot or Langtry coil, and a long circle comb which only little girls in the country used to wear. After you get the hang of Ceylon's customs you know the men by this comb, and unless they have a beard, that is about the only difference you see between the sexes in their street attire.

It was about the same in Rangoon, and there the men wore a long, bright scarf about their heads, their hair coiled in the back, and when you saw one coming and just behind him a woman dressed quite the same, only without the scarf, but with a cigar half a foot long in her mouth, you were excusable for feeling bewildered about who was who. Well, after we left the rest house we entered the jungle–the real thing. A road has been cut for many years–a very good motor road– but on each side lie miles and miles of thick jungle, where, at night, all kinds of wild animals prowl about.

At the end of many miles we came out of the jungle, to the place where the wonderful buried city of Anuradhapura lies, and where a portion of its marvelous ruins have been excavated. These ruins were far beyond our imagination, especially the four great Dagobas, 303 feet in circumference and in height, and the four or five hundred granite posts, which cover a city block at least, and are the foundation of the Brazen Palace, built by King Dutugamunu, 300 years B. C. And there were beautifully carved door steps leading to a temple, curious with astronomical signs; and remains of great baths, luxurious as the baths of the Roman era. This city was in its prime about the same time as Pompeii, but it seemed to be more impressive even than the historic ruin. It occupied sixteen square miles, and now is overrun with a jungle growth of at least a thousand years. But everywhere you look you see granite or marble posts, pillars or slabs, peering out of the rank vegetation and from among the trees, and mounds and hills everywhere, showing that under them lie countless and priceless historic treasures.

They lack money and men to be brought to light. What a delight it would be to have millions enough to use in unearthing these old things!

A remarkable system of waterworks supplied this old city with water, and portions of it are still in use by the new city which has sprung up about the works of excavation. Wherever the jungle has been cleared away most impressive trees stand guard over the ruins, making great parks and gardens of stately beauty.

We remained overnight at Anuradhapura, and took an early start the next morning. Our first stop was near i o'clock, at Dambulla, where there is a famous temple high in the rocks of the mountain, made before Christ, in the era of the King just njentioned. A drove of native boys surrounded our motor car at once; all wanted to act as guides to the temple. Robert selected one and sternly told the others to go away, saying he should pay only one guide. They all smiled and ran along beside us, four in number. Halfway up the mountain, at the second pagoda, I made up my mind that I had gone far enough. The heat was unbelievable; so I sat down in the shade of the pagoda and a sympathic tree, and the smallest of the guides, a little nude bronze Adonis of ten, remained with me. Robert proceeded with his three retainers.

The small Adonis could not speak a word of English, but he did all he could to entertain me. He opened nut shells and picked flowers and climbed trees, and after a long time Robert came back with his retinue, hot and weary, but astonished at what he had seen in the way of old carven images in the Rock Temple, near the top of the mountain. Then he kodaked me with his retainers four, beside the pagoda, where I tried to pose the four bronze retainers and was snapped in the act. Then, of course, despite all resolutions, the four all had to be recompensed; and we were glad to escape from an increasing crowd of importuners and fly away to Kandy through a few more miles of jungle. When we arrived, some hours later, hot and tired and dusty, it seemed to us we had attained Nirvana.

Oh, the beauty of that charming spot and the relaxation of mind and body for five delightful days in that cliff hotel, "The Firs," above the lake, better known as the "Tank," because supplied with water from the mountain artificially; a splendid piece of engineering done five hundred years ago, and now kept in perfect order by the British government.

One morning we rose at dawn, and after coffee and toast we took two rickshaws, and rode for an hour and a half over what is known as Lady Morton's Drive, leading into Lady Gordon's and another drive–all named for the wives of the Governors, who improved the paths laid out by the old Ceylon Kings, and made them into splendid thoroughfares. We thought we had seen the most wonderful drives in the world: the Mount Diavolo drive in Jamaica; the Sorrento to Amalfi drive in Italy; the Sicilian road leading from the station to Taormina; but this drive in Ceylon surpassed them all. Mountain range after mountain range came into view, all with the glory of the dawn; and every variety of tropical tree, vine and plant with here and there a beautiful bungalow of pleasing and picturesque architecture, half hidden in gorgeous gardens; with lakes in the valley below, and temples and shrines and brilliantly attired people moving to and fro. Part of the drive was through deep woods; here trees centuries old were whispering of other people and eras, vanished; and here we left our rickshaws and walked along together, wishing the hour would last interminably.

The very first day in Kandy, we engaged a rickshaw man who proved to be a personage, one of those people with an individuality which takes hold of you and remains with you.

He was slender as a young girl, thirty-three years old, with a sensitive, finely featured face, and a gentle voice. He did not weigh over one hundred and ten pounds at most, and it seemed a cruelty to sit in a rickshaw and let him drive me about town, and up steep hills, through a broiling sun. Yet he was eager for patrons, and assured me he could easily go twenty miles in a day. He spoke an excellent English, learned of an English gentleman, whose servant he was until he married and needed a more lucrative occupation. "Now I make from two and a half rupees to five a day; a very good income for a man in my position," he said, "and I can take very good care of my wife and four little children."

Five rupees is a dollar and sixty-six cents; and I tried to imagine any man in America being grateful for such payment for running ten and twenty miles a day, dragging a heavy load in tropical heat. But this man, Simon, wore no shoes or hose. I doubt if he ever owned a pair of either. He wore only a loin cloth and a thin cotton shirt, he never worried about coal for winter, and fruit and rice are cheap. Yet in spite of all that, the whole situation stirred my heart with sympathy.

Simon was up every morning at six, he told me, and he went to bed at eleven at night. He was very proud of his three little sons and his one daughter. But his hours with them must have been brief, indeed. The happiest memory of all the happy ones in Kandy is Simon's face when I gave him a tip of five rupees after my drive at five o'clock in the afternoon, and told him to go home and spend the rest of the day with his family. He had already earned four rupees that day, and he had taken me up the steep mountain drive, and afterward five miles to and from the Elephant's Bath, where we saw the monsters disport themselves in the river after working hours. Gentle, refined, grateful-hearted Simon; I wonder how long he will be able to keep up his hard work. Yet I heard a tourist woman say: "How those rascally rickshaw men do rob one, don't they?" She had been asked to pay sixty-six cents for being hauled four miles.

To enjoy fully historical scenes, I always want my intellectual interest supplemented by a romantic flavor. My husband supplied this for Tunis and Carthage by giving me "Salammbo" to read on the journey. All the way from Tunis to Carthage, as I rode along in the train, I was sedng with my mind's eye the young giant barbarian, Martho,– not as the warrior, but as the lover,–in his pursuit of Salammbo, daughter of Hamilcar, and every step of the way, as we drove or walked about Carthage, I saw Salammbo making her exit, on her camel, guided by the high priest, as she went on that famous journey to Martho's camp to recover the veil of Janet which Martho had stolen for love of her. So it was Flaubert's genius–rather than dry history alone– which vitalized Carthage for me.

The excavated ruins of three cities, the Christian, the Roman, and the Punic Carthage– all fascinated us; the amphitheater, the statues, the villas, the baths, while less imposing than those we had seen in Pompeii, Herculaneum, Taor-mina, Rome, or Syracuse, were even more impressive because of the wonderful history of the three periods of grandeur which Carthage enjoyed. And the Museum! Never have I seen so alluring a place! Never have I dreamed of such necklaces, jewels of Carthage, and curios as are those on exhibition, taken from the tombs and temples.

My husband was most impressed by the statue of the Punic priestess–which was found lying over her tomb, ever so many feet below the surface. In her sarcophagus we saw the skull and a few bones and scattered ashes–all that remained of her beauty. We returned to Tunis in a magnificent environment of golden clouds and amethyst mountains and deep, deep sapphire seas–a sight to remember forever.

Another afternoon we visited Carthage and, wandering along among the old ruins, we observed a pretty villa projecting out into the robin's egg blue sea. Our guide informed us it was the summer palace of Prince Kazabar Baredine, who had just married the daughter of the Bey, Princess Guchena. He said the Prince and Princess were probably absent and we might look about the grounds if we chose. Looking about the grounds, however, was not satisfying, and I asked the guide to gain permission from the attendant to enter the courtyard. What was my amazement to have the guide return with the Prince himself, a handsome young Turk of twenty-five dressed in uniform, who made a low, Oriental bow and invited us to enter. My husband and the guide were only permitted to remain in the courtyard and an outer room pertaining to it while mine was the privilege to be asked inside to be shown the handsome house and to be presented to the pretty Princess Guchena, a lovely Arab girl of seventeen, and to the aunt of the Prince, a delicate and refined looking Turkish woman of middle age.

Neither of the ladies spoke a word of English or French, but they seemed greatly interested in my tall. My conversation was, of course, entirely with the Prince. He was much interested in hearing about America. Like a large percentage of Oriental people, South America alone was known to him. He had heard of Buenos Aires and Venezuela, but he knew little or nothing of North America. New York, Boston, Chicago, California, were meaningless words to him.

The Prince ordered coffee for the ladies and went out to see that it was served to my husband and the guide. I was left alone to sip my coffee and converse in sign language with the two ladies. Princess Guchena (the name means "a garden") was decorated with the Allah cross on brow, throat, cheeks and wrists, and another of these henna-made marks nestled in the deep dimple of her pretty chin. I touched the pretty dimple with my finger and smiled. She touched my chin in return with a questioning look, repeating this look with a little guttural sound in Arabic, which I interpreted to be a query of some kind. I nodded assent though I did not know to what; then the Princess clapped her hands three times, whereupon she was surrounded by slaves small and great, of all colors from coal black to light tan color. One small mulatto girl was given her instructions. Disappearing from the room, she returned in a moment with the beauty box of the Arab Princess. I was conducted to a deep window seat and the Princess herself began to decorate me with her henna brush. Both wrists, my throat, and my chin received the Allah cross mark. I declined further decorations, which caused the Princess to look disappointed. At this juncture the Prince entered and assured me it was a mark of great distinction for a woman to wear this insignia. The Princess was anxious to stain my fingers to the first joint with henna, but again I thanked her and declined. A swarm of attendants in the room and outside upon the balconies, peering through the windows, had watched the process with great interest.

Finally I bowed myself out, feeling I had had one of the most interesting experiences of my life, and not realizing how long a time had passed since I left Robert in the outer court. I found him waiting in a state of great anxiety, imagining all sorts of Arabian Nights' tragedies. My henna marks, which I had imagined would wash off with the first bath, stubbornly remained for an entire week before they wore away.

Until our last visit to Northern Africa in the winter of 1913 I had never heard of ancient Tiblis (nor of its modern name Annouha). Yet it is one of the most interesting spots it was ever my privilege to behold. We set out from Hammam Meskoutine on a glorious morning with our little Arab guide, who spoke a very good French, to show us the way. We drove through scenery so rare and majestic, with such great vistas opening before us at every turn, that language being inadequate, we could only clasp hands and gaze in silence. The fields for miles and miles were, as Robert expressed it, "covered with God's Persian carpets." We thought we had seen flowers in other lands, but such flowers as we saw that day surpassed anything ever before beheld! Gorgeous poppies, of vivid red, wild narcissus growing in golden opulence, and deep purple and pale lavender flowers, all mingled in one vast carpet for many acres. Olive trees, in great profusion, everywhere, also many other species, making a beautiful blending of shaded greens.

It was an hour's drive to Annouma, where we left the car and began to follow our little Arab guide, who had accompanied us from the hotel, over narrow, stony, winding paths, up and down hill, until we reached the first broken temple of the old Roman town. The gateway arch still stands just as it was found; broken columns cover the earth, an altar is still visible and from the doorway one looks out upon the ruins of what were evidently four other temples, and upon acres of ground completely covered with remnants of houses. Upon hundreds of these stones are Latin inscriptions. There are artistic carvings and every indication that this was a town of wealth and prominence. Its situation was magnificent. Its principal driveway still remains in a good state of preservation.

Robert wandered all over the site of the old city and was more impressed than we had been with Pompeii. I covered about half the distance and then sat down on somebody's old doorstep and talked with the little guide. I took some pictures of my husband, and he of me, and then we both walked back over the hard and difficult road to the motor car. As we walked, an Arab shepherd in a field near by began playing on his reed pipe. We called to him and he came and followed us almost to the car, playing all the time, and went away happy with a few pennies. The guide asked us if we would like to see the Sheik's house on the way back. The Sheik we had seen at the hotel—a sumptuous Arab, dressed in great elegance, in silk burnous and white and gold draperies and large turban, going about in a white and gold motor car. He boarded at the hotel, albeit owning a large estate and a farm besides, and a big house, where he had twelve wives. We stopped at the door of his house and about fifty attendants came to ask our wishes, and finally it was agreed that I might enter and see the house, and still later it was said I might see some of the women. So two of the Sheik's sons conducted me through a ragged curtain, which hid the court-yard from the road, and then through that to another, where I saw three women at work in a large room piled high about the sides with queer-looking bags of a bright red color. One was a girl of eighteen years, who was presented to me as the Sheik's daughter. She was very pretty, pale of skin, with delicate features, and golden brown eyes. Her dress did not seem typically Arabian—a long white cotton garment, on straight lines, and a narrow red belt, and a colored kerchief about her head. No jewels were visible. Another woman sitting in the court, on a pile of cushions, was evidently one of the twelve wives. She was past her youth, dressed in gay colors, and wore much jewelry: she was painted in Arab fashion, white and red, with heavily marked brows. She shook hands with me, and seemed pleased to see me, but could not converse. Then I was taken up a flight of stairs and the young Arab unlocked a door and showed me into a large bed-room with many gay carpets and cushions and a large bed, and all the windows shrouded with orange silk curtains over lavender. He urged me to sit down and began to question me as to how the ladies of Tunis dressed, all of which he repeated to his sister (she not speaking French). Then he took me to see another room, darker and more secluded than the other, and urged me to sit down and take coffee. His brother and sister had not followed us, and I began to feel a bit nervous: when I refused coffee and said I must go he became quite persistent, and urged me not to hurry. I got out with some precipitancy, and assured him I must go, as my husband was waiting outside. I breathed a bit more freely when once in the motor car. The whole place seemed tawdry, squalid, unclean, unwholesome, and more nearly like a den of pirates than anything I had ever seen. When we got back to the hotel we saw the Sheik dining in state at the table. We were told he locked all bis young wives in their rooms when he left the house, and carried the key in his pocket.

In Emperdocle, Sicily, lived my little god-child, Ella Veronica. Little Ella was born in 1908, in Brooklyn, N. Y., where her parents had passed through great trouble and loss of children and money. It was my privilege to be of some mental and social aid to lovely Signora Veronica (the mother) at that time; but my efforts to obtain proper occupation for her and her refined, educated husband proved unavailing. So shortly after the birth of the little girl, named for me, they returned to Sicily, before I had seen my little god-child.

We arrived in Emperdocle at three in the afternoon and found the parents and my namesake at the station. One glance showed us what an exquisite little being had been bearing my name for five years—a most beautiful Madonna-faced child.

with light brown hair and eyes, and a fair complexion and perfect features, and the sweetest possible manners. She was timid at first, but in a few hours she grew confiding and loved to be near us, listening gently while we talked a tongue which she did not understand. Her parents spoke a very good English, and her sweet sister, Minna, twelve years old, had not forgotten the language. We were entertained by her aunt and uncle, charming, cultured and wealthy Sicilians, speaking no language but Italian.

Their home was beautiful; but the desolation of the little town of Emperdocle is beyond words. A mining center for sulphur, there is nothing but dust and deadly monotony in the town of fourteen thousand people—no newspaper or even a moving-picture show. No lady ever walks on the street there, because there is no place to go and nothing to see or do. Yet wealth is to be gained, through the sulphur mines, and so little Ella and her handsome, cultured family were domiciled there.

All my limited knowledge of Italian was brought into play. I began sentences in Italian, continued in French, and finished in English. Ella's father and mother translated our conversation to the relatives and she told us what they said. It must have been a strenuous two days for them.

Sunday we went by carriage to Girgenti, where in 500 B. C. stood great Akraba and a few centuries later Argentium. These cities were opulent and contained millions of inhabitants, magnificent temples and homes, and all the luxuries which wealth produces. But now only broken columns and a few portions of splendid temples, magnificently situated, remain.

Girgenti is some two miles from the old site. It is built about the fort to which the people filed when the great city was taken by its enemies, and around this fort grew up the modern town, while the ancient scene of magnificence is only a desolate plain–dotted with picturesque ruins.

A row of these ruins stands on a steep cliff which extends some miles, and in the days of its glory these temples and the glorious view beyond over the sea, and the great city of luxury in the background, must have made an imposing spectacle for every beholder. The architecture of the temples was exquisite.

and the Temple of Concord, still in outline comparatively complete, stirs one like soine rare piece of sculpture or painting. It was all well worth the hard, hot, dusty ride. Two months after our return to America we received word of the death of Mrs. Veronica.

One of our most gruesome experiences was a visit to the Catacombs at Palermo, where the skeletons of the dead, clothed in grave garments, stand in rows, their skulls grinning at each living observer. Some of them carry Bibles in their fleshless hands; and occasionally a skull was seen bending over his book as if reading the holy words.

It seemed incredible that so many different expressions could be seen in the faces of skulls!

It was an olden custom in Palermo to exhume the dead after a certain period of time allowed for decomposition of the flesh and to stand the skeletons upright in these Catacombs. The horrible and unsanitary custom fortunately has been done away with for many years.

It was by sheer accident that we went to Herculaneum. Every one said it was not worth the trouble, yet we found it one of the most valuable experiences of our months of travel.

Herculaneum is some six miles from Naples by trolley. It is buried eighty feet under the small modern town of Resina. Very little has been excavated, but the treasures recovered are amazing–such beautiful bronzes, magnificent marbles, priceless pictures, marvelous manuscripts! Still they have only picked a tiny hole into this beautiful old buried city, so tragically embalmed many, many centuries ago.

Though Herculaneum was destroyed at the same time as Pompeii and lived under the same licentious influence, its relics show little of the vulgar immorality that marked Pompeiian discoveries. Yet Herculaneum left its "House of Julia" to speak of the Ancient Sin to posterity. In this house were found priceless treasures and money and jewels, proving that "Julia" was one of the last to flee.

Herculaneum was buried under a mountain of lava, Pompeii under a mountain of ashes. After more than i,8oo years they were located by archeologists. It took one thousand dollars to do the same work of excavation in Herculaneum which one hundred dollars would do at Pompeii. The lava is like sohd granite and had to be chipped away, piece by piece.

It was a wonder to us when we went out and saw it to think that so much had been brought to light–the dozen houses perhaps, and gardens and fountains, whose beautiful works of art we had seen in the Naples Museum. Then we went ninety feet underground and saw the theater which was partly excavated, the seats, the stage, the orchestra. How they ever chipped away the solid lava and found so much is a marvel; but, oh, what a glorious work it would be for a billionaire to put five thousand poor men to work there and unearth the other wealth of beauty and art which is buried under one hundred feet of lava! It would do more to educate the world than many libraries.

ON SEEING "THE HOUSE OF JULIA" AT HERCULANEUM

Not great Vesuvius, in all his ire. Nor all the centuries, could hide your shame. There is the little window where you came. With eyes that woke the demon of desire, And lips like rose leaves, fashioned out of fire; And from the lava leaps the molten flame Of your old sins. The walls cry out your name– Your face seems rising from the funeral pyre.

There must have dwelt, within your fated town Full many a virtuous dame, and noble wife Who made your beauty seem as star to sun; How strange the centuries have handed down Your name, fair Julia, of immoral life, And left the others to oblivion.

CHAPTER XIX

Hawaiian Queens and the Sultan of Java f N the wonderful winters of travel I was privileged to enjoy with the man of my heart, none stands out more clearly than the winter of 1908, which we spent in Honolulu.

We were fortunate in obtaining one of the Royal Hawaiian Hotel Bungalows, a tiny house of three rooms, hid in among tropical trees and shrubs, and only a three minutes' walk from Young's Hotel, where we dined (the Royal being closed that year).

Our little bungalow was nearly all doors and windows; four doors and seven windows, with a snug bay window, screened by lace curtains, which made a dream of a reading room nook for my husband. Absolute charm hung about the little toy house. In all the happy weeks that followed we never closed one of those seven windows or four doors; and we were put to sleep by the sighing of palms and the cry of tropical night birds, and wakened by a chorus of riotous day birds in the morning.

Never in any other spot on earth had we found such utter freedom from obligations of all kinds and such absolute peace and serenity as in this darling little bungalow.

We procured the assistance of a little toy Japanese maid, named Meekie, who performed many simple duties for me, while our Chinese boy. Ah Luie, we found a comfort and a delight. (Ah Luie looked like a Chinese Apollo at that time. Yet two years later, when we passed through Honolulu again, he had grown ponderous and middle-aged.)

Shortly after our arrival we met the then very notable person, Governor Cleghom, who moved about among people with the air of one who belonged to a past era, as in truth he did. Governor Cleghorn, a Scotchman, had come to the Hawaiian Islands in his early manhood, made a fortune, and married Like-Like, sister of the then King of the Hawaiian Islands. Their daughter, Princess Kaiulani, was heir apparent to the throne when the United States annexed Hawaii, and it ceased to be a monarchy.

Kaiulani had been sent to Scotland and England to be educated; and her father's entire life had been spent in the endeavor to make his estate worthy of a future Queen. No King or Queen of Hawaii had ever lived in such a lordly place as this estate of Governor Cleghorn's (called Ainahau), which we visited on two occasions. It is a half hour's ride by trolley from Honolulu, on the seashore, and was at that time resplendent with every beauty which Nature, assisted by wealth and good taste, could supply. We walked through the wide-spreading grounds under the shadow of lordly palms, where the childhood of Kaiulani was spent; tropical vines flowered there in audacious colors and flung bold arms about unresists ing trees; and made a riot of strange blooms. Splendid peacocks swept down the spacious paths beside the handsome white-haired host, as he came to greet his guests; soft fountains played and refreshed the air with cooling sounds; and while the calendar declared the month was February, the weather was July.

It was a superb scene; but over it rested the shadow of a great disappointment and a great sorrow. Kaiulani had been abroad at school when the annexation of the Islands took place. She was a young girl, brought up to think of herself as a future Queen, and the blow to her ambitions proved a death thrust. Speaking of his daughter. Governor Cleghorn said: "She died of rheumatism of the heart, a year after the annexation of Hawaii. It may really be said that she died of annexation. All interest in life had gone for her, with the passing of the monarchy."

Everywhere were portraits and pictures of Kaiulani. She was beautiful, as are so many of these "daughters of a double race"; and no name is more revered in all the Hawaiian Islands than that of this young Princess who passed out in the morning of her life. As we walked down the long avenues,

HAWAIIAN QUEENS AND THE SULTAN 285 followed by the haughty peacocks who seemed to want proof that we were not loitering in the grounds, a penetrating melancholy permeated the sunshine; and never did life speak more clearly to us of the transitory nature of happiness which is based on human ambitions.

Later in the day we stood by the Royal Mausoleum where Princess Kaiulani lies entombed beside her mother and royal uncle, and we recalled the words of the Persian poet:

"This, too, shall pass away."

Robert Louis Stevenson had been a devoted friend of tlie little princess, and when she went away to Scotland he wrote these lines:

"Forth from her land to mine she goes, The Island Maid, the Island Rose: Light of heart and bright of face The daughter of a double race. Her Islands here in southern sun Shall mourn their Kaiulani gone; And I in her dear Banyan shade Look vainly for my little maid. But our Scots Island far away Shall glitter with unwonted day; And cast for once their tempests by To smile in Kaiulani's eye."

To these pretty lines Mr. Stevenson appended this exquisite bit of prose, more poetical than his poetry, as always was his prose:

"Written in April to Kaiulani, in the April of her age, and at Waikiki within easy walk of Kaiulani's Banyan. When she comes to my land and her father's land and the rain beats upon the window (as I fear it will), let her look at this page; it will be like a weed, gathered and pressed at home, and she will remember her islands and the shadow of the mighty tree, and she will hear the peacock screaming in the dusk and the wind blowing in the palms, and she will think of her father sitting there alone.

"Written in April, 1889."

After we left Kaiulani's tomb and went back to our little bungalow, I wrote the following verses:

KAIULANI

Dreaming of thrones she grew from child to maid. While under royal palms soft fountains played. She saw herself in Time's appointed hour Ruling her kingdom by love's potent power. Her radiant youth imperially arrayed Where tropic suns were tempered by sweet shade, Protecting love her pleasant pathway laid, And there she dwelt, a Princess in her bower Dreaming of thrones.

Marauding changes brutally invade Her Island home; and yet Time's hand is stayed. Her name has left the fragrance of a flower; And in the regal state that was her dower She sleeps in beauteous youth that cannot fade Dreaming of thrones.

We afterward visited the Kaiulani School, and from a great collection of trinkets belonging to the Princess, I was given a crown of small shells which at first glance seemed to be formed of feathers–a valuable addition to my collection of curios.

Another Hawaiian Princess we met socially, Princess David Kawaananakoa, whose husband was a nephew of the late King Kalaqua, and who therefore would have laid claims to possible queen consortship, had the monarchy continued. Princess David was astonishingly beautiful–the most perfect type of the half Hawaiian that can be conceived. Her mother, an exceedingly handsome full-blooded native woman, married a Scotch-Irish capitalist, Mr. Campbell, in the golden days of the monarchy; and this Princess and several very beautiful sisters were the result of the union. (One of the sisters was blonde as wheat.) Both the Princess and her mother (Mrs. Sam Parker, by her second marriage) were very fond of playing cards, and my husband had the pleasure of being invited to their games on several occasions. An interesting story was

HAWAIIAN QUEENS AND THE SULTAN 287 told me of this family. I cannot vouch for its truth, but I was assured it was a fact and I enjoyed believing it.

The Princess' step-father, Mr. Sam Parker, was many times a millionaire and a man of great intellectual powers. Taking his step-daughters to California to be educated, he entered one of the prominent hotels in that State with his very handsome wife and daughters, intending to lunch there. The head waiter, not knowing who they were, and observing the very dark complexion of some of the strikingly handsome ladies in the party, stepped up to the millionaire and announced that colored people were not allowed in the dining-room. The party withdrew. In a few hours Mr. Parker returned and informed the head waiter that he had purchased the hotel and hereafter would bring his family there to lunch whenever he so desired. My informant added the statement that this hotel was, at that time, bringing a large income to the family.

It was somewhat surprising during our first weeks in Honolulu, as we sat in the dining-room of Young's Hotel, to see a very blonde man enter with a very brown wife in full evening regalia and frequently accompanied by children of variegated colors, but we grew accustomed to this after a time.

One day, through Governor Cleghorn, we were accorded an audience with the deposed Queen Liliuokalani. The Queen kept up a very royal attitude and never became democratic or easy of approach. We found her in her pretty house, set in a tropical garden, attended by her lady-in-waiting, and several little brown maids of honor. The Queen was an impressive-looking person, large, dignified, and unmistakably intellectual. Through her Polynesian beauty there was also a hint of the African somewhere back in her ancestry. She spoke with a quiet, dignified resentment of her dethronement, and believed absolutely in her right to rule. She was very gracious in her treatment of us and permitted me to read the lines of her beautifully shaped hand. In it were clearly shown her powerful intellect, and the artistic talents which enabled her to be a fine musician and to compose the immortal "Aloha Ouie," whose poignant beauty has become known to the whole world. There, too, I saw the savage instinct which had made her insist on her right to decapitate the men who had created a revolution against her in case she remained a Queen under a protectorate. This, we understood, had been the real cause of her complete deposition by the United States.

Some years before we went to Hawaii we had become interested in a protege of the King, who, at periodical times, made himself notorious through political intrigues and revolution. The reason of our interest in the man was because of his name, Robert Wilcox. My husband used to open his morning paper and say to me: "Well, Ella, I see I am in prison this morning." One morning he found he had been sentenced to death, but this Hawaiian Robert Wilcox finally departed from earth through a natural death, several years before our visit. He had received, through the King, a military education in Italy, became an officer in the Italian army, and married an Italian countess who believed him to be of royal blood and straightway divorced him when she learned to the contrary. He then married a native woman who was called Princess Theresa. This Princess Theresa, hearing of our presence in Honolulu, became keenly interested in meeting another Robert Wilcox, and so invited us to a native feast, a Luau. It was given on her husband's birthday, in honor of his memory, and there we met seventy-five natives of all ages and shades of color, and only two other fair-skinned guests. The feast was served at long, rough tables, the guests seated on benches. Big bowls of poi were placed before each of us, which we were expected to consume by the use of our fingers. This poi is the national dish of the South Seas, eaten at all times and in great quantities. We did not find it appetizing, but we managed to dispose of some of it. Other mysterious dishes were placed before us which we had to accept with faith and courtesy.

After the feast there were music and dancing and, as a special favor, two formerly famous dancers gave us the Hula. It might have seemed quite a naughty dance had the women been younger and slenderer. In their day they must have been very attractive in the Oriental manner and in Oriental costumes. Just then they were simply rather good looking, heavy matrons, attired in the Hawaiian dress of that day HAWAIIAN QUEENS AND THE SULTAN 289 (1908),-which, in the States, we call a "Mother Hubbard."

We went forth from the Luau, hung with leis on neck and hat–the native wreaths made of heavily fragrant flowers which are a part of every festival in Honolulu. Many pleasant courtesies were shown me that winter. The Kilohana Art League, which was the largest association of its kind in Honolulu, gave a reception for me. The feature of the evening was the presentation of a little poetical play of mine, entitled "Art vs. Cupid." The leading role was played by Mrs. Ethel Humphries, the wife of Dr. Frank Howard Humphries, the English doctor who had been the royal physician the last year of the monarchy, and who was shortly to return to a larger field in England.

The Doctor himself, a fine actor, played the lover's role, and a pretty child, named Farrington, made an adorable Cupid.

Then there were the usual dinners and luncheons, where I met the distinguished people of Honolulu, official and native, and there was a wonderful flower festival where the native Pau riders performed brilliant equestrian feats.

But, happiest of all, were the leisurely saunterings to suburban resorts just by ourselves. We went out to Waikiki and enjoyed the surf riding, which we found novel and interesting, but not quite as exciting as we imagined it would be. Our jaunts included Wahiwa, Pearl Harbor, and several immense sugar plantations. Such happy days!

Every morning we ate a delicious papia– next to the mango, the most perfect fruit on earth–in our little bungalow, before going over to the hotel for a mid-day breakfast. Then the afternoon was given to sight-seeing until we grew tired and returned to our charming nook for a nap and a bath before dinner. After dinner we received a caller. This caller we called "Our Bungalow Cat." Cats instinctively knowing my interest in the feline race, almost invariably attach themselves to me wherever I go. This Hawaiian cat had appeared the day after we entered the bungalow in a stage of imminent maternity. I fed her sumptuously and prepared a box for her on our veranda and hoped each morning to find it occupied by the cat family. Not until three days afterward did I see

Madam Puss, who came back very hungry indeed and then stole away, evidently to her kittens, which I was unable to find, despite much Sherlock Holmes' detective work, for a period of three days. Then the caretaker of the vacant hotel found Madam Puss and her four kittens in the third story of the empty hotel, in a dark corner of the linen room. I brought her down and gave her wonderful luxury in a very quiet corner of our bungalow, but after two or three more days she again disappeared and returned to the old quarters, carrying each kitten up the three flights of stairs by the back of its neck. Every morning she came for her breakfast and every night for her supper. Then late in the evening she made us a dinner call, rolling at our feet and purring to tell us how she appreciated our attentions. Before leaving Honolulu I had told, written and telephoned to several of my friends, asking for a home for each sturdy kitten. Two years later when I passed through Honolulu again on our trip around the world, we went up to our old bungalow and, finding the caretaker of the now open Hawaiian hotel, I inquired if my friends ever came for the kittens after my departure. "Great Heavens, Madam," ejaculated the man, "what trouble you did make me! There were only four kittens and at least sixteen people came demanding a kitten after you left."

Our leaving was a very spectacular affair, as is usually the case with visitors in Honolulu. Burton Holmes and Alexander Hume Ford had prepared some old-time sports at the dock for my edification. A small regiment of black native boys, attired in nature's costume, came, bringing long wreaths with which to decorate me, and then proceeded to make high dives from the top of the ship into the sea. Bands played, handkerchiefs and flowers waved, as regretfully we sailed away from Honolulu in the golden sunlight of a March day. The decks of the Manchuria were veritable flower shops. There were sixty-seven passengers that day and all were flower-wreathed. My own leis were mainly made of yellow flowers, my friends knowing my fondness for that color. Burton Holmes had his moving-picture camera leveled at us and later displayed these pictures throughout the country. We

HAWAIIAN QUEENS AND THE SULTAN 291 happened always to be somewhere else when they were displayed so we never saw ourselves as others saw us.

That I should be presented to the Sultan of Java, Sultan Hamangkoeboewono VII in the city of Djokjakarta, at the Royal Palace of the Kraton, came about in this way.

We had received letters of introduction from a high official to Captain Happy, a retired naval officer, living at Solokarta, who, upon the receipt of our letters, came at once to call upon my husband and me and to offer his services toward our entertainment. There are two Sultans of Java; and great is the rivalry and animosity existing between the two. An old feud, dating back centuries between two brothers, keeps its smouldering fires smoking to this day. Each Sultan believes he is the only rightful heir to the throne and each speaks of the other with disdain. It was to the palace of the older Sultan that Captain Happy secured our admission during a great festival andarranged to have us presented to His Royal Majesty in person. This particular reception was given at the Kraton in celebration of a ceremony of the previous morning, viz.: the circumcision of twenty-five sons, grandsons and nephews of the Sultan, performed in public in the court of the palace and witnessed by ten thousand people of both sexes. The religion of Java is Mohammedan and this surgical ceremony has both a physical and spiritual significance and constitutes a consecration to the creed of Mahomet. It is followed by a formal ball and a festival lasting three days. The propitious time for the ceremony is decided by astrologers.

It was on the second evening of the festival that we set forth with our naval officer in that state of gleeful expectancy which characterizes the American mind about to be entertained by novel sights and customs. In theory we despise ostentatious courts; in fact we love them as we love spectacular drama. Captain Happy had informed us that our presentation to the Sultan would take place at seven o'clock: and we arrived at the outer court of the Kraton five minutes before seven and proceeded through the shadows of great banyan trees to the inner court, among increasing numbers of retainers and servants. The sudden night of the tropics had fallen aiid as we descended from the carriage to the place of waiting, a curious and weird picture was presented to our sight. Through the purple twilight and by the flickering flames of torches hundreds of retainers were moving about and as many more were sitting upon their haunches. All of these attendants were naked to the waist; clothed from hip to knee in the graceful sarong. Some of them wore peculiar caps, others the fez, others a curious comb set high upon the back of the head: and each head-dress signified the position, nationality, or occupation of the wearer.

A few moments after our arrival we were approached by a soldierly looking Japanese in officer's uniform; this proved to be the Crown Prince, who had come to escort me to the presence of the Sultan. Followed by my husband and Captain Happy, we proceeded through the inner court to the reception hall of the Kraton. At the main entrance just inside the large hall the old Sultan of Java stood waiting to welcome his guests. He was dressed in military uniform and his personality strongly resembled that of Bismarck, as seen in his portraits. He was, at that time (1911), seventy-two years of age, strong of face, gracious of manner, and with a direct gaze when shaking hands which always gives a visitor a sense of being welcome to his host. Immediately behind the Sultan crouched his personal servant, holding in both hands what was afterwards discovered to be the royal cuspidor. When the Sultan walked about the bearer-of-the-royal-cuspidor followed with bent knees and low bowed head, for no servitor of the Palace of the Sultan may walk upright in the presence of his Royal Master.

The Crown Prince conducted me about the room, and presented me to five of his sisters and the Crown Princess, who formed the receiving party. But instead of sitting together they occupied chairs at stated intervals about the large hall.

Behind each Princess crouched two women servants, one holding the box of sweets and the betel nut, so popular in Java, and the other the cuspidor, for the betel nut necessitates the use of this unpleasant utensil, even as does the tobacco used by

Javanese ladies to remove the stains of deep magenta which the betel nut produces.

After having made the tour of the room I was seated near one of the exits and allowed to watch the arrivals of the native men and women of high caste, and the Dutch dignitaries and their wives and daughters. First of all, being a woman, I studied the costumes of the six princesses. Five of them wore a kaim (which is the royal sarong) of the same pattern, a pattern reserved for royal princesses. It was soft brown in color, and composed of small squares the size of checkers. The kaim of the Crown Princess was in a different design. The hair of each was dressed in the same manner; brushed back from the brow and coiled low in the neck; and all were splendid with jeweled pins and combs, and bracelets. The one touch of individuality was the coat of varying color and material. One was of velvet, a fabric much loved by ladies in the tropics, perhaps because it is expensive and unsuitable for general use, and others were of silk and satin in as many colors as there were princesses.

Each princess carried a small fortune on her person in precious gems, and each was bare of foot. This is the law of the Sultan; no man or woman of native blood may appear in his august presence with covered feet, unless it be a son who has arrived at the distinction of wearing soldierly dress.

The faces, necks, hands and feet of the royal ladies were powdered creamy white, and their amiable and agreeable countenances might have been almost pretty but for the unattractive custom (which only recently has begun to decline) of blackening the teeth. It is the distinguishing mark of the married man and woman. Now blackening the teeth does not mean merely to stain them black. It means to scrape off the precious enamel, paint them black, and then re-enamel them, which, once done, is done for ever, or for so long as the teeth last. It is said that the custom originated with an idea of making the dental adornments of the human face differ from those of the animal. Others say it was done to make sacrifice on the altar of marriage. As our eyes see beauty in pearly teeth, so the eye of the Javanese and Japanese of the olden time found beauty in these black pearls. To us it seemed a disfigurement.

When the Crown Prince and the Princess smiled, which was often, and when they spoke their mouths were ugly black caverns. The attendants of the princesses (like all the innumerable servants in and about the palace) were clothed only in the sarong, while in the hair, and on the arms of these special "slavies" shone jewels of the first water.

The courts surrounding the palace were packed with hundreds of these half-bare attendants, and in still another portion of the great gardens, within sight and sound of the reception hall, were crowded hordes of concubines and children. These thousands of nude torsos, gleaming like bronze statues in the half lights, were a curious spectacle to the American eye.

Later we saw the streets leading from the main court, lined on either side with little houses, occupied by the favorites of the Sultan.

The old Sultan is said to be the father of eighty children, the eldest a man of fifty-seven, the youngest a child of three months. The Crown Prince is a son of the legal and official Sultana, for while true disciples of Mahomet, the sultans of Java do not recognize more than one wife as legitimate. However, they legitimize and ennoble many favorite children of concubines.

The Sultan of Solokarta has no children by his Sultana. He has made the son of one concubine heir apparent, yet it is a matter of great concern to him that he has no royal heir to the throne.

The Crown Prince of Djokjakarta is the oldest son of the Sultana, herself a princess by birth. He is thirty-four years of age and has been married less than ten years; but is the father of seventeen children. The Sultan educates his sons in Javanese, Dutch and Malay, but refuses to have them taught other European languages or to allow them to travel in foreign lands. He is intensely jealous of the European countries, and does not wish his own to be contaminated by foreign manners or ideas.

The younger and more progressive Sultan of Solokarta has HAWAIIAN QUEENS AND THE SULTAN 295 sent three of his sons (by concubines) to be educated abroad. Yet he is less sociable with the Dutch residents than his rival.

Our Sultan crossed the large reception hall and took his seat of state (a most simple one by the way) soon after we made our entrance, and there he remained until the march played by the European orchestra in the court announced the coming of the resident general, the official Dutch governor. Descending from his chair, the Sultan met the resident at the door and conducted him to a seat on his left, the chair on his right being occupied by the Crown Prince.

As soon as this ceremony had taken place, the weird, sad, fascinating music of the native gamelan orchestra gave the signal that the feature of the evening was about to begin. The dance of the Eastern performances has an historical basis; and each step and gesture relates some event in a story of mingled romance and glory. It may be performed by a company of dancers, but this evening it was given by four of the younger princesses, all dressed in a costume reserved for such occasions, and all as exactly alike in appearance as four peas in a pod.

Slim, tall young girls (as height goes in Java), they seemed to be not over seventeen years of age, and in their elegantly fantastic and rich costumes, with their powdered white faces and black hair and eyebrows and numerous jewels they were peculiarly attractive. They were not spoiled by blackened teeth.

The young women made a most deliberate and stately entrance. They were preceded and followed by two old duennas, withered dames who had taught generations of princesses this same dance. These royal ballet teachers were attired only in the sarong, fastened above the breast, and falling just below the knees. Their grizzled hair was plainly knotted, and they wore no jewels. It required some ten minutes for the dancers to reach the center of the hall, where they paused, each in her place, forming a square directly in the center of the room and in front of the Sultan and the resident. After a low obeisance was made the four duennas dropped upon the floor and squirmed (something after the combined manner of an inch worm and a crab) back to the main entrance. This movement was repeated eight times by the old dames, who brought four tables and four pistols and placed them beside the princesses, and then writhed back to a position immediately behind the dahcers where they watched the performance as interestedly as if they had not seen it, a thousand times.

A shrill chorus of women's voices, nasal and penetrating, was the signal that the dance had begun, and for ten or fifteen minutes the graceful movements of the heads and arms of the slim young princesses, and the delicate manipulation of the scarf and the pretty little sliding step of the bare feet made a fascinating picture. It was all novel and full of charm.

The remaining thirty-five minutes grew monotonous, for the dance has no variation save the shooting of the four pistols toward the end, a proceeding gone through without a single change of countenance by the princesses, and with no excitement save in the audience.

The Sultan watched the performance with a polite show of interest, but one could not help thinking that in the course of his seventy-two years and with a family of eighty children, he must have seen this same exhibition too many times to be thrilled by it.

Shortly before the entertainment began four young men between fifteen and twenty-two years of age, dressed in Javanese costume of sarong and coat, and with little odd caps on their heads, came salaaming through the main entrance, and immediately dropped upon their haunches and hopped (literally hoptoaded) their way to within a few feet of the princesses, where they sat until the end of the entertainment.

These were four younger sons of the Sultan, who were not yet permitted to wear uniform, and likewise not permitted to walk upright in the presence of royalty. Even in the presence of the Crown Prince must they squat and hop when they need to move.

The weird chant of women's nasal voices died away, the gamelan instruments changed their tuneless tune to a march movement, the four old duennas squirmed forward to the front and rear of the four princesses, arose and stood as erect HAWAIIAN QUEENS AND THE SULTAN 297 as the young maidens. Away they all marched, princesses and duennas, and the royal dance was over.

The Sultan and the Resident went away to sup together, and then something else happened to entertain the foreign eye.

From a row of chairs on a platform a few steps below the reception hall and below the six older princesses who had received the guests came marching forward, led by the Crown Prince, sixteen more royal princesses, all dressed in kaims of exactly the same pattern as those worn by the six older sisters, and looking so much alike as they ranged themselves in chairs ready to be served with refreshments, that one felt it was an optical illusion or a trick of multiple mirrors.

Each of the twenty-one princesses wore a wide comb heavily studded with diamonds just over her coil of black hair; each wore a large diamond butterfly in the middle of her coil; and each wore three little diamond flower pins on either side of her coil. Each sported diamond bracelets, above her elbow; and each was powdered to a creamy tint. But fifteen sets of teeth were pure white and six were jet black.

Then as they sat there a curious thing was made evident. Every royal princess plainly exerted herself to hide her bare feet from view, by means of her tightly fitting sarong. Though they are born and bred to this custom, yet contact with the modern world, slight as this contact is, has rendered the princesses conscious of their bare feet

A sumptuous supper of European dishes was being served to the guests in the various side rooms and courts of the palace; wine flowed, rich course succeeded rich course, and with something like fifteen thousand people in his train, all dependent upon his bounty, all consumers and no producers, save of more consumers, one felt that the royal host had been royal indeed to provide such a repast for his many guests.

The princesses were served in the great reception hall, and a pretty feature of the occasion was the assistance of the Crown Prince, who helped them to cakes and cream and removed their plates with his own hands and laughed and chatted with them, meanwhile, as any other brother might do.

We came away and left them there, the charming young prince with the almost handsottie face, the twenty-one near-pretty princesses in their simple native costumes (which require four months in the making, yet which by the casual glance may be mistaken for a bit of calico or cretonne), the squatting attendants with their two boxes behind each princess, the hundreds of retainers and servants of servants, the scores of concubines, and the innumerable semi-royal children. As we looked back, the mass of half-nude bodies, the variety of strange head-dresses, the glitter of precious jewels, all produced a never-to-be-forgotten picture. We made our way to the outer court through a sudden tropical rain storm to the music of gamelans, and we found our carriage by the flare of torches. We drove away wondering how long this relic of a dying era would continue.

It is the last act of the spectacular opera. Before another century the curtain will ring down–Java will be less picturesque– but will not the human race be benefited?

The ruins of Bbro Boedor, the most magnificent monument Buddhism has ever erected, built in the eighth or ninth century in purely Buddhistic style, are the most remarkable of the many ancient relics that are to be found at Java. One has said of this: "There in the heart of the steaming tropics, in that summerland of the world below the equator, on an island where volcanoes cluster more thickly and vegetation is richer than in any other region of the globe, where earthquakes continually rock and shatter, and where deluges descend during the rainy half of the year, remains nearly intact the temple of Boro Boedor, covering almost the same area as the Great Pyramid of Gizeh.

"That solid pyramidal temple, rising in magnificent sculptured terraces, built without mortar or cement, without column or pillar or arch, is one of the surviving wonders of the world."

During the time that Java was under the rule of the English the temple was laid bare by removing the earth, which probably was heaped up against it by the last worshipers of Buddha in Java.

HAWAIIAN QUEENS AND THE SULTAN 299

Within the last few years, the wall that encloses the lowest terrace had also been divested of its cloak of stone, photographed and then covered again in order to prevent subsidence.

In addition to that wall, which also rests upon a terrace, it consists of two square lower terraces, and five galleries with balustrades, which, with the inside walls of the lower gallery, rise upon the others like an outer wall, on which again four terraces are erected, the three highest of which are circular.

The images of the lower tiers represent the world of wishes; those upon the upper terraces, the world of forms; and the unfinished image in the cupola, the world without forms, agreeing with the three stages for the obtaining of Nirvana.

I went out one morning and wrote, at dawn–

AT THE BORO BOEDOR

Watching the dawn upon its turrets break (New beauties leaping to each ray of light), Methought I heard Christ calling (as one might Call to an older brother): "Buddha, wake! Come toil with me. From thy calm eyelids shake The dreams of ages; and behold the sight Of earth still sunk in ignorance and night. I took thy labor–now thy portion take.

"Too vast the effort for one Avatar,
My brave disciples are not overwise,
Our kindred creeds they do not understand;
My cross they worship, yet thy temples mar.
Dear brother Buddha, from Nirvana rise.
And let us work together, hand in hand."

CHAPTER XX Marriage Customs and Polygamy

TO meet four wedding processions in two hours is not an unusual experience at this season of the year in India. It happened to us. Two of the brides chanced to reach the Jaipur temple, where certain of the rites were to be performed, at the same time, and it was our good fortune to be passing the temple at that moment, also.

The spectacle was brilliant. We had heard the shrill singing of the throngs of people as they approached, and we had seen their rainbow-hued garments from afar. A hundred– possibly two hundred– people were in the first procession, men, women and children–mainly the last two.

Marriage is a four or five days' process in India, and each day has its special features. This day brought the families and women and children friends of the bride and bridegroom to the temple, the bride leading the procession all curtained in her cart drawn by two white bullocks. We were told that we might wait and see her descend from her cart at the temple door, where a stalwart and handsome Hindoo, very much trimmed with gilt braid and wearing a great turban of splendid yellow colors on his head, lifted down this tiny bride, just ten years old.

He was the proud uncle: and when, on counsel of our guide, I approached and asked to meet the little lady of the bullock cart, it was he who granted gracious permission.

. A score of women and a dozen men crowded closely about us, the women peeping with one eye from under their brilliant saris and showing gorgeous necklaces and bracelets and nose-and ear-rings as they arranged their draperies with the evident intention of revealing their jewels. The little bride was so hidden by her cloth of gold wrappings that she seemed only a

MARRIAGE CUSTOMS AND POLYGAMY 301 big bronze package on end, and she reached barely above tay waistline as I stood beside her.

A request to peep at her face was granted with much laughter and good will by the relatives, and I stooped down and drew apart the cloth, stiff with gold embroidery, and saw a dear little brown face, classic as a cameo–a Greek nose, delicate mouth, white teeth and great dark eyes.

Jewels gleamed in the nostrils, ears and upper lip, and the slender throat wore too many necklaces to be counted in so brief a moment. This bride was ten years old, and she was going home from the temple with her husband, an undeveloped lad of fourteen.

The other bride waiting her turn at the temple door was just five years old and her husband eight. She would not consummate her marriage for five years, possibly, though wives of eight and mothers of nine are found in India.

Innumerable instances can be related by those who are in mission or medical work in India of little girls of seven and eight who are actual wives to husbands much older.

The mania of the East Indian mother to marry her daughter young has become insanity. While the better and more educated classes of men are awakened to the evils of this custom and wish to change it, the mothers bar the way.

Should the eight-year-old husband of the five-year-old bride I saw at the temple door die to-morrow, the little wife would be forced by the traditions of her race to live a widow always and devote her life to praying for the dead husband's soul.

The brief little hour of glory which the child wife enjoys during the wedding festivities is her one season of triumph. Never after the wedding feast is she permitted even to dine at her husband's table. The high caste Brahmin will assure you that it is because the Indian so reverences woman that he gives her such seclusion and privacy. It may be. Certainly the East Indian wife is more content with her lot than most American wives.

Progress and the influence of Western ideas have caused a cessation of the old custom of "suttee," the burning of the widow on her husband's funeral pyre, but she is quite as abso- lutely sacrificed in many instances by the traditions of her race to-day, though the process is slower. Yet she seems to love her old customs and to fight against progress.

In Bengal, the province which includes Calcutta, there is a marked change taking place in the minds of the cultivated classes regarding child-marriage, the seclusion of women and the position of widows. Yet when we realize that only one woman in one hundred in India can read or write, and that only one man in twelve is educated, it is easy to understand that the cultivated class is not sufficiently powerful to make a decided change in a thousand-year-old custom.

The great city of Calcutta contains one ex-widow who devoted her life from child-hood to ripe womanhood to her dead husband's family. Then, four years ago, she created a scandal by the unheard-of act of eloping and marrying a second time. She climbed over a garden wall, and her lover awaited her on the outer side. She is a handsome and attractive young woman, and has further literally "astonished the natives" by ascending in an aeroplane, and (it is regretful to state) by smoking cigarettes! She is regarded by the conservative people of Calcutta as a warning rather than an example, because it is declared that her new-found freedom has made her bold and destroyed her modesty. It is further stated by the tradition-bound that the birth of two daughters and no son to this woman gives evidence that God does not bless her re-union to a second husband, albeit he is a descendant of one of the many royal branches of India.

The orthodox people of India will insist upon saying that the child widows of their land live quite happily in their exalted ideals of devotion to the dead. Without doubt there are such cases, and it is impossible for the Western mind to grasp the Eastern view of life.

One young girl who was widowed shortly after she was taken to her husband's home is to-day very unhappy, because her mother-in-law, a poor woman, sent her back to her wealthy parents to live. She was sent as a punishment and feels she is deprived of happiness here and hereafter in not being allowed to work as a slave for her dead husband's mother. This is an absolute fact, and is not an isolated case. Centuries of superstition and time-honored traditions produce in certain idealistic temperaments such examples of hysterical devotion to a cause. But there is another side to the picture.

An Indian doctor, deeply interested in his land and devoting his whole time and efforts towards the betterment of his race, told me there were 1,000 Indian widows under fourteen years of age living improper lives in Calcutta, and many others of a more mature age.

With no outlook toward home, happiness, liberty, love or any of the things which make life for a woman worth living, can we wonder if many of these child widows fall by the wayside?

Dr. K. Deva Shastri called in answer to one of our letters, and proved to be a young man of great mind and learning and one deeply interested in helping to regenerate India.

Dr. Shastri is striving to obtain a public school system also, and Home Rule for India. Surely the hour has come when Home Rule should be given that land.

One afternoon in Benares we went to the Monkey Temple and the Golden Temple and saw sacred bulls and cows, alive and in the flesh as well as represented in bronze, and we beheld people worshiping before innumerable phallic (Hnga) emblems, the worship of Siva, just as they did in the most primitive ages of the world. In fact, everything was phallic and linga; paper-weights and bric-a-brac were for sale at every step.

The Monkey Temple proved to be very amusing. Hundreds of wild monkeys were visible, all seeming to enjoy their life of luxurious ease provided by a wealthy Rajah. They sat on window ledges, roofs, stairs and in doorways, and leaped about asking for the nuts we bought to feed them. One mother monkey with twins was most human as she sat and nursed one of her babies with a look of sleepy pleasure on her face while the baby's hand patted her shoulder.

The next morning we went to see the people bathe in the Ganges–a most impressive sight! We were rowed up the famed river in a queer boat, and for an hour watched the brilliantly colored throng of hundreds of people come and go, bathing and praying, outlined against the background of splendid mansions, for most of the great Rajahs of India have palaces on the Ganges where they come at certain seasons to bathe and worship.

As we rowed by, we saw gruesome sights at the great burning ghat where several bodies were being burned and others were awaiting cremation. People came from great distances, carrying their dead on their shoulders, to cast their ashes in the Ganges. We saw men raking over the cinders where a body had been burned and were told these cinders were made into a paste and used to smoke. The "holy men" of India are considered, they say, too holy to burn, and so they are put into the Ganges after death. We came very close to one of these bodies as we rowed back to the landing stairs. It was sewed in cloth and anchored midway in the river and three vultures were sitting on the breast, picking into it.

As we walked up the stairs from the river, I spied a remarkable looking being in a long, dingy robe and turban, his face painted a deep saffron, with a bright red V in the forehead. He wore a wonderful necklace made of wood, and I stopped him and, by the aid of the guide, managed to get possession of the ornament. The man was a "holy man" and said he could not sell anything for money but he would accept a gift of it. So he went away with four rupees and I went on, happy with my queer trinket.

We dined with Dr. Shastri and four bright young men at his house the next night. It was an Indian dinner where all the food, even rice, was eaten with the fingers by the Indians, we only being given spoons and forks. The room was quaint, the house surrounded by great trees. The conversation was brilliant and instructive, and the evening was delightful. The next day Dr. Shastri took us to the village free school where we saw ten boys under eleven years of age, all married.

It is interesting to look back over one's life and see how small events sometimes lead to great experiences.

MARRIAGE CUSTOMS AND POLYGAMY 305

One day, in a very large mail, a letter came to me in New York City from a stranger. It was an appealing letter and was written by a woman passing through the Garden of Geth-semane.

It led to our acquaintance: and, strangely enough, our acquaintance had, in a circuitous manner, led this woman to India five years before my visit to that ancient and wonderful land.

Now I found my friend, companion and teacher of English to the wife of a progressive Prince of large wealth and with ambitions to have his wife come out of Purdah–that is, give up the life of veils and seclusion, and become modern.

The wife found it a penance, much preferring her native customs; but, like wives in India, she obeyed her husband. My friend wrote me a letter one day, telling me there was to be a Purdah Party; all the high caste women of Calcutta were to meet at a large reception, given in honor of Lady Hardinge, wife of the then Viceroy. I was invited; and here my friend assured me I would see the real beauty and the splendid dressing and the gorgeous jewels of the women of India. Heavy awnings protected the driveway from allowing any rude eye to gain one peep at the form or the veiled face of any woman as she approached the building where the reception was to be held. As my carriage arrived, and I stepped out and entered the covered passageway, I saw bundles of exquisite material perambulating along in front of me, and conjectured that fair forms might be within these bundles. Once in the reception room, my eyes were dazzled with the sights I beheld. Beautiful faces were everywhere; and such radiance of color and such artistic draping in garments it had never been my fortune to behold before this occasion.

The oddest and rarest jewels, too, were to be seen: and though the old custom of wearing jewels in the nose is said to be passing, there were many classic noses so decorated in that room. My friend was at my side and said: "You will see many women here to-day who never before attended any gathering of people save family parties. You will notice their little timid and almost frightened air: and somehow it is sweeter to me than the air of the modern women of India who have come out of Purdah. I have grown to feel that the life of the higher class women of India is very beautiful indeed. The little Princess whose companion I am is not nearly so happy since she came out of Purdah. One has to be long in India, and to get into the close family relations, and to study the minds of the women to be able to understand how happy and how sweet are their lives. It is impossible for a tourist or for a missionary, whose work lies in entirely different lines, to comprehend the real India; the real inner lives of its women. Somehow it appeals to me more strongly than the hurly-burly life of the American woman of our best society."

I could not dispute my friend, being only a tourist; but I felt as I watched these beautiful women in their picturesque attire and their gleaming jewels bundle away down the passage to their tightly closed carriages, and roll off to their secluded homes,–I felt, I say, that I preferred my own life to theirs. My life, not my garments, however; for glancing in a mirror during the reception hours, I had been shocked at my utterly commonplace appearance, although I was clothed in one of New York's latest creations: but the artistic fashions of India, which never change, while centuries roll, had so pleased my eye, that my own costume seemed hateful in comparison. On another occasion I was invited to the home of a man of large wealth, occupying an enviable position in the intellectual world of Bombay. We had letters introducing us from a Hindu Swami we had known in America. As soon as our letter was presented the receiver sent his motor car for us; and at his home were gathered a number of notable men of letters. After a very interesting half hour all the men departed, while the host informed me that his wife and daughters were waiting impatiently to meet me. "Of course you know it is the custom of India," he said, "that the women of the household do not come into the presence of any men save their husbands and sons; and even those they would not, as a rule, see in the presence of strange ladies. But my youngest son will, on this occasion, remain and act as interpreter: for my wife and daughters speak no English."

The youngest son was a big handsome youth of seventeen, speaking an excellent English; and with very modern ideas. His mother and two sisters came into the room like visions– beautiful and gentle and timid; and I talked with them through the young man. They passed their days in household duties, they said, and in sewing and embroidering; their religious devotions took much time. They sometimes drove out in a closed carriage and at times called on friends and received calls– always veiled from the sight of the public. Only the very poor or the undesirable women of India as a rule disregarded this custom, though they knew a modern idea was creeping in which caused some high caste women to come out of Purdah. They shrank from the thought of it, as we would shrink from the idea of walking abroad at high noon in evening dress. It seemed rude and vulgar to them. They were very happy in their sheltered lives, yet they understood how strange it must seem to me. The young man confessed that he believed in modern ideas regarding women; and it was his intention to adopt them, he said, when he married. It was evident that he had to some extent adopted them already, or he would not have been single at seventeen.

There was an atmosphere about that home and something about those sweet women that did not permit me to feel sorry for them. Happiness is, after all, a matter of one's point of view.

I could not think a missionary was needed to convert these deeply religious women to a different creed: or to make them accept a life of fashionable dissipation, bridge, dancing, and extravagant dressing, motor riding and traveling about from resort to resort to find distraction (as do so many of our "best people") in place of the simple secluded lives they lead.

I think I understood my friend's point of view partially when I went forth from that house in India.

By one of those strokes of good luck which so frequently attended our travels, we arrived in Singapore just in time to be taken by the American consul to the Chitty temple, where the Hindu festival of Tanpaniene was in full swing. It occurs, only once a year.

The scene presented to our eyes fairly staggered us; it was like living an Arabian Nights' tale, beautiful, barbaric, splendid, horrible. There were ten thousand Hindus gathered there. The vast temple was ablaze with color and filled with superb and hideous things–superb decorations and hideous gods. The "John Rockefeller, Junior," of the Temple and all his receiving committee were naked save for loin cloths of varying lengths and colors. They wore big diamond bracelets and rings of priceless value and were handsome as bronze statues. One man, it was said, possessed a fortune of fifty million dollars.

We saw ten thousand poor people fed there. It is the custom at this festival. At the end of a vast hall a devout procession was winding up a flight of stairs, bowing before the shrine of Vishnu, throwing ashes on their chests, making a cross of ashes on the brow and saying strange prayers. I followed and performed the same rites to the best of my ability. Weird and insistent music of two tones made its monotonous accompaniment to the ceremonies. The nude participants squatted on splendid, rugs and were surrounded by a mute circle of semi-naked devotees, sitting cross-legged.

In the outer court a religious fanatic was doing penance for his sins and showing his scorn of the body by sticking knives and needles into breast, shoulder and face and letting others do the same for him. He was full of drugs and exaltation but looked like a dying man in torture. A weird chant was sung by the crowd about him; some were fanning him, others were holding wreaths over him. It was an awful sight, yet we were assured by the consul and the harbor master, who had lived there many years, that the man would be about the next day showing no signs of this horrible experience. Robert pressed close to the scene and watched it closely for several minutes to convince himself that there was no legerdemain about it. He stood so close he could have touched the man, and came away convinced as well as sickened at the sight.

This was the one night in the year when invited guests could MARRIAGE CUSTOMS AND POLYGAMY 309 gaze on the sacred bulls in this temple. We were presented to six in all. I never dreamed that the worship of bulls really-existed to-day. I thought that only their pictures and images were kept in the temples, but here they were, beautiful creatures, all of them. One! actually had an angelic face! They never do any labor, save once a year to drag the silver peacock, worth ten thousand dollars, through the streets. That was done the next night; it rained so hard we did not go out among the throngs to see it.

The Chitties are the Hindu money lenders of Singapore. They possess great wealth and their temple is only open to the public once a year and entrance then is only by invitation. It was owing to the thoughtfulness of the charming American consul, Mr. Dubois, that we were permitted this interesting experience.

While we were fairly enthralled and taken out of purselves by the barbaric scene, the magnificent coloring, the burning incense and the strange music, there was a sudden blare of sound and a modern band began playing the "Merry Widow" waltz. Young "Rockefeller, Junior," desired to make the reception wholly up to date and had provided entertainment for foreign guests. It woke us rudely from our pipe dream, and we hurried home to our hotel.

The Island of Singapore is twenty-seven miles long, fourteen miles wide and sixty-six miles in circumference. Between Singapore and the United States the time difference is twelve hours. While you breakfast here your friends are dining there.

The very last day we were in Singapore we met with another piece of luck. We were driving to the Botanical Gardens and came across the funeral procession of a rich mandarin. We have seen Mardi Gras in almost every part of the earth, but never anything that could compare in startling and. original features with this solemn religious ceremony. There was a column of people over a mile long; and some twenty immense, grotesque images, fully fifteen feet high, with faces of animals and demons, and enormous painted bodies moved by men hidden inside were walking in the procession.

Jio THE WORLDS AND I

One statue was a mandarin, thirty feet tall. He was seated in a triumphal car and crowned with a golden coronet and toted by a lot of near-naked coolies. There was a line of Chinamen simply dressed in bracelets and scarfs and carrying splendid flags with many letters and designs.

We were told by our driver that these were club men belonging to the dead man's club and that the jewelry all belonged to the deceased. There were carriages filled with women and children all dressed in white. They were the children and wives of the dead man. Other women, with a brownish costume and lips painted bright magenta, I imagined were concubines. The demons and animals often turned and glanced behind them and the effect was grotesque and awful.

It seems that it is the custom for rich mandarins to leave a sum of money to pay for having this procession march to the cemetery on certain days for one or two months after their death. All the large images are made of paper and are burned at the cemetery as an offering to the gods to make things easy for the dead man in the spirit world. Other images are made to take their place for the next procession, so trade is helped and many people given work.

Beautiful cabinets or shrines were carried on poles at intervals, and there was a small body of perhaps a dozen pig-faced and demon-faced pigmies who cut an occasional pigeon-wing as any small boy might do in a Fourth of July festival.

Important events in one's life often become dim in memory, while lesser incidents stand forth clearly.

A day in Salt Lake City, Utah, I have never forgotten, where I went out to see the remains of the Salt Sea, in company with twenty-two women who had all been polygamous wives.

One Elder accompanied the party; and he had been, until the laws of the Government made polygamy unconstitutional, the happy husband of six wives. He talked to me freely of their ideals, and the deeply religious sentiment on which Mor-monism was founded.

Polygamy, he said, was only adopted by the Mormons in

MARRIAGE CUSTOMS AND POLYGAMY 311 order to populate the community with latter-day Saints. The mistaken idea of the outside world that men took many wives from licentious or self-indulgent reasons, he deplored. It was a serious obligation, he said, for a man to assume the care and maintenance and spiritual growth of six families: but he had felt it incumbent upon him.

He believed the polygamous wives were happier than most of the Gentile woman. Every day, he observed, the newspapers reported how some wife had discovered that her husband was living a double life, and the position of a mistress was far more deplorable, he thought, than that of a respected and well cared for polygamous wife. He believed women were meant for mothers; and the preponderance of spinsters in manj; States he felt was a disaster to the race. He called my attention to the mental and physical superiority of Mormon children over those born in conventional society. This fact I could not deny. The care and protection given expectant mothers by the Mormons naturally produced more normal children than were to be found in any community of people outside, where the bearing of children is so frequently regarded as a calamity, and where efforts at prevention of Nature's most sacred office are prevalent. I assured the Elder I believed men in general had much to learn from the Mormons regarding the right view of fatherhood, and the obligation to protect and care for the expectant mother, but I could not regard the polygamous wife with any feeling, save one of pity. "I would rather," I said, "be a deceived wife, or the unfortunate affinity even, on whom the world looks askance, than accept the position of one of a syndicate owning stock in a husband."

The Elder said there was a moral question involved, and I agreed with him, saying the moral question to my thinking was that the whole ideal of the relation of the sexes rested on the effort to establish the law of one man and one woman living together in constancy and affection; and all the failures of this effort were better for the race than any lower ideal which encouraged promiscuous relations under any religious cloak.

"Never till man learns the higher laws governing sexual love and the glory and growth which comes through self-control, and the deeper emotions and joys which result from consecration of the body to one love, will the race develop to the plane God meant it to reach. Better fail over and over in trying to live up to these laws, than to settle down to self-indulgence, believing such indulgence is God's will," I said.

The Elder grieved that I could not grasp the higher meaning of polygamy, and ceased to argue the question.

The youngest and handsomest woman in the company was the one wife which the Elder was permitted to proclaim at that time.

"Yes," she said to me, "I am, or was, a polygamous wife; do I look like an unhappy woman? My husband had four other wives when he took me."

"Were you the last of all?" I asked.

A slight shadow passed over her face. "No," she said, "there was one after me; she died, and when the law declared only one wife could be recognized, I was chosen. My husband cares for the two others who are living, and provides for them. They are past child-bearing age."

"Do you mean to tell me," I asked, "that you felt no sorrow or jealousy or pain when your husband brought the last wife home?"

"We are not here on earth to be selfishly happy," was her evasive reply. "We are here to live for the good of the human race. I believed my husband was doing God's duty by taking another wife who could bear him children, and so help people the world with Saints. If I suffered it did not matter."

That she had suffered was evident by her voice and expression.

At the end of what was a very interesting afternoon, I was photographed with the party of Mormon women and the Elder.

A day at Funchal, on the island of Madeira, two days in fact, separated by an interval of three years, are clearly outlined by memory. On the first occasion we spent the evening there, going back to the ship after participating at the Casino MARRIAGE CUSTOMS AND POLYGAMY 313 in a brilliant ball, and trying our luck on the roulette wheel, which was in full swing, winning a few dollars and promptly-losing them. The gi; ounds surrounding the Casino and the city below were lighted with thousands of colored globes; and the whole scene was suggestive of the Arabian Nights.

On the next occasion we passed the day in Funchal, and rode in queer and uncomfortable bullock carts over cobblestone streets: we ascended the high cliffs which rose above the town by means of a little funicular railway, and we descended by tobogganing down in curious baskets made for that purpose.

Then I went shopping in a very restful, hammock swung over the shoulders of two stalwart Portuguese carriers.

Happy days!

The very last experience of an unusual nature which I enjoyed with my beloved, in travel, was motoring through the Kabyl Mountains in the late winter of 1913.

We had been in Tunis and Hammam Mousketine, and we came to Algiers–remaining for the day and for the second time visiting some of the interesting spots in this too modernized Oriental town.

My husband photographed me in the "Palace of Abandoned Wives," a very beautiful house, where the Sultan, in olden days before the French invasion, stored the wives of whom he had grown weary. He returned to them the jewels they brought at the time of their marriage, and they were fed and clothed by him, but their only occupation was in wandering about the beautiful halls and rooms of their prison palace, while later favorites dwelt with him elsewhere.

I visited the Turkish baths, where the high class Arab women go with their attendants and often pass the entire day. This is their one opportunity for gossip, and for learning what is going on outside of their own harems.

Only one Arab woman in fifty possesses the beauty we associate with the Oriental woman. The Arab men admire fat, and so the women acquire it early. The very young girls are often beautiful, but their beauty sinks into avoirdupois before thirty.

We took the evening train for Tizi-Ouzou, arriving there at noon the next day, after a steady mountain climb. Soon after lunch we engaged a small Arab guide and set forth on foot to see the sights of the little Arab town. Hearing weird plaintive music, I asked the guide to conduct us to the spot where it originated; and in a few moments we came upon a curious sight. In a large courtyard were congregated fifty women, and three little girls, six, eight and ten years, fantastically yet attractively arrayed in brilliant hued scarfs and bizarre jewels, and all three being coached by a teacher in the old licentious Dance du Ventre, which must be taught in childhood to those who acquire the control of their muscles which alone gives skill in this dance.

It is the only terpsichorean performance which one sees in those lands, and becomes very monotonous to travelers, but it seems never to pall upon the natives. These little girls were being taught to hold the body rigid, and to move the abdomen in a rotary manner, and again to keep the abdomen and limbs motionless, while the breasts quivered like jelly shaken in a mold.

Four Arab men musicians were playing on strange native instruments and the teacher, a very pretty Kabyl woman, was encouraging her pupils by showing them her own perfect command of her muscles: the other score or two of women were clapping hands and giving shrill cries as the dancing proceeded. The Kabyl people occupied Northern Africa before the Arabs invaded it. They fled to the mountains, and were never conquered by the invaders. While they are Mohammedan in religion yet they do not veil their women, and therefore my husband was allowed to stand with me and watch this dancing class, where he would have b6en driven away from such a scene among the other Arab tribes. The Kabyles are an intellectual people and possess much artistic taste: the women are often delicate and handsome of feature, and of a lighter shade of brown than the Bedouin or

MARRIAGE CUSTOMS AND POLYGAMY 315

Tunisians. The dancing teacher wore a most odd and effective necklace, and I signified my wish to buy it. My Httle guide tried to obtain it for three dollars, then four, and finally procured it for five. I washed it in peroxide and other disinfectants and often afterward wore it with much satisfaction. I had made a collection of odd necklaces and chains in various parts of the world: and the next day as we motored up a spiral roadway, corkscrewing about the high mountains in what seemed to me a perilous manner, we came to a curious little town perched on the very top of the Kabyl range, and there we found a native jeweler making the most interesting necklaces and pins we had ever seen. He had never been outside the Kabyl Mountains, and how he had obtained his artistic ideas puzzled us greatly. Doubtless from past lives.

After we returned to America I had sixteen of my odd necklaces photographed. One had been obtained from a harem in Tangier, Morocco—bought off the neck of one of the widows of the defunct Bey: China, Japan, Tunis, the Garden of Allah, Algiers, the Kabyl Mountains, Tizi-Ouzou, Sicily, Venice, Ceylon, Burmah, were all represented in this col-le'tion.

CHAPTER XXI People, Abroad and at Home IT was a rainy afternoon in Paris, i ne late winter day, and my husband and I had gone out to Fontainebleau to loiter about the galleries and bathe our minds in the atmosphere of an historic past.

I was wandering through a room filled with the portraits of famous beauties, painted by equally famous artists, when a lady entered and seated herself just opposite me.

She was attired in a jaunty rain coat and cap, and she was in the full bloom of youth. So attractive and magnetic was she, that I forgot the inanimate paintings on the walls, and devoted my time to looking at the living beauty, endeavoring by every kind of maneuver to prevent the object of my admiration from knowing that I was staring at her.

I found my husband in an adjoining room and advised him to obtain a peep at what I supposed was a French beauty: and he quite agreed with me that she rivaled the portraits of the King's favorites.

It may have been a week thereafter that we were bidden to a banquet at the charming home of Mr. and Mrs. John Adams Thayer, who were residing in Paris. The dinner was in honor of the American Consul, General Mason and his wife. The other guests were Mr. and Mrs. Booth Tarkington, and Mr. and Mrs. Harry Leon Wilson.

When the last mentioned lady was presented to us, imagine our surprise in recognizing our beauty of Fontainebleau; it was no other than Rose Cecil ONeill, the famous artist and author, at that time Mrs. Harry Leon Wilson. She was even more radiant in evening dress, and justified all our former admiration.

Among the scores of banquets recalled by memory, few
PEOPLE, ABROAD AND AT HOME 317 stand forth with such undimmed luster as that dinner of the hospitable Thayers. It was a progressive dinner, and at a signal from the hostess each man took his glass and his napkin, and proceeded to the chair next the lady at his right. In this manner each woman talked with each man at the table: and brilliant was the sparkle of conversation and repartee in that gifted circle.

I remember the surprise I felt when after dinner Booth Tarkington proceeded to sing a series of songs in a most melodious voice and with the air of a professional entertainer.

Eight years afterward my husband and I were again bidden by Mr. and Mrs. Thayer to another dinner at their new home in Westport, Connecticut, and again it was in honor of General and Mrs. Mason, who were visiting America for the first time in years. (This was the first year of the present war.) General Mason told us most interesting experiences he had enjoyed while serving our country in a high official capacity in Germany, where he had frequently dined at the Emperor's table.

A few days later this dear couple called on us at our Bungalow and Nature graciously prepared for them one of the most splendid sunsets Granite Bay ever offered her visitors. Standing by the water's edge bathed in the sunset's glory. General and Mrs. Mason talked with Robert and me of their profound belief, based on personal experiences, of the nearness of the spirit worlds and the desire of our departed dear ones to communicate with us. Many times since have I recalled the hour and scene and talk.

Once in Paris I made a professional visit to Madame de Thebes, the famous psychic and palmist, who predicted the San Francisco earthquake six months before it occurred.

Madame de Thebes possessed unquestionable powers as a clairvoyant and as a palmist, yet like all professional psychics she made great mistakes.

So soon as one possessed of the open mind or psychic power uses it as a means of gaining a livelihood, the menace of trickery must be met. Approached every hour by some one who wants a revelation, the professional psychic forces conditions which should come spontaneously and which do so come at times. The weaker and coarser type resort to stimt-lants and drugs to produce the powers to see and hear claii–voyantly, and in this way open the door to evil influences on both planes. Others simply resort to deceit and still others merely fail. Madame de Thebes was a woman of high moral character, refinement and statuesque beauty. So in demand were her services that I was obliged to wait two weeks from the time I first made my application for an interview. While I waited for her to admit me to her presence I was entertained by studying dozens of royal photographs which were autographed gifts to the Seer ess. And almost every celebrity in Europe was also upon her table or wall in photograph form.

I had gone to Madame de Thebes simply as an American woman who desired to consult her on business. I went the day preceding the presentation in New York of the play, "Mizpah," a drama by Luscome Searelle, the English playwright, with whom I had collaborated. My work consisted in taking his ideas and turning them into verse. The play was based on the Bible story of Queen Esther and it had been produced in California a year previously with great success. It had a most brilliant run in San Francisco and Los Angeles, Oakland and other California towns, and to this day people talk of "Mizpah" with admiration and affection. So decided was its success that Mr. Frohman bought it and put it on nearly a year afterward in Boston with a very expensive cast of stars, where it achieved an artistic success but did not fill the box office requirements. So it was sublet to a less expensive company and was to be produced in New York the evening of the day I called on Madame de Thebes, Once in the presence of that lady I asked if a business venture in New York about to be put to the test would succeed.

Madame de Thebes, without a moment's hesitation, replied: "It will be an absolute failure."

"Has it no future?" I asked.

"It has something to do with an MS.," Madame replied, "and I see it crossing the ocean and coming over here, but that is all. I do not find any appearance of it afterward."

PEOPLE, ABROAD AND AT HOME 319

Her words were verified in every particular.

"Mizpah" made a complete and tragic failure in New York.

Mr. Searelle took the MS. to London and had all arrangements well in hand for its presentation in a large theater there with a brilliant cast, when he suddenly died, as he stood at the telephone sending a message.

"Mizpah" seemed to die with him. The Frohmans for a time used it in stock; there was a sale of its moving picture rights, and talk of a spectacular costly presentation, but that too flashed in the pan. "As dead as a door nail" seemed to be the epitaph of "Mizpah."

Yet in California people say that no other drama ever left upon their minds such beautiful and lasting memories as the love scenes of,"Mizpah" when played by beautiful Adele Block, the ideal Esther, and J. H. Gilmore, that most wonderful Ahasuerus.

It is curious that Madame de Thebes was able to forecast the utter failure of this play, without knowing it was a play, twenty-four hours before its appearance in New York.

And having forecast the San Francisco disaster with equal exactness, it is curious that she so utterly failed in her previsions of the war, which she declared would end in 1915-Madame de Thebes passed into the world of realities two years ago. Her last published Almanac contained many erroneous predictions; yet were all her predictions to be classified, she would doubtless be found to deserve her title of Seeress.

I met Bernhardt in New York, and afterward when I was in Paris the Divine Sarah sent me a telegram one morning asking me to breakfast with her at her charming home. That was a memorable morning: and the two hours I spent in her presence repaid me for all the years of study I had given to her language. Had it been necessary it would have recompensed me too for the price I had paid, previously and all unknown to her, for my introduction. But my manner of introduction was not necessary. Julie Opp, in the early years of her dramatic career abroad, had attracted the attention of

Madame Bernhardt, who became her devoted friend, and whenever the great actress came to New York this source of a personal introduction was open to me. But I had never been a seeker of dramatic celebrities, knowing how occupied they always are, and being myself always a busy person.

There was for several seasons (perhaps three only) a French professor in New York City named Professor W. His name and his personality were distinctly German (as were his ideas of business acumen seen under present illuminating conditions), but he was born and had been reared and educated in Paris, and his diction was perfect. He became a very pronounced success as a teacher and lecturer in New York's ultrafashionable and ponderously rich circles. The Vander-bilts, the Astors, the Crugers, and many others of that class employed Professor W. to give them morning talks in French, and there was even a rivalry shown by certain fashionable women regarding him, each desiring to exploit him as an entertainer more conspicuously than the other.

Society columns of the weeklies and dailies gave Professor W."s name in connection with smart set affairs frequently.

Before he had come into his vogue with the very wealthy, however, I had been in his class for a term of lessons, and he had called at my humble little apartment one Sunday with his pretty wife and handsome daughter. When, the winter following his second season of social success. Professor W. began to be a regular attendant at my Sunday afternoons, I remember feeling a sensation of surprise. I somehow previsioned an ulterior motive. One day he came early and told me his lovely daughter was engaged to be married and he said he wanted to give a social affair in my honor, as his daughter's fiance was a literary man, and for other reasons. The affair came off and was very pleasant. It was several weeks after this that he and his wife came to call, bringing the news that Madame Bernhardt was in town and that she had expressed to them a great desire to meet me. Professor and Mrs. W. were close friends of hers and had been for many years, so they told me. I thanked them for the offer to introduce me to

PEOPLE, ABROAD AND AT HOME 321 the world-famous artist, and saia that before she left town I would avail myself of the opportunity.

The next week Professor W. called and suggested that I write a poem to Bernhardt; and he would see that she gave me an autographed picture in return and that she expressed her admiration for my poetry publicly. All this disturbed more than it pleased me. Never in my life had I found it necessary to plot and plan for praise, or to use a go-between to make the acquaintance of any one. But I understood that the professor wished to appear as a friend to both Madame Bernhardt and myself, and so I allowed his plan to culminate. His wife accompanied me to Bernhardt's dressing-room one night and the matter of the verses and the photographs went through.

My husband and I were starting on a vacation trip, possibly two months later, when there came to me a messenger boy bringing a letter from Professor W. He stated that he was about to be evicted from his apartment through lack of money to pay his rent, now two or three months in arrears. He said that the wealthiest family in New York had gone away owing him four hundred dollars and another owed him two, and still another three. "These people are good pay finally," he said. "I know when they come home they will give me all they owe me. But they have never needed for money, and it does not occur to tfiem that I could be in straits. I dare not dun them. I will lose their patronage in future if I do. But I am in an awful dilemma. My daughter is to be married soon: the date is set; if I am evicted and disgraced it will spoil her pleasure, perhaps prevent her marriage. My poor wife is ill and we are appealing to your good heart as a last forlorn hope."

The letter embarrassed me exceedingly. I realized they believed me to be under obligations to them, and that my refusal to lend the two hundred dollars asked would seem ungrateful. I knew Professor W. had a large patronage among the very wealthy. I knew from other people, sewing women, hairdressers, milk dealers, newsdealers, that the ultra-fashionable folk were most inconsiderate as a rule in the matter of paying small bills promptly. They paid eventually; but rarely promptly. I believed Professor W. would receive all due him and believed he would reimburse me. I had paid in advance for the niece I was then educating. I had sent my mother money; I had helped private charities in which I was interested. By denying some other deserving people

I had planned to assist, I could lend the professor for the months he asked the two hundred dollars. I sent it to him and received a fervent letter of thanks and his note.

The daughter was married and a reception of a most elaborate kind was given, with much feasting and many guests.

When, at the stated time, I asked for payment of the note, Professor W. wrote me his wife was at death's door. Later letters brought no reply. For some years I could not locate him. Inquiries resulted in the information that both the professor and his wife had died some four years or more after my loan, and the daughter was divorced. But, at least, I had my breakfast with Bernhardt out of that experience. And there were present her lovely daughter-in-law, and her two adorable grandchildren, the youngest one then about nine years old and the image of her famous grandmere, I thought. There were, too, several secretaries and a Major Domo; and I read all their palms, even including the Divine Sarah's, and saw therein all the marvelous qualities which had made her what she was: for the palm, even as the Bible tells us, contains the whole character. It never lies. We can train the voice, the eye, and even the muscles of the mouth to conceal what the mind is thinking. But the palm is, second by second, recording every emotion and thought, and he who runs may read.

I think it was two years after this experience of loaning money that I was next called upon to act the part of the good and foolish fairy godmother: the goose of the golden egg.

It was fully ten years later (1917) that I again was bidden to breakfast with Bernhardt, this time in New York, and again was amazed at that wonderful woman's indescribable beauty and charm; and saw again that lovely granddaughter, grown to exquisite adolescence.

PEOPLE, ABROAD AND AT HOME 323 I had met in New York drawing rooms a very gifted artist, Miss B. She was a woman in perhaps her late thirties or early forties; very plain, but exceedingly magnetic and witty and entertaining. Her work in oil was attracting much attention and two years before we met her she had sold some of her landscape scenes for large sums. The best critics ranked her among the immortals. My husband enjoyed talking with her, and we asked her to visit us at our Bungalow the following summer, when we left for the seashore. I wrote her after we were settled, naming a time.

Miss B. replied with a most pitiful letter, saying she had not the price of a railroad ticket, and worse yet, she was to be evicted from her apartment where she had lived ten years, for the lack of means to pay her rent. She said she was to give an exhibition of her paintings in the early autumn, after people came back to town. She valued some of her paintings at five thousand dollars, and her prices ranged from that down to one thousand and even less. If I could lend her two hundred dollars, or if any of my friends could, she would give as security any picture I selected, and her note at the usual rate of interest, payable in a few months, when her exhibition was sure to place her on Easy Street. She reminded me of her last exhibition, where her work had commanded such excellent prices.

I talked with my husband, and he thought it a kindness to a worthy and sister artist to help her out of her difficulty; and he believed it also a good investment. One of her paintings would always command much more than the amount of the loan.

So the money was wired to Miss B., bringing joy to her heart.

Letters of gratitude, and her note followed. She said I must wait for the picture till I came to town so as to select carefully. In the autumn I made my selection, and asked for the picture to be sent me at my apartments. Miss B. suggested that she keep it at her studio to show visitors until I again opened my seashore home, when she would send it there. I consented. She called or wrote me a tender note of apprecia- tion of my kindness almost weekly. Yet when I was ready to go to the Bungalow, and asked her to send my picture, she put me off with so many excuses I began to feel uneasy. After my arrival there it was the same, until I gave up in despair. And when Miss B. died, a few years later, I had not received the picture or the money.

When her studio effects were put on sale I sent in my claim to her brother. He was indignant at my lack of feeling, he wrote m, to mention such a matter at such a time.

The only explanation for these and several other similar experiences which I have had, lies in my old incarnations where I set in motion some vibrations of a like nature, which had to affect my life here and now. But there have been more agreeable events in these matters– things which restore one's faith in humanity. My husband and I both once lent money to an ex-convict in whose reform we implicitly believed. He paid it back to the last farthing, refusing to keep the final five dollars as my husband requested him to do for good luck. "I will feel more of a man," he said, "if I pay it all." And he has proven himself a man ever since, and that is more than twenty years ago.

A fallen woman, who was trying to pick herself up, came across my path once upon a time. I became interested in her, and helped her financially. It was only a matter of sixty dollars; but it meant life or moral death to her at the time.

She repaid every penny of it: repaid it by money earned in honest labor, and there have been others who swelled the list of the honorable and worthy.

So when we sum up our experiences we find life gives us as many happy surprises as painful disillusionments.

But looking back over a long career, I am more and more impressed that in the matter of lending money a great moral responsibility is involved. With parents lies an equally grave responsibility in teaching their children early in life that debt, even temporary debt, borders on weakness and that every possible effort in self-reliance must be made before a loan is requested. One of the many bonds of sjmipathy between my husband and myself was this horror we both felt for any form

PEOPLE, ABROAD AND AT HOME 325 of debt; he as an orphan boy, dependent on his own exertions from the age of eleven, and I as a country girl digging a path out of obscurity with my pen. That we both had known the experience of borrowing, we remembered as a sort of ignominy; and we both had the happy consciousness that our first obligation in life had always been to repay our debts even to the return of a borrowed postage stamp. Only through such a sense of moral obligation can character be developed. Life is a mental and spiritual gymnasium; and it is by using the difficulties and obstacles we encounter and overcoming them OURSELVES that we gain strength. The ready asker for financial help is seldom the ready payer. And beware of the friend who, owing you one debt, however small, asks for a second loan. Something is lacking in his moral make-up. Pride is certainly lacking.

A young woman found herself ill at a hotel and unable to pay her room rent. She had planned to give a recital, but holiday season caused the people who had promised to assist her to postpone the event. She fell ill and despair seized her. Her case was called to my attention and I paid her hotel bill of forty dollars, she to repay me after her recital took place. That was thirty years ago. The lady has since that time sent me engraved cards from a hotel in London where she was living, and she has written me many letters asking my help and influence for various charitable enterprises. She devotes her life to altruistic work; but there is a loose plank in her character or she would feel it imperative to pay that old loan, no matter whether she thinks I need, it or not. She would pay it to build up her own self-respect and to earn my respect. It is impossible to feel respect for those who have no fine sense of honor and obligation in money matters. Money is a coarse and ugly commodity; unless we surround it with fine and delicate thoughts, it will invariably cheapen and coarsen our natures.

I believe our Invisible Helpers would approve of this motto for us all, BE CAREFUL HOW YOU BORROW AND BE CAREFUL HOW YOU LEND.

We should think thrice before doing either.

I fear both my husband and myself have done more toward making weaklings, by our ready loans, than we have done in building up courage and overcoming despair.

It is a discouraging thought, to come late in life. But experience has forced it upon me. If any troubled soul facing financial need reads these lines, let me urge prayer without CEASING FOR LIGHT AND STRENGTH TO SEE THE PATH TO INDEPENDENCE, and constaut quiet assertions of the power within that Soul to bring its rightful share of God's opulence. Then go forth and seek, and the way will open. Look up and look in before you look out to mortal aid.

Yet in this matter of refusing appeals for loans, there must be great delicacy and great unselfishness employed; And self analysis to see that we do not simply follow an avaricious or unsympathetic impulse. We must be willing to take time and trouble and effort to help the would-be borrower to help himself. We must convince him, and ourselves as well, that we are not withholding the money from any mean or ignoble motive. And great discrimination must be used. Out of too many unfortunate experiences to enumerate, I can think of four occasions where had my husband and I refused a loan we would have missed just so many rare privileges to aid the deserving at the psychological moment.

To miss such an opportunity from indifference, thoughtlessness or selfishness, would have been to set ourselves back in growth of character, as well as to discourage worth-while souls struggling to climb over rough roads.

During my several visits to England I had been urged by friends there to request our American Ambassador to present me at Court. The idea seemed at first more absurd than otherwise to me. I associated a presentation at Court with people of large wealth and extreme ambitions to shine socially. I possessed neither.

My English friends, however, convinced me that it was an agreeable form of placing oneself on the right social footing in England, and that as my literary work had already received the commendation of royalty, I ought to receive it

PEOPLE, ABROAD AND AT HOME 327 personally. My London publishers urged the matter also, saying I must view the matter from the English standpoint, not the American. So I made my application, and shortly afterward the American Ambassador died. I believed my chance of being presented to King George and Queen Mary had died with him; my husband took me on a second tour through northern Africa, and I quite forgot about the matter. We reached London on our return from motoring through the Kabyl Mountains on Sunday, at midday, May 4th, 1913. (Right here I digress a bit to relate an amusing incident that occurred as we drove from the station up to the Langham Hotel. Previous visits in London had caused me to find a center of interest in the large department store of Peter Robinson. As we passed it on this Sunday afternoon, my husband glanced up at the building, heaved a sigh, and gave vent to the following impromptu quatrain:

Oh, Peter, Peter Robinson, When you and Ella meet Then things get dark for Robert But very bright for Pete.)

Arriving at the Langham Hotel, we found the accumulation of a three weeks' mail. Among the letters was the following from the American Embassy: ti P- SO0 ccoc.?

It filled me with consternation. I had just three days in which to prepare my gown and to rehearse my unaccustomed part. I telephoned to my most intimate friend in London, Mrs. Frank Howard Humphries, and she came and assured me we could manage the affair if we lost no time. Heir dressmaker would put aside all other work and make my gown. The Charge daffaires and his wife (officiating at the American Embassy until the arrival of the new Ambassador) would tell me everything I needed to know about the presentation. It was a much simpler ordeal, she said, than it had been in the Victorian period. King Edward had abolished the awkward, backward exit, and substituted an easy, straight path from the presence of royalty after the necessary obeisance had been made.

Even as my friend said, the gown was finished a half hour before I was booked to leave the Langham Hotel for Buckingham Palace:–costumed, betrained, befeathered, with a coachman and footman as the law of etiquette demanded. That afternoon was most strenuous. Reporters, male and female, English and American, flocked to the Langham for news about the presentation and description of the costume I was to wear; and personal friends came in numbers. The maids and housekeepers of the hotel asked permission to come in and see me in the attire which was so soon to be looked upon by the eyes of royalty: and their respectful, almost reverent attitude was difficult for an American mind to grasp.

Among my callers was Elsa Barker, who was living in London at that time, and with her came Dr. Murray Leslie. My last few moments before leaving the room were devoted to a rehearsal of my presentation to the King and Queen. Dr. Murray Leslie and Mrs. Barker assumed the role of the royal personages. Lacking a throne, they sat side by side on the bed.

I started by the farthest window of my quite capacious room and slowly approached the distinguished impersonators of royalty, and made my best curtsey separately to each as I had been instructed to do, careful not to allow my gaze to leave the face of the Queen too abruptly. "You must look at her until she looks away to the next one who follows you," they had told me.

As there was no one following me at this rehearsal, I looked at Elsa's handsome face until I passed out of the door and was on my way toward my carriage. I heard a burst of laughter from the royal persons I left behind, and hoped I would not hear such merriment when I left the presence of real royalty.

Perhaps a half mile from Buckingham Palace the carriage I occupied fell into line with innumerable other carriages and motor cars, all containing ladies in court dresses with be-feathered heads: and there I sat for a good three-quarters of an hour inching along a few feet at a time, as the other carriages allowed. Finally the gates of Buckingham Palace were reached–were passed; the door itself was reached and out I bundled, carrying my yards of velvet train over my dissatisfied arm and following the ladies who preceded me through great halls and splendid corridors, into a large room filled with gorgeous costumes and nodding plumes.

Many maids came forward to take our wraps and lift down our trains, and refold them and hang them again over our arms after we had primped a bit before royal mirrors.

Being alone, and having no one to ask "What next?" I simply followed where the crowd led. We wound along through other splendid corridors and through other lordly rooms until at last we came to one half filled with a brilliant crowd of men in uniform and royal flunkies in wonderful habiliments and hundreds of dazzling ladies seated in chairs doing nothing save to look at one another's gowns. Obeying the general rule, I also sat down and looked at the other dresses and there I remained a mortal hour and a half, at least–my train still over my arm because I saw all other trains over arms. It grew very heavy and I grew a bit tired looking at befeathered heads and diamond tiaras and shining satins and lustrous silks, and snowy laces and dazzling complexions.

Then suddenly there was a flutter and a tall, royal flunky came and began to direct the front rows of ladies to move onward, and one by one the seats were emptied and the ladies disappeared into another room and finally my turn came to follow. Down a long hall, the walls lined with priceless tapestries; through a room filled with gleaming statues; past rows of historic portraits of famous personages, done by immortal artists; and finally the door of the throne room was reached. There two brilliant beings in the impressive costumes of court officials stepped forward and deftly lifted my heavy and tiresome train from my grateful arm, and dropped it neatly and squarely upon a rose colored carpet. The lady immediately in front of me wore a corn-colored satin. I walked slowly, intent upon keeping a safe distance from her train. Suddenly I saw her curtsey very low; once, twice; then I became conscious that I was in the presence of royalty: and I too followed in her wake and curtsied low, once, twice; looking straight, first at King George and second upon Queen Mary, at the distance of perhaps twelve feet, sitting on a raised dais sort of throne. The King was in uniform: the Queen in pale blue satin with many jewels. Then I walked forward, following always the lady in yellow satin. At the door, beyond the throne room, two more impressive beings lifted my train and put it back upon my arm. I followed through another long room, filled with beautiful objects of art, its walls covered with many portraits; I stood in line with those who preceded me and watched others who followed me reinforce our ranks. A Guard of the King's Household, nine feet tall, counting wonderful headgear, stood next me, holding a tall spear; and I snugged under his arm and watched the glittering scene, wondering if it were a twentieth century fact or a bit of ancient history shown on a moving picture screen.

One by one the ladies who had been presented came down the center of the two lines of watchers like the head couple in Money Musk, until the last one passed by. Then there was the blare of a trumpet and the orchestra began to play "God Save the King." Men in heavily braided uniforms walked down the centers in twos: and four other men in still more wonderful uniforms backed down the center, salaaming as they backed: and following came the Queen with two small pages bearing her train, and by her side, the King: and behind trailed all the royal family of sisters and cousins and aunts. I had seen them in the throne room, sitting on a dais at the right, gazing at us through their lorgnettes, but I had been warned by the Charge daffaires to pay no attention to them, as only the King and the Queen were to be the recipients of one's attention on presentation night. And then it was all over, save a march of the entire company into the refreshment room; and then the march out past an important personage, who proved to be the first Royal Carriage Caller, who shouted it to a second, who shouted it to a third. Then there was nothing to do but to stand or sit and wait until one's carriage came.

I waited just one hour for mine. But the wait in the great corridor of Buckingham Palace while dukes and duchesses, earls and countesses, and the high officials of Army and Navy passed out to their vehicles was not tedious: for it made a picture for the eye that loves color and it gave food for the mind and imagination. It was the only food which I enjoyed that night, for so hurried had been my afternoon of preparation that I had no time for dinner. A glass of milk had been really my entire sustenance since breakfast. I was faint with hunger when I reached the refreshment room in Buckingham Palace, and the smell of the coffee accentuated my hunger. I seemed to be the only lady who had no escort: and so occupied were all the attendants in serving the guests that most of the ladies appealed to their escorts to bring them refreshments. My turn did not seem to come, while my hunger augmented every moment, and I finally decided to call my carriage and get back to the Langham Hotel before the dining room closed at midnight This I did with a narrow margin of fifteen minutes. Almost falling into my waiting husband's arms, I begged him to conduct his starving wife to the dining room. Now nothing embarrassed my husband more than being prominent in any spectacular scene. He hesitated a moment and softly murmured, "Don't you think you had better go and remove your feathers and your train before going into the dining room?" "There is no time," I waned; "the dining room would close before I could accomplish it, and you must remember, my dear, that we are not in America, and that my attire will cause nothing but the most humble reverence from every one here who beholds it." The statement proved literally true. The waiters in the dining room bowed low before the lady who had been so recently in the presence of the King and Queen, and we were ushered in and out with respectful dignity. My hunger appeased, I went up to my room, glad that I had been presented at Court (because I regarded it as a tribute to American literature) and gladder still that I would not have to repeat the performance the next night.

When I told the story to my publisher the next day, he asked why I did not call on some one in the dining room to bring me refreshments. "Because I did not dare," I answered, "lest among those universally resplendent beings who surrounded me, I should make my appeal to a Crown Prince or a Prime Minister." Another interesting event in which I was asked to take part was to award prizes at the annual competition of "The Children's Salon."

After my presentation at Court I was the recipient of very many interesting invitations which I could not accept as I was leaving England shortly. Captain and Mrs. John P. Boyd Carpenter invited me to meet his Grace, the Duke of Argyle, an event which occurred ten days after our date of sailing; and many other functions of a like nature had to be declined for this reason.

When I received a letter from Lady Emily Lutyens asking my husband and myself to lunch, I had no idea who she was, other than an English woman of rank who had been for some years deeply interested in Theosophy. I knew the term "Lady" in England indicated that a woman was either the wife or the daughter of a titled man. Great was my pleasure on learning, the morning before the luncheon, that Lady Emily was the daughter of Owen Meredith, author of "Lucile" and granddaughter of Sir Bulwer Lytton, author of "The Last Days of Pompeii" and many other great books. This news, while agreeable to me, was particularly

PEOPLE, ABROAD AND AT HOME 333 pleasing to my husband, who was going somewhat unwillingly to the lunch table of a mere woman of title, but who now felt she was something more than that. And glad he was afterwar4 23 Annual Competitions IN ART. LITERATURE. MUSIC AND DANCtnQp ETC

"THE CHILDRENS SALON"

On Saturday, May 31st, 1913

Connaught l oms, Qt, i ueen St,, Kingsway

ADMISSION 2s. 6d. from io hm. dv Paymert at Doorand

F amlcr toe patronoc 0t!

U. R. H. TIIE PRINCESS CBBKTUN na.   B. TOB PRCfcESS BEATRICE (PRINCESS IIRNBY OF BATEESBXtai H. B. I1. TUB DUCOESS OP ALSAHY BJt.1L THE PRINCESS CHARLES OP UOUEnzOIXEfiir B. IL PandiSCES5 MARIE LOUISE OF SCBLESWia-BOLSTEIll THE DDCBCSS OP IfoRPOLK THE DUCUESS OF ABERCORM XBB COVinfisS OF

TUB DUCKESS OP BEAUPORT TJOC MARCHIONESS OP

TliB DUCHESS OF SUTUEBLASD LONDONDEBKT " COOSTESS OP ItaH-ESTEB

TIK DUCHESS OP DEVONSUIRB jq marCHIONSSS OP ZETLAND THE COUNTESS BAXSCnsT

THE DUCHESS OP SOMERSET COUNTESS OP ABERDEEN THE COUNTESS OF UTEKPOOL

THE IIARCHIONESS., j. COUNTESS OP DUPLET THB LADY ABTHUft BILL

Mrs. ELLA WHEELER WILCOX

HAS KINDLY CONSENTED TO

DISTRIBUTE THE PRIZES

TO THE SUCCESSFUL COMPETITORS, of the privilege accorded him of meeting this very charming and brilliant woman.

Lady Emily married an eminent architect and artist and their home was most restful and lovely in its orderly simpli- city– not too much of anything anywhere and everything just right. We met two of her four children, girls of twelve and eight; she asked them to assist serving at luncheon, and the little girl was sent ahead to open doors for us. The home was based on ideals of loving service and simple living. Lady Lutyens was a most serious student of Theosophy and put its principles into daily execution. The children were deeply interested in her philosophy, and the husband tolerant and satisfied to have his family pursue these studies even if he had not the time himself. He was assigned (in 1913) the architectural reconstruction of Delhi, India. With such a gifted father, such an unusual mother, such a grandfather and great grandfather, one might look for something remarkable from the children of Lady Lutyens when they mature; but who can tell?

Sir Henniker Heaton was a prominent figure in London in 1912, and both he and his wife and his son and the son's very brilliant wife, the Honorable Katherine Mary Burrell, showed me many pleasant attentions. Sir Henniker Heaton took me to the House of Lords and presented me to all the distinguished men who were in sight or in sound of his voice; declaring me to be a much more important personage in the world than I had ever before, or have ever since, considered myself. I smiled thinking of the amazement which some of the American high-brow critics would have felt– an amazement mixed with indignation, I am sure, had they heard what this big-hearted, gracious Englishman, on whom the King had bestowed a title, said of me. But of course a man may be a great statesman and worthy of a title, and yet not know the fine distinctions the critics make in literary matters.

Afterward I took tea with Lady Henniker Heaton and a very handsome daughter, Rose, who was a poet as well as a beauty, and met other distinguished English men and women.

The next year I was again indebted to the Henniker Heatons for social favors. Their daughter in law was taking part in a great tournament in Earls' Court, where she rode a horse as Queen Elizabeth, leading a retinue of historic personages.

All royalty was there to witness it; and I was asked to sit PEOPLE, ABROAD AND AT HOME 335 in the Henniker Heaton box, just two tiers away from the Royal Box; and there I saw at very close range, in daylight, King George and Queen Mary, and was much impressed by the very serious faces of both. It was as if they already pre-visioned the grave events which were so soon to follow.

Surely when England opens her heart to strangers she opens it wide. On my departure from England in June, I learned that a large reception had been planned for me at Southampton before sailing from that port on the Olympic. Proceeding to Southampton a day in advance, accompanied by Messrs. Gay and Hancock, my English publishers, I was met at the train by the American Consul, Colonel Albert W. Swalm, and several prominent citizens and conducted to the Polygon Hotel, where a luncheon of ten covers was prepared.

Meantime Mrs. Smith, widow of the Captain of the ill-fated Titanic, was waiting to see me for a half hour alone. It was a difficult and pathetic half hour–this interview with the frail little lady filled with thoughts of her husband to whom she had been married a quarter of a century when his tragic death occurred. She felt I could say something to comfort but I fear I failed, save as there may be comfort in sympathy.

Among the distinguished guests at the luncheon was Dr. Alexander Hill, president of the Hartley University, and Mrs. H. Bowyer, the Lady Mayoress of Southampton. After the luncheon there was a motor drive to Beaulieu and Lyndhurst, places of exquisite beauty and historic charm. Having always thought of Southampton as a dock for steamers, it was a revelation to find it a big beautiful city of subliminal buildings, of which Beaulieu Abbey stands preeminent. After the drive there was tea in the private rooms of the hospitable lady who conducted the Polygon Hotel, and during the tea her small nephew of eleven recited verses of mine with astonishing expression and feeling.

In the evening a reception was tendered me under most picturesque conditions. Carpets were spread upon the velvety lawn, and an artistic electrician had outdone himself in the lighting effects. Hundreds of guests were there and the whole scene was fairylike. An effective musical program ended the very unusual evening.

During my drive in the day I had been shown a window of the most prominent book store in Southampton which had been given over to an exhibition of my volumes as published by Messrs. Gay and Hancock. That day and evening were my last memories of England before the war.

CHAPTER XXII The Beginning of the End

WHEN we returned from our wanderings in the early-summer of 1913, I said to my husband, "I do not want to travel any more for some years. Let us stay here and assimilate the mental food which we have received during ten years of roaming. Let us improve our home and make every spot, within and without, a pleasure to the beauty loving eye. To help create beauty in the world, is to help God's ideals. We have an earthly Eden, and we must try and grow worthy of it by developing all its charms."

This wish of mine found a response in my husband's heart; for he too felt he wanted the repose foimd only at home.

We added a long-talked-of "Flower Room" to our Barracks, and made many improvements which gave comfort to our employees, as well as to ourselves. We laid out a flower garden, in the form of eight triangles, in the back yard of the three little cottages (which we rented each summer to the same tenants year after year) and in this garden I worked a few hours daily, trying to carry out effective color schemes in sequences.

My husband busied himself training the vines over the Bungalow Tower, which he had named "Starling Tower" because it was neighbor to many bird houses, intended for robins and orioles, and bluebirds, but nearly all had been preempted by the starlings. We found those birds to be much like some people. During the courting season, and while fixing up their houses, their voices were like wind harps: so tender and sweet, they filled the air with music. Once they were settled in housekeeping, and rearing their young, they became the noisiest, most discordant birds imaginable; their voices harsh and grating to the ear, and their aggressive qualities causing all other occupants of the houses to depart. A dead cedar tree near by, Robert made into a thing of beauty, by training beautiful fragrant flowering vines over it: and just under this tree were the Elephant Gates leading down into the water; so named because of the pottery elephants we had brought from India, which decorated the posts: and from there the Tower Path led up to our beloved Bungalow.

When the outdoor hours ended, I went indoors to pursue my study of the harp, begun that summer of 1913 under Edith Davies-Jones, the Welsh harpist, who owned a cottage near us: and in two years' time I had made sufficient progress to be able to assist my teacher at a harp recital. It was given at the Stratford Hotel, in Bridgeport, Connecticut, as a testimonial to my first French teacher, Madame Sorieul. I had composed a little air for the harp called "The Dance of the Elves," and Mrs. Davies-Jones and I played it as a duet, while four tiny human elves gave a wild wood nymph dance, which proved so effective they were three times recalled.

1 went to New York from Bridgeport; and the next day my husband (who did not attend the recital) wrote me expressing his delight and pride at the reports he heard of our successful entertainment. No matter what I did, ever were his interest and sympathy and wise criticism sure to enfold me, and make each effort seem worth while. We remained in our shore home, for the first time, those three winters succeeding our return in 1913, and we loved best the storm-bound days, when we were shut from the outside world with just ourselves, our books, our harp and Prince and Kim, the household pets.

And how we loved our beautiful Granite Bay in its winter dress! My husband took some effective pictures of it during the snowy season of two winters, yet the camera could do but scant justice to the gleaming glory of the actual scene. We wondered how we could have left such beauty behind us, to seek far tropic lands for ten winters. Thank God for those three last memorable winters in our ice-wreathed, snow-dressed Granite Bay.

It has been stated that invariably preceding a great war
THE BEGINNING OF THE END 339 people pass through a period of unusual social merriment and frivolity; there seems to be an hysterical element in their amusements, and dancing is always a pronounced feature of their merry-makings.

This condition certainly existed in the social world, both of Europe and America, for two or three years before the war blast blew over Belgium, and dimmed the lights of festivity in the halls of the whole world.

In 1912 and 1913 the dance madness was at its height in London, and old and young alike participated in it.

Always exceedingly fond of dancing, I was swept into the whirl with all my friends; and many afternoons and evenings in London were spent in this grace-developing and health-sustaining exercise.

When I returned to my own country, the craze was at its height, and all my contemporaries were whirling and spinning about in the new dances. At Short-Beach-on-the-Sound a very attractive Inn had been erected by a woman Napoleon (in a business sense), Mrs. Emma Beers. "The Arrowhead" was a social center of the most desirable people from surrounding resorts. Miss Beers (christened Jennie May, but renamed Jane, by my husband) was a finished pupil of three dancing academies; and she had many classes those two winters at "The Arrowhead." From infants to grandparents, the people of our own resort, and neighboring places, flocked to Miss Jane to be taught the newest steps in dancing. Under Jane's tutelage I had a private class for a time at The Barracks; and while I danced my husband played cards, not being himself a dancer.

Jane and I together created a new dance. I gave her the idea, and she fashioned it into a choice classic, which we called "The Dance of the Adoration of the Lilies."

Miss Beers wore all green, and I wore all white; and we carried arms full of lilies when on three occasions we gave our dance in public. Many invitations came to us to repeat it; but we felt it quite too perfect a creation to make common, so after its third rendition, we put away our dance-poem, in rose leaves and lavender, a lovely memory. After the break- ing out of the war, all my interest in dancing died a sudden death. I think I attended a few dancing functions with friends in New York, but the zest had departed, and forever.

We enjoyed many pleasant house parties those winter months when our friends would leave the city gayeties to come to us.

One shining occasion was starred by the presence of Kate Jordan, Theodosia Garrison and Charles Hanson Towne. Jean Pardee Clarke, always a picturesque member of the Bungalow circle, came out one of those days, and we all indulged in reminiscences of beautiful years gone, and still beautiful years with us. Always we talked softly of Martha,

The morning the party broke up, I proposed that we should sit together and write some verse on any topic we chose. So the four of us wrote, while Robert srrtoked his cigar in the poetic atmosphere, and made witty comments. Theodosia, as ever most expert, finished her lines first and Mr. Towne next. Each of us wrote things we deemed worthy of publication later.

Some years previously I had made the acquaintance in London, of a young woman of marked physical and mental attractions–Ruth Helen Davis, of New York. Endowed with beauty and musical talents, she was then devoting her time to French translations and dramatic literature, with the hope of becoming a playwright. In all my experience with humanity, I have never encountered another human being who possessed so much ambition for achievement and so much energy and determination to succeed as Ruth Helen Davis. She was a stimulating companion, full of appreciation and kindness and good will; and both ray husband and I enjoyed having her with us.

One summer she rented a cottage to be near us, and to carry out her ambition to collaborate on a play with me. I have no plots in my mental storehouse, but Ruth Helen supplied the plot, and I was to give lyrics and poetic dialogue. We completed this play, "The Victory," and it was given for charity, as an outdoor entertainment one superb June day at the lordly

THE BEGINNING OF THE END 341 estate of Simon Baruch in Long Branch, in a wonderful nature setting. Mrs. Davis played the leading role; and the caste was-formed of society belles and matrons. It was a great artistic and social success; and Mrs. Davis was fired with an ambition to produce it in Boston. I urged otherwise, feeling it had not the vitality for a professional run. It was withdrawn after a week; but Mrs. Davis regarded it as so much valuable experience and went forth undaunted to undertake more ambitious things.

The next spring she came down to the shore with an Egyptian idea in her bright brain: an idea for a big drama, historic and poetic. She asked Robert to make suggestions, knowing he was a student of history; and he entered at once into our collaboration with interest and gave us valuable information on the subject matter we had in view. We used to work from six to eight on the Bungalow veranda; and then Robert came to take us to breakfast, telling us what he had read up in history regarding the period we were attempting to portray. Those were interesting days and were to be treasured in memory. In the autumn Mrs. Davis went to Boston to take a course of study, and we never finished our drama.

A brilliant dinner guest, we wired her once to come from Boston to meet our delightful friend Colonel Charles Bigelow and his sweet wife, who were just from England. Ruth Helen came, and the dinner party was another of the unforgettable occasions of that last winter of happiness.

My husband had always been fond of his occasional Club night: but that winter of 1916 he seemed to lose interest in it.

I urged him to keep in touch with clubs, for when a man is not in active business these masculine organizations are helpful to him in many ways. But more and more he seemed to begrudge hours spent away from his home. Constantly he talked to me of his pleasure and satisfaction in his home, and of his delight in returning there when absent for even a few hours. Our social life, apart from our own entertaining, had always been in New York. Sometimes we went there for a week or a few days at a time, and one of the last occasions was a dinner party at the home of Hartley Manners, the extraordinarily successful playwright, and his genius wife Laurette Taylor, where we met people of talent in all the various lines of art. Mr. Manners and my husband had been Club friends for years, and one summer Hartley had rented a cottage at Short Beach, while he worked on one of his plays. The very last night in New York we spent together was at the Russian Ballet in the Metropolitan Opera House, where my friends, in whose box we sat, mentioned how noticeably well and vital Robert seemed. He had seemed so all that winter of 1916; and he had often spoken of his satisfaction in, at last, knowing how to take sensible care of himself, and how to get the best happiness out of life. He was making plans for the improvement of a stately piece of seashore property he had recently purchased, "Deepwood Park," and he was planning, also, travels abroad, after the war ended. Yet at the same time he was putting all his earthly house in as careful order as if he had known how brief was to be his stay. Every day that last wonderful winter he gave a portion of his time to making an inventory of every object we possessed: and all his business affairs were attended to after the manner of one who is going on a long journey.

Always interested in matters psychic and spiritual, he was particularly so that winter; and the last book we ever read together was "Patience Worth." Over and over he reiterated his life-long statement to me, that should he precede me to the realm beyond, he would importune God until he was allowed to communicate with me, and he pleaded for a similar repetition of my promise to him.

One stormy March day he said to me, "Every one is longing for the Spring. I never longed so little for it. In fact I do not want this winter to go. It has been the happiest season of my life. I wish it could go on and on like this; just you and I shut in this dear home together." Early in April I was puzzled and disturbed by my own mental condition. With every blessing in life, doing the work I loved, having the recreation I loved, in the place I loved, and with the man I loved, I yet woke every morning filled with a profound melancholy. I could not shake it off. My Flower Room, which for two seasons had been my delight, gave me no pleasure. My window boxes which the previous winter I had found so interesting to prepare in color schemes to suit each room, I now planted in a dull apathy. The Spring wardrobe, which usually fascinated me, while in preparation, now gave me a sensation of nausea. A vast pall seemed to be spread over the whole world. I did not mention this mental condition to my husband. Even a serious mood of mine troubled him. He expected from me, always, bubbling spirits and radiant joy in life. A man of moods himself, and prone to days of melancholy, he looked to me to bring him back to optimism. "What will happen to me and the world," he once said, "if you become despondent? The bottom will drop out of the universe." So I hid my unreasonable and incomprehensible melancholy from him.

I think the pretty French artist who helped me design my gowns, and made them for me, was the only one to whom I mentioned it. I said to her, "I am surely growing old at last. I have absolute distaste at the thought of getting new clothes to wear this Spring." "That sounds very strange from your lips," she replied. Then a curious thing happened. I had been a guest of honor at a very brilliant function. It was the White Breakfast of the Mozart Club in New York. It had been most interesting and I had received every attention, and had reason to feel happy and satisfied with life. I was remaining in town over night. I knew my husband was to spend a happy evening at his Club; and he was in the best of health. Yet I sat down that evening and wrote the following verses. I felt as if the end of the world had come. The universe seemed a vast cavern in which I sat alone and desolate.

THE FINISH

Out of that wonderful world where God is. The Lords of Karma the path have shown. And given us lessons to learn in bodies– Oh, many the bodies our souls have known!

In gem, and blossom, and sentient being. In dull cave dweller and thinking man. All things knowing, and feeling, and seeing– This is the purpose and this the plan.

Forms are fashioned in wide world places
From flame and ether and common clay;
While egos wait in the high star spaces
Till the call shall come, which they must obey.
Oh, never a wish or a hope lies hidden
Of good or evil in any heart.
But back to earth shall the soul be bidden
To live out its longing, and play its part.
Grief and pleasure and joy and sorrow.
Out of old sowings we gather them all–
And the seed of to-day we shall harvest to-morrow.
When our souls come back at the karmic call.
Over and over the lesson learning.
Till, letter perfect, and meaning clear–
Back on the spiral pathway turning
We carry the knowledge we gathered here.
The thought of that last journey back to Him

When there is no more longing or desire
For anything but God left in my soul,
Shines in the distance like a great white flame.
I think the way will lead through golden clouds
Skirting the shores of seas of amethyst!
And winding gently upward; past old worlds.
Where body after body was outlived.
Past Hells and Heavens, where I had my day
With comrade Spirits from the lesser spheres
And paid my penalty for every sin
And reaped reward for every worthy act:
Past Realms Celestial and their singing hosts (Where once I chanted with the cherubim)
Out into perfect silence. Suddenly
An all enveloping vast consciousness
Of long, long journeys finished: one more turn
Then glory, glory, glory infinite
And selfhood lost in being one with God.
The ray once more absorbed into the Sun.
The cycle done.

The next day my husband was attacked with a severe cold, the physician said. It was called a cold for a week. Every afternoon there was fever. I had been a great believer in the power of the spoken word, in matters of all kinds. Whenever any malady had threatened either of us, I had written to Unity, the New Thought Society, at Kansas City, Missouri, and asked for the word of strength and healing to be uttered by the beautiful souls who conserve their lives for this purpose in silent unity. I wrote them on this occasion and received news by letter and by wire that the word was being uttered. Meantime the best medical skill was in attendance. I had no fear whatever. I felt he would recover. But when the hour strikes which God has appointed for a soul to be called out of the body, no mortal has power to hold it back. The hard cold developed into pneumonia. May twenty-first at 11.25 P. M. Robert's soul went to God.

CHAPTER XXIII

The Search of a Soul in Sorrow you promised me
All holy books of earth, all churches and all creeds.
Are based on spirit miracles.
Moses, Elias, Matthew, Mark and John,
Paul and Cornelius, Buddha, Swedenborg,
All talked with Angels, Yea, and many more.
That was a mighty promise that you made me:– not once,
But many a time. Whenever we discussed the topic death– You promised me that were such things possible In God's vast Universe, You would send back a message to my listening soul.
Now am I listening with bated breath.

Always on earth you kept your promises. Why! never once Through all the years, the wonderful great years

We walked together Did you forego your word and break a pledge However trivial its purpose.

Surely that habit of a loyal mind endures;

Surely that soul of yours Has not been changed so utterly because it laid aside The body which had died– That it forgets a solemn promise made to me

Not once, but many a time. Why I such forgetfulness would be a crime Against love, faith and hope, the precious three.

It could not be.

So am I waiting, watching–in the light–and listening in the dark– For any sight, or sound you may have sent: So do I lean and hark– Night in, day out–

Nor will I let my starved and eager spirit doubt

Or sink in discontent Because no answer comes.

You promised me: some day, some way Will open for you, dear, to keep your word. So many eyes have seen–so many ears have heard. Moses, Elias, Matthew, Mark and John– Paul and Cornelius, Buddha, Swedenborg–

All talked with Angels. Science, which once denied, now patiently investigates. I do not seek alone.

And I will knock upon the door of heaven

And shake God's window with the hands of prayer,

Asking for those old Angels, wise with centuries

Of large experience, to come to you.

Oh my beloved, and to show you how

To keep your promise, made in solemn faith–

To bridge the River Death,

And rend the veil between. So many ears have heard–so many eyes have seen–

Why not mine own? I do not seek alone–

You promised me.

Written in California, 1916.

Over and over, solemnly and sacredly, during three decades of years had the promise been made to me. There was belief and faith in my heart that it would be kept. Yet the awful days went into awful weeks and months, and there was no rift in the clouds, no blowing aside of the dark curtain, no sound to break the killing silence of empty space.

Somewhere beyond all this I believed my Robert was living and loving me and longing to communicate with me. I knew it MUST be so. I knew the mere cessation of breath in the body could not destroy such a mighty love as ours. The orthodox idea that he was singing in the heavenly choirs about the throne where God and Christ sat in glory, or that he was lost to me until the resurrection, lying "asleep in Jesus," were both repellent. The Christian Science idea that he was absorbed into the Infinite Spirit, and merely lived as a part of that, left me cold and desolate. That wonderful individuality.

even that wonderful personality, I felt, still existed, and with them, memory and love.

I believed with my brain, but the soul of me cried in anguish for the proof, the proof. Other people, so many other people of sane minds and clear intellect, told me they received proof of the continuity of memory and love from souls gone onward.

I knew that in searching for proof of continuity of life, love and memory on the other side of the grave, and for means of communication with those who had gone across, I was placing myself in goodly company. The world had advanced and its ideas had enlarged since my early girlhood, when to speak of the subject of spirit messages savored of insanity.

I knew that during the last decade many of the world's most gifted and brilliant men and women had entered into this Search for the living dead.

Sir Oliver Lodge, Lombroso, Flammarion, Sir Alfred Turner, Maeterlinck, Conan Doyle, Lillian Whiting, Elsa Barker were but a few of the shining names associated with this study. Since the first year of the great war the ranks of the Searchers after proofs of life have grown almost as rapidly as the ranks of the destroyers of life. The ancient ideas of life to come have ceased to satisfy hearts torn with anguish. Intelligent minds refuse to believe that no revelations have been accorded to mortals since the days of St. John and that no true statements have been made by men who claim to have spiritual vision since Bible days. The words and writings of modem mystics–Besant, Leadbeater, Fechner, Steiner and others whose lives have been devoted to spiritual study, have awakened the thinking world, even as the revelations of Sweden-borg awakened it to a larger understanding of what life after death might mean.

Sir Oliver Lodge's recent works have all been frank avowals of his belief in spirit communication: and from every part of the world I had for several years received letters on this subject from men and women of mental prowess and high moral character.

Therefore I knew I was in worthy company, however many personal friends might be left by the wayside as I pushed forward to the truths waiting to be proven.

While I might regard with unabated affection old friends who had no understanding of the new spirituality, yet only people who had thought on these subjects really interested me. I listened to what they had to tell me, as one perishing from thirst might listen to tales of running brooks near by. Then I went forth to search, search, search for the experience which should cool my own burning thirst. Every breath was a prayer for Light and Knowledge. I woke with prayer– I lived in prayer, I fell asleep in prayer. I went to California, that center of spiritual research. At first I sought only the Wise Ones, the Theosophists. Being a Theosophist, I understood their objections to my seeking information among mediums of the professional class. I was exhausted with sorrow. My nervous system was depleted. My will power had lost the reins of guidance. In such a condition, if I went to a psychic, whose controls were on the lower astral planes, as so many are, I would easily become the prey to some unfortunate obsession. "Wait until you are stronger," the Wise Ones said. "Then seek a psychic who is a trained clairvoyant, understanding the laws of the spiritual planes, and who will bring only the best influences to their own and your aid."

I read the works written by the Wise Ones, and was helped and given strength to endure the days. "The Invisible Worlds About Us," by Rogers; "The Inner Life," and "To Those Who Mourn," by Leadbeater; "Death and After," by Besant, and "The Outer Court," that sacredly beautiful book, by the same author; "Our Life After Death," by that subtle German mystic, Fechner; and the profound works of Rudolph Steiner and Mabel Collins. All these books helped me. All reiterated what I already knew, that excessive sorrow and constant weeping prevent the spirits of those we love from manifesting themselves to us and disturb their peace and progress in God's world. To regain my poise and build up my depleted nervous forces, I went to "The Home of Truth," a metaphysical college, where ten lovely women, teachers, healers and students imder Anna. Rix Militz, lived beautiful and helpful lives. It was my home until I became more normal, yet it gave not the answer to my inquiring grief. They cast no light on Robert's realm. The members of that household comforted my heart and endeared themselves to me forever. But the search of a soul in sorrow did not end there. Wonderful cures were performed on the sick, but the sickness of my soul was not cured.

I visited the Rosicrucians, a noble and intellectual company of people with high ideals, leading ascetic lives; their influence can be only good and uplifting for the race, yet they shed no new light upon my path. I went to the little waning colony of Oshaspians, a strange and earnest handful of men and women, following altruistic ideals, but leaving me sadder than before I visited them. They seemed to have eliminated from life on earth all idea of beauty.

I went one day to hear a famous divine in the orthodox Christian Church. His whole Sunday morning was devoted to a furious attack upon all other organizations save the orthodox Protestant Church. He ridiculed and attacked Christian Science, New Thought, Theosophy, Spiritism, and sent me forth disgusted and melancholy. This is not the spirit of Christ, my Elder Brother, as I know Him and love Him–He who passed through all earth incarnations and became at last one with God, as each of us must eventually–He who left his beautiful example for us to follow when He said, "Love one another."

One day there came to me a letter filled with comfort. Years previously I had met in New York Rev. Frederick Kee-ler, a man possessing both natural and trained clairvoyant powers. He had given me a most interesting reading at that time, foreseeing certain developments in me which afterward proved true in a peculiar way. Mr. Keeler wrote me a letter of sympathy and informed me that he had been able to put himself in touch with the beautiful spirit which had made my earth life so blest; that he was seeking to communicate with me and would when I attained my poise; that he was adjusted to his new realms, and was often near me, striving to comfort and help me. The letter from Mr. Keeler was like a spiritual tonic,

THE SEARCH OF A SOUL IN SORROW 351 and gave me an influx of courage. I began to visit reputable psychics. Many interested me, some distracted me, a few comforted me with what seemed real messages from the Great Beyond. Others gave only what might have been read from my mind. Still others gave the babble of the elementals. None of them satisfied me. One man gave me my first illustration of that curious phenomenon, "precipitation." He sat at one end of a room flooded with southern California sunshine, I at the other. On a table beside me were fifty or more slates. He told me to select two and strap them together (after sponging them well) and to place them under my feet. Then I was instructed to take a skeet of paper from the table, write the names of three people who had gone away from earth, and ask one question; to seal this in an envelope and hold it in my hand. I held this for a half hour, while the man with the occult power saf quietly writing at the opposite end of the room. Suddenly he said: "Look at your slates."

I looked at the slates and found a forget-me-not flower, in water colors, on one corner, and both slates were filled with a message signed by my husband's name. No human hands had touched the slates. They were blank when placed by me under my feet. Yet I was not thrilled or stirred. I was deeply interested in the phenomenon. I knew it was a genuine phenomenon, known to occult students as "precipitation." It is a peculiar mental power which enables the possessor of it to obtain facts from the sitter's mind, and precipitate them upon paper or slates. This man had used the three names I wrote on the slip of paper, no others. He had seen, and read, clairvoyantiy; and that is miracle enough to convince any save the utterly ignorant bigot that our minds are independent of our mortal organs of sight, touch and hearing. But what this man had done did not, to my thinking, prove that he had any connection with the realm of spirits. I did not believe for one instant that my husband had sent the message. It was not the message a spirit, longing for months to communicate with the dearest soul on earth, would send when first the door was opened. It left me utterly cold, and simply curious. For twenty years this man has been producing this kind of phenomenon, and puzzling the minds of investigators. It is interesting, but has no bearing on life after death, save that it proves the independence of the mind in the body, and naturally suggests its continued independence out of the body. I met an eminent attorney afterward who told me he had been studying this "precipitant" for a period of twenty years. He had a chest specially devoted to slates filled with these messages: he carried his own slates, and the psychic never touched them. The Psychical Research Society of London has been considering an investigation of this man's peculiar powers. No pencil was placed between the slates, yet the messages came, clearly and distinctly written. The doubting rea-soner, who questions every statement which he cannot explain with his five senses, will say that the slates I placed under my feet were prepared chemically by the medium before my arrival. He will be very sure that the man knew who was coming and knew my name and that of my husband. But could he know that I was to write the name "Martha" on the slip of paper?

For the education of Mr. Reasoner, I will add to my own experience that of a friend who went with me. She was a lady in private life, and she was mourning for her beautiful daughter, Zaida. She preceded me into the room and had her sitting before I went in. She went through the same formula; selected her slates and placed them under her feet, took her slip of paper and wrote thereon three names: that of her father, long dead, and Zaida. At the end of a half hour her slates were filled in the main with messages from her father (doubtless because her father's name came first on the slip she held in her hand) and only a line at the bottom was signed "Zaida." The messages brought her no satisfaction, but her experience proved that neither she nor I were hypnotized, and that we did not imagine what occurred. No slates could have been prepared before her coming, for so odd a name as Zaida would hardly have been expected by the medium to be demanded by a sitter. It was only additional proof that the medium depended upon our minds and upon what we wrote upon the slip of paper (which his mortal eyes did

THE SEARCH OF A SOUL IN SORROW 353 not behold, but which he nevertheless saw clairvoyantly) to produce his message, precipitated upon the slates. A marvelous power indeed it is which this man possesses, but it did not bring me nearer to Robert.

Another medium, a little old lady, with a grandmotherly personality, produced messages for me in the clear light. I took my own slates, and she held them in my view, just under the table edge, because she said her controls needed to have the slates protected from too clear light, as the negative of a photograph has to be developed in a dark room. Many scrawly messages came, but they seemed to me the work of very crude elementals on the astral plane. My husband's name was written and the usual banal messages which come from that sphere where the undeveloped entities dwell. I received no enlightenment from them.

One of the most interesting psychics I met in the search of my soul through the valley of sorrow was John Slater. He is a man of high moral character, and clean life, a man who has given demonstrations of his remarkable clairvoyant powers all over the earth, and whose messages breathe the spirit of the higher spheres. Mr. Slater gave me much comfort, assuring me my husband was near me, and that as soon as my turbulent state of mind grew calm he would be able to communicate with me. "You do not need to visit mediums and clairvoyants," Mr. Slater said. "Save your time and money by staying quietly in your own room, and through prayer and concentration attaining that state of tranquillity which will enable your husband to reach you." Mr. Slater did not know who I was, and had he known he still would not have known the facts which he proceeded to state. "You do not belong in California," he said. "Your home is distant from here. Your environment here is not congenial. Its atmosphere is antagonistic to progressive spiritual thought. Your husband can never reach you clearly and positively until you return to your home. Then he will come. Meantime you will receive other assurances than mine of his proximity before three weeks pass."

I did receive other assurances, but not proofs, while in Cali- fornia. Two lovely cultured women, sisters, living quietly in Los Angeles, were both clairvoyants and mediumistic. They gave their services to friends in sorrow, never accepting money. They came to the house of a dear friend who had little knowledge of things psychic, and who was rather timid regarding such manifestations. She allowed me to see the psychics in one of her rooms. There were four investigators and two psychics. The room was darkened, for the reasons given above. We formed a circle about the small center table, clasping hands. On each side of the two mediums sat an investigator. Had the circle been broken we would have known. There were flowers on the table and a small trumpet. Voices spoke through the trumpet and the flowers were drawn from under my hands and pinned in my hair. Soft touches on my head and arms, and soft whispers in my ears sent thrills through me. Yet I did not feel that my husband was there. In truth the voice which spoke through the trumpet claimed to be the voice of the father of the two sister mediums; and he spoke my name, and said my husband was trying to reach me, but was not yet strong enough in his spiritual powers to achieve the desired result. "To reach a material world by immaterial means is not easy," he said. "It requires study. Your husband will come to you when you return home. He bids me tell you this."

I felt after this experience that I had been given real spiritual messages of a high order, yet that which I sought had not come to me. In the home of Hon. Lyman Gage at Loma Lodge, San Diego, very interesting phenomena, trumpet voices, and other demonstrations were given one evening by a professional medium. Again I was interested, and my feeling of loneliness and desolation was lightened. But I was not convinced. Hon. Lyman Gage had been an investigator and a believer in spiritual communication for more than fifty years.

I met that wonderful man of ninety-five years, J. M. Peebles, scholar, traveler (he has compassed the earth five times), lecturer, and famed for his lifelong proclamation of the truth of spiritual communication, and was strengthened by his conversation on the all-absorbing topic. Mr. Peebles, nearing the THE SEARCH OF A SOUL IN SORROW 355 century mark, has perfect hearing and excellent eyesight, and his magnetism and eloquence affect all who approach him. He writes with vigor and power. One very dear friend of mine in California, who held crude ideas on subjects psychic, grieved over my interest in spiritual research, lest I lose my health and my mental powers. I pointed to Mr. Peebles as a reassuring example of a seeker in the occult realms of study.

Mr. Peebles advised me, as did my Wise Ones, to avoid ordinary seance rooms and circles, and to place little faith in the average professional medium, because so soon as a money consideration enters into a spiritual power that power becomes vitiated. We have seen this proven many a time in the orthodox Christian Church. Young clergymen filled with the love of God and man, and desiring to lead a holy life, have been placed in fashionable churches, where their silence on certain ideas dear to them, or their clinging to worn-out dogmas, meant their continued salary: and we have seen these men of God become mere men of society, growing in popularity with their congregation, but growing farther and farther from God. So the psychic, who follows his profession for a livelihood, sometimes opens the door of his mind to the devils of greed.

I met Dr. Austin, who was once upon a time a minister of the gospel, after having graduated from a theological college. From this position he was asked to resign, because he announced his belief, through remarkable experiences, in spirit communication. Dr. Austin became a preacher of this faith and an editor of a mazagine devoted to the subject. He and his lovely daughter assured me I would one day find that which I sought. Their own experiences had been so numerous I could not question their truth, but why did they not come to me?

During that year of the search of my soul in the valley of sorrow, I was newly and painfully impressed with the spirit of intolerance and prejudice rampant in so many religious organizations.

Each little or large center which I approached seemed more anxious to convince me of the falsity of all other roads which claimed to lead to God than to cast light upon my troubled way, or comfort on my aching heart. From the orthodox Christian element came the most bitter opposition to anything which deviated one jot from its own ideas, forgetting how absolutely all those ideas depend upon spirit miracles for a foundation. Yet among church members of various denominations I found large souls who had developed into an understanding of the great truths which vibrate through space to-day. One was a communicant in a prominent church, the leader of its hundred-voiced choir, and a man whose mental, moral and artistic qualities made him a distinctive character. This man possessed psychic powers to a marked degree, and had been brought prominently before the public eye in this respect through a curious incident. At a church picnic one of his choir had used an ordinary camera and "snapped" the choir director as he stood under a tree. When the picture was developed a most remarkable phenomenon was observed. Directly above the figure was a clearly defined head of Dante, an exact duplicate of a marble bust in the studio of the choir director. At the left appeared a face so strikingly like that of the director's dead father that a member of his family grew faint at sight of it. Several other faces were outlined: one very much resembling the photographs of Longfellow, the poet. The director had been for months making a careful study of Dante's works, with the hope of writing fitting music for some of them. The head which appeared in the photo graph was, according to theosophical lore, a "thought form," one which the musician's mind had impressed so powerfully on the ether that the camera had been able to reproduce it. The face of the father was quite another thing: an unquestionable spirit face, "caught in the act" of visiting earth.

Etheric and vibratory conditions chanced to be just right for this most interesting result.

The photograph caused a sensation among the friends of the director, and the newspapers heard of it and one reproduced it with an interview in which the director talked freely of matters spiritual. Thereupon the church elders, deacons and pillars of traditions called a meeting, with the intention

THE SEARCH OF A SOUL IN SORROW 357 of having Mr. Director apologize, recant, or resign from the church, because, forsooth, he had believed in things upon which every religious organization on earth is founded– viz., spirit appearances on this sphere.

Mr. Director calmly asserted his knowledge of these facts: and told of many occasions in his life where he had been in touch with spirit realms and had received help and strength from spirit friends. So firm and strong and unwavering were his statements that his clergyman put an end to the "trial" and even preached a sermon soon thereafter speaking of this subject leniently, if not favorably.

I was given a copy of the spirit photograph, and it and the story as related to me by the director himself were my first proofs that such things as spirit photography really existed. That was a phase of spiritism which had seemed questionable to me. Later I investigated many other cases of spirit photography, and became fully convinced that under certain etheric conditions, and with the right personalities producing right vibrations, such pictures are obtained. Efforts of my own in that direction, however, were failures. The musical director whose story I have related was one of my most comforting and sustaining friends. He assured me that the hour would arrive when that which I sought would come to me. A soul which made his earth happiness, gone on a decade ago, came to him continually, he said, and gave him counsel and enlightenment. His advice Yas, "Go about your duties, do the tasks nearest, meditate and pray, be faithful to your musical studies, conquer your grief, trust in God, and wait till your illumination comes. To some it comes in one way, to others in other ways, but it will come to you." Surely it would not seem that a man holding such views needs to be excommunicated from a Christian Church! Yet he said to me, "My views on spiritual subjects have led to much persecution, and the most bitter of all has proceeded from my own Church."

The greatest tolerance and liberality toward other organizations of all kinds which I encountered in my search was in the Krotona Center of Theosophy. They had few words of criticism for anything or any one, preferring to see and talk of the good latent in all human nature. Opposed to spiritualism which degenerates into fortune telling, and which delays the souls of those gone on by continual appeals to return for trivial purposes, they yet approved of my investigations into the occult, knowing my purpose was not a selfish one and knowing any truths which came to me from any source would not be misused, or abused. They even accompanied me in some of my investigations, and helped me to discriminate between mere mind reading, chatter of elementals from the borderland, and messages from higher planes.

And they helped me to wait. And to grow while waiting. During all those long months I was not forgetting my life motto of service. I knew that the lords of Karma demand service of us while we pass through the valleys of tribulation, as well as while we walk on the hilltops of joy. I sought to help others who came into my daily life in all ways possible for me. To do that which would be pleasing in the sight of God and the generous soul gone into His keeping, was my effort. There were no longer any worldly pleasures which lured me. I had no ambitions for personal achievements of any kind. Light on my path, knowledge of God and Robert, service to humanity— these were all I asked. I devoted hours each day to meditation and prayer. I made a paraphrase of an old Moody and Sankey hymn, and began my meditations with it.

Oh, I am nothing, nothing– I only can lie at His feet: A broken and emptied vessel For the Master's use made meet. Broken that He may mend me, Emptied that He may fill: Teach me, O God in the silence,– How to be still.

That is the great need– to know how to be still in the silence until we receive the messages waiting in space to be delivered. I knew this was my need. Yet after trying to still the pain and the sense of loneliness exhaustion followed. And the messages could not be delivered.

There was another h3min I loved away back in the old singing school days of my early girlhood. I had loved it and sung it. Now I said it every morning as an ending of my first devotional exercises and a beginning of the long day.

Guide me, O Thou Great Jehovah, Pilgrim through a barren land: I am weak but Thou art mighty. Lead me with Thy powerful hand. Though I wandered Thou hast found me. Though I doubted sent me light; Still Thine arms have been around me. All my ways are in Thy sight. Bread of Heaven, Bread of Heaven– Feed me from Thy bounteous store. Bread of Heaven, Bread of Heaven– Feed me till I want no more.

To me this "Bread of Heaven," meant knowledge of Robert: that knowledge which he had over and over promised should be given, with God's consent. There was a storehouse of evidence to me, that other seekers for this knowledge had been fed by the Bread of Heaven. Every day this evidence increased, yet it did not come to me.

It must. Every morning at "The Home of Truth" Mrs. Militz and her students and teachers held a half hour silence meeting. While I did not attend any of their classes, or take up their studies (already familiar to me) I always participated in the half hour of silence. I found the vibrations stimulating and uplifting as they must be where a number of pure and unselfish souls are gathered together in His name.

Mrs. Militz usually gave a thought for us to hold in the silence; sometimes I accepted it, and sometimes I selected my own thought. One morning shortly before I separated from this lovely home to go elsewhere, the sentence given was, "I am the living witness." Mrs. Militz amplified the sentence to apply to her philosophy, but I amphfied it to meet my own needs. I composed a little Mantra, which was as follows:

"I AM THE LIVING WITNESS: THE DEAD LIVE: AND THEY SPEAK THROUGH US AND TO US: AND I AM THE VOICE THAT GIVES

THIS GLORIOUS TRUTH TO THE SUFFERING WORLD. I AM READY, GOD. I AM READY, CHRIST. I AM READY, ROBERT." I have never failed one day since that morning to repeat my assertion. In the next chapter will be related when and how and to what extent has the spoken word been verified.

CHAPTER XXIV

The Keeping of the Promise

T T is never quite safe to make positive assertions regarding our capacity for suffering. I once knew a woman to say she could bear every kind of sorrow but one kind. That, she said, she could never endure. Yet that was g ven her, and she had to endure it.

When I went away to California, I had said, "Life has no new pain to offer me; I have received its supreme blow." Yet, during the next sixteen months I found that life held other blows for me, and that I could still smart with pain. In that land of bloom and beauty, I found souls welling with God's own sjmipathy and love, and by many old friends, and many new ones, was consoling kindness poured upon open wounds, and never to be broken ties were formed that will unite us even beyond this earth. Yet, from some sources where the greatest understanding, sympathy and affection were expected only cold neglect and indifference came. And from some of those to whom, in my anxiety to be of service, I had given my heart to put under their feet, came unbelievable cruelty and unkind-ness.

I found that I could still suffer, and wondered why these seemingly needless hurts were given to one already bleeding at every pore. But now I have come to understand God's purpose. Holding in store for me the greatest gift the Lords of Karma have to bestow to those on earth, God wanted me to cast away, one by one, every prop on which I leaned, and to break every tie which bound me to material things, or held me closely to earthly affections. To no one and nowhere must I look for comfort and help, save to God Himself, and the realms where dwell the souls released from earth.

In a previous chapter, I have said that the last book Robert and I read together was "Patience Worth," that most interesting work, called by thinkers, "The Psychic Mystery of the Century." "Patience Worth" was dictated through the Ouija Board, which Mrs. Curran and some friends in St. Louis were using, more as an amusement than otherwise; its very remarkable literary and historic value has won the attention of eminent scholars and thinkers all over the land. Patience Worth proclaimed herself a spirit that had lived upon the earth three hundred years ago, and her diction is of that period.

This book, and others which have followed it in the same manner, brought the Ouija Board into new prominence, and gave it a dignity never before possessed by it. Many years ago I had owned a Ouija Board; all my interests at that time were on this earth plane. Family and friends and lover were all here; I sat with various friends, and we received the usual curious, erratic things which come to those who idly experiment in such matters. Each accused the other of causing the board to move; and, when convinced this was not just, the results were laid to subconscious mind or involuntary muscles.

This was my acquaintance with the Ouija Board, when after sixteen months in the valley of sorrowful search, I decided again to test its power as a means of communication with worlds beyond. I had returned from California and was at my home– my "Paradise Lost" at Short-Beach-on-the-Sound.

In their artistic home, "The Terrace," next to our Bungalow Court, live our very dear friends, Mr. and Mrs. W. H. Ritter. It is a friendship cemented by sixteen years of intimate association. They were most eager to experiment with me on the Ouija Board. We were disappointed when Mr. Ritter and I could not produce the least quiver of the implement. Mrs. Ritter and I had better success, but it was slow and tedious work; each knew the other was not moving the board, and some of the sentences which came seemed very characteristic of the soul we were seeking.

Of the purpose of these messages I shall speak later. Mr. Ritter (one of the few fine American business men who are

THE KEEPING OF THE PROMISE 363 awake spiritually) was more impressed with their being genuine phenomena than was I. I had so long doubted every manifestation received, in my search of sorrow, that it was difficult for me to feel satisfied with anything short of the miraculous. Distracted and interested for a half hour with the slowly spelled messages, I would go home and weep myself to sleep, wondering why my Beloved could not keep his lifelong promise to reach me from the worlds beyond. I knew how souls bound by affection which is more mental and spiritual than merely physical long to communicate with those left behind, and I knew that such communication, when understood by those on earth and not misused or belittled, comforts the soul which has gone on, and strengthens it for its later higher flights to more subtle spheres. I knew Robert would be as gratified, and as benefited, once the way opened for him to say "Hail," as I would be. I knew Heaven could never satisfy him until he came in touch with me.

And each day I said my Mantra over and over; each day I prayed for light, and guidance, and knowledge of life beyond. It was in late July that I wrote the following verses:

DAILY TALKS

So much I miss those daily talks with you, O my Beloved! Though you answer not, (In any manner that of old I knew) Yet will I seek in each familiar spot, To bring your sympathetic spirit near

Where it may hear My inmost thoughts, in written words revealed. Perchance my bleeding heart may thus be healed. Of that deep wound this silence makes therein.

The world has no harsh sound, no clash, no din So hard to bear as silence day on day. And night on night, the while we plead and pray For some faint echo from the world unseen.

Dear, you have been A year and three score days lost to my sight. And to my touch and hearing; and despite My life-long faith in Heaven's proximity. And in communion of souls linked by love,

Yet do we seem divided by a sea

Across whose still unatlassed waters move

Out-going silent ships, that come not back.

Still do I watch the track Of that strange midnight craft, whereon you sailed. Believing love like yours which never failed On earth to keep its promises will find Some way to give mine eyes, which now are blind. Their clearer sight, and to prepare my ear Its message from the other world to hear. The while I wait, perchance you, too, wait near. Attentive, smiling, in the olden way. Beloved, day by day.

It was in the early evening of September loth that the door opened. Mrs. B, a New Haven friend, came to call. I had just purchased a Quija Board of my own. At Mrs. Ritter's I had used hers. My board was lying on the table. I asked my caller if she had ever tried the Quija. "No," she said, "and I should like to; I think it would be most interesting." In a light and laughing mood she placed her hands on the Board, and in one moment the heavens opened! Both my caller and I were shaken by a power which beggars description; it was like an electric shock. The Board seemed to be a thing alive; it moved with such force that we could not follow it. I called to Mrs. Randall, who was in an adjoining room, to come to our assistance. She came and gave her whole attention to the letters; neither my friend nor I was able to read them, so great was the speed of the pointer. When the table rested, she read these sentences, "Brave one, keep up your courage. Love is all there is. I am with you always. I await your arrival."

When I heard these sentences read out, after experiencing the electric shock of their transmission, there was no longer any doubt in my mind. My message had come! I was in touch with my Robert! He had kept his promise! I asked how long I must wait in the body before going to him. The answer was, "Time is naught; hope for bliss with me; I am incomplete without you. Two halves make a whole; we will finish in Nirvana."

I attempted to obtain some advice about business; the answer was, "Material things are unimportant." I then asked questions regarding my heauh. "Fill yourself with God,– health will come."

This was the beginning of a series of most remarkable conversations with a freed soul in the worlds beyond. And these conversations grew steadily in value and importance, as will be seen by what follows. On the next sitting, September 13th, we had been perhaps half an hour at the Board, receiving remarkable communications, when Mrs. B 's husband came in, quietly, trying not to disturb us. I remarked, "Robert, can you tell me who just entered the room?" The answer was, "Yes." "Then tell me," I replied. Mrs. R., who was acting as our scribe, said the letters seemed to make only jargon. They were given again, and the sentence was– "Quinnipiac Club, our last game." To us this sentence carried no meaning, but my friend's husband, a practical business man and popular club man, said quietly, "The last time your husband ever appeared at the Quinnipiac Club I was his partner at auction." Neither his wife nor I knew of this incident. Surely there can be no explanation of "subconscious mind" or "involuntary muscles" given to this message! I then asked:

"Robert, have you a message for your friend?"

Instantly the message came: "Better try some other game.

V. W. B. quitter." I felt embarrassed, until Mr. B with a quiet laugh said, "That night I played with your husband until after midnight, when I said I must go home. He replied, You are a quitter; you had better try some other game!"

Again the subconscious mind must be omitted by the sceptic; neither my friend nor I had any knowledge of this incident, which was evidently repeated to Mr. B as a proof of the identity of the sender.

Our next meeting was at the home of my friend. The room in which we sat had recently been done over in a most effective Oriental fashion. No sooner were we seated with our hands on the Board, than it wrote, "Arabian Nights' Room! Scheherezade." This impressed us at once, as during his last winter of earth life Robert had loaned this friend a valuable edition of the "Arabian Nights' Tales," and they had discussed them together frequently. I then asked this question: "Robert, if this is you, tell me what are you doing in the invisible realms?"

The answer was rapidly written,–"I am doing a great work; meeting souls shot into eternity. That is why I left you." Many questions were then asked and swiftly answered, and so remarkable was the impression left by this sitting, that I sent records of it to Mr. Robert Walton of California, a man eminent in theosophical work, then in New York. My first month in California had been spent in the mountain home of the Waltons at Nordhoff. I wrote, asking Mr. Walton to come and be a witness of the messages we were receiving, and to use all his analytical powers in studying them. Mr. Walton came, and the sitting took place in my home. Mrs. Randall was as usual the scribe, and Mrs. Davies-Jones was a witness of the test conditions under which the messages came. I proposed that Mrs. B and myself be blindfolded during the sittings, in order that no least suggestion might come to the mind of Mr. Walton that we in any way influenced the Board. This was done and the messages came as swiftly and powerfully as before, the pointer moving with unerring certainty to the letters. So remarkable seemed the force that I spoke of it, and the Board wrote, "Scota is helping to-night." We had no idea what this meant, but in later sittings we became very familiar with "Scota." I asked why, since the communication seemed so fully established now, had he not come to me during those terrible months of lonely search. At once came the reply:

"Your tears hung a veil between."

"Tell me what your life is like now," I questioned.

"The same life, only tised more intelligently."

I asked if he had met a friend who had died recently, "No, he is not on my plane; my work is different, meeting souls shot into eternity. All is confusion for them. Equanimity is my gift; I supply it to those killed in the shock of battle."

This sentence, strange as it sounded, did not seem incom- prehensible to me. Every student of occult lore knows that the Episcopal prayer, "From sudden death, O Lord, deliver us," is founded on a knowledge that souls driven from the body by sudden death suffer from fright and confusion on the astral plane, and that it requires the aid of older spirits and messengers of God to convince them they are out of the body. In my husband's early business career he had always been sent by his firm to bring order out of chaos where unpleasant entanglements existed.

Equanimity was his gift here, and it would follow as a matter of course that it was his possession there.

Ques.–"Can you give me the name of a distinguished guest we have here?" (I was referring to Robert Walton.) Ans.–"Mine."

I asked if he would give us the names of those who were associated with him in his work on the astral plane. "It is forbidden."

I asked if he would help me to retain health while on earth. " am but an instrument in His hands. Health is of the soul."

Reminded that once, through Mrs. Ritter, he had suggested my taking some treatment, he wrote–"Means are not to be despised."

Ques.–"How can you attend to your work of meeting and helping the souls of soldiers, and yet come at once whenever my friend and I sit together?" "Spirit is omnipresent. Love is my guide, love is all."

Ques.–"Do you long for the time when I shall leave my body and be with you?" "Yes; Devachan is a state of bliss unalloyed."

Mrs. Randall found no meaning to the word, but Mr. Walton explained that it was the theosophical word for heaven. I then said, "But you will not go so far ahead in your heaven world, Robert, that you cannot meet me when I come?" Ans. "I will meet you; how could you have bliss unalloyed without me? Everything you long for will be given."

I asked if he could give a message or a word that would indicate the presence of another guest. I was referring to my harp teacher, Mrs. Davies-Jones. The room had become very warm, and we had removed the bandages from our eyes, as the sitting was nearing its dose. The pointer moved to H-A-R- when I interrupted and said, "I think it must mean harp." Emphatically the pointer went back and wrote HARMONY. My suggestion was scorned, and my interruption rebuked. On another occasion while messages were coming rapidly, I had spoken to Mrs. B, and the pointer rushed to form this sentence: "Ella, stop interrupting": then added, "Ella is scolded!" After one of the early sittings, I had written the two sonnets which follow:

At last! at last the message! Definite As dawn that tells the night has gone away. The silence has grown eloquent with it. The silence that late filled me with dismay. So dumb it was; triumphant now I sit So near to God and you I need not pray. For only words of thankfulness were fit For this estate wherein I dwell to-day.

You live! you love me! You have heard my call,
And answered it in your own way. The proof
So satisfies the soul of me, were all
The hosts of earth henceforth to stand aloof
Till I recanted, my reply were this:–
One men call dead, has sent me messages.

0 my Beloved! Through these months like years, 1 know you might have reached me sooner here Had I not blurred the trail by storms of tears. And yet, how could, how could I help it, dear? Now you have found a way to make God's spheres Seem very intimate and very near.

And radiant my lonely path appears, The light you cast upon it is so clear.

I stand victorious at the longed-for goal.

With open vision, where I once was blind.

And cry aloud to every suffering soul:

"Pray without ceasing, seek and ye shall find.

Though Science sneer, and school and church condemn,

Your dead dwell near, you may commune with them."

THE KEEPING OF THE PROMISE 369

We were barely seated at the Board, on our next meeting, when the hurried sentence came, "Ella, send your sonnets at once to England: at once." (I had not mentioned to Mrs.

B that I had written the sonnets, and they were not in my mind.) I replied that I had sent them to my English publishers. The answer was, "No, to Sir Oliver Lodge; you owe it to him, and the world; such proofs are rare. Though many doubt, seers will be convinced, and we must work together."

On this occasion we sat in the room where Robert's soul took flight. I asked, "Do you remember this room, Robert?" "My darling nurse, I do!"

"Do you remember those last hours with me here?" (He had been seemingly unconscious those hours.) Reply–"As plainly as you do."

It was a later sitting when the following questions and answers were received:

"How long after your soul left your body was it before you woke on the astral plane?" "Seven days."

"Did you know when your body was cremated on the fourth day?" "No, my astral body was out."

"What did you first see when you awoke?" "Your face– Memory."

"What spirit first met you?" "Our son."

"How did you recognize him, since he died when an infant?" "He was so like you."

Asked if he had met a young friend recently deceased, he replied: "I see her when I wish; she is, as you know, undeveloped, but safe and happy."

Then came the parting messages:

"Be strong; my help is constant, I am always with you."

I had been away on a two weeks' visit to old friends in Jersey. While there, very interesting messages had come through one of these friends, T. G. The force was not quite as powerful or rapid as that which came through Mrs. B, yet it was remarkable. This friend had never experimented in any occult matters. One day when very interesting per- sonal messages were coming, T. G. was called away. When she returned, the pointer suddenly swept several times across the Board, and wrote–"Make room for me, make room for me.

We asked who "me" might be. The answer was, "Martha."

Eight years had passed since Martha Jordan Fishel died. And this was the first intimation that we had received of her wish to communicate with us. T. G. was her very close friend. The messages that followed were intimate, and breathed of her characteristics. She said Robert had told her to come and talk to us, that she was doing God's work, and had no desire to return to earth.

When I returned to my home, the first sitting with Mrs.

B brought the following greeting. (All these messages, be it understood, were received by Mrs. B and myself blind-folded, with Mrs. Randall taking down the letters by pencil.) The first word spelled was "Robert," then, "I am glad you are back."

Ques. "What have you to say to me?" Ans. "Great things; events are shaping on your plane and mine; our lives are one."

In my first somewhat laborious messages received with Mrs. Ritter, there had been one most insistent message, "Go to France," followed by, "Take very little with you: only one trunk." This message came so regularly when we sat down that Mrs. Ritter and I both began to laugh when the pointer approached "G." I now, while under the perfect test conditions with Mrs. B asked if he had any suggestion for my winter. Instantly the answer came, "Go to France; humanity has need of you. Wonderful things will happen. Your spark of God is greater than that of ten ordinary mortals."

Until that message came, I had not seriously considered the journey to France. Then I asked if the messages received through Mrs. Ritter and T. G. had been authentic. He replied, "Yes, but I reach you better through Isis." This was a name used by Mrs. B in a humorous Oriental Society she had founded. Several sentences then followed so rapidly that Mrs. R became confused, and asked to have them re- written. They were spelled out slowly, and then came, "Is May blind?"

Still later, when confusion resulted from too rapid writing, he said, "Oh, May, you make me tired."

These very human and characteristic touches gave the experience more reality, as did a later reproof to me, when I interrupted his dictation by speaking to Mrs. B. He stopped and wrote, "Ella, don't butt in." (His little imperious ways with me on earth, rebuking me when he felt I needed it, were part of his many attractions for me.) When we heard Mrs.

R read out this sentence, we all burst out laughing, and the pointer scurried over the Board, and wrote, "That sounds good; everybody laughs."

This, too, brought him nearer, for his delight was in having his home echo with laughter. (Alas! what pain he must have felt those sixteen months gone, when coming near me.) I was then contemplating writing for the Occult Review the chapter which has been given herein, entitled "The Search of a Soul in Sorrow."

I asked him if I should do this. He replied, "I will give you the title of a book. Wait." We rested for a time and after our return he wrote: "This is so delightful; now I will give you the title of the book."

"The Goal"

Chapter ist, "Immolation."

Chapter and, "Suttee."

Chapter 3rd, "Juggernauth" (Insisting on the final "h").

Chapter 4th, "The Holocaust."

Chapter 5th, "Sesame."

Chapter 6th, "The Key."

Chapter 7th, "The Goal."

Then he went on to say, "I will write it." "When?" "I have begun it."

Q. "How will you write it?" A. "I will put the words in your hand."

Q. "Alone, or with Isis?" A. "Both ways."

)372 THE WORLDS AND I

Then he wrote, "All you gave me, and all I gave you, through seven incarnations will be incorporated in this book. Our seven love lives live in the book." I asked when we would begin. He answered, "At once."

THE GOAL

CHAPTER ONE Immolation

A scorching heat, a blue mist, a tinkle of rippling water within the shelter of their cave. Pan and Ilia rest. How came they here? ons ago, on Saturn, a Monad's thought took shape; form, newly donned, seeks resting place. Search stirred into being, by divine discontent, senses vibration. In sympathy he vibrates, and lo! motion is born. He rolls, rolls, rolls, unsatisfied. But what delicious softness is this! He sinks into her yielding embrace. Ages pass. O sweet mud! Though you cling to me forever, yet we are not one body. Stirred by a great devotion, mud vibrates. The Lord of Will accepts her sacrifice of Ego, and bestows the gift of growth to solidarity upon mud. Ages pass in the process. She yields her attribute of softness to his hard substance; folded each within the other, they become one at last. Her immolation complete. Mates in Primos, nodules in matrix. End of Chapter One.

It was not until this very remarkable dictation was read over carefully, that I realized its purport. It was a condensed exposition of the first descent into matter of the Divine Spirit, and "thought," which had becomef mineral and had been embedded in soil, "sweet mud." After aeons of time, the mineral and the mud became one substance. And this was the first incarnation of Pan and Ilia.

As a result of an accident to their motor we had only a hurried sitting with Mrs, B on October 21st, 1917, at

"The Barracks." There were present tv. W. B. and Mrs. Randall. He began at once, "Ella, dearest, you are with me." I said, "It is too bad, Isis can only stay a few minutes." Reply, "She will come again soon."

Then he began again on the book. I interrupted and said, "You'd better not write on the book to-day; we have so little time." "But this is so important; wonderful impressions, peculiar combinations of atomic forces give Manu of Race this opportunity of sending truths hidden from mankind."

I then asked if he could not give some one nearer me power to go on with the work when Mrs. B could not be here.

"I have no control." Then I said, "I suppose it just happens that Isis has the power with me to get your messages." "Nothing ever just happens. " I asked if May could not be given the power. "May is not Isis." I asked if I could in any way develop myself to receive the messages alone. "Yes, go to our room, sit in my chair. Empty your mind and I will fill it. The pitcher that goes to the well, full, gets nothing. Keep trying, do not tire. Power comes with use." I asked for messages for each of us, beginning with V. (I did not use his name.) Reply, "V., you old robber!" This caused a great laugh, as at the card games Robert often called him that.

For Isis, "Graciousness personified."

For May, "A more joy-filled future."

For Ella, "For you, my soul's bond."

The next sitting was with Mrs. B at her home October 24, 1917.

First sentence, "Isis has on my gift." Mrs. B said,

"Yes, you see I am wearing the pendant Robert brought me from Africa."

Then, "Take off your wrist watch, Ella," I took it off. "Isis too."

She said, "I have no watch, only a bandage on my wrist, where I have a bum. The doctor told me to keep it covered." He said, "Take it off; the Lords of Love will protect it." Then he began on the second chapter of the book.

CHAPTER TWO Sesame (I asked if he had made a change in the order of the chapters. "Yes." Then followed:)

A long rest in cosmic sleep. The hardness of our physical bodies is dissolved; we become pure spirit. Then comes the call into being. The Lords of Wisdom summon us to our station in the sun. Our chosen path leads finally to earth. Impulse to push permeates us with a quivering stream of compulsion. We respond and the stream flows through us with accumulated force. We push through that which on Saturn was ourselves, now far above it in evolution. We feel air for the first time.

O joyous sense! Around us are vast thick clouds of gorgeous color, filled with angel forms. We grow, grow, grow, two in one, when lo! upon our life-filled stem unfolds a lotus bud, first offspring of Ilia and Pan. Our Lord of Wisdom smiled, well pleased with our sacrifice of sap and strength, and his smile took form. In that form clung our inestimable gift, our etheric self. Sesame to higher planes.

End of Chapter Two

Again I realized that a perfectly scientific explanation was given in this chapter of the progress of the spirit through the mineral into the vegetable state. Pan and Ilia were now a lotus tree.

CHAPTER THREE (On October 22nd was dictated the third chapter.) Cradled in the womb of Time, we develop though we sleep, and when our time is fulfilled, liie Lords of Motion summon us. We stir and struggle into astral birth on the moon. We roam, we breed, we leap, we sleep. Within our forest home, beneath his wattled hut, dwell Milidh and Scota, with their two sons, Eiram-Hon and little Arannan. They fear us not, nor fear we them. But to play by day and guard their sleep by night, become our greatest joy. In return we give them love and thought, and in their likeness we develop fast.

At length there comes a fearful night. From out the forest depths an horde of ravening beasts, with slimy scales and deadly fangs. They storm the hut, with horns and claws and horrid din. Heedless of selves, we leap into the fray. Mighty Milidh gives battle to the monsters, but all in vain. He falls, pierced by many wounds. Before our very eyes little Aran-nan's bones are crushed to pulp. The sturdy Eiram-Hon, in terror, clings around the neck of Ilia, and cowers in her thick soft fur.

With one tremendous leap Ilia gains the topmost branch in safety with the boy. With the fainting Scota clasped tight in his hairy arms. Pan follows. Sudden to our ears comes the dying groan of Milidh. "Save him," in anguish Scota cries. With one impulse, animated by a desire to serve and save, we leap to earth, and cast ourselves protectingly on his prostrate body.

The maddened monsters, with jaws agape for flesh of man, thrice angered by their loss of victims two, deal us our death blow. With dying blessings of Milidh in our ears, we feel a mighty flood of power from the vast Cosmos of love through us flow.

On wings of flame, the Lords of Personality appear, and on us bestow the great gift of Ego. Key to the goal. Humans at last we die.

End of Chapter Three

Again I realized that this was the exposition of the progress of divine spirit through vegetable to animal life, and then to human through service and sacrifice. Pan and Ilia would be reborn in their next incarnation as human beings. We were all filled with a madness of desire to know in what way they would appear, and in what era, when we next sat at the Board on October 30th. With great force the Board wrote, "Ella, momentous things are upon us. I have come to a new path. I had to decide; I will tell you all. The Deva who protects us, caljed me to a choice of paths; there were two.

One would open a glorious service for me. I could be a messenger for the Logos, one of his agents." I said, "What is the other path?"

"Helpfulness toward earth dwellers, and those newly arrived."

I said, "You must not give up the higher work for me; I will be able to go on alone now, if you are called onward."

"I could not leave you; millenniums are before us for service and development, so why should I go ahead? I give you to-night this great proof of my love. I had to plead our cause with Deva, who carried the prayer to Logos. Can you not feel how I was torn by struggle between duty to God and love for my mate, my Ella? I pleaded our oneness from Saturn to Earth and gained the, favor of a little reprieve."

I asked how long he would be able to continue giving me messages.

"I do not know; they did not tell me." Then he said,

"I want to tell you about the book. The next chapters naturally grow more complex. My idea is to give you a S3mop-sis of each chapter, thus saving time and strength. You can elaborate later. For me, time is limited; means, clumsy." I replied, "No, I shall give it just as you send it to the public when the time is ripe. I wish to state positively that I had no part in it."

We asked for personal messages and he wrote:

For May, "That which the fountain gives, into the fountain returns."

For Isis, "A splendid destiny."

For Ella, "Strength divine for the goal."

Asked for a word about the war, he wrote, "If all nations were wiped out, yet in the plan of the root and seed Manu this were as naught. Everything that is, is right."

Sitting with Mrs. B at her residence, November I2th, 1917.

"You are doing finely, Ella; courage!" Then, "I have part of the new chapter ready." il said, "Shall you give it to-day?" "Not all; it takes time to evolve a chapter." I then asked, "How do you evolve it?"

"The next chapter was revealed to me by the graciousness of Viavasate Manu by means of pictures stored in the archives of the universe, made by vibrations.

Each object, each act, each thought which ever existed in any world, is recorded in indestructible films of etheric matter by means of vibration.

"Viavasate Manu permitted me to see unrolled the whole picture. I saw myself and you, and all the multitude in the Golden City of Atlantis, and our daily lives, our friends, our bridal couch, the pathetic sacrifice of Rhada, High Priestess of the Sun, who gave herself for love of her sister Isis, the temple dancer, beloved and branded by Eiram-Hon, Crown Prince, and only son of Emperor Milidh and Scota. You were the lovely Princess Ilia, and I was Pan, General of the Emperor's army. You were the star far above my head. I saw the hosts of Arhinan, Lord of Evil, tuler of the nether world, advancing upon the city. I saw us die, murdered on our bridal couch. One blow severed our two heads, so tightly were we clasped together. I saw the incomparable Isis dragged from the temple crypt, and torn to bits before the eyes of Eiram-Hon. I saw the rod of the four Kumuras raised to destroy all this evil. Floods, earthquakes, storms, electricity, volcanic eruptions, convulsed the earth, until with one fearful shudder, it was swallowed up in the oblivion of the sea. Holocaust of the Kamuras. This is the truth."

One month after these dictations had been received he asked one day, "Let May read aloud my chapters of the story; I will point to No' where there are errors, and correct them." This was done, and like the most careful proofreader he went over every phrase, and corrected many punctuations and changed some passages.

It was not until some months after this dictation had been given me, that I began the study of that remarkable book, "The Secret Doctrine," and found in the "Stanzas of Dzyan" the following description of the descent of the soul from the first cause into matter.

My husband had never read this book or any other on that particular phase of our creation, so his knowledge must have come from the infinite realms. The stanzas read as follows: "The Spark hangs from the Flame (God) by the finest thread of Fohat (creative thought). It journeys through the seven worlds of Maya (seven globes of the planetary chain). It stops in the first and is a metal, a stone. It passes into the second, and behold, a plant! The plant whirls through seven changes and becomes a sacred animal: from the combined attributes of these Manu, the Thinker, is formed. Who formed him? The seven lives and the one life. Who completes him? The five sons of Mind. Who perfects the last body? The Immortal Being."

At the next sitting his messages began:

T wish you could take May to France with you; you may need an earthly friend, and May is so unselfish and devoted."

Then suddenly, "Do you remember the time I sent you a telegram before we were married? You were at the hotel in Chicago."

I said, "Yes, with Mrs. Talman."

"Tell me aloud what was in the telegram."

I replied that it was to announce his coming. Answer, "Yes, and I was late. Do you remember the time, shortly after our marriage, when I had to make long trips; how we missed each other, and how often I wrote to you?"

I replied, "Yes, I do, and I remember the day before you started, the 29th of July, how, lover-like, you told me there were no other women who could compare with me, to your thinking."

Answer: "Same yet, and there are angels here."

Mrs. B remarked,

"Doesn't that sound just like Robert?"

Answer, "It is I."

I said, "You know, do you not, that this is my last sitting with Isis, and so my last chat with you for a long time?"

Answer, "This is not our last meeting." "You will talk to me many times in the future?" "As long as you are in the flesh."

THE KEEPING OF THE PROMISE 379 I asked if I should use the Board, and also pencil and paper, to try and get messages. "Yes, both."

"Is there any other way?"

"A blank mind, so I can make a record, like the Hindoo seers and adepts. Practice every day.

"How long?" "Begin with ten minutes."

Then we asked for good-by messages.

"My devotion and gratitude for our Isis."

"To May we owe more than you know."

I asked for a little good-by word for me. "Never a good-by for us! Take with you, my only love, the supreme watchfulness of a husband and of a lover."

On December 19th I again visited T. G. The Board which had done great work for us in October now refused to move; a relative, L, a church member and deeply religious woman, placed her hands on it and at once it was seized with the same tremendous power which Mrs. B had brought to it. L had never experimented in such matters before. The pointer wrote with great force, "Ella, listen, stay where you are until Monday. Vitalize your physical powers for the great adventure, Monday next, Scota will come and talk." I asked what the great adventure might be.

"Your message; it will give comfort to many. The Comforter will come, but you must be patient; Scota bids you wait. The ethereal body at this moment is in control: it is very near now; Robert is here. Comfort will come–r-pa- tience. To-morrow L will receive a message from me: remember, and vitalize for the great adventure. Your message will come, and give comfort to all mankind now in darkness. Listen, wait, vitalize."

December nth, 1917. The pointer wrote at once, with great force, "Ella, listen, Heaven is opened to me: I am moving in the circle of Divine Essence, in the transcendent Source of all Being. God is infinite love, and His manifestations infinite wisdom. Nature rises out of Him and we sink into Him. Scota had brought me into contact with Jacob Boehm, a great soul who has given messages. He bids me tell you, that you are far along on the path. The path is

380 THE WORLDS AND I long and difficult, but you are farther along than most, and your Chela is sure that you will soon be an Independent Soul. Remember always our hour at dawn, and worry not, as I am with you. Nothing is gained by worry. Sleep well. I am to learn from Jacob Boehm things that you taught me first, but I shall see

them in the full daylight now. His words make it seem like the sunlight in the Flower Room."

"Can you give us any idea when and how this war will end?"

"God, the center of all, controls; and the end will justify all."

I attempted several more questions about the war, and was interrupted with, "Stop asking questions; I will return in two days, Ella; wait and rest."

We had none of us ever heard of Jacob Boehm. We looked in the Encyclopedia and were amazed to find two pages devoted to him. His philosophy was given in these words, "Nature rises out of God, and we sink into Him." This struck us as remarkable evidence of the absolutely spiritual source of our messages; our subconscious minds did not hold this knowledge.

December 13th there was a hurried sitting, and for the first time the messages contained references to business. Once I had asked if he approved changes made in my will, and the reply had come, "Yes, ingratitude is abhorrent." Again, when questioned about business and its outlook, the board had written with seeming impatience, "This is not fortune telling." But on this evening I had been talking after dinner regarding my possible death abroad, and had mentioned what seemed to me wise disposition of my own small personal patrimony.

A message had come to L; then suddenly this came, "Tell Ella not to be in a hurry about disposing of her possessions. There are greater causes waiting." Asked to suggest them, the reply was, "I will come in two days, and advise you. Wait, rest, vitalize." But circumstances beyond my control rendered it impossible for me to remain where I was until Monday; I could neither wait, rest, nor vitalize. Instead I was obliged to take a railroad trip in zero weather, and in a THE KEEPING OF THE PROMISE 381 crowded train where there was standing room only. The next two days found me quite ill, and so I was not enlightened regarding the Great Adventure promised.

It seemed like scorning the voice of Heaven, but it could not be helped. Just as one on earth cannot transmit a telegram without an operator who understands telegraphy, so a spirit must depend on one who has the right vibrations to get the messages to earth. After I left T. G. and L, many friends desired sittings with me, but all failed to bring any convincing results until, some three weeks after this, Miriam French, a beautiful and gifted woman, with whom I had had some correspondence, called on me at the hotel. Deeply interested in all spiritual matters, she was much impressed with my experiences. I asked her to try the Board with me, and, the moment her hands touched it, it wrote rapidly, "Keep this woman with you; I can work through her. She has the power." Mrs. French was obliged to leave, however, but came again the next day. The first sentence was, "This lady is the one for our work in hand." I then introduced her to him as "Miriam," and he continued, "Miriam's purpose is pure; she can help you to develop so that you can use pencil and paper; try a few moments every day; it must come. Scota knows Miriam's incarnations. Be of good courage, for the God of the Ages is with you."

An old friend, Lida Melhuish, had come in during this sitting, and was watching the messages for me. I asked for an idea regarding the poem Robert wanted me to write. Suddenly this came, "You might write on The Birth of Two Souls, a few lines to the twins." Mrs. Melhuish started up and cried out, "Why, my niece gave birth to twin girls yesterday: do you suppose Robert means that?"

He said, "Lida is a good sport, and Ella is the dearest thing on earth. Time will reveal God's plan to you. Good-night."

In the next sitting with Miriam French, a very interesting message came. The first was, "Scota says Miriam was a priestess in the Temple of Rameses in the Egyptian period. Scota was then a hand maiden in the temple. She has never incarnated since." I asked about the husband of a friend, and said she was breaking her heart, because no messages came from him.

"I never knew him on earth; it would help if you had a picture of him. If he came here without God in his heart it would make it harder for him to communicate and she must have God in her heart to succeed. Many come here who had only material desires in their hearts: they try to live the same way here. When they find they cannot they seek the same vibrations of those 6n earth: they live in a cloud near earth. Intense love and desire is the only way out. Desperate grief of those on earth makes the burden heavier for souls here." I remarked that this seemed a flaw in God's system, as without some direct ray of light to prove immortal life, and with our dear ones wrenched away, we could not help the bitter grief. He replied: "It is the greatest proof of unselfishness a human soul has to meet." Then added, "I take you with me every night in your sleep, and show you the higher realms, and you see all I do."

"But why do I not remember any of it?"

"That comes with growth."

I asked about Christ, and what he knew of Him.

"Christ is at the head of the spheres which belong to the Christian era. To see these spheres we have to ascend; a band of Devas took me, and then I only glimpsed His glory."

"And do you know if Buddha, who went from earth 500 years before Christ, has spheres belonging to his era?"

"Yes, the region is so high that we have to raise our vibrations to approach it, and then only sense its radiance." Suddenly came this message: "Ask Miriam to show you the small Buddha in her handbag." Miriam, who had been sitting with closed eyes during the coming of these messages which were taken down by Mrs. Randall, started up in surprise and took from her handbag a small silver Buddha no larger than a pea. "Ask her to open it." Opened, it revealed five tiny dice. I exclaimed with pleasure over this unexpected stunt? I wanted you to know I could look into handbags!" test. Then came this: "Are you pleased, Ella, at this little I remarked that I wished he could give us more quotations to

THE KEEPING OF THE PROMISE 383 verify, as he did in the Jacob Boehm incident; at once came this,

"Thou for me at Allah's shrine, I at any God's for thine." Moore.

We were not familiar with the words, but afterwards found them in Moore's poems, with only one word changed. I asked if he lived in a house. The answer was, "We only have houses when we desire them: I am moving constantly." I asked, "Is it from realm to realm you move?" "Yes, and from glory to glory." I reminded him that once, standing on our veranda at the Bungalow" in the moonlight he said he wanted no more beautiful heaven then a duplicate of our Bungalow. "Well, then, we will build a Bungalow," was the answer, evidently meaning that when I came we would desire a house and that we would at once build it.

I asked if beautiful Aunt Hattie could sometimes come and talk to me. There was a pause, then, "Bless you, my child, this is Aunt Hattie." I asked whom she was with over there. "The light, of which you get only glimpses, shines around each soul: we do not see others unless they are in that ray." I asked if it was not a lonely life.

"It is life as you cannot conceive it. Immortal life is doing the rarest duty, not always the easiest one. It is Aunt Hattie who gives this message."

Then Robert came and wrote, "Unless souls are in the same work they do not meet. We are so busy, we seldom see each other; our lives are devoted to duty and service." I remarked that Miriam had to go, and asked for a parting message. He came directly to earth matters, and to his earth habit of looking after my health. "Take care of yourself, and do not take cold when you go to the country; wear rubbers, take fresh milk and fresh eggs every morning. My beloved, I am always with you, asleep or awake. We shall see each other again: have patience. Sit every day, alone in the silence, until you learn the use of the higher laws, then you will not need the Board. Fill yourself with God; when you are developed enough I will appear to your sight; be patient."

Then—"You must not call for Scota, she has gone to higher realms to prepare for initiation. When she has finished her studies she will speak to you."

At the next sitting I asked, "Did you see me reading over your old letters last night, and crying to think I never saw any more letters in your penmanship?" Answer. "You will not make any progress until you give up wanting letters." Then— "I have very important things to say to you."

"Well, our minds are very peaceful and ready to receive."

"That is good; some one has said the Infinite is always silent, the Finite only speaks, but I want you to prepare for very vicious attacks made by the world on the gigantic work you have undertaken; many will be jealous and vindictive. You must write an article saying you have not received these messages through professional mediums or clairvoyants." Reply, "I have written this in the Epilogue to my Memoirs."

"But you must write another short article at once; to be published right after you go away. Get Mr. Brisbane of the Journal to publish it without fail." I replied that I would do so before I slept. "Remember, your promise is recorded in the soundless sound."

I spoke to Miriam then, and said with a good deal of emphasis that the world would have to listen to my story of messages received under test conditions, and their absolute proofs of life beyond. The Board wrote, "Tige!" Miriam asked what that could mean, and I replied, "It is one more proof, another link in the chain. Robert used to call me that, when I showed a bulldog tenacity of purpose. It is the first time I have heard the word, or thought of it since he went away."

At our next meeting we were barely seated when the telephone called me. I returned to the sitting and said, "Robert, a man you met on earth is on the way up to my room. Tell me if you know who it is." Instantly the answer came—"It is a dark man from the far East—from Benares— the land of Krishna." It was indeed an eminent Hindoo, philosopher and scholar, Dr. Shastri, who had entertained us in Benares. Dr. Shastri had learned of my experiences on the

THE KEEPING OF THE PROMISE 385

Ouija Board, and had asked to be present with an American friend of ours, Dr. B. Both came in and took part in the sitting. Dr. Shastri acting as scribe. On this occasion both Miriam and I were blindfolded. We had not done this before; Miriam had always sat with closed eyes. I of course knew neither she nor I produced the messages, but a doubting friend had asked me if Mrs. French was blindfolded, so I decided to cover our eyes. We did so, and the messages came as clearly as before. Dr. Shastri wrote down each letter. "Good-evening; my Ella, I love you." Question–"Did you talk through a spirit named Lottie yesterday?" Dr. B had called and told me that a clairvoyant girl of his acquaintance had given him a message from "Lottie," a friend who had died in France five years previously, and whom I had never known. According to the clairvoyant (who had never known or seen Lottie in

Hfe), Lottie desired Dr. B to give me a pendant he had in his collection, bearing the head of Joan of Arc. She said

R wanted me to have it, so also did Joan of Arc, who would watch over me in France. Dr. B had to hunt through his collection to find it, and he brought it to me. So I now asked Robert if he had sent such a message. Miriam knew nothing of this. "Yes, tell B— I am obliged for the pendant; get a fine gold chain for it." I said I had thought of using a small silk cord. "No, a cord gets soiled so soon. You should get a good history of Joan of Arc to read on the ship and write a strong poem about her."

Then he wrote, "Krishna told Arjina that the mind is more fickle than the wind." Dr. Shastri laughed and said that was a verbatim quotation from the Veda. I said I hoped Robert's mind was not so fickle. Reply, "I keep it on you." Miriam and I had been fussing about the bandages over our eyes, and twice we had to stop and adjust them. Then with emphasis Robert wrote, "You ask me to say great truths to you, and I feel I am having a hard time. As soon as I try to get a message over there is all this fuss and nonsense about blindfolding! I am bored; now if I have given you all the reproof needed, we will proceed to business." I said, "First let me tell you. Robert, that I understand how foolish this blindfold- ing our eyes seems to you; you know you send the messages, and we know it. We only do this to be able to say to a doubting world that we could not see the letters as they were written down. Dr. Shastri is also able to verify this fact. Now proceed with what you have to say."

"When I first came here I was treated like a guest and privileged to meet many great souls; now I am an older resident. It is a life of sacrifice, but I come to you because you call me."

Then followed a lover's quarrel between a mortal and a soul in space. I replied, "Do I understand that I am interfering with your duties? Last fall you told me that you had begged the Deva who has charge of us to be allowed to stay near and help me, because we had millenniums for progress after I came to you. Now if you are tired of this, and want to go on without me, I certainly will never call you again." "No, no, no! Forgive me, beloved Ella, my Lady of the Lilacs! I have said you were destined for great things, and I am going to keep my word. And the world will have to listen; you are expecting messages, but you forget that we must have peaceful minds, and hearts filled with love for humanity. We must not be selfish or hurried."

I assured him the whole effort of my life now was to be unselfish and patient. I then asked where he was while I was in such terrible anguish in California. "I had to awaken; you know I liked the things of earth and of flesh. I had much to learn, and your sorrow made a heavy burden for me to bear. It hung a veil between us."

On the day preceding our departure for France, after giving me wise counsel about the care of my diet on ship board, just as he used to do when in the body, he wrote, "This is our last sweet message on this side. Pan and Ilia are going on one of their long voyages. Remember, I shall be with you constantly. Now I must go to my lessons."

I asked, "What are your lessons?"

"The cosmic consciousness."

"How do you receive the lessons?"

"Through the great teachers from higher realms."

THE KEEPING OF THE PROMISE 387

"How long was it before you began these studies?"

"I had to wait. I had not sacrificed enough on earth for humanity."

I replied that his whole life was sacrifice, of time, money, labor, for his relatives and for me; that his whole life was unselfish.

"It is not a great virtue to do for our own. We must sacrifice for the stranger within our gates, for humanity. On earth we fashion our bodies through desires; and after we get here nearly every one wants to make himself over. That takes time, and only comes by change of desire and thought."

"How did you go about the change?"

"Watching others; then I got busy." Just then the Board seemed to be taken possession of by a different force, and the word "Fanny" was written. I asked who Fanny was, and why she had broken in, saying I did not like Robert to be displaced in this way. He answered, "I had to give way to the lady. It is Fanny Crosby."

"The blind hymn writer who died a few years ago, at nearly ninety?"

"Yes, and she wants you to write a great battle hymn.

"Very well," I said. "Tell her to give me the inspiration while on the voyage." Then he went on with the story of his own progress. "Watching others, I gathered my wits together and asked to be taught; then great angels came and put me in classes." I asked him how they traveled– what was the sensation.

"A floating sensation; you float, too, in your sleep when I take you with me. Now you had better say good-bye, as I shall have to leave soon. Eradicate ytur fears; tell B to confirm the Joan of Arc matter, and get a history. May, you will watch out for the Lady of the Lilacs. Beloved Lady of the Lilacs, my Ilia, Mizpah."

The use o the name Lady of the Lilacs is most curious. I had never been called that, or heard the term, till in California at the home of Honorable Lyman Gage I attended a private seance at which a professional medium officiated. One of her controls, "Deer Hunter," spoke through the trumpet, and called me Lalita, the Lady of the Lilacs. I asked what it meant, and he said they called me that in his realm: therefore it struck me as an odd thing when Robert used the name three times. Then he added this final message: "Do not talk this on the boat; you cannot convince people by talking about it openly. They will simply regard you as unbalanced. Keep these great truths with the dignity and in the silence of the great masters till the opportune time comes to give them to the world. Mizpah."

Sailed for France the following day, February 17th, on the Espagne.

CHAPTER XXV From France

KEEPING in mind the earnest messages from Robert to avoid talking of my experiences, save when the moment seemed propitious, I remained silent on the subject ever uppermost in my thoughts, until one night, ten days after my arrival in Paris. We had come over midwinter seas, seething with dangers, in the most ominous period of the world's history, and the voyage had been one of the most peaceful and pleasant in the memory of the ship's crew. Interesting people made up the passenger list– people all bent on service and sacrifice; and voyaging humanity appeared to me in a new and fairer light, recalling, as I did, other voyages taken in times of peace, when frivolity and dissipation often sounded their staccato notes on ship board.

One night there was an auction of all sorts of objects for the benefit of wounded soldiers. I was asked to donate my advance copy of "Sonnets of Sorrow," just published by George H. Doran Company of New York. I had sailed on the 17th of February and Mr. Doran had sent me this advance copy, saying the book would go on the market February 23d. The auction took place on February 23d, and I regarded it as a good augury for the future of the book, that this little dollar volume brought sixty dollars at the auction. Lieut-Col. de Billet, a French officer, was the purchaser. The spirit of liberality was everywhere on this ship, and whatever meant helpfulness met with generous assistance. Miss Elsie Janis was the life of the ship; and her charming powers of persuasion aided greatly in the realizing of over two thousand dollars for the wounded soldiers on that night. It was my first meeting with this lovely young American comedienne since her tenth year. At that time, not so very long ago, she was a child prodigy, and was offered large sums by enterprising managers to sing a few songs each evening in New York. While Httle news girls and little slaves, in shops and factories all over our Land of the Free and our Home of the Brave, pursued their labors unmolested, little Miss Janis, carefully protected by her mother and only called upon to sing a few numbers each evening, was made a shining ejcample of the vigilance of a worthy society, in its anxiety to protect our young children from wrong usage. Elsie Janis was told she must not sing in public until she reached the age of sixteen. Mrs. Janis came to call on me, and to ask the assistance of my husband and myself in obtaining for her little girl the privilege to continue her engagement, which meant a salary sufficient to enable her to receive an education later. Just what was done about the matter had quite gone from my memory; but here on the Espagne was Miss Elsie Janis, now in the splendor of her fame and success, and she was coming over to Europe to help entertain our soldier boys, by whom she is regarded as little short of a goddess.

We reached Paris on the 27th of February, and it was on the 8th of March, just after we were settled in Hotel Vernet, that we had our first experience with an air raid. That night the siren whistle and the sound of dropping bombs and the guns of the barrage held no special meaning for me or my friend and companion, Mrs. May Randall (the friend Robert had selected, as will be recalled in his messages, to go abroad with me). We remained in our room writing letters all the evening, and retired before the berlogue sounded its note of "All clear," Indeed, when we heard that musical note, at a quarter to twelve, we did not know its import. However, the next day we drove with friends to see the place which had been destroyed by the German bombs, and the sight of this wanton destruction and the knowledge of the deaths which had resulted, left an indelible impression on my mind. The morning I left America I had received a telegram from Dr. Stillmanof Albany, President of the Red Star Society, containing a commission for General Pershing. As the representative of the society, I was asked to learn if General Per- shing would accept the gift of a veterinary ambulance from them, costing five thousand dollars. On my arrival in Paris I wrote a letter to the General, enclosing the telegram. Some time thereafter I received a reply, saying General Pershing would be in Paris and would communicate with me. One evening in March Mrs. Randall and I returned from our daily war duties in the Grand Palais (where with a bevy of other American ladies we found work to do with the convalescing French soldiers) and a letter was placed in my hand" summoning me to meet General Pershing in a half hour's time. Calling a taxi, we were enabled to keep the appointment at the place indicated by the General, where we were most graciously received, and where we enjoyed a delightful quarter of an hour with the handsome and impressive head of the American Army.

General Pershing consented to receive the gift from the Red Star Society, with the proviso that it should be purchased in Europe, to save transportation. Among the American and French women who met at the Grand Palais, in this rather monotonous and very unpicturesque, yet important, branch of war work, was one American who since her girlhood had been famed for her beauty. This was Mrs. Hatmeiker. In her apron and cap, and in the full daylight, pouring through the big glass dome, Mrs. Hatmaker was a vision of beauty and enduring youth. Indeed, that circle in the Grand Palais was remarkable for its women of beauty and culture, giving a part of every day to hard, patriotic labor in a dull, dusty room. That evening, after meeting General Pershing, the siren again sounded, and we were urged by ladies in the hotel to gather with them in the room of the wife of the Pa)rmaster of the U. S. Navy, Major Wills. Our rooms were on the fourth floor; there were two floors above us, but Mrs. Wills was on the third floor, and believed her rooms much safer. Whether bombs fell on the street or on the roof she felt her apartment would be protected. So ten ladies gathered there, and Major Wills came back and forth from his visits to the street to report to us the progress of the violent raid. There were sixty German aeroplanes in the skies, and these, with the

French barrage guns, caused a noise like unto the roar of ten thunder storms. There was much well-controlled nervousness among the brave and brilliant women in that room, for all were women of unusual mental and social powers–all women engaged in serious war work. Suddenly it seemed to me that the psychological moment had arrived for me to tell them of my knowledge of the worlds which lie beyond this world, and of my messages from my husband. So I said, "You must not feel afraid or nervous–I am a mascot. I am eager to go out of the body, and reach the realms which are more beautiful and satisfying than this earth, but I have to stay until my work is done. That work is to make those who have ears hear what the spirit of my beloved husband has said unto mankind." Then I began to tell them of the messages which have already been given in the preceding chapters.

All listened with the most intense interest; we forgot the bombing guns and the exploding bombs. When the berlogue sounded its joyous note, and Major Wills came in and said, "It is all over," Mrs. Wills remarked to me, "I feel as if death were indeed a beautiful adventure, as if it were something to anticipate instead of dread. Some tinie you must let me try to obtain messages with you." Every one of tlie ten women expressed the same wish, and all did try, during the next few days, but with no success, until Mrs. Wills sat down with me, quite alone one morning when another air raid was in progress. Then suddenly the same mysterious power took possession of both of us which had been the forerunner of the messages I had received in America; and swiftly and with unerring directness the message was written: "A great battle rages on the Oise; the odds are fearfully against the Allies but a change will come. France will suffer terrible losses– later, glorious America will come in, and bring success; boastful Germany will be beaten." At that moment neither Mrs. Wills nor myself knew there was a battle raging on the Oise. I did not read the papers, because I knew how unreliable were all published reports of war matters, and because I found myself disturbed and made tmcomfortable by such reading. It was not, however, until the next day that the story of the

Battle of the Oise was given in print. That day Mrs. Wills and I received this message written with tremendous force– "Ella, go at once to Dijon–at once. Terrible air raids are coming; a strong will tries to hold you, and a great force is around you. Gro at once; go to-morrow."

The next day the command was repeated. Obstacles to a sudden departure from Paris seemed insurmountable. I had not thought of leaving the city for more than a day or two at a time; but I set about making an effort to get away and, curiously enough, every obstacle in my path melted like wax in a warm fire. We found ourselves on the evening of March 26th all ready to leave Paris at six the next morning, our baggage gone, and our tickets bought, but we were told we would have to stand all the five hours to Dijon, as there were no compartments to be obtained. That night Mrs. Wills and I received this message: "Go in peace–I go with you; with all my strength I am strengthening you: have no fear; you will be safe. Write a poem on the war as soon as you reach Dijon; give new effort to your work. Do all you can to keep vibrations coming to this world. You are taking your first brave stand in your efforts to help humanity; get all together helping in your great work– the dedication of your life to knowledge of life eternal. One giving as much as you are giving is a glorious light in the world; nothing shall hurt you. I am very near you to-night."

I then asked for a message for Mrs. Wills, and this came– "This lady has made great headway; she will cause new vibrations between us; I can see you, dear Ella; I am very near you; be brave." Asked if I must remain much longer on earth, the answer was–"You must stay and do your work for humanity. I will wait for you; go to bed and know you are safe."

When I reached the train the next morning mobs of people filled the station, but a clear path seemed to open for us, and we found an empty compartment awaiting us. In Dijon we found much to occupy our time in visiting the American Hospital and entertaining the convalescents; and in going atnong the blind French soldiers, helping to distract them by taking them to walk and to dine and to concerts. We also visited various canteens and camps. But I had Ceen two months in France before I found what Robert had meant by the work waiting for me, and by his puzzling words–"You have taken your first stand for humanity." One night we went to a large camp, where we expected to hear a concert, after visiting the various points of interest and having "mess" with the officers. As we entered the entertainment hall three thousand men began to cheer. The secretary of the entertainment informed me that the men expected me to speak to them. Never having addressed an audience in my life, I was for the moment startled and even frightened; then suddenly a sense of power came over me, and when the secretary called upon me I arose and gave my first of a series of talks to soldiers, which have since proved extremely successful.

The next messages which came to me were through a beautiful French woman in Dijon, Madame Soyer, who had lost her only son in the war a year previous. She is a most earnest Theosophist and a woman of much culture. She was my next link to heaven, and while the power was spasmodic and not equal to that of Mrs. Wills, it came at times with great force. This was especially notable one evening at the Theosophical rooms. A little circle of very earnest Theosophists, all French people, gathered every fortnight in the apartment of Miss Le-veque, an accomplished woman professor in a school at Dijon. The vibrations in her rooms were most powerful, and when Mme. Soyer and I met there for research our first message was, "Mighty forces are here, and great knowledge helps you. Keep the truths I give you to finish your book; heaven is the goal of each soul after death, and my work here is to help souls; Go on in your work for humanity; speak to the soldiers of spiritual things; give them courage to go into battle; tell them death is not the end of life, but the beginning; go to Tours; great new help will come to you there." I then asked if he knew what the 21st day of May commemorated; this was the date of his death. He replied, "All life for me, and life universal for you." On several occasions the only sentences were brief words–"Get going." Finally this was enlarged into, "Go to many places; get new ideas; write every day. I will come at night and help you; trust my powers of divination. Help will be given the Allies; their cause is just. Time will testify to all I say. Get the idea of God in your daily life; learn to keep quiet; remember, life is eternal." Asked if I should go to England June ist, as planned, it wrote, "Go before June, go May isth." I saw no reason why I should go so soon, and did not obey. When June came the German offensive was on and in full blast, and Paris and England were both impossible places to approach. My friends in London wrote me to stay away till things quieted.

I had become interested in the works of Leon Denis in Dijon, and learned that he lived in Tours. Robert's urgent request that I should go to Tours decided me to make the journey and meet M. Denis, and if possible obtain the right of translating his great work, "The Problem of Life and Destiny." His books had been brought to my attention by a beautiful young French woman, Mile. Camille Chaise, a refugee from Rannes. Mile. Chaise came to Tours to spend ten days while I was there, and through her I met M. Denis, who was her friend and teacher in Occult Philosophy. She also brought about my meeting with Madame Colnard, another rare soul, widowed by the war. Madame Colnard and I received several messages at various times while Mile. Chaise was in the room. Curiously enough, we had little success for weeks after Mile. Chaise left us to return to Dijon, yet Mile. Chaise and I alone could produce no results. The laws governing these vibrations are evidently complicated and difficult for mortal minds to understand. Through Mile. Chaise I met, too, M. Rossignoue, author of "The New Scientific Horizon of Life." M. Rossignoue, now a man of eighty years of age, published his book under the name of "Albert La Boucie" in 1907, after a long life devoted in the main to the scientific study and analysis of spiritual phenomena. The proofs which M. Rossignoue has found of life beyond the grave, through his researches, have made his philosophy a religion for him, a religion of reverence for the Creator and love for humanity.

Before leaving Paris I had met through a letter from Sir Oliver Lodge another man, eminent in the world of psychical research. This was M. de Vesme, Editor of the "Annds of Psychic Science." M. de Vesme is a man past the half century mark, possessing high culture and a serious and earnest demeanor. The chief aim of his life is to convey the truths of his researches to the world at large. Soon after arriving in Tours I obtained from Leon Denis the rights to translate his book, and the first messages received from my husband after I began the work were of approval and satisfaction. He wrote, "Keep on with the translation. The book contains great truths on life and death, and will help your development." At the time this chapter is being written the translation is half finished, and the interest of my lover in the spirit world is unabated. Only yesterday he wrote, "Try and finish the book before you return to America."

After a period of weeks, wherein we could obtain no results, the power was again restored to Madame Colnard, and some remarkable results followed. I had been desirous of finding a certain order of specialist, and had been assured I could find one only in Paris or London. I supposed this to be the case and gave up the idea of further inquiries; yet suddenly there came a message urging me to continue my search, and assuring me I should find what I sought. I made a new effort and found a famous specialist in that line, living in Tours. Madame Colnard, who neither writes nor speaks English, was also unaware of this man's existence and equally unaware that I had made such a search. It was one more evidence that my beloved in the spirit world watches over me and helps me, with the same solicitude he showed on earth. One day I received a call from Count Gilbert de Choiseul, bringing an introduction from Leon Denis. Count de Choiseul informed me that he was deeply interested in matters occult, and I was invited to visit friends of his also interested in the subject. A few days later I spent a most memorable afternoon in one of the most beautiful chateaux of Touraine, where an interesting family of wide culture and evident large wealth was eager to hear what I had to say on the subject of communication with our beloved ones in spirit worlds. My charming hostess and her distinguished mother were both ip possession of incontrovertible proofs of such communication.

Through Count de Choiseul I also entered into correspondence with Felix Remo, author of "The Pilgrimage of Life," and Editor of "Le Monde Invisible," M. Remo's book is of literary and scientific value and importance. His letters indicate profound culture and feeling. Convinced by innumerable proofs of the truth of life after death, and the continuity of love and memory, and the possibility of spiritual communication under right conditions, M. Remo is devoting his life to the promulgation of these ideas. At the time of writing this chapter I have been six months in France, and I can but smile, remembering the violent opposition raised by a number of my American friends to my coming. I was told that I had no right to come and take up room in ships and consume food needed by troops, that I had no place or work waiting me here. The fact of my having a literary reputation was declared by these friends of no value now, as "in times of war," so said one pert lady, "the world could get along very well without poetry." Mr. Arthur Brisbane, of the New York American, was violently opposed to my coming for the reasons mentioned. Yet having received orders from the astral world to come, I came.

On the first Decoration Day of soldiers' graves ever observed in France it was my great privilege to be asked to write a poem for the occasion in Toura The request came from Mr. Cook, chaplain of the Y. M. C, A., and my acceptance was applauded by all the United States Army in Tours. The poem was superbly read by Major Pierce to an enormous audience gathered in the beautiful cemetery where a cluster of graves marked by a cross and an American flag signified the resting place of our American boys fallen early in the fray. The day was one of golden glory; and I was able to view the wonderful picture from the platform where I was honored by sitting with the highest officials, French and American, in Tours. After the ceremonies, consisting of brief addresses, song and reading, four aeroplanes flew down from the clouds close to the cemetery, scat- tering showers of blossoms over the graves and over the congregation of people. It was a wonderful and impressive hour, and my mind went back to that first Decoration Day of my early youth when Major Meyers had read my poem at Madison, Wisconsin; and all the scenes of my life seemed to pass in review before me.

DECORATION DAY POEM FOR SOLDIERS GRAVES, TOURS, FRANCE, MAY 30, 1918

Flowers of France in the Spring, Your growth is a beautiful thing; But give us your fragrance and bloom– Yea, give us your lives in truth. Give us your sweetness and grace To brighten the resting place Of the flower of manhood and youth. Gone into the dust of the tomb.

This is the vast stupendous hour of Time, When nothing counts but sacrifice, and faith. Service, and self-forgetfulness. Sublime And awful are these moments charged with death And red with slaughter. Yet God's purpose thrives In all this holocaust of human lives.

I say, God's purpose thrives. Just in the measure That men have flung away their lust for gain– Stopped in their mad pursuit for worldly pleasure And boldly faced unprecedented pain And dangers, without thinking of the cost, So thrives God's purpose in the holocaust.

Death is a little thing. All men must die; Yet when ideals die, God grieves in Heaven. Therefore I think it was the reason why This Armageddon to the world was given. The soul of man, forgetful of its birth. Was losing sight of everything but earth.

Up from these many million graves shall spring A shining harvest for the coming race; An Army of Invisibles shall bring A glorified lost faith back to its place.

And men shall know there is a higher goal Than earthly triumphs for the human soul.

They are not dead, they are not dead I say, These men whose mortal forms are in the sod. A grand Advance Guard marching on its way, Their souls move upward to salute their God. While to their comrades who are in the strife They cry–"Fight on! Death is the dawn of life."

We had forgotten all the depth and beauty. And lofty purport of that old true word Deplaced by pleasure–that old good word, duty. Now by its meaning is the whole world stirred. These men died for it. For it now we give. And sacrifice, and serve, and toil, and live.

From out our hearts had gone a high devotion For anything. It took a mighty wrath Against great evil to wake strong emotion And put us back upon the righteous path. It took a mingled stream of tears and blood, To cut the channel through to Brotherhood.

That word meant nothing on our lips in peace–
We had despoiled it by our castes and classes.
But when this savage carnage finds surcease
A new ideal will unite the masses.
And there will be True Brotherhood with men.
The Christly Spirit stirring earth again.
For this our men have suffered, fought, and died.
And we who can but dimly see the end.
Are guarded by their spirits glorified
Who help us on our way, while they ascend.
They are not dead, they are not dead I say.
These men whose graves we decorate to-day.

America and France walk hand in hand. As one, their hearts beat through the coming years. One is the aim and purpose of each land. Baptized with holy water of their tears. To-day th worship with one faith, and know Grief's First Communion in God's House of Woe.

Great Liberty, the Goddess at our gates,
And great Jeanne darc, are fused into one soul.
A host of Angels on that soul awaits
To lead it up to triumph at the goal.
Along the path of Victory they tread.
Moves the majestic cortege of our dead.

Flowers of France in the Spring, Your growth is a beautiful thing; But give us your fragrance and bloom– Yea, give us your lives in truth. Give us your sweetness and grace To brighten the resting place Of the flower of manhood and youth. Gone into the dust of the tomb.

The next public occasion in which I took part in France was at the presentation of a flag by the Marquise de Rochambeau to the camp named in honor of her family. Given a seat beside the Marquise (whose two young sons were killed in war), I witnessed the simple ceremony, and that evening while in her home was requested by her to commemorate the occasion in verse, which I did.

Lines Written on the Presentation of an American Banner to Camp Rochambeau, by the Marquise de Rochambeau at Tours, France, June, i, 1918.

Here is a picture I carry away On memory's wall; a green June day– A golden sun in an amethyst sky, And a beautiful banner floating as high As the lofty spires of the city of Tours, And a slender Marquise, with a face as pure As a sculptured Saint; while staunch and true In new world khaki, and old world blue. Wearing their medals with modest pride. Her stalwart body-guard stand at her side.

Simple the picture, but much it may mean To one who reads into and under the scene. For there in that opulent hour and weather. Two Great Republics came closer together;

A little nearer came land to land.

Through the magical touch of a woman's hand.

And once again as in long ago

The grand old name of de Rochambesu

Shines forth like a star, for our world to see.

Our Land of the Brave, and our Home of the Free.

On the Fourth of July the American officers in Tours decided to give an entertainment beginning with patriotic moving pictures and a concert and ending with a ball. It came to my ears that the French residents were criticizing the idea of dancing at such an hour in the world's history. It impressed them as frivolous and indecorous. I wrote the following verses, and sent them to the committee of entertainment, who published them with the program:

ON WITH THE DANCE

We have come over death charged seas, to fight the foes oi

France; The foes of France, the foes of earth, the foes of God on High. Oh think not that because we laugh, because we sing and dance. We have forgotten this grave fact– to-morrow we may die. The ocean billows leap and lilt, when tides are at full flow. But never yet a wave forgot the depths that lay below.

As David danced before the Lord, we dance now in our joy At being part of this great force for justice and for truth. Strong as the old Olympian gods that won the siege of Troy! We glory in our brawn and brain, and in our splendid youtii. We glory in the right to live and use our manhood's dower. And if need be, the right to die in this stupendous hour.

America holds out her hand to beautiful brave France, Her friends are ours, her foes are ours. On! On, now with the dance!

This little incident served to stem the tide of criticism; and on the evening of the entertainment I was asked to occupy a box, to which came many French and American people thank- ing me for the verses. In just two weeks thereafter our American boys did indeed show their willingness to fight and die for France.

Again I could not help recalling the objections of my friends to my invasion of France. They had said that only Red Cross nurses or Y. M. C. A. canteen workers were needed here. Yet it seemed to me that my humble muse had found on these three occasions a place waiting for her. Later I made a tour of camps and hospitals and, assisted with the recitations of Mrs. Randall, gave most successful entertainments to thousands of American soldiers, who everywhere greeted us with an ovation. Indeed, it has seemed to me that I had to come to France to realize how beautiful was the spirit of appreciation which our American boys felt for me and my work. Added to this is the knowledge I have gained of the great part poetry and verse play in the soldiers' lives. Hundreds of boys after our evening entertainments came to Mrs. Randall and me, asking for copies of various verses recited during the evening. Especially interested were they in those relating to the war, yet others of a spiritual or romantic trend, too, found favor in their sight. Letters of appreciation often came to me afterward from the boys in the trenches, so that I knew my pert friend had erred in saying "the world had no need of poetry in war times."

These experiences in Europe were most agreeable after some which had preceded them in my own land. In America my open declaration– first of my intention to make a thorough study of spiritual phenomena, and my later declaration that I had received absolutely authentic messages from my husband, met with numerous rebuffs from friends and acquaintances, not one of whom had ever made serious investigations in psychic science. Many of these rebuffs were simply expressed by a manner of cold indifference or badly concealed contempt when the topic was mentioned. Others were outspoken and combative. Some orthodox people, whom in my agony of loneliness and sorrow I had reached out to for companionship, casting my heart and my purse under their feet and asking for nothing in return but sympathy, showed their ideal of a tender compassionate Christ by turning on me with vindictive ingratitude because I could not believe my Robert was asleep, awaiting the Resurrection morning, but alive and blest in God's great kingdom, and eager to commune with me. Others regarded me with a sort of silent pity and patient tolerance.

Among the most intolerant of all my theosophic ideas of immortal life, and particularly of my final declaration of having received communications from my husband, has been Mr. Arthur Brisbane, the brilliant editorial writer, and orator, and long the golden mouthpiece of Mr. W. R. Hearst. Mr. Brisbane has been my intellectual friend for fully twenty years. I have admired his brain and his courage and his wit. But I have always regarded him as what I would term a distorted triangle. Each human being is intended to be a perfect triangle, with a well developed and healthy body, an educated, thinking mind, and an aspiring, up-reaching spirit. It is indeed rare to find the perfect human triangle. Many splendid physical specimens are dwarfed in mind and spirit. Many intellectual giants are weak in spirit and body. Among mediums and psychics we often encounter those of rare spiritual knowledge who are uneducated, and frail physically. Others have two sides of the triangle developed finely, but lack the third. Mr. Brisbane belongs to this category; he has a splendid athletic body and a brilliantly educated mind. He speaks several languages, having been educated in three countries– America, France and Germany. But Mr. Brisbane has had no spiritual education; he has made no researches along psychical lines. These researches have engaged the attention and made converts of such men as Lombroso, Sir William Crookes, Sir Oliver Lodge, Flammarion, Prof. Hyslop, Prof. Myers, Dr. Chas. Richet, Sir Alfred Turner, Conan Doyle, and a score of other eminent and highly educated men.

No, Mr. Brisbane has made no researches. His experience in things psychic consists probably in some time having visited a cheap fortune teller; and finding nothing of further interest in the subject he has gone on his intellectual way, with his eyes resolutely turned away from these hidden paths where lie wonderful truths for man's discovery. He has listened to what other people of his own order of mind had to say on the subject, but he has shut his ears to what such great men as are named above have to say, while the material philosophers of France and Germany have influenced his thoughts. Mr. Brisbane reminds me of one thing. Imagine a bowlegged baby, allowed to use its limbs too soon, and in the wrong manner, brought up in an asylum filled with other bowlegged and deformed babies. When this baby, accustomed only to seeing its own kind, grows to puberty and is shown a statue of Hercules, or a moving picture with Sandow doing his acts of prowess, the baby, grown up, says, "That's just pictures; there are no such men alive; there are only bowlegged babies." Mr. Brisbane boldly and egotistically (and alfeo quite pitifully) says in the New York Sunday American, May 19, 1918, "There is no real knowledge, of course, on this subject of death. The dead in this day do not come back. Mrs. Wilcox and her friends are deceiving themselves; the spirits that are dead do not talk to us while we live. Mediums and others, some of them sincere, more mere swindlers, impose upon the sorrowful." This is exactly where the spiritually bowlegged baby makes his entrance in the personality of Mr. Brisbane.

Mr. Brisbane also declares that my experience on the Ouija Board would have been just as successful with a "Chief from the Congo" as with my four friends. Perhaps so, if the Chief had possessed the peculiar vibratory power needed. But if my messages came because I so much wanted them, as he asserts, why did I have to experiment with a hundred friends, as eager as myself, before the real power came, as I have described?

Why were the most intimate friends of both my husband and myself unable to obtain these amazing results, and why were others able to sit with me (both of us blindfolded) while these messages came? How could the last words of my husband to a Club friend be given when neither I nor the friend with me knew he had been with this man at the Club, or spoken those laughing words? How could a quotation be given from the philosophy of Jacob Boehm, when the three people in the room were alike equally ignorant that such a man as Jacob Boehm ever existed? Eager as I have been for these communications, Mrs. Randall and I have never been able to produce any results; how would Mr. Brisbane explain this?

We all know the good old story of the country woman, who had been brought up in the narrow confines of a country farm, and accustomed to think of animals as horses, cows and dogs. When the traveling circus exhibited a giraffe, she looked at the strange creature and turned away, saying, "There ain't no such animal." Mr. Brisbane's mind, despite its brilliancy, is of this order. An old lady in California told me a droll story of herself. Living in the rigorous climate of Massachusetts until the age of fifty, the family moved to California in mid-winter. Arriving at Los Angeles late one February night, she awoke early the next morning and, looking out of her window, saw green fields and joyous birds building nests in glorious trees. 1 Turning away from the window, she said, 7 don't believe it." This will doubtless be Mr. Brisbane's attitude after he leaves this mortal body, and faces the reality of the astral world. His will be a long, lonely and difficult path after death, because of the obstacles he has set in his own path of attainment. He will be astonished to find himself on a lower plane in the heavenly realms than many a simple, uneducated person he has known on earth whose awakened spirituality he regarded as proofs of ignorance. But teachers will be sent to Mr. Brisbane in the Beyond, and he, and every other delayed soul, will eventually come up into the light and knowledge and understanding of God's great universe. In truth I anticipate the satisfying experience of perhaps being myself given the role of instructor of Arthur Brisbane in the astral world and of hearing him say, humbly, "Oh, how I wish T had listened to you on earth; I would now be so much farther along on the ascending path!"

Beside Lombroso, Sir Oliver Lodge (who ranks with Edison), Flammarion and Prof. Frederic Myers, Mr. Brisbane does not seem a giant of intellect, yet he dares dispute these men's statements. Frederic Myers, the eminent professor of Cambridge, was compared (by Prof.

Floumoy of the University of Geneva) to Copernicus and Darwin. Prof. Floumoy said, "Myers completes the triad of geniuses who have profoundly revolutionized scientific ideas, in the order of cosmology, biology, and psychology." In his "Survival of Human Personality," Myers says, "I have come to the conclusion slowly, and at the end of a long series of reflections, based on increasing proofs, that the consciousness and faculties of man assert themselves in all their plenitude after death. For every enlightened and conscientious seeker in this realm, there awaits logically and necessarily a vast philosophical and religious S3mthesis. dare state that there exists a method of arrivifig at a knowledge of things divine with the same certitude aifd assurance with which we arrive at earthly things. Through Slich methods the authority of churches will be replaced by observation and experience; the impulse of faith transformed into reasonable convictions; and an ideal will be born superior to those which humanity has until now known."

Sir William Crookes of England won the grand prize of Ashburton at seventeen. Then he became Inspector, Professor and Director successively of the Scientific Review and Chemical News, and the Quarterly Journal of Science. His achievements and discoveries, and his classic writings in the domain of chemistry and astronomy, won the gold medal for him, and the prize of 3,000 francs. He was made an honorary member of all the Academies, and was ennobled by the Queen. After years of psychical research this man says, "I do not say perhaps the soul of man lives after death–I say, it does." And he gives volumes of evidence. Yet to these serious and important statements made by these men of giant intellect, after fourteen years of careful study, Mr. Brisbane dares give the lie! He dares say, "It is not so; no one has obtained such knowledge. Only fools and impostors assert such things." Surely the words of Mr. Brisbane on this profound subject should be regarded as the babble of the bowlegged baby who looks at Sandow and says, "He is only a picture; there is not such a man." With all Mr. Brisbane's education, and originality of mind, he would not think of disputing Luther Burbank in some of his most advanced statements regarding the habits of plants–results gained by long years of close study by Mr. Burbank, and only possible to be obtained by such study. He would not think of disputing some of Mr. Edison's ideas, even if he found himself unable to grasp their true import. He would allow the astronomer, doubtless, to assert facts that seemed well nigh unbelievable. Yet psychic science (as great men have said, and demonstrated) has reached a state where it is as exactly provable to one willing to give the same amount of time and patient research to it as any of the other sciences. It marks a man now as a bigot and reflects upon his intelligence when he makes sweeping assertions such as Mr. Brisbane has made in the quotation given above on this all-important subject of life after death. For this is the one subject of any lasting import. If any of us had failed to realize or had lost sight of the utter vanity and ephemeral nature of all earthly achievements, aims land pleasures, the last four years have served to bring home these things to even the dullest minds. Glorious works of art, great buildings, mighty works of engineers, proud cities, lordly empires, what are they all when war, earthquakes or tidal floods sweep over the world, and what is human life and mortal happiness but a puff of thistledown on the wings of the tornado? Mighty continents and vast civilizations have gone down in convulsions of nature, and no vestige of them remains. But the souls who lived on those continents live still, for the soul is indestructible. As we think, act, and live here to-day we build the structures of our homes in spirit realms after we leave earth, and we build Karma for future lives, thousands of years to come, on this earth or other planets. Spiritual knowledge is therefore the one lasting education to obtain, the all-important subject for man to investigate while here. We can build bridges, construct cities, launch ships, follow the arts, establish worthy industries and endow colleges while we yet pursue the more profound study, of the spirit, and learn to know its indestructible nature, and its vast potentialities. Life will assume new dignity, and labor new interest for us, when we come to the knowledge that death is but a continuation of life and labor in higher planes. That is.

higher planes if we build them while here by our thoughts and acts.

These are the truths which are taught by psychical research and by communion with our dead. Enormous accumulations of facts have been obtained by an army of investigators all over the world; greater revelations await us in the near future. Where of old the erratic, the unbalanced and the uneducated formed the rank and file of spiritual investigators, the work is now conducted by the most brilliant and highly endowed men and women of the day. It is no longer regarded as "fortune telling"; it is revelation. The dead live! They do speak with the living; he who seeks may find. But beware how you seek, and for what purpose! When the x-ray was first discovered, with all its revealing and healing powers, many rash physicians rushed blindly forward in their investigations without caution, or precaution, and suffered injury and death in consequence. Now, no such results come from the use of the rays. Science has placed it on an intelligent foundation; so with psychical research. The rash, the curious, the ignorant, have often suffered from its dangers; but science and religious devotion are together placing the study where it belongs. Only to lift the soul nearer to God, and to come more closely in contact with the spirits of our beloved ones, and to gain larger knowledge of the eternal laws of life everlasting, should we approach this holy work of psychical research. The effort to obtain communication with our dear dead should begin with prayer and supplication for light and guidance, followed by a season of quiet tranquil meditation on the Omnipotent Power who rules the universe. He of whom Christ our Elder Brother said, "Why call ye me good? There is but one good, and that is our Father who art in Heaven."

From ten minutes to an hour should be given to our meditation at least once a day. When the mind is under the control of the will, and the thoughts are kept to the one subject of God, and His great universe, we set vibrations in motion which make it possible for those who have left the body to approach us. In my hus- band's communications he has constantly urged me to give more time to meditation and to hold pencil and paper in readiness, so that when the vibratory force becomes strong enough he can direct messages through my hand alone. This power has not yet come to me alone but it has come to many of my acquaintances (people of as great intelligence and education as Mr. Brisbane) whose integrity cannot be questioned. Lady Blake, a woman of rare culture and wide education, lost her devoted husband, Sir Henry Blake, during the last year. The blow was almost crushing her great soul, and she wrote me letters of despairing anguish, which opened anew the still fresh wounds in my own heart. Then suddenly came a letter from Lady Blake, with a ringing note of triumph rising over the miserere of her former letters. A psychic friend, a lady in private life, had visited Lady Blake in her beautiful old home in Ireland and this friend had attained to the power of automatic writing. Messages came through this friend from Sir Henry Blake under such test conditions and containing such authentic messages that Lady Blake no longer questions the fact that her husband lives, and watches over her, with love intensified by his spiritual life.

The following letter from Lady Blake she has kindly allowed me to give to the public:

Myrtle Grove, Youghal, Ireland, July 3, 1918. My dear Mrs. Wheeler Wilcox: I am quite willing that you should quote my name as a believer in the fact that our loved ones who have passed "behind the veil" can communicate with us. As you know, I have recently had the supreme anguish of losing my beloved husband. I felt that if indeed death were not the extinction of identity he who had so loved and cared for me would find means of giving some sign that he had not left me forever, and so save me from despair. Thank God, he has done so, and the communications I have received, as I believe from him, have been a ray of comfort in the dark night of my overwhelming sorrow. When on earth, my husband was greatly interested in occult subjects and hail his life been spared intended studying them further.

Believe me, yours affectionately,

Edith Blake.

Sir Oliver Lodge has given a great many books of scientific value to the world, but nothing to my thinking of such vast import to humanity as one small detail in his recent book, "Raymond: Life after Death." This detail is the incident which he describes wherein he received from the spirit world a message from his son Raymond, describing a photograph taken before his death. The negative of this photograph was found undeveloped several months after the message was received. A small incident, but coming from a great man who had devoted years to psychical research it is of enormous value to humanity. "Physical" science is of temporary importance to the world, but "psychical" science,– the science proving by incontrovertible facts that the soul lives on, loves on, and remembers those on earth after it leaves the body– that is the science which is eternal, indestructible, and everlasting.

I speak of the things that I know to be, For my Spirit Lover has talked with me.

Referring to the class of people known under the various names of mediums, clairvoyants, psychics and sensitives, the time will come when, instead of being punished by unjust laws, and persecuted by a cheap class of detectives, they will be studied and classified by science, and the wheat winnowed from the chaff. People born with this clear, open vision usually display it in early life, and such children should be carefully protected and educated under wise masters as future aids to spiritual science. A little girl of eight years stopped in her playing one day, and said to her mother, "Papa has gone down in a hole in the street, but he is hanging by his hands." A little later she said, "Some one helped him. Papa is out." The mother rebuked her for foolish chatter, but a half hour later the father came home and reported that he had fallen through a manhole in the street, and had held himself by his hands until help arrived. The child, now a young woman in private life, still has this clairvoyant vision. Had she been trained by wise teachers, and learned the laws controlling this power, she might be of vast value to psychical research or to the students of theosophy to-day in explaining astral planes. As it is, she hides her powers from most people, because her family think her "queer," and she has become sensitive regarding her ability to see occurrences at a distance, and to receive from people long dead messages which have startled the recipients on earth, by their authenticity.

These occult powers should never be used for material gain. So soon as they are, the individual possessing them attracts a low, undeveloped order of spirits who are earth bound, and both those spirits and the mediums are injured in consequence. To elevate ourselves to the state where lofty spirits dwell, not to bring spirits down to our earth plane, should be our aim.

Until that high state of development is attained, where messages come direct to our minds from the disincarnate souls, we must lean on more material means for communication. It is the material nature in us, which compels the denizens of the spiritual world to use these material means. In several of his messages here in France, my husband has asked this curious question, "Why do you not answer me?" or "Try and answer me." And when I begged for an explanation, his reply was, "You stop too soon in concentration." By this I understand that he is trying to impress directly on my mind what he has to communicate, and fails only because I do not attain to the high state of vibratory power, gained only in the silence, and in the complete tranquillity which permits such spiritual intercourse. Turbulent sorrow, unrestrained grief, rebellion toward death, non-resignation, all are obstacles to communication, and so is scattered thought where the mind never holds to one resolute idea. In talking with Max Heindel, the leader of the Rosicrucian philosophy in California, he made very clear to me the effect of intense grief. Mr. Heindel had assured me that I would come in touch with the spirit of my husband when I learned to control my sorrow. I replied that it seemed strange to me that an omnipotent God could not send a flash of His light into a suffering soul to bring its conviction when most needed. "Did you ever stand beside a clear pool of water," asked Mr. Heindel, "and see the trees and skies repeated therein? And did you ever cast a stone into that pool and see it clouded and turmoiled, so it gave no reflection?

Yet the skies and trees were waiting above to be reflected when the waters grew calm. So God and your husband's spirit wait to show themselves to you when the turbulence of sorrow is quieted." And so, months afterward, it proved to be, and so will it be to every loving suffering heart that seeks without pausing, and prays without ceasing, for proof of the living dead. That proof will be given. For God and His great cabinet of archangels want the denizens of earth to come up higher and to know the glories that await them in Life Everlasting. The search may be surrounded with difficulties, and the way long, but the goal awaits those who have love enough, reverence enough, and patience enough to keep on until success crowns their efforts.

For the ceaseless prayer of a soul is heeded.
When the prayer asks only for light and faith,
And the faith and the light, and the knowledge needed.
Shall gild with glory the path to death.
Oh heart of the world by sorrow shaken,
Hear ye the message I have to give.
The seal from the lips of the dead is taken.
And they can say to you, "Lo, we live!"

EPILOGUE

WHEN anaesthetics were first discovered the orthodox Church and the clergy loudly denounced their use, as opposed to God's assertion that women should bear children in pain and suffering. Mcuiy violent sermons were preached, declaring the merciful anesthetics were agents of the devil, and that those who employed them were defying God.

N. A. Richardson, in "Industrial Problems," states that in Lancaster, Ohio, in 1828, the school board refused to permit the school house to be used for the discussion of the question of a proposed railroad. The old document reads as follows; "You are welcome to use the school house to debate all proper questions, but such things as railroads and telegraphs are impossibilities and rank infidelity. There is nothing in the word of God about them. If God had designed that His intelligent creatures should travel at the frightful speed of fifteen miles an hour by steam, He would clearly have foretold it through His Holy Prophets. It is a device of Satan to lead immortal souls down to Hell."

We laugh at these ideas to-day and we would laugh at the man who declared the use of electricity to be a sin. Imagine one so bigoted and so ignorant who would say, "If God had wanted man to employ such a power for the transmission of light, or messages. He would have placed it in his hands, and not made the discovery of it so difficult. God made sunlight for the day and moonlight for the night. He gave man his feet on which to run with messages. It is wicked and at variance with God's wishes to use electric light or to send messages by telephone or telegraph: the Holy Prophets did not foretell them. Whoever does these things is in league with the devil." Such words would be no more absurd and silly than the words of those who claim that God's secret of life beyond the grave should not be sought; and that no effort at communication with those who have gone onward should be made because the fneans of that communication are not obtained without effort.

Just as crude oil gave place to gas, and gas to electricity, so will a still more subtle source of light be discovered one of these daysi God has no secrets He does not intend to share freely with human beings who aire adventurous enough, reverent enough and patient enough to seek the way of knowledge.

Man is an unawakened god; not one man, but every man. We are heirs to every thing in the vast universe. It is because the Great Creator wants us to search for these higher truths, and this glorious knowledge of life immortal and the wonder of sphere upon sphere filled with super beings, that He is permitting the race to see the awful result of thinking only of material successes and earthly power and glory. The world war has prepared the minds of human beings as nothing before ever prepared it for study of the worlds beyond. Never before was such a spiritual awakening on earth, and it has but begun. That study cannot and will not be confined to the creeds and dogmas of established churches. It will leap over hurdles and barriers set by the clergy, and soar into space, seeking its own trail to truth. And those whose minds are awake, whose souls are purified through suffering, whose hearts are cleansed of all selfishness and all earthly lusts and longings, will meet the spirits of their dear dead in the silence and be instructed by them. L. W. Rogers tells us that by a series of sustained efforts to live the highest life of which one is capable, it is possible to attain a level of consciousness where one has personal knowledge that the dead live. That is of course the highest road and the safest one to tread. But when we are suddenly separated from those who have been torn by death from our sight, touch and hearing, we are not possessed of the poise and strength to go through these scientific methods of development. As in times of great emergency, we cannot be content to write a letter in long hand and send it to India, and await an answer from a friend, but rush to the wireless operator and ask that our message be sent, so do we turn in the time of awful need to some more material means of communication with our dead. A woman said to me: "I cannot imagine my husband needing a third person between him and me, or a material object like a Ouija Board or a table to bring messages. When he was on earth he did not do these things. Why should he in the spirit world? He always came directly to me here." "I think not always," I replied. "When he was only a block away from you and needed to send a message he called up an operator to connect the telephone wires. He could not do this himself. He used the telegraph operator and the wireless operator at other times to reach you. They may not have been people of education or culture: but they knew how to connect the wires and

RENDER IT POSSIBLE FOR YOU AND YOUR HUSBAND TO COMMUNI-CATE."

There is nothing more unreasonable or absurd in the use of a Ouija Board, a table, a planchette or a trained clairvoyant to afford our disembodied friends the power to transmit their messages than in the use of the wires and operators on earth. Death does not make souls omnipotent. Immortal life is a matter of slow growth toward greater power and knowledge. Freed from the physical body, souls are for many years in the astral body; and that body has its limitations. Upon etheric and vibratory conditions the possibility of transmitting messages from the astral to the physical world depends. An individual may be of an inferior type of mind and without knowledge on these subjects, he who produces the phenomenon which brings messages from the worlds beyond, or may be of the highest order of development. It is simply a matter of the right vibratory combination.

The astral realm is filled with souls in all states of development, from the lowest to the highest; and whoever seeks persistently for messages will receive them. But beware of seeking idly or without a high and holy purpose. Beware of seeking in mere curiosity or for knowledge of mere earth matters. The state of mind you take into your investigations will attract the same order of disembodied mind. Whoever approaches this study with an idle, banal mind will receive idle and banal messages from the borderland. But it is an imper- tinence for such people to go forth and say that only such messages are to be obtained. These statements are repeatedly made by individuals who have never gone more deeply into the matter than a visit to a fortune teller, or an hour spent with a rollicking party of friends experimenting with table tipping.

There are just as many differing localities in the worlds beyond as here on earth. When a ship lands its passengers at a dock in New York there are those who stay about the dock; they are only fitted for its duties and its lodging rooms. There are others who pass on, to be lost in the slums and the underworld of the city until settlement workers or Salvation Army angels hunt them out and help them to better things. Others go on to the business localities; to Wall street and the crowded places where the busy toilers are. Others go to upper Fifth Avenue and Riverside Drive, to homes of opulence and beauty. Precisely so do the voyagers on the ship of death scatter when the further shores are reached. But in that world it is not money, title or influence which decides the locality of the passenger. It is thought. The kind of thought which each one of us entertains in the mind, year in and year out, establishes our position in the world beyond. The frivolous, selfish voluptuary from Riverside Drive, suddenly called from the body, will find him or herself in the slums and underworld with very undesirable company in the astral realms: and all the death-bed repentance and holy ceremonies at the last moment cannot alter this situation immediately, or give the soul admission to higher planes until it works out its own salvation by a complete change of thought. The unselfish, pure-minded, God-loving, simple toiler, who has tried to do as he would be done by, and to return good for evil, will be happily surprised to find himself among the scenes of beauty he has starved for on earth, and given at once glimpses of the glories beyond–glories of which he has only dreamed in his earth life.

I was told not long ago, by a friend opposed to this subject, that Edison did not believe in spiritual life. My friend seemed to think that was a conclusive argument. One might as well quote him on music or sculpture, neither subject being familiar enough to him to render his opinion of value.

Mere intellect or genius in some one direction does not make a man capable of speaking authoritatively on a matter which he has not deeply investigated. A great statesman, a great architect, a great writer, a great warrior, all would carry no weight in arguing about the worlds spiritual unless they had given serious and respectful and persistent study to the matter. Sir Oliver Lodge and Lombroso, while great men in the world of science, were not competent judges of this subject until they investigated. Mr. Bolton Hall said to me, "Why not live in one world at a time? If I am writing a book in English, would it not be wise to try and improve ray English, rather than stop and attempt the study of the language of Hindustan?"

"That is not a good simile," I answered. "Suppose your nearest and dearest ones had gone to Hindustan to live. They could not come back. You knew you were to go there and to remain a very long time. You knew you might be called any moment.

Would it not seem sensible to give a portion of each day to the study of the language of Hindustan, and to learning all you could of the ways and habits of that land from reports of those who had gone ahead? You could still perform your duties while here: you could write your book in English, but you would be preparing meanwhile for a journey you knew you must take."

But while we put ourselves In communion with the travelers who have gone on, we must learn to be as considerate of them as we would of our friends who have gone to foreign lands on some great commission. We would not think of writing or cabling to our nearest kin who had become an ambassador abroad, or who was holding a position In some college, to give us points on the market, or to advise us in our domestic affairs. We would feel his time too valuable for that. All our dead are in God's colleges, and we should ask of then! only such help and information as would better prepare us to enter into their world and help us to rise above petty ideals while here.

Nor should we too long and too persistently seek even this direct assistance from them. Once positively convinced of their identity and their continued life and love, we should be considerate of their highest good, and not demand too much of their time and attention. Such demands delay them and weaken us. Just as it may help and comfort and increase the happiness of a diseftibodied soul to have communion with those left behind for a time, so it may hinder a soul's progress, if we cling too persistently to it, and demand its continual ministrations: as a college junior, striving to pass his examinations so that he might enter the senior class, would be delayed if his brothers and sisters at home were constantly asking him for answers to their own primary school problems.

In the very instructive book by L. W. Rogers, "Elementary Theosophy," he speaks of this point and illustrates it by the story of the woman of Endor who, at the request of Saul, obtained communication with the spirit of Samuel and advice about the impending battle. Samuel's first words were, "Saul, why hast thou disquieted me, to bring me up?" The dead king was studying things more spiritual than the wars of earth, and did not want to be disturbed. Let us remember this incident when we approach our dead, and ask only of the things which pertain to the growth of the spirit.

Out of these messages which I have received under conditions and through people who are above suspicion, the following convictions are indelibly impressed upon my mind: I–Reincarnation in many forms and bodies, from the mineral to the mortal being, is a scientific fact. The divine spirit of the Logos-God enters into all things and exists always, and when all experiences have been obtained in various forms, and through all sorrows and joys, we return home again, once more pure Spirit.

2–Death is only a doorway to a larger life and does not destroy memory or ailection or personal characteristics. Death ushers each soul into the place and plane it has made for itself while on earth by the nature and habit of its thoughts.

3–The fact that we have belonged to some church and subscribed to some creed and belief will not help us in the least to find the heavenly planes after death unless our thoughts have been heavenly with love and sjnupathy for our fellow men. Only by changing our thoughts can we change our plane of consciousness.

5– Just as on earth Salvation Army and other helpers are sent to those in need of light, so will messengers of God come to those after death who need to be helped upward and onward. It will aid such souls to pray for them after they have left the body.

6–Christ is the latest and greatest of the masters who have been sent by the One whom He called "The Father" to enlighten and uplift the race. He rules the spheres belonging to the Christian era. There are other chains of spheres governed by other great spirits.

7–Death does not admit a soul, however pure, at once into the presence of Christ. All must first pass through many planes, and be purged of all earthly desires, before they can reach the high vibratory state which enables them to enter the Christ realm.

Back of all the spheres, at the center of all things, is the Solar Logos–God–from whom all the universe proceeds. In the immensity of space are vast heaven worlds, filled with spirits in various states of development from the earth-bound souls to the great archangels– all bent on returning to the source eventually and becoming "one with God." A wise teacher has said truly, "Orderly gradation is Nature's method of expression. Just as a continuous chain of life runs down from man, so also it must rise above him until it merges into the Supreme Being. Man is merely one link in the evolutionary chain." And Alfred Russel Wallace, who was called the grand old man of science, said, "I think we have got to recognize that between man and God there is an almost infinite multitude of beings, working in the universe at large at tasks as definite and important as any we have to perform. I imagine the universe is peopled with spirits, intelligent beings, with duties and powers vaster than our own. I think there is a spiritual ascent from man upward and onward."

And from this mighty storehouse we may gather wisdom and knowledge and receive light and power, as we pass through this preparatory room of earth, which is only one of the innumerable mansions in our Father's house.

Think on these things.

Few lives are so full of incident and romance that they lend themselves to interesting portrayal in pictures. These photographs, the accumulation of adventurous years at home and abroad, present in a unique and appealing way the chief events of Mrs. Wilcox's life to the beginning of 1919.

It was here that Ella Wheeler was born, and here she lived until her marriagev Her first attempts a, t writing were made in order to win comforts for her family, and she was overjoyed when she was at last able to remodel the old homestead.

It is to the prenatal influence exerted upon her by her mother that Mrs. Wilcox ascribes her literary career. "My child will be a girl," declared Mrs. Wheeler; "and she will be a writer." So, for months before her daughter's birth, she committed to memory many books of poetry.

Her father had moved to Wisconsin from Vermont, where he had been a teacher of music, dancing, and deportment. It was not surprising that his efforts at farming were far from successful and that he again was forced to teach dancing to replenish the family purse.

At this school, where little Ella studied from the time she was eight until she was fourteen, she was regarded as a child prodigy. "Composition Day," the bug-bear of most of the scholars, was to her a delight.

Mill i- Du UI

At the age of nine she had written a novel in ten chapters, called "Minnie Tighthand and Mrs. Dunley." It was printed by her childish hand on chance scraps of paper and bound in paper torn from the kitchen wall.

Here is the little writer, just ten years old. In her serious face one can read the determination that was to carry her on to fame and fortune.

It was when she was only fifteen that she first appeared in print through prose essays published in the New York Mercury. Her verses were the subject of ridicule by its editor who "trusted that she would never again attempt poetic expression."

Crushed only temporarily, the little poet continued to bombard magazines with her verses. She grew so accustomed to "respectfully declined" enclosures that when Frank Leslie's Magazine sent her a checlj for forty dollars, she almost had a nervous shock.

After a short and not very happy term at Madison University, where her family had made great sacrifices to send her, she begged to be allowed to stay at home and write. But life was not all work, and the country dances, held at "Miller's Hall," were to Ella, at sixteen, brilliant functions.

With constantly increasing success, her world grew larger at every sunrise. People from Madison, Milwaukee, and Chicago began to seek out the little country girl with the inspired pen; and to visit their city homes was to her a delight bordering upon ecstasy.

A A

By 1880, the "Milwaukee School of Poetry" was at ijts height, and EUa Wheeler was its shining light. Her first verses to be read in public were written for a Decoration Day celebration in Madison.

The publication of "Mau rine" served to bring her into prominence; but "Poems of Passion" caused the name of Ella Wheeler to reverberate from one end of the land to the other.

Her romantic temperament had impelled her to imagine herself the heroine of many sentimental experiences, but when the compelling lover who was to dominate her life appeared, no tremors gave her warning of his presence. Here she is in the costume she wore on that fateful occasion.

Ella Wheeler at the time of her marriage to Robert Wilcox, whom she met by chance while visiting in Milwaukee. They were both attracted from the first and the correspondence which followed served to heighten friendship into love. They were married in a year from the time they met.

Mr. WUcox's business affairs took them to Meriden, Connecticut. This is the house on Colony Street, where they spent the first three years of their married life. The house is just as it was then except for the flags which decorated it for celebration.

But their first real home was the little New York apartment, which soon became a center for the most distinguished figures in the literary circles of the period. Here is EUa Wheeler Wilcox as she looked in those intoxicating days of congenial society.

This is tlie gown she wore when she recited "The Birth of the Opal" at Mrs. Frank Leslie's salon. She tells us that it was her one and only attempt at recitation in public, and that she was convulsed with mirth when an imitation of it was given later.

In 1894.

In 1902.

In 1907.

-rt.

In 1913.

In 1916.

"The Bungalow" from the water.

In 1890, Mr. and Mrs. Wilcox fell in love at first sight with Short-Beach-on-the-Sound, on beautiful Granite Bay, and there, that summer, they built "The Bungalow," perched high on the pink rocks above the water. The next year "The Barracks," as they christened the living house, was built close by. Gradually the months in New York grew shorter, and longer and longer the season at the shore.

Totliem heit camt. rttany. friends to revel in the outdoor life and in the cheer and good. fellowsliip within. One day when Theodosia Garrison and Rhoda Hero Dunn were-. visiting. EUa. Wheeler Wilcox,, an enterprising photographer captured the three poets arid posed them Olii the sea-wall.

For fifteen years there was an annual Bungalow Costume Ball. In this flashlight, Mrs. Wilcox is shown as "Princess White Wings," the name bestowed upon her by the Sioux Indians she met at the Pan-American Exposition and by whom she was adopted into the tribe.

Many winters were spent in travel, and everywhere people delighted to honor their distinguished guests. In England a window display devoted to Mrs. Wilcox's books shows a photograph of her in the costume in which she was presented at the Court of St. James.

One of their happiest winters was spent in Jamaica, where they saw a great deal of Jack London and his wife, Charmian. This is a snapshot of them talsen on the porch of the Hotel Tichfield, San Antonio, in 1909.

Mrs. Wilcox is a talented musician, and her mandolin always accompanied them. During her travels in Africa and India she learned to play many native airs upon it.

At Salt Lake City. Ella Wheeler Wilcox with a group of Mormon ladies and an Elder.

Luther Burbank and Ella Wheeler Wilcox.

In Africa. Mrs. Wilcox with her mandolin.

Before a great cathedral.

limit l- isandj. J? F '-jd–i M In Tunis at the Gate of the Bey–April, At Tiblis. 1913.

On the Island of Madeira.

At the Bardo Palace, In Sicily. Ella Wheeler Wilcox with her godchild.

Kf: wljmw

At sea.

In Jamaica.

In 1913 they decided to settle down after their ten gears' roaming. Never had "The Bungalow" seemed more inviting, and happy were the days spent there in work and in play. Here is Mrs. Wilcox reading, in "the cabin," surrounded by some of her trophies of travel.

Swimming had always been a joy to Mrs. Wilcox, though in lier youth it was regarded by her mother-as anything but a ladylike accomplishment, and she had had to(, iiidulge in it surreptitiously. She is shown here taking a sun-bath after a recent swim. She says that she rejoiced as much after learning a new stroke as after finding a new metre.

Domestic pets were welcomed at their fireside. Cats had always been wonderful companions to Mrs. Wilcox and even as a child she had found dolls cold and unresponsive wheff compared with kittens or puppies.

Into this contented life, tragedy entered when Robert Wilcox passed from this earth on May 21st, 1916, after thirty-two years of marriage made radiant by mutual devotion. This picture shows Mr. Wilcox in 1912.

It was on September 10th of the following year that, after months of unceasing struggle to win a message from the void, Mrs. Wilcox hadthe inefeable happiness of ail undoubted communication from-his spirit through the medium. of the; Ouija Board. Told a little later to go to France, she sailed on February 17th, Iftls.

J5- -:–jr.

Here she is in the courtyard of an old French chateau, surrounded by her fellow workers and by the soldiers into whose lives she was able to bring happiness. She is still receiving wonderful communications from the husband who has been hers through many incarnations, as his messages from beyond the grave have proved to her complete satisfaction.

Lightning Source UK Ltd.
Milton Keynes UK
171605UK00009B/18/P